Western Civilization
Volume 2

14th Edition

Early Modern Through the 20th Century

EDITOR

Robert L. Lembright

James Madison University

Robert L. Lembright teaches World Civilization, Ancient Near East, Byzantine, Islamic, and Greek/Roman history at James Madison University. He received his B.A. from Miami University and his M.A. and Ph.D. from The Ohio State University. Dr. Lembright has been a participant in many National Endowment for the Humanities Summer Seminars and Institutes on Egyptology, the Ancient Near East, Byzantine History, and the Ottoman Empire. He has written several articles in the four editions of *The Global Experience,* as well as articles in the *James Madison Journal* and *Western Views of China and the Far East.* His research has concentrated on the French Renaissance of the sixteenth century, and he has published reports in the *Bulletins et memoires, Société archéologique et historique de la Charente.* In addition, Dr. Lembright has written many book reviews on the ancient world and Byzantine and Islamic history for *History: Reviews of New Books.*

 **Contemporary Learning Series**

2460 Kerper Blvd., Dubuque, IA 52001

Visit us on the Internet
http://www.mhcls.com

Credits

1. **The Age of Power**
   Unit photo—Library of Congress (LC-USZ62-690)
2. **Rationalism, Enlightenment, and Revolution**
   Unit photo—Library of Congress (LC-DIG-prok-10099)
3. **Industry, Ideology, Nationalism, and Imperialism: The Nineteenth Century**
   Unit photo—Fototeca Storica Nazionale/Getty Images
4. **Modernism, Statism, and Total War: The Twentieth Century**
   Unit photo—Library of Congress (LC-USZ62-7449)
5. **Conclusion: The New Millennium and the Human Perspective**
   Unit photo—Yousuf Karsh/Library of Archives Canada/PA-212510

Copyright

Cataloging in Publication Data
Main entry under title: Annual Editions: Western Civilization, Vol. 2: Early Modern Through the 20th Century.
    1. Civilization—Periodicals.   2. World history—Periodicals. I. Lembright, Robert L. *comp*. II. Title: Western Civilization, Vol. 2.
ISBN-13: 978–0–07–351622–6   ISBN-10: 0–07–351622–8   901.9'05   82–645823   ISSN 0735-0392

Fourteenth Edition

Cover image © Neil Beer/Getty Images
Printed in the United States of America   1234567890QPDQPD9876   Printed on Recycled Paper

Editors/Advisory Board

Members of the Advisory Board are instrumental in the final selection of articles for each edition of ANNUAL EDITIONS. Their review of articles for content, level, currentness, and appropriateness provides critical direction to the editor and staff. We think that you will find their careful consideration well reflected in this volume.

Preface

In publishing ANNUAL EDITIONS we recognize the enormous role played by the magazines, newspapers, and journals of the public press in providing current, first-rate educational information in a broad spectrum of interest areas. Many of these articles are appropriate for students, researchers, and professionals seeking accurate, current material to help bridge the gap between principles and theories and the real world. These articles, however, become more useful for study when those of lasting value are carefully collected, organized, indexed, and reproduced in a low-cost format, which provides easy and permanent access when the material is needed. That is the role played by ANNUAL EDITIONS.

What does it mean to say that we are attempting to study the history of Western civilizations?

A traditional course in Western civilization was often a chronological survey in the development of European institutions and ideas, with a slight reference to the Near East and the Americas and other places where Westernization had occurred. Typically it began with the Greeks, then the Romans, and on to the medieval period, and finally to the modern era, depicting the distinctive characteristics of each stage, as well as each period's relation to the preceding and succeeding events. Of course, in a survey so broad, from Adam to the atomic age in two semesters, a certain superficiality was inevitable. Main characters and events galloped by; often there was little opportunity to absorb and digest complex ideas that have shaped Western culture.

It is tempting to excuse these shortcomings as unavoidable. However, to present a course in Western civilization which leaves students with only a scrambled series of events, names, dates, and places, is to miss a great opportunity. For the promise of such a broad course of study is that it enables students to explore great turning points or shifts in the development of Western culture. Close analysis of these moments enables students to understand the dynamics of continuity and change over time. At best, the course can give a coherent view of the Western tradition and its interplay with non-Western cultures. It can offer opportunities for students to compare various historical forms of authority, religion, and economic organization; to assess the great struggles over the meaning of truth and reality that have sometimes divided Western culture; and even to reflect on the price of progress.

Yet, to focus exclusively on Western civilization can lead us to ignore non-Western peoples and cultures, or else to perceive them in ways that some label as "Eurocentric." But contemporary courses in Western history are rarely, if ever, mere exercises in European tribalism. Indeed, they offer an opportunity to subject the Western tradition to critical scrutiny, to assess its accomplishments and its shortfalls. Few of us who teach these courses would argue that Western history is the only history which contemporary students should know. Yet it should be an essential part of what they learn, for it is impossible to understand the modern world without some specific knowledge in the basic tenets of the Western tradition.

When students learn the distinctive traits of the West, they can develop a sense of the dynamism of history. They can begin to understand how ideas relate to social structures and social forces. They will come to appreciate the nature and significance of innovation and recognize how values often influence events. More specifically, they can trace the evolution of Western ideas about such essential matters as nature, humans, authority, the gods, even history itself; that is, they learn how the West developed its distinctive character. And, as historian Reed Dasenbrock has observed, in an age that seeks multicultural understanding there is much to be learned from "the fundamental multiculturalism of Western culture, the fact that it has been constructed out of a fusion of disparate and often conflicting cultural tradition." Of course, the articles collected in this volume cannot deal with all these matters, but by providing an alternative to the summaries of most textbooks, they can help students better understand the diverse traditions and processes that we call Western civilization. As with the last publication of *Annual Editions: Western Civilization*, Volumes 1 and 2, are Internet References that can be used to further explore topics that are addressed in the essays. These sites are crossreferenced by number in the topic guide and can be hotlinked through the Annual Editions home page: http://www.mhcls.com/online.

This book is like our history—unfinished, always in process. It will be revised biannually. Comments and criticisms are welcome from all who use this book. For that a postpaid article rating form is included at the back of the book. Please feel free to recommend articles that might improve the next edition. With your assistance, this anthology will continue to improve.

Robert Lembright
Editor

Contents

Preface   iv

Topic Guide   xi

Internet References   xiii

UNIT 1
The Age of Power

Unit Overview   xvi

1. **The Gunpowder Plot: Terror and Toleration in 1605,** Simon Adams, *History Today,* November 2005
   The author investigates the political and religious options of the Catholics in early Jacobean England and asks why some chose to attempt the November, 1605 plot. Was it the product of ***Catholic discontent*** or was it a last episode of "***Elizabethan extremism***"?   2

2. **The 30 Years' War,** Graham Darby, *History Review,* September 2001
   What began as ***religious war*** of the Protestants and Catholics in 1618 Hungary, developed into a European war, involving the great powers of Europe—Hapsburgs, France, England, Prussia, and Sweden. Graham Darby recounts the ***religious, social, economic, and military*** aspects of the war.   7

3. **Cardinal Richelieu: Hero or Villain?,** Robert Knecht, *History Today,* March 2003
   Robert Knecht looks at Cardinal Richelieu and considers how his image, carefully crafted during his lifetime, has become that of a demonic schemer. Richelieu controlled public opinion, the press, historical writing, and the theater in order to support the monarchy. Yet, in later centuries he became the villain to men such as ***Voltaire***, the ***Romantic writers, and the theater in the nineteenth century***.   11

4. **From Mercantilism to 'The Wealth of Nations',** Michael Marshall, *The World & I,* May 1999
   Mercantilism was the practice of measuring a country's wealth by how much gold and silver bullion it could amass. This theory was challenged by Adam Smith in his ***Wealth of Nations,*** who believed that economies worked best when they had the least government interference.   15

5. **400 Years of the East India Company,** Huw V. Bowen, *History Today,* July 2000
   The East India Company proved to be one of the longest commercial enterprises ever undertaken in Britain. It was chartered in 1600 and finally dissolved after 1857. It was charged with the commercial ***exploitation and defense*** in a large part of India. What brought about its demise was excessive administrative costs and charges of misrule.   20

6. **John Locke: Icon of Liberty,** Mark Goldie, *History Today,* October 2004
   Mark Goldie traces the ways in which people have used and abused the ideas of the philosopher who died 300 years ago. Locke's ***Two Treatises of Government*** (1689) argued that a government required the consent of the people, and he was hailed as the philosopher of freedom and founder of liberalism. Yet panics of the ***American and French Revolutions*** smashed his reputation which was not revived until the second half of the twentieth century.   25

The concepts in bold italics are developed in the article. For further expansion, please refer to the Topic Guide and the Index.

UNIT 2
Rationalism, Enlightenment, and Revolution

Unit Overview   30

7. **Descartes the Dreamer,** Anthony Grafton, *Wilson Quarterly,* Autumn 1996
Descartes advanced, even epitomized, **rationalism**. Anthony Grafton explains why this seventeenth century thinker seems **modern** three and one-half centuries after his death.   32

8. **Empires Ancient and Modern,** Paul A. Rahe, *Wilson Quarterly,* Summer 2004
Paul Rahe examines what two Frenchman, **Voltaire and Montesquieu**, had to say in the 18th century about forces that sustain or shatter great powers. Voltaire visited England and then wrote his **Philosophical Letters** (1734) which compared the **religious freedom and government** to the **absolute monarchy** of his native France. Montesquieu also visited England and wrote **The Spirit of Laws** (1748) and found the chief passions of the English were **fondness for liberty and commerce**.   39

9. **Declaring an Open Season on the Wisdom of the Ages,** Robert Wernick, *Smithsonian,* May 1997
Although the enemies of the **Encylopedists** said they were responsible for the **French Revolution, the Reign of Terror**, and the horrors of the modern world, their friends credited them for **the rise of liberty, universal suffrage, freedom of the press,** and all the progress of the modern world. Robert Wernick recounts the impact Diderot and d'Alembert's work had on France.   46

10. **Thomas Young: the Man Who Knew Everything,** Andrew Robinson, *History Today,* April 2006
Andrew Robinson marvels at the breadth of knowledge of Thomas Young in physics, philology, and physiology. Young first demonstrated that **light was a wave**; he cracked two scripts of the **Rosetta Stone** and explained how the human eye focuses on objects. Robinson examines his relationship with his contemporaries, particularly with the **French Egyptologist François Champollion** and how he has been viewed by later historians.   51

11. **The Passion of Antoine Lavoisier,** Stephen Jay Gould, *Natural History,* June 1989
Many people paid the price for the **French Revolution**. One was France's greatest scientist, Antoine Lavoisier. A proponent of some of the Revolution's early accomplishments, the famous chemist ran afoul of the **Committee of Public Safety**. Stephen Jay Gould cites Lavoisier's accomplishments and ponders why in revolutionary times even a brilliant scientist was not immune from political extremists.   55

12. **The First Feminist,** Shirley Tomkievicz, *Horizon,* Spring 1972
Mary Wollstonecraft, author of **Vindication of the Rights of Women** (1792), cogently argued that the **ideals of the Enlightenment** and of the **French Revolution** should be extended to **women**. This is her story.   60

13. **Napoleon: A Classic Dictator?,** Laurent Joffrin, *History Today,* July 2005
Laurent Joffrin looks at the paradoxes surrounding a man who has fascinated the French for two hundred years. With his **will, anger, repression and control of public opinion**, Napoleon is seen as a classic **dictator** and favorite of the French republic.   65

The concepts in bold italics are developed in the article. For further expansion, please refer to the Topic Guide and the Index.

UNIT 3
Industry, Ideology, Nationalism, and Imperialism: The Nineteenth Century

Unit Overview   68

14. **Slavery and the British,** James Walvin, *History Today,* March 2002
    Although the British were not the originators, by the mid-eighteenth century they
    dominated the **Atlantic slave trade**. This trade was part of the global exchange
    of goods that added to the "greatness" of England. James Walvin examines the
    economic and social consequences of the trade.   70

15. **Victoria,** Lynne Vallone, *History Today,* June 2002
    Lynne Vallone reviews the lie of the woman who occupied the English throne
    longer than any other individual. She details the conflicts between the demand of
    masculine government and of the feminine home located within the woman
    who was from 1837 until her death in 1901, the head of both.   74

16. **Bismarck, Prussia, & German Nationalism,** Edgar Feuchtwanger,
    History Review, March 2001
    Otto Von Bismarck **masterfully used diplomacy and Prussian armies** in order
    to defeat Austria and France to create the **German Reich of 1871**. Edgar Feucht-
    wager assesses Bismarck's career and his legacy.   79

17. **Napoleon III: 'Hero' or 'Grotesque Mediocrity'?,** Roger Price, *His-
    tory Review,* March 2003
    Louis Napoleon used the memory of Napoleon Bonaparte to get elected president
    for the **Second French Republic**. He then staged a coup in 1852, as Napoleon
    I had done. The **Second Empire,** with its authoritarian and repressive nature and
    its collapse in the Franco-Prussian war, earned its bad reputation. Author Roger
    Price details differing views on Napoleon III.   83

18. **The Russians Shall Not Have Constantinople,** Roman Golicz, *His-
    tory Today,* September 2003
    English views on Constantinople varied from the **Crimean War** against Russia in
    1854 to neutrality at the beginning of the Russo-Turkish War of 1877. But when
    the Russians seemed to become superior over the Turks by the Treaty of San
    Stefano, English "**jingoism**" helped to call the **Congress of Berlin**. Roman Golicz
    surveys the changing geo-political situation in England.   87

19. **The Evolution of Charles Darwin,** Frank J. Sulloway, *Smithsonian,*
    December 2005
    Frank Sulloway tries to correct the view that Darwin's visit to the **Galapagos
    Islands** immediately persuaded the naturalist of **evolution**. He says that Darwin
    had been a **creationist** and only grasped the full significance of the unique wildlife
    he found there after he had returned to London.   93

20. **Florence Nightingale as a Social Reformer,** Lynn McDonald, *Histo-
    ry Today,* January 2006
    Florence Nightingale, heroine of the **Crimean War**, is most known as founder of
    the modern **profession of nursing and as a hospital reformer**. Yet her contri-
    bution to **public healthcare and social reform**—a public health care system and
    disease prevention—is scarcely known.   99

21. **Benjamin Disraeli and the Spirit of England,** T. A. Jenkins, *Histo-
    ry Today,* December 2004
    T.A. Jenkins reviews the life and legacy of Benjamin Disraeli, **statesman, nov-
    elist, and man-about-town**. She relates that his critics viewed him as a **cynical
    adventurer, a political charlatan motivated by personal ambition,** but new
    insights into his character say that Disraeli possessed a clear set of ideas of
    England's national character and destiny as well as his own unique position.   103

The concepts in bold italics are developed in the article. For further expansion, please refer to the Topic Guide and the Index.

22. **The Incurable Wound,** Lizabeth Peak, *History Magazine,* October/
November 2004
Rabies, or hydrophobia, afflicts victims with light sensitivity, paralyzed throat muscles and aggressive behavior. Lizabeth Peak explores the history from the ancient
period to the nineteenth century when veterinary medicine emerged. It was only
when *Louis Pasteur* began his groundbreaking experiments that the world to be
safer from this plague. **107**

23. **Quinine's Feverish Tales and Trails,** Louis Werner, *Américas,*
September/October 2003
Before the discovery of cinchona bark, *malaria* had no known cure and had ravaged the world for centuries. Louis Werner recounts the search for a treatment
of the disease, which involved international disputes and theft until *quinine* was
finally synthesized. **110**

UNIT 4
Modernism, Statism, and Total War:
The Twentieth Century

Unit Overview **114**

24. **The Divine Sarah,** Joseph A. Harriss, *Smithsonian,* August 2001
Born in 1844, *Sarah Bernhardt* was a sickly child and not expected to live. But
live she did and grew to become the first worldwide "*superstar diva,*" making her
reputation as a great tragedienne, mistress of nobles, and political activist. **116**

25. **Germany, Britain, & the Coming of War in 1914,** Richard Wilkinson,
History Review, March 2002
Richard Wilkinson asks why the quarrel happened between *Germany and Britain.*
What went wrong and who were the *Guilty Men* in 1914? The article considers
the role of the *Kaiser* and looks critically at the *Anglo-German naval rivalry,*
considered to be the prime cause of hostility between the two nations. **120**

26. **Queen of the Sands,** Kerry Ellis, *History Today,* January 2004
In the turmoil of modern Iraq, one need only turn back the clock to World War I
and the remarkable career of *Gertrude Bell.* She was the first woman graduate
from Oxford in Modern History, a Near East traveler, archaeologist, political ad-
viser, and creator of the pro-British kingdom of Iraq at the war's end. **124**

27. **Art Deco: High Style,** Stanley Meisler, *Smithsonian,* November
2004
Art Deco was the name given to the commercial, streamlined style that emerged
in Europe prior to World War I and lasted until World War II. Whereas the previous
arty style *Art Nouveau* involved naturalist themes, Art Deco artists loved *machinery and power.* They used modern materials such as plastic, chrome, rich fabrics,
and gems in *patterns of circles, zigzags, squares, bright colors* that depicted
speed. **128**

28. **Auschwitz: The Forgotten Evidence,** Taylor Downing, *History Today,* February 2005
In 1944, Allied bombers took pictures of the *Nazi Death Camp at Auschwitz.*
Taylor Downing ponders the uncomfortable questions—if the camp could be seen
so clearly from the air why was it not bombed? And why were the gas chambers
not destroyed and the killing stopped? Are the Allies to be blamed for a terrible
moral lapse in not stopping the *genocide of the Jews*? **131**

29. **Contemplating Churchill,** Edward Rothstein, *Smithsonian,* March
2005
Edward Rothstein surveys the life and reputation of Sir Winston Churchill on the
opening of the *Cabinet War Rooms* in London. After the First World War Churchill
was considered a failed politician, but his constant warnings about the *Nazi menace* eventually made him the greatest *Wartime Prime Minister.* **134**

The concepts in bold italics are developed in the article. For further expansion, please refer to the Topic Guide and the Index.

30. The Mystery of Stalin, Paul Wingrove, *History Today,* March 2003
How was *Josef Stalin* able to appear to his comrades as a reticent, patient, and imperturbable. To his allies in war—Churchill and Roosevelt—he was someone they could work with and believe in; to the masses, his picture appears everywhere and he had a unerring capacity to lead them to Communism. It was a false representation, so says Paul Wingrove, who examines different interpretations of Stalin's character. **139**

31. Kim Philby Had a Remarkable Long Career with British Intelligence—Spying for the Other Side, Richard K. Munro, *Military History,* June 2001
Although *Kim Philby* came from an illustrious English family, in his college years at Cambridge, he joined three other young men—*Guy Burgess, Anthony Blunt, and Donald McClean*—who were all strongly Marxist and pro-Stalinist. These four men became famous *Soviet moles,* passing information from the British and Americans to the Russians. Richard K. Munro recounts Philby's activities and his discovery. **142**

32. The World According to Wells, Joel Achenbach, *Smithsonian,* April 2001
Well known for his science fiction—*The Time Machine* and *The War of the Worlds*—H.G. Wells was a futurist and progressive idealist in that he predicted *the invention of the A bomb, the fourth dimension, the automobile revolution, a sexual revolution, and the United Nations.* Yet, he was criticized for his advocacy of a strong, scientific utopia, which many felt bore a resemblance to the totalitarian regimes of Germany and Russia. **145**

UNIT 5
Conclusion: The New Millennium and the Human Perspective

Unit Overview **150**

33. Beloved and Brave, Kenneth L. Woodward, *Newsweek,* April 11, 2005
The reverberations of Pope John Paul II's life and pontificate resounded through every nation on earth. He is seen as a *geopolitician, evangelist, and mystical believer, doctrinal disciplinarian, scourge of feminism, and the champion of ecumenicism* in this article by Kenneth Woodward. **152**

34. The Rise and Fall of Empires: The Role of Surplus Extraction, Harold Perkin, *History Today,* April 2002
The key to the formation, survival, and decline of all societies has been their use of *surplus income.* Without an extraction, by an elite, of products—in the form of *food, arms, luxuries, goods, and services*—no society could afford a high standard of living. Harold Perkins surveys the rise and fall of societies and wonders if America will last or decline as others have done. **156**

35. The Maestro of Time, Patricia Fara, *History Today,* April 2005
Patricia Fara discusses the centennial of *Albert Einstein's* three great scientific papers which revolutionized *physics.* The first was a new way to describe the *movement of atoms and molecules in liquids;* the second dealt with the *photoelectric* effect of light on metals; and the third was *relativity* which *reversed the Newtonian thinking of time and space.* **161**

36. 'You Say You Want a Revolution', Mikhail Safonov, *History Today,* August 2003
"Music hath charms to soothe the savage beasts", might have been another title for this essay that recounts the reasons for the fall of the totalitarian *Soviet regime.* Mikhail Safonov argues that *Beatlemania* did more to unravel the government than the Nobel prizewinners *Alexander Solzhenitsyn and Andrei Sakharov.* **165**

The concepts in bold italics are developed in the article. For further expansion, please refer to the Topic Guide and the Index.

37. **Europe's Mosque Hysteria,** Martin Walker, *Wilson Quarterly,* Spring 2006

Terrorist bombings, riots, and an uproar over satirical cartoons have inspired talk of a Europe under siege by Muslim immigrants. Martin Walker undertakes to demolish three myths of the situation—first is that there is any such phenomenon as *European Islam*; second is that native Europeans have been so sapped of their reproductive vigor that *Muslim immigrants' higher birthrate threaten to replace traditionally Christian Europe with a Muslim majority*; and finally that a *shrinking* and aging population of native Europeans and a growing population can only be alarming.   **168**

38. **Folly & Failure in the Balkans,** Tom Gallagher, *History Today,* September 1999

Although Otto von Bismarck said that the Balkans were not worth the bones of a single Pomeranian grenadier, for 200 years the major European powers have intervened in the region. The results of this interference created small, weak states while *neglecting differing religions, ethnic identities, and rising nationalism.* This has led to the difficult situations that now confront the West.   **174**

39. **The End,** Michael D. Lemonick, *Time,* June 25, 2001

Since the 1960's scientists discovered that the universe is about 15 billion years old but the question remained—what will happen at the *end of time*? Will galaxies fly apart forever until all is cold and dark, or will the expansion of the universe reverse direction and worlds will collide? Michael Lemonick recounts several new scientific observations, which lead many to believe that the universe will not end with a bang, but a whimper.   **178**

40. **Why We Study Western Civ,** Steven Ozment, *The Public Interest,* Winter 2005

In this defense of the study of Western Civilization, Steven Ozment says that History is every civilization's *clinical record of human nature and behavior.* We study the past *not to avoid repeating it but to learn how previous generations survived the same mistakes we make.*   **183**

Index   **187**

Test Your Knowledge Form   **190**

Article Rating Form   **191**

The concepts in bold italics are developed in the article. For further expansion, please refer to the Topic Guide and the Index.

Topic Guide

This topic guide suggests how the selections in this book relate to the subjects covered in your course. You may want to use the topics listed on these pages to search the Web more easily.

On the following pages a number of Web sites have been gathered specifically for this book. They are arranged to reflect the units of this *Annual Edition*. You can link to these sites by going to the student online support site at *http://www.mhcls.com/online/*.

ALL THE ARTICLES THAT RELATE TO EACH TOPIC ARE LISTED BELOW THE BOLD-FACED TERM.

Art

27. Art Deco: High Style

Business

4. From Mercantilism to 'The Wealth of Nations'
5. 400 Years of the East India Company
34. The Rise and Fall of Empires: The Role of Surplus Extraction

Cities

18. The Russians Shall Not Have Constantinople

Cold war

29. Contemplating Churchill
30. The Mystery of Stalin

Culture

15. Victoria
20. Florence Nightingale as a Social Reformer
24. The Divine Sarah
27. Art Deco: High Style
32. The World According to Wells
40. Why We Study Western Civ

Economics

4. From Mercantilism to 'The Wealth of Nations'
5. 400 Years of the East India Company
14. Slavery and the British
34. The Rise and Fall of Empires: The Role of Surplus Extraction

England

1. The Gunpowder Plot: Terror and Toleration in 1605
5. 400 Years of the East India Company
6. John Locke: Icon of Liberty
8. Empires Ancient and Modern
10. Thomas Young: the Man Who Knew Everything
14. Slavery and the British
15. Victoria
19. The Evolution of Charles Darwin
20. Florence Nightingale as a Social Reformer
21. Benjamin Disraeli and the Spirit of England
26. Queen of the Sands
32. The World According to Wells

Enlightenment

7. Descartes the Dreamer
8. Empires Ancient and Modern
9. Declaring an Open Season on the Wisdom of the Ages
10. Thomas Young: the Man Who Knew Everything
11. The Passion of Antoine Lavoisier

Ethnic issues

37. Europe's Mosque Hysteria
38. Folly & Failure in the Balkans

Fascism

28. Auschwitz: The Forgotten Evidence

France

2. The 30 Years' War
3. Cardinal Richelieu: Hero or Villain?
7. Descartes the Dreamer
8. Empires Ancient and Modern
9. Declaring an Open Season on the Wisdom of the Ages
11. The Passion of Antoine Lavoisier
13. Napoleon: A Classic Dictator?
17. Napoleon III: 'Hero' or 'Grotesque Mediocrity'?
24. The Divine Sarah

Germany

16. Bismarck, Prussia, & German Nationalism
25. Germany, Britain, & the Coming of War in 1914
28. Auschwitz: The Forgotten Evidence

Ideology

4. From Mercantilism to 'The Wealth of Nations'
6. John Locke: Icon of Liberty
9. Declaring an Open Season on the Wisdom of the Ages

Imperialism

5. 400 Years of the East India Company
18. The Russians Shall Not Have Constantinople

Liberalism

6. John Locke: Icon of Liberty
8. Empires Ancient and Modern

Middle East

18. The Russians Shall Not Have Constantinople
26. Queen of the Sands

Nation-state

16. Bismarck, Prussia, & German Nationalism
38. Folly & Failure in the Balkans

Nationalism

16. Bismarck, Prussia, & German Nationalism
38. Folly & Failure in the Balkans

Philosophy

4. From Mercantilism to 'The Wealth of Nations'
6. John Locke: Icon of Liberty
7. Descartes the Dreamer
8. Empires Ancient and Modern
9. Declaring an Open Season on the Wisdom of the Ages
19. The Evolution of Charles Darwin
40. Why We Study Western Civ

Prussia

2. The 30 Years' War
16. Bismarck, Prussia, & German Nationalism

Religion

2. The 30 Years' War
19. The Evolution of Charles Darwin
33. Beloved and Brave
37. Europe's Mosque Hysteria

Revolution

6. John Locke: Icon of Liberty
9. Declaring an Open Season on the Wisdom of the Ages
11. The Passion of Antoine Lavoisier
36. 'You Say You Want a Revolution'

Russia

18. The Russians Shall Not Have Constantinople
30. The Mystery of Stalin
36. 'You Say You Want a Revolution'

Science

10. Thomas Young: the Man Who Knew Everything
11. The Passion of Antoine Lavoisier
19. The Evolution of Charles Darwin
22. The Incurable Wound
23. Quinine's Feverish Tales and Trails
35. The Maestro of Time
39. The End

Slavery

14. Slavery and the British

Society

12. The First Feminist
15. Victoria
24. The Divine Sarah
27. Art Deco: High Style

Totalitarianism

28. Auschwitz: The Forgotten Evidence
30. The Mystery of Stalin
36. 'You Say You Want a Revolution'

Values

34. The Rise and Fall of Empires: The Role of Surplus Extraction
37. Europe's Mosque Hysteria
40. Why We Study Western Civ

War

2. The 30 Years' War
16. Bismarck, Prussia, & German Nationalism
17. Napoleon III: 'Hero' or 'Grotesque Mediocrity'?
18. The Russians Shall Not Have Constantinople
20. Florence Nightingale as a Social Reformer
25. Germany, Britain, & the Coming of War in 1914
28. Auschwitz: The Forgotten Evidence
29. Contemplating Churchill
30. The Mystery of Stalin
38. Folly & Failure in the Balkans

Women

12. The First Feminist
15. Victoria
20. Florence Nightingale as a Social Reformer
24. The Divine Sarah
26. Queen of the Sands

World War I

25. Germany, Britain, & the Coming of War in 1914
26. Queen of the Sands

World War II

28. Auschwitz: The Forgotten Evidence
29. Contemplating Churchill
30. The Mystery of Stalin

Internet References

The following Internet sites have been carefully researched and selected to support the articles found in this reader. The easiest way to access these selected sites is to go to our student online support site at *http://www.mhcls.com/online/*.

AE: Western Civilization, Volume 2

The following sites were available at the time of publication. Visit our Web site—we update our student online support site regularly to reflect any changes.

General Sources

Archaeological Institute of America (AIA)
http://www.archaeological.org

Review this site of the AIA for information about various eras in Western civilization.

Archive of Texts and Documents—Hanover College
http://history.hanover.edu/texts.html

This Hanover College historical texts project is very creative. Sources are available on Europe and East Asia.

Discover's Web
http://www.win.tue.nl/~engels/discovery/index.html

Data on historical voyages of discovery and exploration from ancient to modern times are available from this Web site.

The History of Costumes
http://www.siue.edu/COSTUMES/history.html

This distinctive site illustrates garments worn by people in various historical eras. Clothing of common people is presented along with that worn by nobility. The site is based on a history of costumes through the ages that was originally printed between 1861 and 1880.

Library of Congress
http://www.loc.gov/

Examine this Web site to learn about the extensive resource tools, library services/resources, exhibitions, and databases available through the Library of Congress in many different subfields of historical studies.

Michigan Electronic Library
http://mel.org/index.jsp

Browse through this enormous history site for an array of resources on the study of Western civilization, which are broken down by historical era, geographical area, and more.

Smithsonian Institution
http://www.si.edu/

This site provides access to the enormous resources of the Smithsonian, which holds some 140 million artifacts and specimens in its trust for "the increase and diffusion of knowledge." Here you can learn about social, cultural, economic, and political history, particularly about the United States, from a variety of viewpoints.

Western Civilization: Act 3
http://www.omnibusol.com/westernciv.html

An interesting mix of information can be found at this eclectic site whose span is from the French Revolution to the present day. Thirty-seven pages lead to many other Internet sites.

UNIT 1: The Age of Power

EuroDocs: Primary Historical Documents from Western Europe
http://www.lib.byu.edu/~rdh/eurodocs/

This collection from the Brigham Young University Library is a high-quality set of historical documents from Western Europe. Facsimiles, translations, and even selected transcriptions are included. Click on the links to materials related to "Europe as a Supernational Region" and individual countries.

1492: An Ongoing Voyage/Library of Congress
http://lcweb.loc.gov/exhibits/1492/

Displays examining the causes and effects of Columbus's voyages to the Americas are provided on this site. "An Ongoing Voyage" explores the rich mixture of societies coexisting in five areas of the Western Hemisphere before European arrival. It also surveys the polyglot Mediterranean world at a dynamic turning point in its development.

World Wide Web Virtual Library/Latin American Studies
http://lanic.utexas.edu/las.html

Maintained by the University of Texas, this is the site of first resort for the exploration of a topic dealing with Latin America. It lists resources available on the Web for historical topics and related cultural subjects.

UNIT 2: Rationalism, Enlightenment, and Revolution

Adam Smith
http://cepa.newschool.edu/het/profiles/smith.htm

At this site there are links to the major works of Adam Smith, including the *Wealth of Nations,* and a list of additional resources.

Eighteenth-Century Resources/JackLynch
http://andromeda.rutgers.edu/~jlynch/18th/

Open this page to find links in eighteenth-century studies, including History, Literature, Religion and Theology, Science and Mathematics, and Art. Click on History, for example, for a number of resources for study of topics from Napoleon, to piracy and gambling, to a discussion of Catalonia in the eighteenth century.

Napoleon Bonaparte
http://www.napoleonbonaparte.nl

According to this site, you will find the best Napoleonic Internet sites in the world right here. In addition to many articles, there are many links to other sites as well as newspaper articles edited by Beryl Bernardi, called "News From the Front."

Western European Specialists Section/Association of College and Research Libraries
http://www.lib.virginia.edu/wess/

WESS provides links in regional and historical resources in European studies, as well as materials on contemporary Europe. Visit this site for texts and text collections, guides to library resources, book reviews, and WESS publications.

UNIT 3: Industry, Ideology, Nationalism, and Imperialism: The Nineteenth Century

The Victorian Web
http://www.victorianweb.org/victorian/victov.html

The Victorian Web offers a complete examination into all aspects of Victorian life.

Historical U.S. Census Data Browser
http://fisher.lib.virginia.edu/census/

At this site, the interuniversity Consortium for Political and Social Research offers materials in various categories of historical social, economic, and demographic data. Access here a statistical overview of the United States, beginning in the late eighteenth century.

Society for Economic Anthropology Homepage
http://nautarch.tamu.edu/anth/sea/

This is the home page of the Society for Economic Anthropology, an association that strives to understand diversity and change in the economic systems of the world, and hence, in the organization of society and culture.

UNIT 4: Modernism, Statism, and Total War: The Twentieth Century

History Net
http://www.thehistorynet.com/THNarchives/AmericanHistory/

This National Historical Society site provides information on a wide range of topics, with emphasis on American history, book reviews, and special interviews.

Inter-American Dialogue (IAD)
http://www.iadialog.org/

This is the Web site for IAD, a premier U.S. center for policy analysis, communication, and exchange in Western Hemisphere affairs. The organization has helped to shape the agenda of issues and choices in hemispheric relations.

ISN International Relations and Security Network
http://www.isn.ethz.ch/

This site, maintained by the Center for Security Studies and Conflict Research, is a clearinghouse for extensive information on international relations and security policy. The many topics are listed by category (Traditional Dimensions of Security, New Dimensions of Security) and by major world regions.

Russian and East European Network Information Center/University of Texas at Austin
http://reenic.utexas.edu/reenic/index.html

This is *the* Web site for exhaustive information on Russia and other republics of the former Soviet Union and Central/Eastern Europe on a large range of topics.

Terrorism Research Center
http://www.terrorism.com/

The Terrorism Research Center features original research on terrorism, counterterrorism documents, a comprehensive list of Web links, and monthly profiles of terrorist and counterterrorist groups.

World History Review/Scott Danford and Jon Larr
http://members.aol.com/sniper43/index.html

Associated with a college course, this site will lead you to information and links on a number of major topics of interest when studying Western civilization in the twentieth century: Imperialism, the Russian Revolution, World War I, World War II, the cold war, the Korean War, and Vietnam.

UNIT 5: Conclusion: The New Millennium and the Human Perspective

Center for Middle Eastern Students/University of Texas/
http://menic.utexas.edu/menic/Society_and_Culture/Religion_and_Spirituality/

This site provides links to Web sites on Islam and the Islamic world. Information on Judaism and Christianity is also available through this Middle East Network Information Center.

Europa: European Union
http://europa.eu.int/

This site leads you to the history of the European Union (and its predecessors such as the European Community and European Common Market); descriptions of the increasingly powerful regional organization's policies, institutions, and goals; and documentation of treaties and other materials.

The North-South Institute
http://www.nsi-ins.ca/ensi/index.html

Searching this site of the North-South Institute—which works to strengthen international development cooperation and enhance gender and social equity—will help you find information and debates on a variety of global issues.

Organization for Economic Co-operation and Development/FDI Statistics
http://www.oecd.org/home/

Explore world trade and investment trends and statistics on this site that provides links to related topics and addresses global economic issues on a country-by-country basis.

U.S. Agency for International Development
http://www.info.usaid.gov/

This Web site covers such issues as democracy, population and health, economic growth, and development. It provides specific information about different regions and countries.

www.mhcls.com/online/

World Bank
http://www.worldbank.org/

Review this site and its links for information on immigration and development now and in the future. News (press releases, summaries of new projects, speeches), publications, and coverage of numerous topics regarding development, countries, and regions are provided here.

World Wide Web Virtual Library: International Affairs Resources
http://www.etown.edu/vl/

Surf this site and its extensive links to learn about specific countries and regions, to research various think tanks and international organizations, and to study such vital topics as international law, human rights, and peacekeeping.

We highly recommend that you review our Web site for expanded information and our other product lines. We are continually updating and adding links to our Web site in order to offer you the most usable and useful information that will support and expand the value of your Annual Editions. You can reach us at: *http://www.mhcls.com/annualeditions/.*

UNIT 1
The Age of Power

Unit Selections

1. **The Gunpowder Plot**, Simon Adams
2. **The 30 Years' War**, Graham Darby
3. **Cardinal Richelieu: Hero or Villain?**, Robert Knecht
4. **From Mercantilism to 'The Wealth of Nations'**, Michael Marshall
5. **400 Years of the East India Company**, Huw V. Bowen
6. **John Locke: Icon of Liberty**, Mark Goldie

Key Points to Consider

- What caused the Gunpowder Plot in England?

- Why was the 30 Years' War to involve religion, social, and economic aspects?

- How was Cardinal Richelieu viewed over the centuries?

- How did Adam Smith's economic theories challenge European thought?

- How did the East India Company evolve from a business enterprise into a governing body? What were some of the results of this influence?

- How did John Locke's ideas influence constitutional government? Why was he not always liked?

Student Web Site
www.mhcls.com/online

Internet References
Further information regarding these Web sites may be found in this book's preface or online.

EuroDocs: Primary Historical Documents from Western Europe
  http://www.lib.byu.edu/~rdh/eurodocs/
1492: An Ongoing Voyage/Library of Congress
  http://lcweb.loc.gov/exhibits/1492/
World Wide Web Virtual Library/Latin American Studies
  http://lanic.utexas.edu/las.html

The early modern period (c.1450–1700) was a time of profound change for Western civilization. During this era the medieval frame of reference gave way to a modern orientation. The old order had been simply, but rigidly, structured. There was little social or geographical mobility. Europe was relatively backward and isolated from much of the world. The economy was dominated by self-sufficient agriculture in which trade and cities did not flourish. There were few rewards for technological innovation. A person's life seemed more attuned to revelation than to reason and science. The Church both inspired and limited intellectual and artistic expression. Most people were prepared to suppress their concerns to a higher order—whether religious or social.

This narrow world gradually gave way to the modern world. There is no absolute date that marks the separation, but elements of modernity were evident throughout Western civilization by the eighteenth century. In this context the late Medieval, Renaissance, and Reformation periods were transitional. They linked the medieval to the modern. But what were the facets of this emerging modernity? Beginning with the economic foundation, an economy based on money and commerce overlaid the old agrarian system, thus creating a new and important middle class in society. Urban life became increasingly important, allowing greater scope for personal expression. Modernity involved a state of mind as well. Europeans of the early modern period were conscious that their way of life was different from that of their ancestors. In addition, these moderns developed a different sense of time—for urban people, clock time superseded the natural rhythms of the changing season and the familiar cycles of planting and harvesting. As for the intellect, humanism, rationalism, and science began to take precedence over tradition—though not without a struggle. Protestantism presented yet another challenge to orthodoxy. And, as economic and political institutions evolved, new attitudes about power and authority emerged.

The early modern period is often called the Age of Power, because the modern state, with its power to tax, conscript, subsidize, and coerce, was taking shape. Its growth was facilitated by the changing economic order, which made it possible for governments to acquire money in unprecedented amounts—to hire civil servants, raise armies, protect and encourage national enterprise, and expand their power to the national boundaries and beyond.

Power, in various early modern manifestations, is the subject of the articles assembled in this unit. Two articles describe religion and war—"The Gunpowder Plot" and "The 30 Years' War," while two others reveal how one governs and the right to dissent—"Cardinal Richelieu: Hero or Villain?" and "John Locke: Icon of Liberty." Several articles deal with monetary power, "From Mercantilism to 'The Wealth of Nations,'" describes new economic ideas that revolutionized Europe, while "400 Years of the East India Company" shows how one business venture used economic power to become a government agency.

CLIPPER SHIP THREE BROTHERS, 2972 TONS.
THE LARGEST SAILING SHIP IN THE WORLD.

The Gunpowder Plot: Terror and Toleration in 1605

Simon Adams investigates the political and religious options available to the Catholics of early Jacobean England, and asks why some chose to attempt the spectacular coup in November 1605.

SIMON ADAMS

Everyone knows what the Gunpowder Plotters looked like. Thanks to one of the best-known etchings of the seventeenth century we see them 'plotting', broad brims of their hats over their noses, cloaks on their shoulders, mustachios and beards bristling—the archetypical band of desperados. Almost as well known are the broad outlines of the discovery of the 'plot': the mysterious warning sent to Lord Monteagle on October 26th, 1605, the investigation of the cellars under the Palace of Westminster on November 4th, the discovery of the gunpowder and Guy Fawkes, the flight of the other conspirators, the shoot-out at Holbeach in Staffordshire on November 8th in which four (Robert Catesby, Thomas Percy and the brothers Christopher and John Wright) were killed, and then the trial and execution of Fawkes and seven others in January 1606.

However, there was a more obscure sequel. Also implicated were the 9th Earl of Northumberland, three other peers (Viscount Montague and Lords Stourton and Mordaunt) and three members of the Society of Jesus. Two of the Jesuits, Fr Oswald Tesimond and Fr John Gerard, were able to escape abroad, but the third, the superior of the order in England, Fr Henry Garnet, was arrested just before the main trial. Garnet was tried separately on March 28th, 1606 and executed in May. The peers were tried in the court of Star Chamber: three were merely fined, but Northumberland was imprisoned in the Tower at pleasure and not released until 1621.

The leader of the plot was Robert Catesby, a Northamptonshire gentleman who lived at Chastleton House, the now well-known National Trust property in Oxfordshire, during the 1590s. Most of the others, with the exception of Fawkes (a late recruit), were related to Catesby or to each other. There are strong similarities to an earlier Catholic conspiracy, the Babington Plot to free Mary, Queen of Scots in 1586, but where in 1586 the government had both written evidence and the testimonies of most of those involved, Catesby's death has left a large hole in the inner story of the Gunpowder Plot. The government's investigation was dependent initially on the admissions of

Fawkes, but the survivors of Holbeach could add little more. All that could be established was that in May 1604 Catesby had devised a plan to mine the House of Lords during the next opening of Parliament.

Thanks to the fact that nothing actually happened, it is not surprising that the plot has been the subject of running dispute since November 5th, 1605. James I's privy council appears to have been genuinely unable to make any sense of it. The Attorney-General, Sir Edward Coke, observed at the trial that succeeding generations would wonder whether it was fact or fiction. There were claims from the start that the plot was a put-up job—if not a complete fabrication, then at least exaggerated for his own devious ends by Robert Cecil, Earl of Salisbury, James's secretary of state. The government's presentation of the case against the plotters had its awkward aspects, caused in part by the desire to shield Monteagle, now a national hero, from the exposure of his earlier association with them. The two official accounts published in 1606 were patently spins. One, *The Discourse of the Manner*, was intended to give James a more commanding role in the uncovering of the plot than he deserved. The other, *A True and Perfect Relation*, was intended to lay the blame on Garnet.

But Catesby had form. He and several of the plotters as well as Lord Monteagle had been implicated in the Earl of Essex's rebellion in 1601. Subsequently he and the others (including Monteagle) had approached Philip III of Spain to support a rebellion to prevent James I's accession. This raises the central question of what the plot was about. Was it the product of Catholic discontent with James I or was it the last episode in what the late Hugh Trevor-Roper and Professor John Bossy have termed 'Elizabethan extremism'?

The primary focus of Catholic discontent was what had become known by 1605 as the penal laws. On one level they included all the Elizabethan religious legislation back to the Supremacy and Uniformity Acts of 1559, but the term was usually applied to a specific series of statutes passed between 1581 and 1593. The 1559 acts involved an oath to the royal supremacy over the church and obligatory attendance at a parish church every Sunday. Absence, soon described as recusancy (disobedience, hence recusant), incurred a one shilling fine. The later statutes made it treason to withdraw the Queen's subjects from their allegiance by converting them (1581) and treason for Jesuits and priests trained in foreign seminaries to enter England (1585). The 1581 statute also increased recusancy fines to the deliberately penal level of £20 a month.

The penal laws were not the product of a clearly articulated policy, each of the statutes was a compromise of greater or lesser incoherence. Their target, however, was clear: the Catholic missionary clergy and those who sheltered them. The Catholic 'mission' began in 1568 with the founding of the first seminary for exiled clergy at Douai in the Low Countries, but after 1580 the Jesuits became increasingly dominant in the mission. Their dominance was intellectual and moral rather than numerical, for the Society was not large. There were only about five Jesuits in England at any one time during the 1580s, rising to fourteen in 1598. Of the 180-odd persons executed under the penal laws in Elizabeth's reign the overwhelming majority were seminary priests, not members of the Jesuit order.

Legislation was one thing, enforcement another. Although it had its enthusiastic priest hunters, the Elizabethan government was not a bloodthirsty regime. Catholic polemic which (very successfully) portrayed the Elizabethan persecutions in a similar fashion to the way John Foxe had portrayed the Marian made the Elizabethan elite (who knew their Foxe well) very uncomfortable. The use of torture was a particularly controversial issue. It was not part of the Common Law process, but was permitted in treason cases, to force the suspect to reveal his accomplices, though not incriminate himself.

The relatively minor role torture played in the Gunpowder Plot investigation is a good example of the myths that surround this emotive subject. Permission was given to employ torture on Fawkes, who initially refused to say anything, but whether it was actually used and how much is unclear. By 1605 the torture debate had spawned another, over what had become known as the 'doctrine of equivocation'. This was the argument that it was legitimate for Catholics to be economical with the truth, even when questioned under oath, in order to protect their friends and family, but it was not difficult to twist this into the claim that nothing a Catholic said could be trusted. Equivocation was attributed to the Jesuits, and Garnet had written a treatise on the subject, a point of major importance at his trial.

The years after 1588 saw the worst phase of the persecutions, culminating in execution of Fr Robert Southwell in 1595. This seems to have been the turning point, and thereafter executions dropped off sharply as Elizabeth's government began looking for a way out. Their solution was an oath of allegiance distinct from the oath to the supremacy that would enable Catholics to prove they were not treasonous. This oath had first appeared in 1581 and a version of it ('a form of submission') was resurrected in the 1593 statute.

On Elizabeth's death there were over 200 Catholic clergy active in the country. Estimates of lay Catholics are particularly vexed. The best modern estimate, John Bossy's, is some 40,000 on Elizabeth's death. For the laity the heaviest burdens were re-

cusancy fines and the exclusion from public life caused by the oath to the supremacy. Open recusants (those fined) were merely the tip of the iceberg, the number of nominal conformists, whom Protestants came to call 'church papists', was another matter. The missionary clergy blamed the penal laws for intimidating many into conformity; once they were removed a large number of conversions could be expected.

What did Catholics want—or rather what solutions were possible? There were four: England's return to the Church; some form of formal toleration similar to that granted French Protestants; repeal of the penal laws; or simple non-enforcement. None, however, was as straightforward as it appeared.

The return to the Church could be accomplished either by a Catholic monarch or by force. Until 1587 the possible succession of the Queen of Scots had provided a straightforward solution. After her execution, however, things became complicated, thanks to the enigmatic stance of James VI. On the eve of the Armada, Philip II of Spain with the support of the leaders of the mission, Cardinal William Allen and the Jesuit Robert Persons, decided to cut James out of the succession in favour of his own daughter the Infanta Isabella Clara Eugenia. It was the Infanta's claim that Persons notoriously made public in *A Conference on the Next Succession* in 1595. By then Spain was not in a position to implement it by force and the Pope (Clement VIII) was hostile to the Spanish monarchy and opposed to its expansion. Under pressure from English exiles, Philip III hesitantly committed himself to the claim privately in February 1601, but Isabella herself was not interested.

One reason Persons and Allen supported Isabella was a residual hostility in Catholic circles to a Scottish succession, a hostility shared by some of the Gunpowder Plotters, especially Fawkes. The paralysis in Spain led to a revived interest in an English alternative to James and Isabella, in particular Arbella, heiress of the junior Stewart line. When Elizabeth died in March 1603 the Spanish government had itself abandoned the alternatives in favour of reaching an agreement with James.

Persons' tract undoubtedly strengthened English Protestant support for James while at the same time stiffening hostility to the Jesuits. Yet James was also convinced that Clement VIII would excommunicate him to assist Isabella's claim. This fear inspired possibly the most dangerous of his pre-1603 manoeuvres, various hints of leniency to Catholics. Rome read this evidence that his conversion was imminent. As a result Clement viewed his accession with benevolence.

A formal toleration offered the most sophisticated solution for the English Catholics, but there were insuperable difficulties. The French edicts of toleration, from the first in 1563 to the Edict of Nantes of 1598, offered two broad concessions: freedom of conscience (no Inquisition and no heresy prosecutions) and freedom of public worship under greater or lesser geographical restriction. This was never a solution Rome wanted, but from 1563 a number of foreign lay Catholics, predominantly, but not exclusively, French, had urged it on Elizabeth. She had refused on the grounds that her subjects already enjoyed freedom of conscience and that English Catholics did not acknowledge her, while French Protestants accepted they were the subjects of the king of France.

The remaining two options would free Catholic clergy from fear of execution and relieve lay Catholics of recusancy fines, but the 1559 Acts would remain in place and Catholic worship would be semi-legal at best. Repeal would demand the co-operation of Parliament, while non-enforcement would involve the Crown overriding the law of the land, an aspect of royal absolutism that would become a major constitutional issue in the Restoration. There was also the tricky political issue of even-handedness, for since 1559 Puritans had repeatedly contrasted attempts to discipline them with the apparent tolerance of Catholics.

In the mid-1590s the Catholic mission fragmented. The underlying issue was hostility among the seminary priests to the Jesuits and their influence, and this came into the open in disputes over the future organization of the mission after the death of Cardinal Allen in 1594. The seminarians wanted a bishop appointed, but this was blocked by the Jesuits, and instead in 1598 George Blackwell, a seminarian sympathetic to the Jesuits, was appointed to the novel office of 'archpriest'. The result was the archpriest or appellant controversy, so-called from the attempts of the seminarians to appeal to Pope Clement VIII against Blackwell's authority. In the spring of 1601 the Bishop of London, Richard Bancroft, secretly offered assistance to the appellants, both in sending a delegation to Rome and in printing tracts against the Jesuits in England.

Bancroft's aim was not merely to encourage the enmity between the appellants and the Jesuits, but also to win the agreement of the appellants to an oath of allegiance. Bancroft had the support of Robert Cecil and the more guarded approval of Elizabeth, although she indicated there were limits to the concessions she would be prepared to make. The Pope was prepared to make some organizational changes to the mission, but he saw no reason to negotiate with Elizabeth with James's accession in the offing. At the end of 1602 the appellants had agreed a form of oath, but they were not prepared to renounce the apostolic authority of the papacy. Nevertheless, by Elizabeth's death the breach with the Jesuits had become open, not least because the appellant controversy was conducted with a remarkable degree of personal animus. This has left its mark on subsequent historical treatment; even Lady Antonia Fraser has referred to the appellants' 'worst qualities of bitterness and self-pity'.

Despite almost universal expectation of a major disturbance, James's accession in the spring of 1603 was uncontested. But the enigma remained. He retained the key figures of Elizabeth's privy council, but added to them several peers of Catholic sympathy (including the Earl of Northumberland). His own solution to the religious question was a new general council to restore the unity of Christendom. Clement remained convinced that James's conversion was imminent. However, James then vacillated over recusancy. In May 1603 it was announced that recusancy fines would still be imposed, but in July, in response to Catholic appeals, he agreed to remit them.

July 1603 also saw the discovery of the Bye and Main Plots. The Bye Plot involved a prominent appellant priest, William Watson, as well as Thomas, Lord Grey de Wilton and George Brooke, brother of the 10th Lord Cobham; the Main Plot involved Cobham himself and Sir Walter Ralegh. Cobham gave the plots their names when he apparently told his brother that he and Lord Grey 'were but upon the Bye, but he and Sir Walter Rawleigh were upon the Mayne'. The plots were discovered when the government was warned by other appellants, Blackwell and the Jesuit Fr Gerard.

The Bye Plot involved seizing James and his eldest son Prince Henry, and forcing him to replace his chief ministers; the Main getting Spanish support to replace James with Arbella Stewart. Both plots intended to impose some form of liberty of religion, Watson being convinced that James had reneged on an earlier promise to implement toleration. This and an (ultimately) mistaken belief that 'discontentment' with James would provide popular support were the only features shared with Gunpowder Plot. Although Ralegh was a friend of Northumberland's, none of the political figures involved in the 1603 plots was a Catholic, and all were notorious enemies of Essex.

At the beginning of 1604 James's government undertook three major political initiatives almost simultaneously: the Hampton Court Conference (January), the first Parliament of the reign (March 19th to July 7th) and negotiation of a peace treaty with Spain (eventually signed in August). James did not have much of a religious policy to announce to Parliament other than the general council scheme; his real interest lay in the Union with Scotland. Only late in the session did what became 'The Act for due execution of the statutes against Jesuits etc.' appear, a statute confirming that the penal laws were still in force. It is possible the inspiration came from Cecil, who may have wished it to strengthen his position in any future negotiations over religion. Another aspect may have been the desire to retain evenhandedness. After Hampton Court a proclamation was published on February 19th ordering all priests to leave the country. In early 1605 a substantial (if debated) number of Puritan clergymen lost their livings, this may account for James's announcement in February that he would enforce the penal laws and collect recusancy fines.

The Anglo-Spanish treaty was the product of considerable behind-the-scenes diplomacy. Philip III intended to obtain some form of alleviation for English Catholics, but he did not want to wreck the treaty by demanding it first. As a result the Spaniards did not have any concrete proposals for a formal toleration like the Edict of Nantes. Instead they floated a scheme whereby Spain would finance recusancy fines for twenty-one years, provided priests were not executed. Although no agreement was reached in the immediate term, great faith was placed in the discussions of a marriage between James's heir Prince Henry and one of Philip III's daughters.

Why did Robert Catesby therefore propose in May 1604 to destroy Parliament? The best explanation is a fatalistic conviction that the penal laws were here to stay and that Spain had abandoned English Catholics for James. However, the plan was also based on the assumption that Parliament would reassemble in the autumn. Because of the plague, on Christmas Eve 1604 it was prorogued to October 1605, forcing Catesby to leave his gunpowder decaying in the cellar for almost a year.

Had the planned explosion been successful, James, Henry and the Lords and Commons would have been eliminated. What

TIMELINE

1586	Babington Plot against Elizabeth; Catholic mission begins
1587	Execution of Mary Queen of Scots
1588	Defeat of the Armada
1595	Execution of Robert Southwell
1601	Essex rising against Elizabeth. Robert Catesby involved
March 1603	Death of Elizabeth; accession of James Stuart
July 1603	Discovery of Bye and Main plots
Jan 1604	Hampton Court Conference
Feb	Priests ordered to leave England
May	Catesby and others, including Thomas Percy and Guy Fawkes, meet to swear oath to blow up the King and Parliament. The conspirators hire lodgings close to Parliament House
Aug	The Somerset House Conference concludes peace between England and Spain
March 1605	Thomas Percy rents a cellar within the Parliament building, and places gunpowder there
June	Catesby hints of plot to Fr Henry Garnet
Oct 26th	Lord Monteagle receives letter by unknown messenger warning of plot
Nov 4th	Guy Fawkes is arrested in Parliament buildings
Nov 5th	Scheduled opening of Parliament
Nov 5th	Remaining conspirators leave London for Dunchurch (Warwickshire), where they meet other supporters
Nov 7th	Conspirators arrive at Holbeach House
Nov 8th	Sheriff of Worcester arrives; Catesby, Thomas Percy and two others are killed; others arrested
Jan 1606	Parliament passed Acts for the repression of recusants and oath of allegiance
Jan 27th 1606	Fr Henry Garnet is arrested
Jan 27th	Trial of eight surviving conspirators
Jan 30th-31st	Conspirators are executed in Old Palace Yard, Westminster
May 3rd	Fr Henry Garnet executed

was to happen next was vague, one of the major mysteries of the plot. Instead of crowning one of the known claimants, Catesby proposed to place James's nine-year old daughter Elizabeth on the throne (a curious choice given the plotters' hostility to Scots). There would also be a Lord Protector drawn from those peers who survived the explosion. It was this intention that ultimately incriminated Northumberland and the three other peers, for it suggested that the warning sent to Monteagle was not unique and that other Catholic noblemen had been advised to be absent, as the four (for various reasons) intended to be. The rest of the evidence against Northumberland was (it was admitted) even more circumstantial. James had appointed him captain of

the gentleman pensioners. He in turn appointed Thomas Percy, his cousin and man of business, a gentleman pensioner in 1604 and Percy had rented the cellar where the powder was laid.

The role of the three Jesuits was more important and more controversial. Gerard had celebrated mass for the plotters after they had taken their decision in May 1604, although it was claimed he was ignorant of their purpose. Tesimond had heard Catesby's confession in the summer of 1605, during which Catesby had asked for advice in general terms about the killing of innocents. Tesimond in turn had revealed his disquiet to Garnet. Thanks in part to Tesimond, Garnet knew Catesby was up to something. He told Catesby that the Pope did not want English Catholics to create a disturbance at this point, but Catesby replied he did not care. Given the willingness of the Jesuits to expose the Main Plot, it was difficult to explain Garnet's silence as other than consent. His failure to do anything effective to stop the plot was perhaps the crucial episode of the whole affair.

As he approached his second parliamentary session James was far more concerned with the Union with Scotland than religion. This makes it difficult to argue that the Plot was a government trap, for it served no obvious immediate political purpose. The official response was surprisingly muted. On discovery of the plot, Parliament was prorogued until January 1606. That session produced two relevant statutes, 'An Act for better discovery and repression of Popish Recusants', and 'An Act to prevent and avoid dangers that might grow by Popish Recusants'. They included a number of provisions that had been proposed and rejected in Elizabeth's reign, of which the most important was an obligation to take communion once a year as well as Sunday attendance. These, however, were only the stick, as there was also a large carrot in the form of the oath of allegiance. This had been revised by Bishop Bancroft after 1602, and encompassed both a theoretical section, denial that the Pope had any power to depose heretical rulers, and a practical, refusal to obey should he attempt to do so. Although not spelt out the implication was that taking the oath would lead to lenient enforcement of the penal laws.

The oath of allegiance was the centrepiece of James's response to the Gunpowder Plot. The 'archpriest' Blackwell, who had condemned the Plot on November 7th, was prepared to take it, but Rome would not consent to any Catholic doing so, and the dispute over the oath kept the Plot alive. That the Plot would be seized on by Puritans as evidence that the Catholic danger was still there was hardly surprising. This was why the Plot did real damage to Catholics, for one of the old arguments in favour of toleration had been that Puritans were seditious republicans and that Catholics were more reliable supporters of monarchy. It cannot be said that, had the Gunpowder Plot not occurred, James I would have implemented a toleration for his Catholic subjects; but the complexity of the situation in 1600-05 meant that a number of outcomes were possible. The plot closed many of them down.

For Further Reading

Antonia Fraser, *The Gunpowder Plot: Terror and Faith in 1605* (Weidenfeld & Nicholson, 1996); Mark Nicholls, *Investigating*

Gunpowder Plot (Manchester UP, 1991); Arnold Pritchard, *Catholic Loyalism in Elizabethan England* (Scolar Press, 1979); Paul C. Allen, *Philip III and the Pax Hispanica, 1598–1621* (Yale UP, 2000); Roland G. Usher, *The Reconstruction of the English Church* (Appleton, 1910); *The Oxford Dictionary of National Biography* (www.oup.com/oxforddnb); James Sharpe, *Remember, Remember the Fifth of November* (Profile, 2005).

From the History Today Archive

David Prior, 'Remember, Remember, The Fifth of November?' (July 2005); Pauline Croft, 'The Reputation of Robert Cecil' (November 1993); Roger Swift, 'Guy Fawkes Celebrations in Victorian Exeter' (November 1981); Jenny Wormald, 'James VI & I' (June 2002); Simon Thurley, 'The Early Stuarts and Hampton Court' (November 2003); Robert Lawson-Peebles, 'The Many Faces of Sir Walter Ralegh' (March 1998). See www.historytoday.com

SIMON ADAMS is Reader in History at the Univeristy of Strathclyde.

The 30 Years' War

Graham Darby examines the nature and effects of the war that dominated the first half of the seventeenth century.

GRAHAM DARBY

For those who wrestle with seventeenth-century Europe there is no more complex topic than the Thirty Years' War. It is also an issue that generates a large number of questions in examinations—on the origins, course and consequences of the war. In addition, there can be questions about its nature: how far was it a war of religion, what was its social and economic impact and what were its military and financial implications? It is the purpose of this article to help clarify the latter topics, beginning with religion.

A Religious War?

This is a difficult issue. For one thing, in early modern times religion and politics were inextricably intertwined, so that our present-day approach, which makes a clear distinction between the two, is often inappropriate. Secondly, early modern language was couched in religious terminology to such an extent that it is often difficult to distinguish between what was, perhaps, formulaic or habitual and what was sincere and meaningful. And thirdly, in our secular age, it is quite simply very difficult to appreciate the extent and depth of religious feeling in the seventeenth century.

Was this the last religious war? Given that Protestant England and Catholic Spain had made peace in 1604, and the Protestant Dutch rebels had reached an accommodation with Catholic Spain in 1609, it could be argued that the outbreak of war in Germany, in which the fate of Protestantism seemed to be at stake, brought religious issues back to the forefront of European politics. Historians have usually suggested that the Thirty Years' War began as a religious war, but became more secular as it progressed, and this formulation is a useful one.

If we begin at the beginning, in 1618, we can clearly see that religious issues were fundamental to the Bohemian Revolt. Religious toleration within the Habsburg lands became a major issue in the first decade of the seventeenth century, but the growth of Protestantism in Austria, Hungary and Bohemia represented a political challenge to Habsburg sovereignty as well—so that events clearly had political implications too. However, it was the Catholic reaction in Bohemia—the pulling down of Protestant churches, the election of the Jesuit-educated Ferdinand of Styria

as king-designate, the appointment of a (largely) Catholic regency council and the banning of Protestants from civic office—that led to the outbreak of hostilities. Moreover, the way events unfolded was interpreted in religious terms too. In the Defenestration of Prague, the fact that the Catholic regents survived the fall was clearly interpreted as divine intervention. Similarly the defeat of the Protestants at White Mountain in 1620 was to some extent credited to the intervention of a priest, Father Dominicus.

The issue here, then, seems pretty clear: the revolt was a struggle between Catholics and Protestants. Or was it? Even at the beginning, when the war might be viewed as being at its 'most religious', we discover that John George of Saxony, a Protestant, allied with the Catholic Emperor to defeat the Protestant rebels of Bohemia in return for some of their territory. Clearly this was a political decision. John George did not like rebels; nor indeed, as a Lutheran, did he like Calvinists. So he opposed Frederick of the Palatinate, whom the rebels embraced as their leader, because he was a Calvinist—but not just because he was Calvinist. Quite clearly by placing himself at the head of a Protestant revolt Frederick had challenged what John George felt to be his rightful leadership of the Protestant princes in Germany. From this example it can be appreciated that the war cannot be easily reduced to any simple formula.

Possibly the easiest way into this topic is to try to determine the motives of the principal participants. There is no doubting Emperor Ferdinand II's motivation: he was devoted to the Catholic church. He equated Protestantism with disloyalty and saw it as his duty to revive and reimpose the 'true faith' throughout the Empire where this was possible. Thus the successes of the Spanish, Imperial and Catholic League armies in the 1620s came to be seen as victories for the Counter Reformation too, and spawned contrary Protestant alignments. But the equation of Habsburg success with the cause of Catholicism became too much even for some Catholics—particularly Maximilian of Bavaria and especially Cardinal Richelieu of France.

The Edict of Restitution in 1629 represented the peak of religiosity in the war. But what was to Ferdinand a genuinely religious measure, to impose religious uniformity, was seen by the Princes of the Empire as a way of establishing Imperial absolutism, a political measure. Thus not only were neutral, moderate Protestants alienated, but Catholic allies too. The opposition to the Edict came as a great disappointment to Ferdinand. Indeed when he made the Peace of Prague with Protestants in 1635, and was prepared to suspend the Edict for 40 years, it is a clear indication that the nature of the war had changed. If Ferdinand was prepared to compromise and drop his ideals for a practical settlement, then clearly it had become a different war.

What had changed matters was the intervention of Sweden and France. From the time of his intervention, Gustavus Adolphus has been portrayed as not only the champion of Protestantism but its saviour too. More recently this interpretation has been called into question. It has been pointed out that Swedish security was his main motive and that his deal with Catholic France was an indication of the pragmatic nature of much of this policy. Yet religion and politics were inseparable in Sweden. Catholicism—in the form of the legitimist Vasa line, Sigismund of Poland—represented a fundamental challenge to the Protestant line of the family represented by Gustavus Vasa. Indeed it was fear of a Habsburg-Polish (Catholic) invasion that prompted Swedish intervention. The defence of the Protestant faith was therefore not just a propaganda ploy to win allies: it was a matter of great importance for the survival of the Swedish monarchy. Ultimately, however, Swedish policy came to be subordinate to that of France.

There is irony in the fact that it was a prince of the Catholic Church who probably did most to 'deconfessionalise' the war. Cardinal Richelieu may have justified his policy by claiming that it was God's will to create a general universal peace, but his anti-Habsburg position was a negation of Catholic unanimity. His approach appears to be entirely secular, putting French interests first. However, it would probably be more accurate to state that he put his own interests above everything else. After all, he had staked his reputation and his position as first minister on the successful outcome of an anti-Habsburg policy. Accordingly he was prepared to make deals with Protestants in order to bring down Spain and the Emperor. After 1635, as French influence grew, the war took on an increasingly secular character.

In the peace negotiations a less extreme religious position was taken by both sides. There is no doubt that after this war, and as a result of it, religious issues receded and were no longer a major destabilising influence in European politics. So, was it the last religious war? Of course religion continued to be politically important. For example, the fight against the Turks in the 1680s was undoubtedly a religious war with the fervour of a crusade. But generally speaking the Thirty Years' War did lead to a decline in the importance of religion as an issue of war. It was certainly the last religious war in Germany. The fact that the Pope's condemnation of the peace settlement was not only ignored but anticipated and ignored in advance speaks volumes about the new religious climate. Secular issues would now come to the fore, though it should be remembered that secular questions of security, prestige, reputation and dynastic rights had been important even during the times of greatest religious fervour.

Did Warfare Change?

In 1955 Michael Roberts suggested that there had been a Military Revolution in Europe between 1550 and 1650, which originated with Maurice of Nassau in the Dutch Revolt and was further developed by Gustavus Adolphus during the Thirty Years' War. Gustavus increased firepower with field guns, the double salvo and brigades in arrow formation. He also increased mobility and used the cavalry charge. Yet, though the battle of Breitenfeld in 1631 is usually cited as the triumph of new tactics over old, what is striking about the battles of the Thirty Years' War is that the victor was usually the possessor of the larger army, regardless of tactics.

Despite (allegedly) being at the cutting edge of military change, the Swedes fought an inconclusive engagement in 1632 and were thoroughly defeated in 1634: When Torstennson won the battle of Jankov in 1645 with a force of 15,000, equal to that of his opponents, he did so by outmanoeuvring them and attacking from the rear. If, then, victory tended to go to the larger army, Roberts' stress on new tactics is probably misleading.

As far as the growth in army sizes is concerned, both Wallenstein and Gustavus Adolphus were able to put together huge forces in excess of 100,000 men. However, only a small proportion would be mobile and used in battle; the rest would garrison captured territory or be involved in supply. Moreover, as the war progressed, army sizes actually declined, as military capacity diminished considerably. Thus army sizes reverted to about 10-15,000 men. What is in fact striking about all this military activity is how indecisive battles and even whole campaigns were. Thus Wallenstein was unable to deliver the knock-out blow against Denmark in 1628; Nordlingen (1634) was not followed up; the Swedes' success at Wittstock in 1636 was soon reversed; and after Jankov the Swedes advanced to Vienna but then had to retire. Victories, then, were most often not followed up at all. Why was this?

Basically the inconclusive character of warfare owed much to problems with the supply of men, money and provisions, and to the strength of fortifications. Logistics (supply) and finance were the real problems. The early modern state was just inadequate to the task. Whatever military innovations there were, logistics counted for more. There could be no total victories, no total defeats. It is no wonder warfare was indecisive, when armies were constantly in search of supplies. Indeed the war became a struggle for resources as whole regions were devastated. Defending and keeping areas for supply often took precedence over the development of an offensive strategy.

So far from witnessing a military revolution, what we can say about the Thirty Years' War is that it was probably one of the longest and most indecisive wars in all history! Peace really only came about when a state of exhaustion had been reached on both sides.

Government Finance

Basically the governments involved in the war could not afford to raise armies from their current resources. Consequently they relied on military entrepreneurs to advance the cash to recruit mercenaries from a wide variety of nationalities. The entrepreneurs did this in the belief that they would recoup their outlay and make a profit by defrauding the government (by receiving pay for exaggerated numbers of soldiers, by underpaying the troops, by forced contributions from the locality, and by pillage when on a campaign). The greatest of the military entrepreneurs were Count Mansfeld, Bernard of Saxe-Weimar and, of course, Albrecht von Wallenstein.

Initially the Emperor Ferdinand II was able to survive and prosper because he did not have to rely on his own meagre resources. He received Spanish and Papal subsidies as well as the contribution of Maximilian of Bavaria, perhaps the wealthiest of the German princes, and Christian IV of Denmark, who was able to finance his own campaign. Subsequently Ferdinand enjoyed the services of the most successful entrepreneur, Count Wallenstein. All commanders exacted contributions from occupied territory, but Wallenstein extended this system to friend and foe alike, and was so efficient that his dismissal in 1630 was not unrelated to the unpopularity he had engendered by these means. In later years, campaigns out of a given region could not be funded and whole armies could be wiped out by famine, disease and desertion, as happened to the Imperial army in 1644. Indeed Imperial effectiveness after 1635 was greatly reduced, not only because of the loss of Wallenstein and the lack of Spanish help after 1640, but because increasingly the Swedes came to occupy territory that deprived the Emperor of tax revenue. In short, when he had to rely on his own resources, the Emperor found the going tough.

The Swedes, on the other hand, had a system of conscription which gave them a relatively cheap core of reliable native troops. Obviously under Gustavus Adolphus, the army was augmented by vast numbers of mercenaries—so much so that eventually only about 10 per cent of the army was manned by Swedes—but they remained a reliable, loyal and efficient component (and were usually the officers). Swedish taxation only provided a tiny fraction of the cost of these forces and the Swedes adopted Wallenstein's methods to extract resources from occupied territory. Indeed the motto bellum se ipsum alet (the war must pay for itself) was very much the basis for Swedish policy. However, after the defeat at Nordlingen this policy was no longer possible and, while exactions were sufficient for the conscripts in the garrisons in northern Germany, the Swedes came to rely entirely on French subsidies to provide central funds for their mobile forces. Indeed between 1638 and 1648 the French supplied the Swedes with over 3.5 million thalers. Yet, despite this, the funds were not enough. Hence the Swedes could not follow up their successes and insisted on an indemnity in the peace negotiations in order to make up unpaid wages.

By far the wealthiest of the participants was France. It did not have American silver mines for credit purposes as the Spanish did; it could not meet costs out of occupied territory, because the French army did not really occupy any; and its tax system was illogical and inefficient. Yet France was a relatively rich country with a large population (possibly as many as 20 million) and a diverse agriculture, and was, accordingly, able to finance the war by increased domestic taxation and borrowing. Indeed French taxation more than doubled between the 1620s and the

1640s, and the inadequate means of collection led Richelieu to appoint intendants, accountable government appointees, in order to ensure the monies reached the treasury. Thus inadvertently the Cardinal was able to extend government control. Even so, funds were inadequate and France had to muddle through by borrowing on the basis of future tax receipts. Moreover, all this change met opposition and resistance, which led directly to the end of the Thirty Years' War.

So, all in all, we can see that the war was often inconclusive because adequate resources were just not available to fund what could have been a decisive campaign. Hence only mutual exhaustion could bring about an end—and that is what happened.

Economic and Social Effects

Despite a wealth of local records, historians have been unable to agree on the economic, social and demographic effects of the war. In the nineteenth century the belief was that the war had created widespread death and destruction, decimating about two-thirds of Germany's population and causing massive economic damage which set her back about a century. Yet such views were the result of generalising about the whole of Germany from a few incidents and taking unreliable contemporary sources at face-value. Town councils, for instance, often exaggerated the damage they had suffered in order to obtain tax cuts, and some rulers (e.g. the Great Elector of Brandenburg) exaggerated the effects of the war to enhance their achievements in postwar restoration work.

More recent research in the localities has demonstrated that the amount of devastation had been inflated. There was a decline in population in Germany, but in the region of 20-40 per cent, rather than two-thirds. In many cases what appeared to be population loss was really migration, as inhabitants abandoned villages in campaigning areas and became refugees. And of course geographically the picture was very varied. Clearly there were war zones, which experienced repeated devastation, but other areas were wholly untouched. North-eastern Germany suffered considerably; but north-western Germany saw very little population loss.

What were the principal causes of population loss? Death from direct military action does not seem to have been the major reason, though there were many atrocities. In the 1620s exactions seem to have been imposed in a relatively orderly manner (when soldiers were reasonably paid they were unlikely to burn or loot). From the later 1630s onwards, however, half-starved soldiers were a real threat to the civilian population. The worst period seems to have been the years 1634-40 when all the armies experienced logistical problems. Moreover, we have to distinguish between the undisciplined behaviour of individual groups of soldiers and the systematic devastation perpetrated by an entire army. The latter was rare, but did occur in Bavaria twice, in 1632 and 1646, at the hands of the Swedish army. Thus the indiscriminate slaughter of civilians and the burning of villages and towns seem to have been the exception rather than the rule. Although many villages and smaller towns were burned down, larger towns were generally spared as they were considered to be valuable as fortresses and sources of wealth (Magde-

DATE	BATTLE	NUMBERS
1620	White Mountain	28,000 beat 21,000
1631	Breitenfeld	42,000 beat 35,000
1632	Lutzen	9,000 on each side: a stalemate
1634	Nordlingen	33,000 beat 25,000

TIMELINE

I) THE BOHEMIAN AND PALATINE WAR 1618-23

1618	Defenestration of Prague
1620	Defeat of Bohemian rebels at White Mountain
1621-2	Palatinate overrun
1623	Maximilian of Bavaria obtains electoral title

II) THE DANISH EPISODE 1625-9

1626	Christian IV defeated at Lutter
1627-8	Wallenstein overruns much of Denmark and Mecklenburg
1629	Edict of Restitution; Peace of Lubeck

III) THE SWEDISH EPISODE 1630-5

1630	Gustavus Adolphus lands in Germany
1631	He wins the battle of Breitenfeld
1632	He is killed at Lutzen
1634	Wallenstein assassinated; Habsburg victory at Nordlingen
1635	Peace of Prague

IV) FRENCH INTERVENTION 1638-48

1638	Franco—Swedish Treaty of Hamburg
1639	France takes over Rhine army
1641	Hamburg renewed
1643-5	War between Denmark and Sweden
1645	Imperial defeat at Jankov
1648	Peace of Westphalia

burg was a singular exception). By far the most common cause of death in the conflict was war-related food shortages (brought about by requisitioning, abandoned farmland and irreplaceable livestock losses) and epidemic diseases such as typhus, influenza and dysentery (spread both armies and refugees) which struck the vulnerable (the very young and the very old) already weakened by malnutrition. Clearly the plague was also a factor but this had little to do with the war. In addition, many marriages became infertile and families disintegrated. In many places the normal social structure broke down.

Although the verdict now is that the effects of the war have been exaggerated, we should not play down the enormous suffering the population endured. Many were ruined and lost everything. The statistics to some extent disguise a myriad of personal catastrophes. And there can be no adequate appreciation of the anxiety, uncertainty and fear that was generated by the war over such a long period. It is little wonder that contemporaries believed that they had lived through a nightmare or that many lost their traditional religious beliefs.

It has been suggested that there was an overall decline in economic activity which began before the war and was a part of a long-term trend, and this seems convincing—though there were exceptions such as Hamburg and Bremen which prospered. Agriculture undoubtedly suffered, as farmland was devastated by soldiery and peasants deserted the land. It is true that agriculture recovered quite quickly and that traditional rural society was preserved, but a reduced population accentuated serfdom, as peasants were increasingly tied to the land. Changes in agriculture outside Germany tended to stem from population pressures, but the Empire remained underdeveloped and her peasantry unfree. The better off managed to survive—large landowners and wealthy peasants—but small tenants and cottagers were bankrupted and their property snapped up by others.

Many lords took advantage of their peasants. In many cases wealthy families were displaced by loyal ones, an occurrence that was not just confined to Bohemia. Thus there occurred a considerable redistribution of capital and wealth. But even the very rich suffered. Many nobles and mercantile families were bankrupted. Certain occupational groups did benefit—brewers and those involved in military supplies—but overall trade was disrupted, and what we see is a general disruption of economic activity and a considerable growth of debt, at personal, municipal and governmental level. Overall the princes were strengthened by the war: the scope of government activity was greatly increased, the level of taxation went up enormously and the church was now more strictly under government control.

Although there is evidence to suggest that many regions of central Europe experienced a rapid recovery after 1650, those who had lived through the previous 30 years had experienced a most traumatic time and had reason to give thanks when the last Swedish troops left occupied territory in the 1650s

Further Reading

There are many books on the Thirty Years' War, each with that title. The most recent and up-to-date are by Geoffrey Parker (Routledge, 2nd ed. 1997), Ronald Asch (Macmillan, 1997) and Graham Darby (Access series, Hodder 2001). Graham Darby is Head of History at King Edward VI School, Southampton. His The Thirty Years' War is published by Hodder & Stoughton in 2001.

Cardinal Richelieu: Hero or Villain?

Robert Knecht looks at the 'eminence rouge' and considers how his image, carefully crafted during his lifetime, has become that of a demonic schemer.

ROBERT KNECHT

Among Foreign Statesmen of the past who are well-known to the average educated Briton, Cardinal Richelieu (1585–1642) occupies an almost unique position. He turns up in the most unlikely places, such as *Monty Python's Flying Circus* and the children's cartoon *Dogtanian and the Three Muskehounds*. Yet his career did not impinge particularly on English history. His role in defeating Buckingham's expedition to the Ile de Ré hardly explains the exceptional place he has come to occupy in British historical thinking. The only other foreign statesman who enjoys a comparable status is Bismarck. We need to ask ourselves whether we have been brainwashed by Richelieu's own propaganda or by the fictional portrayal of the Cardinal generated by the Romantic movement in the nineteenth century.

Richelieu, who dominated French foreign and domestic politics as Louis XIII's chief minister from 1624 until his death in 1642, took great pains to ensure for himself an enviable reputation. His skilful use of propaganda has left its mark on history, though recent research has helped to put the record straight. From the start of his ministry he took care to amass extensive personal archives. The many reports which he sent to Louis XIII (r.1610–43) and his letters to other important contemporaries bear the stamp of a man writing for posterity. He supported extensive archival research by men such as Pierre Dupuy (1582–1651) and Théodore Godefroy (1580–1649) in the hope of giving his policies a historical perspective. He sponsored the composition of pamphlets in his favour, reviewed and corrected the works of historians writing about contemporary events. The history of Louis XIII's reign written by Scipion Dupleix, a militant Catholic and protagonist of absolutism, is an excellent guide to the estimate Richelieu wanted to leave of himself. Dupleix lists the qualities needed of a minister: judgement, reason, diligence, assiduity, knowledge, experience of state affairs, uprightness, reputation, nobility of birth, eloquence, skill and courage. He finds them all in Richelieu and even asserts that the Cardinal was divinely chosen and inspired.

Controlling public opinion is, of course, a two-way process. Criticism needs to be stifled, and Richelieu did this with much success. He submitted the press to a brutally repressive regime. Most pamphlets published in France in his day supported the government; those taking the opposite view emanated from abroad. The Cardinal extended his concept of *lèse-majesté* to any publication critical of the government. He employed more writers to boost his administration than any other statesman of his time. They included Mathieu de Morgues, who began by supporting Richelieu, but turned against him after the Day of Dupes (November 10/11th, 1630, when the Queen Mother, Marie de Médicis, jealous of the Cardinal's rising influence over the King and disapproving of his anti-Spanish policy, plotted unsuccessfully to topple him), and François Langlois, *sieur* de Fancan. After the Day of Dupes, which consolidated Richelieu's position and resulted in Marie de Médicis' exile to the Low Countries, Richelieu assumed the role of 'schoolmaster to the French people' and gathered around himself a group of subservient writers, including the poet Boisrobert (1592–1662), who played a leading role in the foundation of the *Académie française* in 1635. This body, while it was intended to enhance the artistic and intellectual prestige of France, also had a political motivation. Richelieu was determined that its members should be only his known servants. He employed some to write his speeches, others to check his theological writings, and others still to write pamphlets supporting his policies.

The 1630s saw the creation of an official French press. *Le Mercure françois*, which already existed when Richelieu rose to power, appeared only once a year. The need for a more regular and frequent newspaper was met by the creation of the *Gazette* in 1631. This was edited by Théophraste Renaudot (1586–1653), who hailed from Poitou, like Richelieu. The *Gazette* appeared every Saturday. It was four pages long at first, then grew to eight and even twelve pages. Three presses could produce 1,200 to 1,500 copies in one day. Richelieu's influence on the *Gazette* ranged from making suggestions to assigning articles to specific individuals and to writing and editing complete dispatches himself. Richelieu enjoyed being an object of adulation. According to the gossip writer Tallemant des Réaux, the Cardinal once deleted the word 'hero' from a dedication to himself, substituting the word 'demi-god'.

The theatre, too, fell under Richelieu's influence. Writers from whom he commissioned plays were the so-called 'Five authors', including Corneille, Boisrobert and, above all, Desmarets. In 1641 a tragi-comedy by Desmarets (1596–1676), called *Mirame*, celebrated the opening of the theatre in the Palais Cardinal. *Europe*, another play by Desmarets, was an allegorical glorification of Louis XIII's foreign policy. Alongside these works, a flood of pamphlets defending Richelieu's policies poured out of the printing shops. The *Coup d'État de Louis XIII* praised him for rediscovering the art of governing like Tiberius or Louis XI. Many pamphlets equated obedience to Richelieu with submission to the King. 'Ministers', wrote Sirmond, 'are to the sovereign as its rays are to the sun' Achille de Sancy compared Richelieu's relationship with Louis XIII to that between Moses and God. Guez de Balzac in *Le Prince* (1631) addresses Richelieu as follows:

> After the King you are the perpetual object of my mind. I hardly divert it from the course of your life, and if you have followers more assiduous than me ... I am certain that you have no more faithful servant nor one whose affection springs more from the heart and is more ardent and natural.

Richelieu also used painters or sculptors to proclaim his achievements as a royal servant. He commissioned galleries of portraits in all his residences, the most famous being the *Galerie des hommes illustres* in the Palais Cardinal, in Paris. This consisted of portraits of royal servants from Abbot Suger in the ninth century to Richelieu. The Cardinal commissioned numerous portraits of himself, most of them from Philippe de Champaigne. None shows any sign of age or illness, for the painter was instructed to retouch them all to conform to one painted in 1640, which he liked best of all. All except three show the Cardinal standing and in full length. Normally, churchmen were portrayed seated; only rulers and statesmen were shown full length. Richelieu evidently wanted to be among the latter.

Richelieu's mastery of propaganda, however, was not able to guarantee him an unblemished reputation. A host of pamphleteers, mainly based outside France, did their utmost to counter his self-glorification. Thus, Mathieu de Morgues in his *Catholicon français* (1636) accused him of manipulating religion for political ends:

> You make use of religion, as your preceptor Machiavelli showed the ancient Romans doing, shaping it, turning it about one way after another, explaining it and applying it as far as it aids the advancement of your designs. Your head is ready to wear the turban as the red hat, provided that the Janissaries and the Pasha find you sufficiently upright to elect you their Emperor.

In another work, de Morgues attacks Richelieu's foreign policy thus:

> ... his anger has brought the Goths into the state; his madness has called the Poles, Cossacks, Croats and Hungarians into France and has brought us enemies, wars, and disorders such as France has never seen since her beginning.

Morgues' solution is the tyrant's overthrow:

> ... all good Frenchmen, open your eyes to see what a miserable condition you are in; open your minds to foresee the great desolation that menaces you. Do not permit a puny man, sick in body and mind, to tyrannise over the bodies and minds of so many sane persons, nor an apostate monk [Father Joseph], his principal counsellor, to treat you as galley slaves. Cast off these two evil instruments.

News of Richelieu's death on December 4th, 1642, was greeted with rejoicing in France. According to Father Griffet, writing in 1768, the Cardinal

> ... was disliked by the people and I have known old men who could still remember the bonfires that were lit in the provinces when the news [of his death] was received.

Even Louis XIII seems to have had mixed feelings. According to Monglat, the keeper of the King's wardrobe, 'within his heart, he was much relieved and delighted to be rid of him, and he did not conceal this from his familiars'. All kinds of stories were spread about Richelieu after his death. He was accused of sacrificing all, including justice, to his insatiable ambition. Cardinal de Retz (1614–79) claimed that he had created 'within the most lawful of monarchies the most scandalous and most dangerous tyranny which may ever have enslaved the state'. He 'blasted rather than governed the King's subjects'. Michel Le Vassor wrote in his history of Louis XIII (1712) 'I can look only with horror on a prelate who sacrifices the liberty of his fatherland and the peace of all Europe to his ambition'. A similar charge was levelled by Voltaire in his *Le Siècle de Louis XIV* (1751): 'there was fighting since 1635 because Cardinal Richelieu wanted it; and it is likely that he wanted it in order to make himself necessary'. While conceding that Richelieu had begun to make France great internationally, Voltaire accused him of neglecting prosperity at home: the roads were in a poor state and overrun by brigands; the streets of Paris were filthy and full of thieves. He dismissed Richelieu's *Testament politique*, a personal memoir written under Richelieu's close personal supervision, probably for the King, and covering the essentials of the Cardinal's social and political ideology, as 'stuffed full of errors and misconceptions of every kind'. Montesquieu called him a 'wicked citizen'.

With the advent of the Romantic movement in the nineteenth century Richelieu was relentlessly vilified by poets and dramatists. Alfred de Vigny in his novel, *Cinq-Mars* (1826), suggested that all the ills of France stemmed from Richelieu's attack on the nobility. In the preface, Vigny draws a distinction between reality (*le vrai*) and truth (*la vérité*). The historian searches for reality, he argues, but reality without truth is not worth the search. It is truth which gives reality a moral dimension without which reality is nothing, and it is the responsibility of the novelist or poet to draw the truth from reality by using his imagination. *Cinq-Mars* offers the reader a portrait of Richelieu so vivid as to suggest that truth and reality are one and the same. The novel recounts an episode from the nobility's resistance to Richelieu. Its heroes are two young noblemen, Cinq-Mars and de Thou, who were executed by order of the Cardinal. In their punishment Vigny sees the death sentence of the monarchy which, by suppressing the nobility, prepared the turmoil which was to bring about its own downfall. *Cinq-Mars* provided the painter Paul Delaroche (1797–1856), with the subject of one of his most successful works, now in the Wallace Collection, in London. This shows the aged and ailing Richelieu slumped against cushions in his barge, towing the boat in which the young and healthy conspirators are being taken to their place of execution.

The popular reputation that Richelieu enjoyed in England during the nineteenth and early twentieth centuries owed more to fiction than to history. *Cinq-Mars* inspired Edward Bulwer-Lytton to write a play, called *Richelieu or the Conspiracy*. This amalgamated the conspiracy of the duc de Bouillon with the Day of Dupes and the treason of Cinq-Mars. Bulwer-Lytton saw Richelieu as France's dictator, but also as her benefactor; a man with a dual character, both witty and sinister. He captured the interest of the famous actor James Macready, and tried to make him see Richelieu's dramatic potential. The correspondence between the two men is fascinating. On September 16th, 1838, Bulwer-Lytton wrote:

> Richelieu would be a splendid fellow for the Stage, if we could hit on a good plot to bring him out—connected with some dramatic incident. His wit—his lightness—his address—relieve so admirably his profound sagacity—his Churchman's pride—his relentless vindictiveness and the sublime passion for the glory of France that elevated all. He would be a new addition to the Historical portraits of the Stage.

On the same day, he wrote to John Forster: 'Richelieu has never been brought on the Stage, but his character is most dramatic. And he has always what Macready wishes for—one leg in Comedy, the other in Tragedy'. On November 17th, Bulwer-Lytton sent Macready a bibliography of works on Richelieu including the Cardinal's *Political Testament*, describing it as 'apocryphal'. He explained:

> In France there is a kind of traditional notion of his Person much the same as we have of Henry VIII or Queen Mary—or almost of Cromwell, viz. A Notion not to be found in books, but as it were, orally handed down. And this seems general as to his familiarity with his friends—his stateliness to the world—the high physical spirits that successful men nearly always have & which, as in Cromwell, can almost approach the buffoon, when most the Butcher.

Macready read *Cinq-Mars* assiduously, but had great difficulty understanding Richelieu's character as conceived by Bulwer-Lytton. He took the unusual step of consulting Alfred de Vigny himself, when the latter came to England early in 1839. Vigny prophesied:

> He will make a fine Richelieu, and I will have much to say to him about that man whose intimate enemy I

have been during the entire period when I was writing Cinq-Mars.

Macready met Vigny on February 16th, and reported 'Count de Vigny gave me more than two hours on Thursday, and brought the man Richelieu directly before me'. The correspondence between Bulwer-Lytton and Macready may be read as an attempt to bring Reality and Truth into line; in the end Truth won. It was Macready's portrayal of Richelieu as a villain, not Bulwer-Lytton's more tempered version of the character that conquered the English stage. When *Richelieu* was first staged on March 7th, 1839, it proved a triumph. In his old age, the playwright John Westland Marston (1819–90) remembered that first night:

> I fought my way with another young enthusiast to the pit door of old Covent Garden on the first night of Bulwer's *Richelieu*. What a human sea it was, and how lit up by expectation, that surged and roared for two hours against that grim, all-ignoring barrier! But its stubborn resistance, and the dense pressure which, at last, almost wedged out the breath of every unit in the crowd, gave an almost stern delight, a zest of contest for a prize, of which the lounger into a reserved box or seat has no conception.

Macready did not disappoint. The grandest scene was the last in which Richelieu, on the verge of death, attends Louis XIII to submit his resignation:

> How touching was the proud humility of the weak old man as he relinquished, seemingly forever, the splendid cares of State; how arresting the sight of him as, supported in his chair, his face now grew vacant, as if through the feebleness of nature, now resumed a gleam of intelligence, which at times contracted into pain, as he gathered the policy of his rivals—a policy fatal to France! One noted the uneasy movements of the head, the restless play of the wan fingers, though the lips were silent, till at last the mind fairly struggled awhile through its eclipse, as, in a loud whisper, he warned the King his succours would be wasted upon England. Then came the moment when, recovering the despatch which convicted his foes of treason, he caused it to be handed to the King, and sank supine with the effort. Slowly and intermittently consciousness returned, as Louis thrice implored him to resume his sway over France. So naturally marked were the fluctuations between life and death, so subtly graduated (though comprised within a few moments) were the signs of his recovery, that the house utterly forgot its almost incredible quickness when, in answer to the King's apprehensive cry as to the traitors—'Where will they be next week?' Richelieu springs up rescuscitated, and exclaims—'There, at my feet!'

At the end 'it was an audience dazzled, almost bewildered by the brilliancy of the achievement, that, on the instant fall of the curtain, burst into a roar of admiration that, wild, craving, unappeasable, pursued, like a sea, the retreating actor, and swept him back to the front'.

Richelieu was revived by Henry Irving in September 1873 with enormous success. It was performed on 120 nights at the Lyceum. The following account of Irving's performance appeared in the *Standard* on October 14th, 1873:

> In the first act, hugged in his furred robe, darting with arrowy keenness vulpine glances from beneath his shaggy brows, a smile, bitter or benevolent, ever hovering about the stern pursed-up lip, the senile gait still preserving remnants of vigour, made up a perfect picture to the eye, while the measured and significantly terse speech, illustrated by ever-varied and appropriate attitude, the thoughtful by-play, as it is called, completed to the sense, in the most satisfactory fullness, both of character and situation. The rhapsody ending this act, delivered with an eloquent fervour, gaunt arms and glistening eyes uplifted, worthy of words weighted with more genuine metal, gives the first hint of Mr Irving's emotional intensity. As the play proceeds, these vivid outbursts of strongly realised feeling become more frequent, upheaving like volcanic commotions, and pouring out words in a boiling torrent, fiery and scathing as lava. Such was the threat of Rome's anathema ... when the tempest of the soul seemed to act outwardly on the frame, swaying and lifting it bodily from the ground, like an uprooted tree, towards the object of the Cardinal's terrific wrath. The physical grandeur of the explosion, combined with the overbearing moral force, is unmatched by any other similar exhibition of the actor's power throughout the play, and only approached by the triumphant springing up of the Cardinal from his arm-chair at the close of the action, and after the finely-wrought scene of feigned exhaustion, when, trampling the state paper, so perplexing to poor Louis, beneath his feet, he lowers up in savage exultation at the recovery of his lost power, and the distant prospect of dire vengeance over his discomfited enemies. The concentrated malignity with which, as he half-glided, half-tottered towards Baradas, his clenched teeth and parched throat, rather than his lips, force out the words 'thou hast lost the stake', could scarcely be surpassed for spell-like power over the imagination—the man seemed transformed into some huge cobra.

Thus did Richelieu become a well-known stage villain in England. Bulwer-Lytton's play continued to be performed across England for many years in many theatres that no longer exist. It brought Richelieu to the attention of a public not otherwise particularly cognisant of French history and may serve to explain why he has become such a frequent presence in examination papers. Ultimate responsibility for the play's success lay with Alfred de Vigny, but other figures of the Romantic movement contributed to this portrayal of the Cardinal, notably Victor Hugo whose verse drama, *Marion Delorme* (1831), portrayed Louis XIII as a cypher, the real ruler of France being the tyrannical and bloodthirsty Cardinal. Richelieu in this play never appears on stage. His voice, however, is heard from behind a curtain saying at the end 'No pardon!' as the hero, Didier, is about to be executed. For the historian Jules Michelet (1798–1874) the Cardinal was the 'sphinx in a red robe' whose dull grey eye said: 'whoever guesses my meaning must die', the 'dictator of despair who in all things could only do good through evil', a soul tormented by 'twenty other devils' and torn by 'internal furies'. The Cardinal, according to Michelet, 'died so feared that no one dared speak of his death, even abroad. It was feared that out of spite and with a terrible effort of will he might decide to return'.

An unflattering portrait of Richelieu was also widely disseminated in the nineteenth century through the popular novels of Alexandre Dumas, particularly the *Three Musketeers* (1844). This shows the Cardinal as a man without faith or sense of justice who uses his red robe to conceal his depraved appetites. Louis XIII in his presence is little more than a whimpering child. In 1896 Richelieu reappeared in Stanley Weyman's popular novel, *Under the Red Robe*, which was successfully dramatised at the Haymarket Theatre in London. In the face of so much public exposure, is it surprising that Richelieu became almost a household name this side of the Channel?

The most sweeping indictment of Richelieu's policies is to be found in Hilaire Belloc's biography of 1930. This presents the Cardinal as the creator of modern Europe in which nationalism has replaced Catholicism as the state religion:

> We are what we are, as divided and in peril of dissolution through our division, because Richelieu applied his remote, his isolated, his overpowering genius to the creation of the modern state, and, unwittingly to himself, to the ruin of the common unity of Christian life.

Through him, writes Belloc, 'modern Europe arose; until there came, two hundred years after Richelieu, to confirm its divisions, and to render apparently irreparable the schism in our culture, the corresponding genius of Bismarck'.

For Further Reading

W.F. Church, *Richelieu and Reason of State* (1972); H.M. Solomon, *Public Welfare, Science and Propaganda in Seventeenth-Century France* (1972); R.J. Knecht, *Richelieu* (1981); H. Gaston Hall, *Richelieu's Desmarets and the century of Louis XIV* (1990); A.S. Dower, *The Eminent Tragedian William Charles Macready* (1966); L. Irving, *Henry Irving the Actor and His World* (1951).

ROBERT KNECHT is Emeritus Professor of French History, University of Birmingham.

From Mercantilism to 'The Wealth of Nations'

The Age of Discovery gave rise to an era of international trade and to arguments over economic strategies that still influence the policies of commerce.

MICHAEL MARSHALL

We live in an era when continual economic growth is almost considered a birthright, at least in the developed world. It has become the benchmark of the health of a society, guaranteeing an ever-expanding prosperity. The current president of the United States even finds that his extensive misbehavior is overlooked by a majority of Americans because he happens to be presiding over an extended period of economic growth and optimism.

If annual growth drops below about 2 percent, planners and politicians start to get nervous, while a recession (negative growth) is considered a serious crisis. Where will it all end? Can such growth continue—with periodic setbacks, of course—indefinitely? We do not know and usually do not care to ask.

One thing is clear, however. It was not always so. For most of human history it has not been so. In western Europe in the period 1500–1750, output increased by a mere 65 percent, by one estimate, or an average of 0.26 percent a year, even though the population grew about 60 percent. For most of this period, 80 percent or more of the population worked the land. Studies of wage rates in England and France suggest that the working poor had to spend a full four-fifths of their income on food alone.

So this was not an economically dynamic society. There was relatively little disposable income, that being enjoyed by the prosperous elite of landed aristocracy and, increasingly in this period, merchants. Consequently, there was no prospect of creating a mass domestic market for new products. Most wealth was still tied up in the relatively static commodity of land, and agriculture was the major measure of a country's wealth.

Yet in the period from the voyages of discovery in the late fifteenth and early sixteenth centuries [see "Columbus and the Age of Exploration," THE WORLD & I, November 1998, p. 16] up till the Industrial Revolution there occurred what has been called a "commercial revolution."

The story of that revolution, which I will tell here, weaves together a number of significant themes. The upshot of the Age of Discovery was the emergence of a network of global trade. The consequences of that trade, and the measures taken by increasingly centralized European governments [see "The Ascent of the Nation-State," THE WORLD & I, March 1999, p. 18] to control and direct it, produced the system later labeled, most notably by Adam Smith, mercantilism. This was the practice of imperial rivalry between European powers over global trade, and it gave impetus to the disagreements between Britain and its American colonists that led to the American Revolution. Critical consideration of these issues gave birth to Smith's theoretical study of economics, which culminated in the publication of his masterwork *The Wealth of Nations*.

Protecting Bullion Reserves

Smith wrote: "The discovery of America and that of a passage to the East Indies are the two greatest and most important events recorded in the history of mankind." No doubt he exaggerated, but nothing was more important in the unfolding of this story. The Spanish conquistadores went to the New World in search of El Dorado. They found little gold but plenty of silver at Potosi in Peru and in northern Mexico. This silver became the lubricant of the machinery of an emerging global economy.

It flowed into Spain, from where much of it went to the rest of Europe, especially Holland, to pay the debts the Hapsburg rulers had incurred through the religious and dynastic struggles in their German possessions and in the Spanish Netherlands. Some of it then flowed to the Baltic to pay for the timber, rope, and other shipbuilding materials that the region supplied, especially to Holland and Britain. The bulk of it, though, went to Asia to satisfy the growing European demand for spices, silk, Indian calico, and later, Chinese tea.

Without the silver that demand could not have been satisfied: Europe had nothing that Asia wanted to import in exchange. That situation would not change until after the Industrial Revolution, when clothing from the Lancashire cotton industry in the north of England found a market in Asia. Even then problems remained. The economic reason for the shameful opium trade in the early and mid-nineteenth century, when opium grown in In-

The Commercial Revolution

Voyages of discovery in the fifteenth and sixteenth centuries resulted in a growing network of international trade. Silver from the New World became the lubricant for the machinery of an emerging global economy.

Fearing the success of their rivals, European governments imposed trade restrictions to protect their national interests.

Viewing commerce as an arena of conflicting national interests at times thrust competing European powers into war.

Advocates of free trade criticized mercantilist policies, suggesting peace could arise from mutually beneficial terms of trade.

Clashes over trade were significant factors in the antagonisms that led to the American Declaration of Independence.

The growth of economic relations between America and Britain after the Revolutionary War suggests that the free traders were right.

dia was exported illegally to China, was to earn exchange to pay for tea without having to export silver.

Silver was not without problems. So much of it flowed into Europe in the sixteenth century that it caused serious price inflation. The Spanish economy, in particular, was considerably disrupted, a significant factor in Spain's gradual decline. During the seventeenth century, from a peak around 1600, the supply of silver began to decrease. The demand for goods from Asia, however, did not. The result was a net outflow of silver bullion from Europe, a shrinkage of the money supply, and as a result, economic recession.

No economic theory existed at the time, and no contemporary thought argued that governments should not regulate such matters affecting national wealth in the national interest. So they did. The ad hoc system of tariffs and other measures influencing trade and manufactures that came to be known as mercantilism began to emerge.

The context in which this happened was one of increasingly centralized emerging nation-states that were spending a greater portion of the total national income than in the past, especially in the frequent times of war. They exercised closer control over more aspects of life in pursuit of national policy than in the past, especially through the taxation needed to fund wars. Trade with the New World nurtured the idea that commerce could be a source of national wealth and strength just as much as agriculture and should be developed to that end.

Spain, Britain, and France all banned the export of gold or silver bullion, but this proved to be like trying to stop water from running downhill. The belief was that bullion represented the national wealth or treasure, and that trade should be conducted so as to amass a surplus of it. A country would then have a reserve to cushion itself from the economic effects of adverse fluctuations in the supply of gold and, especially, silver.

Underlying this thinking was the assumption that markets and the amount of trade were relatively fixed, and that gaining a larger share of the pie necessarily meant depriving another

country of part of its share. Trade was thus conceived as an arena of national competition and even conflict, a form of war by other means.

Colbert and French Mercantilism

Advocates of free trade in the late eighteenth and the nineteenth centuries strongly criticized this aspect of mercantilist policy. They proposed that peace was one of the benefits of free trade, since it tied trading partners in mutually beneficial exchanges that could only be lost through war. Neither side was totally right. Circumstances always affect cases, and the mercantilist policymakers were pragmatists who reacted to the situation before them.

The most systematic practitioner of mercantilist policies was undoubtedly Jean-Baptiste Colbert, finance minister for France's Louis XIV in the later seventeenth century. Colbert used the considerable power of the Sun King's state to increase its wealth through the promotion of French trade and manufactures. He certainly banned the export of bullion, but his policy was aimed at replacing bullion as the means of payment for necessary imports with the earnings from the export of French manufactures.

To that end he developed selected industries by state subsidies and bringing in skilled foreign artisans. He particularly encouraged high-value products such as quality furniture, glass, and tapestries, and the quality of French workmanship in these areas became legendary throughout Europe. He used tariff barriers to protect industries that faced serious foreign competition. Wanting to develop the French cloth industry in the face of the well-established British cloth trade, he doubled the duty on imports.

Thus emerged the classic mercantilist pattern that, because it came about in a piecemeal, pragmatic manner, has only existed in its complete form in the writings of historians. The export of domestic raw materials was largely discouraged, so that domestic manufacturers could enjoy their use. The export of sheep and raw wool from Britain, for example, was heavily regulated for the benefit of the domestic textile industry. The export of manufactures was encouraged as the means to a favorable balance of trade and the bullion inflows that came with it.

The import of foreign manufactures was restricted since this adversely affected the balance of trade. Raw material imports were looked on favorably to the degree that they could be used in or support domestic manufactures, although a large agricultural country like France, under Colbert, aimed at as much self-sufficiency as possible.

Colbert realized that encouraging French industry had little point if its products could not then be exported. That meant commercial shipping and a navy to protect it. Colbert had before him the example of the Dutch. They were the dominant economic power in Europe in the early and mid-sixteenth century through their skills in trade and shipping.

The Dutch dominated North Sea fishing, annoying the British by taking huge catches of herring from Britain's east coast, developing a factory-style industry for salting the catch, and then exporting it throughout Europe. They dominated the carrying trade from the Baltic to western Europe, were major carriers of imports to Europe from the Americas and from the East, and grew rich through their control of the lucrative reexport of those imports throughout Europe from their initial port of entry in Amsterdam.

To support these efforts the Dutch dredged and improved their rather shallow harbors and developed specialized forms of shipping, both for fishing and for moving bulk materials. They also developed financial instruments to ease the flow of trade and extend the use of credit. Most notably, they established the Bank of Amsterdam, a public bank that offered a source of capital very different from the government funding of chartered companies that had marked the enterprise of discovery and trade in the sixteenth century.

Colbert built up a merchant marine to rival that of the Dutch and ensure that French trade was carried in French ships. Under his direction the merchant fleet grew from a mere 60 ships of 300 tons or more to over 700 ships of that size. He provided for the protection of French maritime commerce by building up the French navy from 20 ships to 250 by the time of his death in 1683.

He always viewed commerce as an instrument of national policy, and merchants had little say in his decisions. This was unlike the situation in England, where various merchant groups formed influential lobbies on the Crown's commercial policies. The prizes of commerce remained for him a zero-sum game: France's gain must be someone else's loss. He created a successful glass industry in Paris by inviting Venetian glassblowers to teach their skills. He later boasted that the successful royal mirror factory that resulted was depriving Venice of one million livres a year.

Commerce and Conflict

Colbert's attitude was much derided by the later free-trade economists, most notably Smith. The Scottish philosopher David Hume, a contemporary and good friend of Smith's, wrote on the subject: "I shall therefore venture to acknowledge that, not only as a man, but as a British subject, I pray for the flourishing commerce of Germany, Spain, Italy and even France itself."

It was an irony, too, and one that later critics did not fail to point out, that a considerable contribution was made to the growth of French transatlantic exports by industries that did not receive Colbert's nurturing support. Iron and coal, hardware, and the cheaper cloths produced by the textile industry in Normandy all developed through their own enterprise.

Advocates of free trade proposed that peace was one of its benefits.

Nevertheless, Colbert's legacy was a foundation for rapid and successful French commercial development in the eighteenth century. Between 1715 and 1771 the total value of French foreign trade grew eightfold until it almost matched British trade. The value of French exports multiplied more than four times between 1716 and 1789. Colbert must have been doing something right.

Nor were the policymakers of the time completely wrong in their view of commerce as conflict to gain the largest share of a fixed prize. It is certainly true that bilateral trade is mutually beneficial. If a country wants to export its goods, its potential trading partners must have the means to pay for those goods. So it is in the exporter's interest that partners have their own successful export markets, perhaps in the original country's own home market, to generate the revenue needed to buy its exports.

This is not true of the carrying and reexport trade, however. The Dutch had grown rich on this trade, and the British and French set out to take it away from them. Both ended up fighting trade wars with the Dutch over the issue. In the second half of the seventeenth century, Britain passed a series of Navigation Acts, which required that goods shipped in and out of British ports, and to and from British colonies, had to be carried in British ships.

This struck at the heart of the Dutch trade, hence the tensions that led to war. At issue was who would distribute the new colonial imports throughout the rest of Europe. The Dutch gradually lost out to the French and British. Between the 1660s and 1700 British exports grew by 50 percent. Half of that increase came from the reexport of colonial imports, mostly to Europe.

As a result, the eighteenth century was the Anglo-French century in terms of commerce. I have already mentioned the spectacular growth in French trade. The value of British trade grew threefold between 1702 and 1772, and British shipping grew at a similar rate, reaching over one million tons by 1788. This phenomenal growth represented a tremendous amount of new wealth, most of it associated with colonial trade, especially that of the New World.

The bulk of British trade in 1700 was still with Europe, but by 1776 two-thirds of its overseas trade was outside Europe. Between 1700 and 1763 the value of British exports to America and the West Indies multiplied fivefold, while the value of imports from those areas grew fourfold. Anglo-French rivalry resulted in a number of wars throughout the century. It is small wonder, given the importance of colonial trade, that parts of those wars were fought in North America and in India, over strategic control of its sources.

'Badges of Slavery'

The Atlantic trade not only was the most substantial but it also formed an interlocking network. From the plantations of the southern colonies of America, the Caribbean, and the Brazilian coast, tropical staples—tobacco, cotton, sugar, coffee, cocoa, rice—flowed to Europe. European manufactures flowed back west, supplying the plantation economies with necessities they did not produce themselves. European cities, especially those on the Atlantic, grew and prospered on this trade. From Cadiz and Lisbon in the south, through Bordeaux and Nantes in France, to Bristol, Liverpool, Glasgow, and the burgeoning entrepôt of London in England, they all became part of the Atlantic economy.

A city like Liverpool benefited from importing, refining, and reexporting sugar and tobacco. It also benefited from a new and increasingly significant part of the Atlantic economy—slavery.

LIBRARY OF CONGRESS

Slaves on the deck of the bark *Wildfire*, brought into Key West, Florida, on April 30, 1860. Carrying 510 slaves, the ship violated the 1809 slave trade law that prohibited slave importation. This engraving was made from a daguerreotype for *Harper's Weekly*, June 2, 1860. Blacks were rarely allowed on deck except for occasional "exercise."

Plantation agriculture is labor intensive, and the plantations of the Americas looked to West Africa to supply that need. Ships from Liverpool or Bristol, or Lisbon for that matter, would sail to West Africa and trade cheap manufactured items to local chiefs in return for live bodies.

These were then shipped across the Atlantic—the Middle Passage—to the Caribbean or the American South, where those still alive after the horrors of the voyage were sold. The ships then returned home laden with cotton, tobacco, or sugar. In the case of Portuguese ships, they would sail to Brazil and return with Brazilian produce.

European manufactures were also exported to the settler societies of the Americas. The half million Spanish settlers in Mexico and Peru paid for these with silver. As the supply of silver slackened and Latin American society became increasingly self-sufficient, this trade became less important.

The North American trade continued to burgeon. European manufactures were paid for by the products of the region. The question arose as to what those products were to be, and who should determine that: the colonists or the government in London? At this point, questions of mercantilist policy become questions about the future of the American colonies, in other words questions about independence. Adam Smith addressed both sets of questions in *The Wealth of Nations*.

He described the regulations by which London sought to control the American economy as "impertinent badges of slavery." They were intended to ensure that the American economy would complement the British economy, but that, of course, also meant subordinating the one to the other. The American colonies were viewed as a supplier of those staples mentioned above and a protected market for British manufactures.

The colonies were by no means expected to develop industries that might compete with those in Britain. In 1699, Britain sought to ban the woolen industry in America and prevent any intercolony trade in woolen goods. In 1750 a similar ban was applied to steelmaking and the manufacture of finished products from iron.

The role of the New England colonies was to reduce British reliance on the Baltic region for naval materials and certain types of shipbuilding timber. Thus, these strategically sensitive materials—essential for building the ships of the Royal Navy that protected British commerce—would be under British political control. These products were allowed into Britain duty-free, as was pig iron, in that case to reduce British reliance on Swedish and Russian sources. But the pig iron was not to be any further refined in the colonies, lest it compete with the British iron industry.

Being true Englishmen jealous of their liberties, the colonists chafed under these restrictions. Political conflict inevitably resulted, and many commentators in Britain considered that the costs of that conflict outweighed any economic benefit from trying to restrict the natural economic development of the colonies. Matters came to a head in 1776, the year in which both the Declaration of Independence and *The Wealth of Nations* were published.

New Economic Directions

Smith had definite views on the American economy and on the system of tariffs and trade regulations that had helped produce the conflict. Unlike the views advocated by other contributors to the debate, however, his arose from the context of an extensive theoretical consideration of how wealth is created. It is only a slight exaggeration to say that he invented economic theory.

He can certainly be considered the originator of classical economics. It was his ideas that were first developed and interpreted by David Ricardo and then by John Stuart Mill in *Principles of Political Economy*. At the end of the nineteenth century they were revived and revised as "neoclassical" economics by Alfred Marshall. Even the economic ideas of Karl Marx and, in this century, John Maynard Keynes, started from the principles first enunciated by Smith, although they then moved in very different directions.

His book discusses systematically the basic economic questions: a theory of price or value; wages, profits, and rents; the role of labor; how wealth is distributed among owners of the different factors of production; the role of capital, money, and the banking system; and taxation and the national debt. He famously introduced the concept of the division of labor, explaining how it increases productivity and also is limited by the extent of the market.

He held a dynamic view of the economy. National wealth resulted from the flow of income over time rather than from the size of the stock of capital held. His theory anticipated the actuality of burgeoning economic growth produced by the Industrial Revolution. It differed significantly from the assumptions that lay behind mercantilist policies.

Smith and his good friend Hume refuted the argument that trade should be managed in such a way as to maintain a positive balance so as to earn bullion. Hume pointed out that if bullion flowed out of a country its prices would fall, which would render its exports more competitive, thus increasing the flow of export earnings into the country until balance was restored. In other words, Hume and Smith thought of the economy as a dynamic self-regulating system. In Smith's most famous phrase, it was as if an "invisible hand" harmonized individual economic actions pursued out of self-interest into an overall balance that served the public good. It worked best without government interference.

Economic historian Peter Mathias sums up Smith's arguments on this topic admirably, saying that

> a system of freely operating market prices, under naturally competitive conditions, would ensure the lowest effective prices to the consumer and produce the most efficient allocation of resources between the different branches of economic activity. The ultimate test of efficiency and welfare thus became a freely moving price level not distorted by legislative interference.

On the basis of this argument, Smith launched into a critique of tariffs, subsidies, and monopolies, all the tools of the commercial policy of the era that he dubbed mercantilism. "Consumption," he argued, "is the sole end and purpose of all production," yet under the mercantilist system the consumers' interest was sacrificed to that of producers, who sought special favors from the government for their particular industries.

With such views he could not help but be critical of contemporary British policy toward the American colonies. He thought that Britain could rightly impose its own taxation system on the colonies but only in the context of colonist representation at Westminster. (He was, incidentally, a friend of Benjamin Franklin's, and the two discussed these issues when Franklin was in London.) He thought, too, that Britain could extend its customs laws to America provided that *all* internal barriers to trade were abolished.

Smith thus conceived of the British Empire as a vast and free internal market for each and all of its component regions. He even envisaged that the seat of the empire should not remain fixed in London but should move "to that part of the Empire which contributed most to the general defense and support of the whole."

The Discussion Continues

Economic relations between Britain and America after the Revolutionary War suggested that the free-trade arguments promoted by Smith and his fellow critics of the system of colonial regulation were right. After 1782, British exports to the United States began to grow more rapidly than those to any other region. By 1836 about a quarter of Britain's total exports went there, while the United States provided 80 percent of Lancashire's cotton.

Such evidence boosted free-trade ideas, which became increasingly influential in the nineteenth century, especially in Britain—whose manufacturers, of course, stood to gain the most by them. But the argument that Smith first articulated against mercantilist policy is still going on today. Countries still remain very sensitive about their balance of trade. In the United States, a Republican presidential candidate, Pat Buchanan, argues for greater protection for American industry, in the face of widespread free-trade thinking in both parties.

Back in the 1970s, the Carter administration bailed out Lee Iacocca's Chrysler Corporation because it was thought that the damage to the economy as a whole and the social cost of the resulting unemployment were worse than paying the cost of a bailout. Right now the United States is entering into a tariff war with western Europe over Caribbean bananas. The Europeans want to reserve 25 percent of their banana market for producers in their former colonies. Without that guaranteed market those producers probably could not survive. The United States is arguing for unrestricted free trade in bananas, which would benefit the mighty Dole Corporation. Whoever is right in the argument, its roots lie in the system of Atlantic trade and colonies that developed in the seventeenth and eighteenth centuries.

The "commercial revolution" of the eighteenth century generated a huge increase in trade and wealth. This all happened under a system of mercantilist policy. Whether that policy nurtured the development or, as Smith argued, it took place despite the policy is a question that can probably never be resolved.

What can be said is that the commercial revolution was an important prelude to the Industrial Revolution. Some of the capital generated from trade found its way into the new manufacturing industries. Perhaps more important was the development of extensive new global markets, for it is questionable whether in the absence of those markets European domestic demand could have grown enough to sustain the rapid growth of the new industries. As it was, those industries found an already established international network of markets through which their new products could flow.

MICHAEL MARSHALL is executive editor of *The World & I*.

400 Years of the East India Company

Huw V. Bowen asks whether the East India Company was one of the 'most powerful engines' of state and empire in British history.

HUW V. BOWEN

The year 2000 marks the 400th anniversary of the founding of the English East India Company, the trading organisation that acted as the vehicle for British commercial and imperial expansion in Asia. For over two hundred years, the Company stood like a colossus over trade, commerce and empire, and contemporaries could only marvel at its influence, resources, strength and wealth. Writing at the beginning of the nineteenth century, the political economist David Macpherson was unequivocal in his assessment that the Company was 'the most illustrious and most flourishing commercial association that ever existed in any age or country.'

Today even the most powerful firm pales by comparison in terms of longevity and wide-ranging economic, political and cultural influence. In an era before fast travel and instant communication, the East India Company established a far-flung empire and then set about governing, controlling and exploiting it from a great distance in London. It managed to do this until it was finally rendered obsolete by the tumultuous events surrounding the Indian Mutiny in 1857.

The Company was granted its first charter by Elizabeth I on the last day of 1600, and it had to survive an uncertain first century or so as it sought access to Asian markets and commodities. At home, it was restructured several times, notably between 1698 and 1708 when an 'old' and 'new' East India Company co-existed before merging to form the United Company of Merchants Trading to the East Indies. In the East, the Company came under such pressure from its Dutch rivals during the mid-seventeenth century that it was obliged to shift the main focus of its activities from the Malay archipelago and the Spice Islands to South Asia. Over time, it managed to establish a commercial presence in India centred upon three 'presidencies' established at Madras, Bombay and Calcutta. These tenuous footholds were fortified and defended by the Company as it sought to consolidate its position in an often hostile commercial and political world. This in turn gave rise to the growth of a small private army that was eventually to rival the regular British army in terms of size and manpower. The Company's role in India was thus defined by both commercial activity and a military presence: it was considered legitimate to use force in support of trade, and the overseas personnel were organised and

HT Archives

The frontispiece of Isaac Pike's Journal of the Stringer (1713) showed the Company robustly defending its trading position.

deployed accordingly. In the words of one contemporary, it was a 'fighting company'

By the mid-eighteenth century, the Company had begun to assert itself over rival European companies and Indian powers alike, and this placed it in a position from which it could begin to carve out an extended territorial and commercial empire for itself. The actions of men such as Robert Clive (1725–74), Warren Hastings (1732–1818) and Charles Cornwallis (1738–1805) helped to transform the Company from trader to sovereign, so that during the second half of the eighteenth century millions of Indians were brought under British rule. As William Playfair put it in 1799:

> From a limited body of merchants, the India Company have become the Arbiters of the East.

The Company created the British Raj, and as such it has left a deep and permanent imprint on the history and historiography of India. The story, once almost universally described as the 'rise of British India', not so long ago formed part of the staple reading diet of British schoolchildren and students. In the post-colonial era, when imperial history has ceased to be fashionable, the legacies of British India are still hotly debated and contested. It is within this context that the history of the East India Company remains to the fore.

Today's casual observer finds few signs of the leading role the Company once played in the life of the nation.

Rather less obvious, perhaps, is the part played by the East India Company in the domestic development of Britain. Indeed, today's casual observer finds few signs of the leading role it once played in the nation's business, commercial, cultural and political life. In terms of architecture, for example, there is little surviving evidence in London of the Company's once-extensive property empire. The London docklands, home to the East India dock complex, has been reshaped. Although Commercial Road and East India Dock Road—the purpose-built link with the City—survive, the docks themselves have been filled in and redeveloped, leaving only a few poignant reminders of the Company's once formidable presence in the area. To the West, the great fortress-like warehouses built by the Company at Cutler Street were partially demolished and refurbished in controversial circumstances during the late 1970s. There is no trace remaining whatsoever of the Company's headquarters in Leadenhall Street. Charles Dickens once described the 'rich' East India House 'teeming with suggestions' of eastern delights, but it was unceremoniously pulled down in the 1860s, and in its place today stands the new Lloyd's Building, also a monument to commercial capitalism, but displaying rather different architectural qualities. In recent years, the only obvious local clue to the Indian connection was provided by the East India Arms, a tavern in nearby Lime Street, but that too has now fallen victim to the modern re-naming and re-branding process. As a result, the East India Company is now out of sight and out of mind.

It was not always like this. During the late eighteenth century, the Company played a key role in London's economy, employing several thousand labourers, warehousemen and clerks. Returning fleets of East Indiamen moored in Blackwall Reach, before their Indian and Chinese cargoes were transferred via hoys and carts to enormous warehouses where they awaited distribution and sale in Britain's burgeoning consumer markets. The profile of the Company in London was always high and the eyes of many were on Leadenhall Street. Political infighting at East India House regularly captured the attention of the metropolitan chattering classes. The Company itself was repeatedly subjected to inquiry by a Parliament uneasy about the turn being taken by events in the East.

The Company's domestic tentacles extended well beyond London, however, and its influences were widely felt across the south of England. Provincial outposts were established in the form of the agencies in ports such as Deal, Falmouth, Plymouth and Portsmouth. Over the years the Company maintained camps for its military recruits at Newport in the Isle of White, Warley in Essex and at Chatham in Kent. Educational establishments were set up for the purpose of preparing those destined for service overseas. During the first half of the nineteenth century, the East India College at Haileybury in Hertfordshire educated boys for the civil service, while Addiscombe Military Seminary near Croydon trained military cadets.

More generally, the Company touched many sectors of British society and the economy, as some contemporaries acknowledged. In 1813, for example, a friend to the Company, Thomas William Plummer, set about identifying what 'proportion of the community' had a connection with the Company. Without mentioning several million purchasers of tea, spices, silks, muslins and other Asian commodities, he listed investors, Company employees of many types, tradesmen, manufacturers, shipbuilders, dealers, private merchants, military personnel and ship crews, before concluding that:

> Scarcely any part of the British community is distinct from some personal or collateral interest in the welfare of the East India Company.

There was more than a grain of truth in what Plummer wrote, and by the beginning of the nineteenth century many interests across the country had been tied closely to the Company. This was particularly the case with the several thousand or so well-to-do individuals who chose to invest in Company stocks and bonds. For much of the eighteenth century East India stock was the most attractive investment available in the nascent stock market, not least because it always paid out an annual dividend of more than 5 per cent. The India bonds that provided the Company with its short-term working capital were also highly prized, with one early stock market analyst describing them as 'the most convenient and profitable security a person can be possessed of'.

The fortunes of Company and nation had become so tightly intertwined that they had begun to move in tandem with one another as those who took a broad view of political and economic matters were able to see. When the Company flourished, the nation flourished. Equally, as Edmund Burke put it, 'to say the Company was in a state of distress was neither more nor less than to say the country was in a state of distress'. Such logic dictated that the effects of any crisis or catastrophe experienced by the Company in India would be deeply felt in Britain and the wider British Empire, and this was well understood by close observers of the imperial scene. One pamphleteer wrote in 1773 that the loss of India would occasion a 'national bankruptcy' while the imperial theorist Thomas Pownall suggested that such an event would cause 'the ruin of the whole edifice of the British Empire'. These concerns lay behind the increased levels of government anxiety about Company adventurism, misrule, and mismanagement in India that became evident after 1760.

By the 1770's the Company was akin to a semi-privatised imperial wing of the Hanoverian state.

Late eighteenth-century concerns about events in the East reflected the fact that the East India Company was no longer an ordinary trading company. It had evolved into an immensely powerful hybrid commercial and imperial agency, and after the conquest of Bengal it fundamentally reshaped its traditional commercial policy based upon the exchange of exported British goods and bullion for Asian commodities. Instead, the Company concentrated its efforts on the collection of territorial and customs revenues in northeast India. The right to collect these revenues had been granted by the Mughal Emperor Shah Alam II in 1765, an event which both confirmed British military supremacy in the region and served to elevate the Company to the position of *de facto* sovereign in Bengal and the neighbouring provinces of Bihar and Orissa. Thereafter, trade was used to facilitate the transfer of 'tribute' from Asia to London as surplus revenue was ploughed into the purchase of Indian and Chinese commodities for export to Britain. As Edmund Burke later remarked, this marked a 'revolution' in the Company's commercial affairs.

The Company's empire had now become self-financing to the point that further military expansion could be sustained, but it was also believed that generous payments could be made to domestic stockholders and the British government alike. This proved to be a vain hope, but the transfer of tribute helped to define the essential characteristics of the late-eighteenth-century state-Company relationship. Successive ministers declared the state's 'right' to a share of the Bengal revenues, but in return for the promise of annual payments into the public treasury they allowed the Company to continue in its role as the administrator, defender and revenue collector of Bengal. This brought the British government the benefits of empire without any expensive administrative or military responsibilities. It was a welcome and convenient arrangement at a time when the national debt was spiralling ever-upwards and parts of the Empire, most notably North America, were proving increasingly difficult to control and subdue.

By the 1770s the Company thus found itself as something akin to a semi-privatised imperial wing of the Hanoverian state, with its operations being defined by the dual pursuit of both private and public interest. It was charged with the protection, cultivation, and exploitation of one of Britain's most important national assets, and contemporary observers described its new role accordingly. In 1773 the prime minister, Lord North, declared that the Company was acting as '[tax] farmers to the public', while a late-century pamphleteer suggested that the Company had become 'stewards to the state'. In this scheme of things, there was a greater need for the Company to become more accountable, efficient, and reliable, and this desire lay behind the reforms embodied in North's Regulating Act of 1773 and Pitt's India Act of 1784.

The Company's importance to the British state was not, however, simply to be assessed in terms of its role as the licensed agent through which metropolitan administrative, fiscal and military influences were brought to bear upon the Indian empire. The Company had been present at the birth of the eighteenth-century state during the troubled period following the 'Glorious Revolution' of 1688–89. As a hard-pressed nation struggled to cope with the demands of the Nine Years' War, ministers had drawn heavily on the financial resources of the 'new' East India Company that had received its charter in 1698. This meant that when the United Company was established in 1709 it was already deeply embedded in both the public finances and the City of London where, together with the Bank of England, it formed part of the 'monied interest'.

The financial relationship between state and Company took several different forms, all of which were a variation on a theme that saw the Company's monopoly privileges periodically confirmed or extended by the Crown in return for loans or payments made to the public purse. Indeed, by the 1720s the entire paid-up share capital of the Company, almost £3.2 million, was on longterm loan to the state at 5 per cent interest. This sizeable advance was extended to £4.2 million before prime minister and chancellor Henry Pelham's restructuring of the national debt in 1749–50 saw the reduction of interest payments to 3 per cent and the creation of the East India annuities. This extensive underwriting of the post-settlement regime was such that a Chairman of the Company, Jacob Bosanquet, was later to borrow a phrase from Adam Smith and declare that the Company, together with the Bank of England, had become one of the 'most powerful engines of the state'. As Chairman of a company under great pressure from critics by 1799, Bosanquet was hardly likely to say anything else, but his comments were not altogether inaccurate. His organisation had established itself as a cornerstone of the City of London, and as such it had played a key role in supporting the state and public credit.

By the end of the eighteenth century, apologists were thus arguing that the Company formed part of the very foundations of Britain's state and empire, yet within sixty years it had ceased to exist at all. What happened to make the great 'engine' run out of steam so rapidly?

There are a great many answers to this question but the most basic one is undoubtedly the most important. Quite simply, in economic terms the Company failed to deliver what it had promised since the 1760s. As the military and administrative costs of empire multiplied, the Company proved itself unable to generate a revenue surplus for transfer to Britain. A great many attempts were made to remodel the Company's fiscal and commercial operations but successes in one area were always off-set by failures and setbacks elsewhere. Only the striking growth of the China tea trade offered the Company any prospect of success, but that in itself was not enough to satisfy the demands of profit-hungry stockholders and ministers. Indeed, the annual flow of 'tribute' to the state Treasury promised by the Company in 1767 had dried up almost at once. By 1772 the Company was teetering on the edge of bankruptcy, having failed to master the complexities of its new role in India, and a degree of desperation forced it into the measures that ultimately led to the Boston Tea Party the following year. Thereafter, the Company staggered from crisis to crisis, requiring government loans to enable it to continue functioning. In effect, this meant that roles had been reversed, and the Company had become dependent upon the state for financial support.

The Company failed to argue convincingly that it offered the best way forward for the Anglo-Asian connection.

A dose of economic reality, coupled with widespread metropolitan unease about 'despotic' Company government in India, caused many commentators rapidly to reassess their views of Britain's eastern empire. Nowhere was this more evident than with Edmund Burke who became one of the Company's harshest critics and campaigned long and hard for reform and the punishment of British misdemeanours in India. Initially, though, Burke had been as captivated as any observer by the prospect of Britain gaining very real material advantage from the Company's successes in Bengal. He had outlined the economic potential of India to the House of Commons in 1769 before concluding that 'The Orient sun never laid more glorious expectations before us.' This type of view was commonplace during the 1760s, but it was replaced by much gloomier assessments of the situation in the decades that followed. Commentators soon tired of hearing about the promise of Indian wealth being used to the advantage of the metropolis, and began instead to expose the flaws that were evident in the Company's calculations and methods. The figures did not seem to add up, leaving one MP, George Tierney, to complain that 'Our Indian prosperity is always in the future tense'.

Criticism such as this only strengthened the case of those in Britain who were campaigning vigorously for the East India trade to be opened up to free competition. Just as the utility of the Company to the nation began to be discussed, old mercantilist assumptions about the organisation of trade were being called into question. Taking a lead from Adam Smith, who had condemned chartered companies as being 'nuisances in every respect', critics exposed the Company to searching analyses of its methods and practices.

Under such attack, the Company proved unable, indeed almost unwilling, to answer the charges levelled against it. Although it began to emphasise the contribution it made to intellectual and scientific life in Britain, it failed to argue convincingly that it alone offered the best way forward for the further development of the Anglo-Asian connection. Part of the reason for this was that the Company believed it had already taken the organisation of its commercial and financial affairs to the highest possible level. It proved to be remarkably complacent and, together with a deep-rooted institutional conservatism, this meant that any change was regarded with the deepest suspicion. As one director of the Company put it, 'Innovations in an established system are at all times dangerous'. Few friends of the Company could see any need to alter an organisation that was thought to be beyond improvement, and this case was restated time and again. Most would have agreed with Thomas Mortimer who argued during the 1760s that the Company had 'brought the commerce and mercantile credit of Great Britain to such a degree of perfection, as no age or country can equal.' To alter anything would be to invite trouble. Sustained failure and. disappointing performance, however, flew in the face of such opinion, and this ensured that pressure for change continued to grow from outside the Company.

In the end, the Company's failure was essentially two-fold as far as many of those in the metropolis were concerned. It failed to deliver to Britain the great financial windfall that had been anticipated after the conquest of Bengal; and because of this it was unable to sustain much beyond 1760 its position as one of the major institutional and financial props of the Hanoverian state. When charges related to misrule, despotism, unfair monopoly practices and a host of other complaints were added to the scales, they served eventually to tip the balance of political opinion.

The immediate and outright abolition of the Company, however, was never an option because the state did not possess the resources, skills or will necessary to govern a large empire in India. Instead, successive breaches were made in the Company's commercial position. Trade with the East was opened up to a limited degree in 1793; the Indian monopoly was ended in 1813; and the exclusive trade with China was abolished in 1833. The Company survived for another twenty-five years as Britain's administrative and military representative in India, but by then it was a trading company in name only. The Company had achieved the full transition from trader to sovereign, amply fulfilling Adam Smith's prediction that trade and government were incompatible within a 'company of merchants'.

The Company ended its days in the aftermath of the Indian Mutiny when no case at all could be advanced for its survival in any form. Its powerful legacy endured in India for many more years in the form of the Indian army and civil service, but sight was soon lost of the importance of its contribution to the development of the metropolitan state and to imperial Britain itself. Today the Company has been almost entirely removed from the geographical and historical landscape and it has been more or less erased from our national consciousness. As the 400th anniversary of the founding of the Company approaches, this makes it all the more necessary for us to reflect on the deep, but now hidden, impression left on British history by this quite extraordinary institution.

For Further Reading

H.V. Bowen, 'Investment and Empire in the Later Eighteenth Century: East India Stockholding, 1756–1791', *Economic History Review* (1989); K.N. Chaudhuri, *The English East India*

Company: The Study of an Early Joint-Stock Company (Cass, 1965); John Keay, *The Honourable Company: The History of the English East India Company* (Harper Collins, 1991); Philip Lawson, *The East India Company: A History* (Macmillan, 1993); Martin Moir, *A General Guide to the India Office Records* (British Library, 1996); Jean Sutton, *Lords of the East: The East India Company and its Ships* (Conway Maritime Press, 1981). Information about the records of the East India Company can be found on the British Library's website http://www.bl.uk/ (follow the links to the Oriental and India Office collections).

HUW BOWEN is Senior Lecturer in Economic and Social History at the University of Leicester and the author of War and British Society 1688–1815 (Cambridge UP, 1998).

This article first appeared in *History Today*, July 2000, pp. 47-53. © 2000 by History Today, Ltd. Reprinted by permission.

John Locke: Icon of Liberty

Mark Goldie traces the ways in which people across the political spectrum have used and abused the ideas of the philosopher who died 300 years ago this month.

MARK GOLDIE

The english do not celebrate their philosophers. In Paris there is a rue Descartes. In Edinburgh there is a statue of David Hume. But in England there is no public fanfare for John Locke (1623–1704), the tercentenary of whose death falls on October 28th this year. You will find his portrait in the National Portrait Gallery, but demand is insufficient for a postcard to be on sale. Perhaps Locke would not have minded that accolades are conferred instead on his friend Isaac Newton. He modestly wrote in the preface to his *Essay Concerning Human Understanding* (1689) that he was but an 'under-labourer in clearing ground' for such 'master-builders' in the 'commonwealth of learning' as Newton and Boyle.

Nor would Locke have wished his life to be remembered. He was indifferent to biography and reticent, even secretive, about himself. When the philosopher Damaris Masham wrote her memoir of him, she could not report his year of birth, though they had lived together for fourteen years from 1690. Like another of his friends, Sir Christopher Wren, whose epitaph in St Paul's Cathedral invites us to 'look around', Locke's epitaph at High Laver in Essex invites us to 'learn from his writings' rather than engage in 'dubious eulogies'.

Yet Locke has not escaped canonisation, and it was for his writings that he became an icon. Today he is lauded in the United States far more than in his own country. There, because of his *Two Treatises of Government* (1689) in which he argued that, to be legitimate, a government required the consent of its people, he is hailed as 'the philosopher of freedom', the 'founder of liberalism'. The American political tradition is grounded in Year One, the Revolution, and it invokes Founding Fathers. The belief is ingrained that Locke was the inspiration behind Adams, Jefferson, and Washington. When the American newspapers of the 1760s denounced George III they quoted the *Two Treatises*. Governments, wrote Locke, may not 'levy taxes on the people' without 'the consent...of their representatives'. In 1773 the *Boston Gazette* hailed the American edition of the *Second Treatise* as providing 'a better view of the rights of men...than all the discourses on government...in our language'.

In contemporary America Locke or, rather, an imagined heritage 'Locke', is a mascot of right-wing think-tanks. The Locke Foundation and Locke Institute teach the virtues of free enterprise and the evils of big government. LibertyOnline offers the *Two Treatises* in its virtual library, where it is placed in a litany of great texts of freedom from Magna Carta to Ronald Reagan's 'evil empire' speech against the Soviet Union. The National Rifle Association cites paragraph 137 of the *Second Treatise* as an authority on the right to carry arms. The Arizona State Court Building, opened in 1991, has inscribed upon it words from paragraph 202: 'Where law ends, tyranny begins'.

Locke had once been a British icon too. British Whigs thought of their own regime as grounded in Year One, the Revolution of 1688. Only later did the British insist on telling themselves a myth of organic continuity. The Whigs made Locke a hero of 'Revolution Principles'. Locke encouraged this reading by a remark in the preface to the *Two Treatises*. He announced that his book would 'establish...King William...in the consent of the people'. An exile in Holland in the 1680s, where he had fled the regimes of Charles II and James II, Locke had sailed back to England in the wake of William of Orange's invasion, and published his *Two Treatises* in the autumn of 1689.

He did not become an icon immediately, however, and he was never an uncontested one. He was revered more for his philosophy than for his politics, and it was his *Thoughts on Education*, not the *Two Treatises*, that ran second to the *Essay Concerning Human Understanding* in numbers of reprints during the eighteenth century. As many historians have insisted, there was far more to political thought in the eighteenth century than Locke and the ideas of consent, the social contract and the right of revolution. The Tories castigated him as a fanatic 'Commonwealth-man', a fomenter of rebellion and anarchy, and a deistical underminer of Christianity. The first pictorial representation of 'Locke on government' appeared in 1710 in a Tory cartoon attacking the Whig pamphleteer Benjamin Hoadly, where Locke appears on the bookshelf behind Hoadly's desk. In one version, Oliver Cromwell stands over Hoadly's shoulder, with regicide's axe in hand; in another, it is the devil who stands there. Ironically, in the reign of Queen Anne Tory hatred of Locke served to make his name better known as a theorist of politics. One of his critics was the Tory

Life and Works

Locke was born in Wrington, Somerset, in 1632, the son of a country attorney who fought on the Parliamentary side in the Civil War. He attended Westminster School and Christ Church, Oxford, and in 1667 he entered the household of the Earl of Shaftesbury, who became Lord Chancellor but who later led the Whig movement against Charles II. Locke fled to Holland in 1683, returning in the wake of the Glorious Revolution of 1688-89. He then began to publish his books, which had long been in gestation. In the 1690s he served on the Board of Trade and Plantations, advising on colonial and commercial policy. He was involved in the Great Recoinage and the end of press censorship. A polymath, he wrote on philosophy, politics, religion, education, economics, and medicine. He spent the last fourteen years of his life at Oates in Essex, in the household of Damaris Masham, a philosopher. He died in 1704.

Locke's chief philosophical work is the *Essay Concerning Human Understanding* (1689). It insisted that the purpose of philosophy was not to produce systems but to clarify thinking, and argued that all human knowledge derived from experience. *The Two Treatises of Government* (1689) attacked divine-right absolutism and advocated a right of revolution against tyranny. The task of government was to protect our natural rights and no government was legitimate unless grounded in the consent of the people. In *A Letter Concerning Toleration* (1689), he argued against coercion in religion. Churches were voluntary associations and the saving of souls was no business of the state. *Some Thoughts Concerning Education* (1693) was a handbook for parents in the nurturing and character formation of children.

The last of Locke's principal works was *The Reasonableness of Christianity* (1695), minimalist as to Christian doctrine, and reflecting his fear of clerical power and of religious 'enthusiasm' or fanaticism.

feminist Mary Astell, who attacked Whig philosophy because it deposed monarchical tyrants while leaving husbandly tyranny intact. 'If all men are born free, how is that all women are born slaves?'

Despite Tory assaults, Locke became an icon. The trend was set round 1730 by George II's consort, Caroline of Ansbach, who commissioned a bust of Locke for her hermitage at Richmond. He was one of five heroes installed there, with Boyle, Newton, and the latitudinarian clerics Clarke and Wollaston. *The Gentleman's Magazine* ran a poetry Competition which made the grotto famous, and yielded reams of egregious verse.

> *Within on curious marble carv'd compleat,*
> *Majestic Boyle claims a superior seat,*
> *Newton and Locke, Clarke, Wollaston appear,*
> *Drest with the native robes they us'd to wear,*
> *Immortal bards, and as divine their name,*
> *Dear to their country and as dear to fame.*

The *Magazine* published panegyrics to the wisdom of Caroline, the people's princess:

> When her majesty consecrated these dead heroes, she built herself a temple in the hearts of the people of England; who will, by this instance of her love to liberty and public virtue, think their interests as safe in the hands of the government as their own.

If Caroline brought Locke to Court, other adepts at political garden art placed Locke among the heroes of the Country opposition. About the same time, Lord Cobham transformed his estate at Stowe near Buckingham into a rural allegory of the fate of political liberty under the rule of perverted Whiggery. In his Elysian Fields he built a sturdy Temple of Ancient Virtue and a ruinous Temple of Modern Virtue. The ensemble culminated in the Temple of British Worthies. Here he placed busts of Elizabeth I, William III, John Hampden, Milton, and Locke. To these he added the Black Prince, a model for the current Prince of Wales, Frederick, who, it was hoped, would restore liberty when his father died. Lastly came King Alfred, whom Cobham called the 'founder of the English constitution'. The inscription under Locke is as follows:

> JOHN LOCKE, who, best of all philosophers, understood the powers of the human mind; the nature, end, and bounds of civil government; and, with equal courage and sagacity, refuted the slavish systems of usurped authority over the rights, the consciences, or the reason of mankind.

Stowe became a site for tourists, and remains so. Gilbert West's versified guidebook of 1732, *The Gardens of...Lord Viscount Cobham*, hailed each bust in turn, dwelling in Locke's case on religious toleration:

> *Next Locke, who in defence of conscience rose,*
> *And strove religious rancour to compose:*
> *Justly opposing every human test,*
> *Since God alone can judge who serves him best.*

Shortly afterwards, Voltaire published his *Letters on England*, which ignited Locke's European fame. In Georgian England, Locke became constantly vaunted. John Clarke's *Essay upon Study* (1731) recommended reading Locke's books every year, 'even the driest'. Samuel Richardson's novels *Pamela* and *Clarissa* treated the reader to meditations on Locke's *Thoughts on Education*. In Francis Coventry's children's book *The History of Pompey the Little* (1751), young Lady Sophister tells Dr Rhubarb that Locke is her favourite philosopher. It was said of William Warburton that he had Locke's works 'bound up in small detached pieces, for the convenience of carrying them with him'. Locke was lauded in poetry, for instance in Isaac Watt's *To John Locke* (1706) and in James Thomson's *Seasons* (1730).

The radical publisher Thomas Holles named a Dorset estate 'Locke Farm'. The merchant Sir Gerard Vanneck decorated his library at Heveningham Hall, Suffolk, with medallion portraits, Locke standing alongside Homer, Virgil, Shakespeare, Milton, Dryden, Pope, Prior, Voltaire, and Rousseau. In 1809 a subscription was launched to place a statue of Locke in St Paul's

Cathedral. Richard Westmacott's model was open for inspection at his workshop and subscribers were to receive from Messrs Boulton—the firm that built Watt's steam engine—a bronze or silver medal. In 1835 a statue of Locke was placed by the Duke of Bedford in his Temple of Liberty at Woburn. The tympanum carried a relief of Liberty, bearing her spear and cap of liberty, attended by Peace and Plenty.

Locke became a plastercast saint of the blandest kind. In the 1730s, Samuel Strutt had remarked that in Locke 'a great many as implicitly believe, as Roman Catholics do transubstantiation'. A century later Henry Acton wrote that 'his life appears to have been one uninterrupted course of innocence, piety, and goodness', he was 'one of the noblest intellectual benefactors of his race'. To Locke, wrote Leigh Hunt in 1810, 'every Englishman owes love and reverence'.

Yet the story of Locke's reputation is more complex. Politically, he seems to have become domesticated and tamed during the first half of the eighteenth century. In a compilation of 1753 called *Of Civil Polity*, selections from Locke were combined with extracts from popular sermons. Locke was cast as a preacher of social duties and family values. Then, after 1760, he was seized upon by radical movements which, in the wake of panics provoked by the American and French Revolutions, provoked renewed Tory counterattacks against him.

During the last thirty years of the eighteenth century a struggle ensued for his soul. The engagement began with the use of Locke by pro-Americans in the Stamp Act crisis, and, in domestic politics, in debates over George III's alleged ambitions to revive royal power. Between 1778 and 1783 there were half-a-dozen tracts specifically addressing Locke's politics. In 1785, the philosophical writer William Paley (1743–1805) observed that, in recent years, in

> . . . the language of party, in the resolutions of popular meetings, in debate, in conversation, in the general strain of those fugitive and diurnal addresses to the public, which such occasions call forth, it was impossible not to observe the prevalency of those ideas of civil authority which are displayed in the works of Mr Locke. The credit of that great name, the courage and liberality of his principles, the skill and clearness with which his arguments are proposed, no less than the weight of the arguments themselves, have given a reputation and currency to his opinions.

In 1783 a Dublin tract complained that 'even shopkeepers might be heard quoting Locke'.

Locke had become the common currency of a new populist politics. He was cited by the Wilkites, the Societies for Constitutional Information, and the London Corresponding Society, in their campaigns for a wider franchise and regular elections. Locke became a hero of the Dissenters, who demanded an end to their civil disabilities. He was the cynosure of latitudinarian Anglicans who wished to ease their consciences of the doctrinal impositions of the Established Church. He was quoted by the friends of the American and Irish causes.

In the House of Commons in 1776, John Wilkes recited from the *Two Treatises* in demanding 'fair and equal representation'.

For the political reformer John Cartwright, Locke's remark that every man must consent upon coming of age was used to support his campaign for annual parliaments, on the ground that prolonged parliaments were a deprivation of each young man's right of formal entry into civil society. In 1795, the radical lawyer Thomas Erskine contrived to turn paragraphs 157–8 of the *Second Treatise* into an argument for universal manhood suffrage. It was a usage which persisted in the *Black Dwarf* and *Northern Star*, the newspapers of the Chartists in the 1840s.

By the late eighteenth century, Locke was doing service in a decisive shift in political ideas away from the traditional ideal of the tripartite constitution of King, Lords and Commons, towards the democratic conception of the sovereign people, and a theory of representation grounded in personhood rather than property. A critic of these movements, Baptist Noel Turner, complained that the old idea of the aristocracy as the 'intermediate power', the counterbalance between crown and people, was in danger of destruction by the craze for a 'democratical' reading of Locke. 'The majesty of the people' will reduce the king to 'a mere signing clerk'.

Locke underpinned the two most signal political testaments to appear from the leaders of Rational Dissent, Joseph Priestley's *Essay on the First Principles of Government* (1768) and Richard Price's *Observations on the Nature of Civil Liberty* (1776). Here a distinctively modern liberalism emerged, marked by an accent on free enquiry and the value of pluralism in modes of life and opinion. In 1787 Charles James Fox cited Locke in a Commons debate on the repeal of the religious Tests. Dissent and pro-American sentiment came together in a cartoon of 1768. Called 'An Attempt to Land a Bishop in America', it showed a ship carrying a bishop being attacked by colonists. One man shouts 'No Lords Spiritual or Temporal in New England'. Another carries a flag declaring 'Liberty and Freedom of Conscience'. And a third waves a book, inscribed 'Locke'.

In the 1780s and 1790s Locke's *Two Treatises* was abridged and anthologised in a series of popular tracts. Extracts appeared in Thomas Spence's brazenly populist *Pig's Meat* (the title a reference to Edmund Burke's sneer against 'the swinish multitude'). A handy forty-two page pamphlet, *The Spirit of John Locke*, extracted Locke on consent, constituent power, restraints on governmental tyranny and revolution. 'Men being all free, equal, and independent' was its opening line, from paragraph 95 of the *Second Treatise*. The jurist Sir William Jones translated Lockean precepts into vernacular simplicities in his *Dialogue between a Scholar and a Peasant*. His brother-in-law was prosecuted for sedition for distributing it.

That Locke became the instrument of libertarian politics will not surprise modern readers. That he became an instrument of what might be called, at least in shorthand, 'socialist' politics, will surprise some, especially in the American neo-con think tanks. By the close of the eighteenth century, at a time of rural poverty, economic dislocation, crisis in Poor Law provision, and steadily diminishing scope for commoners' rights of access to natural resources, manifestos multiplied on behalf of the rural poor against oppressive landlords. Locke's basing of property-right in labour and his stipulation of a natural right to the means of subsistence served such campaigners well. An intellectual tradition of 'Lockean socialism' ran from Thomas Spence's *Rights of Man* in 1775 through to Thomas Hodgskin's *Natural and Artificial Right of Property* in 1832. Spence imagined communitarian utopias. Hodgskin used the newly coined word 'capitalism' to define an economic system which he saw as contrary to Locke's principles. In 1796 the radical John Thelwall, with Locke in hand, denounced the 'territorial monopolist' and defended the right of common access to 'the means of being usefully industrious . . . the common right of all'. George Dyer, in his *Complaints of the Poor People of England* (1793), cited Locke for the principle that the gifts of nature remain in common till a man 'by his own industry' acquires a right over them. Providence had never decreed that

> . . . the squire may shoot a partridge or a pheasant, though the labourer shall not; or that Sir Robert may draw the fish out of the river, and that his poor tenant shall be imprisoned for the same action.

For conservatives, Locke had become a dangerous figure, an icon in need of smashing. In 1783 Baptist Noel Turner issued a *True Alarm . . . A Descant on the Present National Propensity*. The 'present national propensity' was the deployment of Locke on behalf of the 'many-headed majesty' of 'king-people'. Yet, even in Turner there was a note of apology for Locke, a desire to protect him from himself, for Locke's exaggerations were, he said, 'natural enough . . . at the first dawning of liberty'.

A breeze of criticism of Locke gathered into a storm. The sense that Locke's philosophy had been misappropriated increasingly turned into a conviction that it was erroneous. An intense debate on Locke in the years 1778–83 opened with the pugnacious Josiah Tucker's *The Notions of Mr. Locke and his Followers*. Tucker became obsessed with repudiating Locke. He turned his tract into a much longer *Treatise Concerning Civil Government* (1781). It was the most intelligent and sustained critique of Locke of the century. He again repeated himself in an essay of 1783, on 'The Evil Consequences Arising from the Propagation of Mr. Locke's Democratical Principles'.

These were not just books for scholars. The cartoonists noticed the bookish battle for Locke too. A radical print of 1783 showed a pile of books, by Locke and the republican Algernon Sidney and Catherine Macaulay, on the floor, parcelled up for sale. On the desk were books by Josiah Tucker and his colleague, Soame Jenyns. Seated at the desk, a government fox pens a manifesto in favour of kingly prerogative and war against America. Out of doors, a speaker addresses the crowd, 'Lord North . . . butchered your American brethren . . . The king is your servant—Each of you gentlemen ought to have voices in the House of Commons'. The poets joined the fray too. William Mason's *The Dean and the Squire* lampooned a conversation in a Bond Street coffeehouse between Dean Tucker and Squire Jenyns. Tucker opens:

> *Squire Jenyns, since with like intent*
> *We both have writ on government,*
> *And both stand stubborn as a rock*
> *Against the principles of Locke.*

> *Let us, like brother meeting brother,*
> *Compare our notes with one another.*

Jenyns, who was a facile and shallow polemicist compared with Tucker, breezily announced that he had refuted the Whigs' philosophy:

> *I controvert those five positions,*
> *Which Whigs pretend are the conditions*
> *Of civil rule and liberty;*
> *That men are equal born—and free—*
> *That kings derive their lawful sway*
> *All from the people's yea and nay—*
> *That compact is the only ground,*
> *On which a prince his rights can found—*
> *Lastly, I scout that idle notion,*
> *That government is put in motion,*
> *And stopt again, like clock or chime,*
> *Just as we want them to keep time.*

'Sblood! . . . controvert them all?', exclaimed the dean, impressed at Jenyns' brisk temerity.

The attack on Lockeanism signalled the revival of Toryism and the emergence of modern conservatism. The new conservatism was of diverse sorts. In Tucker, it took the form of a secular argument which viewed liberty and authority as the fragile products of political evolution, threatened by the naive dogma that by natural birthright men are 'free and equal' and subject to nothing but what they choose. Others appealed to divine providence and the sanctity of ordained hierarchies.

The French Revolution, and Edmund Burke's savage assault upon it, dealt a heavy blow to Locke's reputation. Burke himself was silent about Locke in his *Reflections on the Revolution in France* (1790), but others filled the gap. 'Mr Locke', blustered William Jones in 1798, is

> . . . the oracle of those who began and conducted the American Revolution, which led to the French Revolution; which will lead (unless God in his mercy interfere) to the total overthrow of religion and government in this kingdom, perhaps in the whole Christian world.

'With Mr Locke in his hand' that 'mischievous infidel Voltaire' had set about destroying Christianity. In 1798 there appeared the first edition of the *Two Treatises* to carry editorial footnotes. This was the work of an Irish Protestant bishop, Thomas Elrington, whose aim was to mitigate Locke's text by adding conservative readings in the notes. One footnote, on the right to overturn governments (paragraph 223), said that 'the answer Mr Locke gives is . . . partial and imperfect . . . as the events of the present time but too clearly prove'.

Whether Locke was an author of sedition became a matter of courtroom debate in the treason trial of the boot-maker and agitator Thomas Hardy in 1794. His defence counsel insisted that Hardy had said no more than what Locke had said, and hoped that Locke remained a sufficiently respectable symbol to save Hardy from the gallows. Hardy was indeed saved, but Locke fell victim to the Counter-Enlightenment. In 1815 his portrait was taken down from the hall of his old college in Oxford, Christ Church, from which he had been expelled by order of Charles II in 1684. The Dissenting journal *The Monthly Repository* lamented that this was 'Locke's second expulsion from Oxford'.

In the nineteenth and early twentieth centuries, Romantics, utilitarians, Marxians, Evangelicals, and high churchmen all had their different reasons for passing Locke by. In the second half of the twentieth century, interest in Locke's political ideas revived, especially after the collapse of Marxism and with the resurgence of several contested varieties of liberalism. Today, of the one hundred volumes in the series Cambridge Texts in the History of Political Thought, Locke's *Two Treatises* is the best-selling item.

For Further Reading

John Locke, *Two Treatises of Government*, ed Peter Laslett (CUP, 1988) or ed. Mark Goldie (Everyman, 1993); *John Locke, Political Essays*, ed. Mark Goldie (CUP, 1997); John Locke, *Selected Correspondence*, ed. Mark Goldie (OUP, 2002); John Locke, *A Letter Concerning Toleration*, ed James Tully (Hackett, 1983); John Dunn, *Locke: A Very Short Introduction* (OUP, 2003).

MARK GOLDIE teaches history at Cambridge University. He is editor of *The Reception of Locke's Politics* (6 vols., London, 1999) and *John Locke: Selected Correspondence* (Oxford, 2002).

UNIT 2

Rationalism, Enlightenment, and Revolution

Unit Selections

7. **Descartes the Dreamer**, Anthony Grafton
8. **Empires Ancient and Modern**, Paul A. Rahe
9. **Declaring an Open Season on the Wisdom of the Ages**, Robert Wernick
10. **Thomas Young: the Man Who Knew Everything**, Andrew Robinson
11. **The Passion of Antoine Lavoisier**, Stephen Jay Gould
12. **The First Feminist**, Shirley Tomkievicz
13. **Napoleon: A Classic Dictator?**, Laurent Joffrin

Key Points to Consider

- What did Descartes contribute to modernity?

- For what purpose did Voltaire and Montesquieu write their works?

- What was the impact of the Encyclopedists on the modern world?

- Why was Thomas Young known for both scientific thought as well as linguistics?

- Why was France's greatest scientist victimized by the French Revolution?

- Was Mary Wollstonecraft's feminism similar to or different than today's?

- How does Napoleon compare to other dictators?

Student Web Site

www.mhcls.com/online

Internet References

Further information regarding these Web sites may be found in this book's preface or online.

Adam Smith
   http://cepa.newschool.edu/het/profiles/smith.htm
Eighteenth-Century Resources/JackLynch
   http://andromeda.rutgers.edu/~jlynch/18th/
Napoleon Bonaparte
   http://www.napoleonbonaparte.nl
Western European Specialists Section/Association of College and Research Libraries
   http://www.lib.virginia.edu/wess/

This unit explores facets of the Age of Reason (the seventeenth century) and the Enlightenment (the eighteenth century). These two phases of Western tradition had much in common. Both placed their faith in science and reason, both believed in progress, and both were skeptical about much of the cultural baggage inherited from earlier periods. Yet each century marked a distinctive stage in the spread of rationalism. In the seventeenth century, a few advanced thinkers, such as John Locke and Rene Descartes, attempted to resolve the major philosophical problems of knowledge—that is, to develop a theoretical basis for the new rationalism. The eighteenth century saw in the work of Immanuel Kant and David Hume continuation of that theoretical enterprise. But there was a new development as well: Voltaire, Denis Diderot, and others campaigned to popularize science, reason, the principles of criticism, and the spirit of toleration. Increasingly, the critical attitudes engendered by rationalism and empiricism in the seventeenth century were brought to bear upon familiar beliefs and practices in the eighteenth century.

Several articles in this unit show the advance of critical reason. "Descartes the Dreamer" profiles the seventeenth-century thinker who epitomized the new rationalism, as does "The First Feminist" by Mary Wollstonecraft's life and her arguments for "enlightened" treatment of women.

The new attitudes were often troublesome, even revolutionary. During the seventeenth and eighteenth centuries no tradition seemed safe from criticism as is seen in the article "Declaring an Open Season on the Wisdom of the Ages", which describes the famous *Encyclopedie* of Denis Diderot. Even the Bible was searched for contradictions and faulty logic. Universities and salons became intellectual battlegrounds where the classicists confronted the modernists. The struggle went beyond a mere battle of books. Powerful religious and political institutions were subjected to the test of reason and often were found wanting as in "Empires Ancient and Modern". The goal was to reorganize society on a rational basis and to develop a new morality based on reason, not religious authority.

Of course, rationalism was not confined to these centuries, as anyone familiar with the works of Aristotle or St Thomas Aquinas knows. Nor did the influence of the irrational disappear during the Age of Reason. The period witnessed a great European witch craze and a millenarian movement in England. And those who doubt that irrational attitudes could surface among the rationalists need only read about the craze for phrenology, or Sir Isaac Newton's interest in alchemy and Blaise Pascal's mysticism.

As for the Enlightenment, many have questioned how deeply its ideals and reforms penetrated society. On occasion, radical ideas and social change produced unanticipated consequences. Sometimes the peasants stubbornly resisted the enlightened legislation passed on their behalf. And we are hardly surprised to learn that the enlightened despots on the Continent stopped short of instituting reforms that might have lessened their authority. Or else they manipulated education and the arts in order to enhance their own power. Nor did modern rationalism cause the

great powers to rein in their ambitions, as international wars often broke out.

And while the doctrines of the Enlightenment may be enshrined in the noblest expressions of the French Revolution, it also witnessed mass executions and systematic efforts to suppress freedom of speech. The excesses of the Revolution are exemplified by the execution of the most brilliant French scientist, Antoine Lavoisier (see Jay Gould's article " The Passion of Antoine Lavoisier"). In "Napoleon: A Classic Dictator?" Laurent Joffrin shows how Napoleon could be a ruthless dictator and still be one of the most honored Frenchmen.

In the last century, with its mass atrocities, world wars, and nuclear weapons, it is difficult to sustain the Enlightenment's faith in reason. But even before our recent disillusionments, rationalism provoked a powerful reaction—romanticism. In contrast to the rationalists, romantics trusted emotions and distrusted intellect; they were not interested in discovering the natural laws of the universe, but they loved nature as a source of inspiration and beauty. They were preoccupied with self-discovery, not social reform; and they often drew upon medieval experience for their images and models. Indeed, Rationalism has survived and lives on in our modern programs of education and social uplift under the concept called liberalism.

Descartes the Dreamer

No single thinker has had a more decisive influence on the course of modern philosophy—and general intellectual inquiry—than René Descartes (1596–1650). On the 400th anniversary of Descartes's birth, Anthony Grafton considers the forces that shaped the man and his thought.

ANTHONY GRAFTON

All philosophers have theories. Good philosophers have students and critics. But great philosophers have primal scenes. They play the starring roles in striking stories, which their disciples and later writers tell and retell, over the decades and even the centuries. Thales, whom the Greeks remembered as their first philosopher, tumbled into a well while looking up at the night sky, to the accompanying mockery of a serving maid. His example showed, more clearly than any argument could, that philosophy served no practical purpose. Those who take a different view of philosophy can cite a contrasting anecdote, also ancient, in their support: after drawing on his knowledge of nature to predict an abundant harvest, Thales rented out all the olive presses in Miletus and Chios. He made a fortune charging high rates for them; better still, he showed that scholar rhymes with dollar after all.

At the other end of Western history, in the 20th century, Ludwig Wittgenstein held that propositions are, in some way, pictures of the world: that they must have the same "logical form" as what they describe. He did so, at least, until he took a train ride one day with Piero Sraffa, an Italian economist at Cambridge. Making a characteristic Italian gesture, drawing his hand across his throat, Sraffa asked, "What is the logical form of that?" He thus set his friend off on what became the vastly influential *Philosophical Investigations*, that fascinating, endlessly puzzling text which the American philosophers of my youth took as their bible, and to the exegesis of which they brought a ferocious cleverness that would do credit to any seminarian. If Helen's face launched a thousand ships, Sraffa's gesture launched at least a hundred careers.

In each case—and in dozens of others—the story has passed from books to lectures to articles and back, becoming as smooth and shiny in the process as a pebble carried along by a swift-flowing stream. In fact, these stories have become talismans of sorts: evidence that the most profound ideas, the most rigorous analyses, have their origins in curious, human circumstances

and strange, all-too-human people. Such anecdotes accessibly dramatize the heroic originality and rigor of philosophers—qualities that one cannot always appreciate only by studying their texts, slowly and carefully.

It seems appropriate, then, that no philosopher in the Western tradition has left a more fascinating—or more puzzling—trail of anecdote behind him than the Frenchman René Descartes. Like Wittgenstein's philosophy, Descartes's began from curious experiences; but in his case the provocation was—or was remembered as—nothing so banal as a train ride.

Early in his life, Descartes became a soldier, serving two years in the Dutch army, before joining the Bavarian service. He writes that in the late fall of 1619, while stationed in the German city of Ulm, he "was detained by the onset of winter in quarters where, having neither conversation to divert me nor, fortunately, cares or passions to trouble me, I was completely free to consider my own thoughts." He refused all company, went on solitary walks, and dedicated himself to an exhausting search for… he did not quite know what. Suddenly he stumbled on what he called "the foundations of a marvellous science." After an almost mystical experience of deep joy, Descartes fell asleep, in his close, stove-heated room. He then dreamed, three times.

In the first dream, terrible phantoms surrounded him. His efforts to fight them off were hindered by a weakness in his right side, which made him stagger in a way that struck him as terribly humiliating. Trying to reach a chapel that belonged to a college, he found himself pinned to the wall by the wind—only to be addressed by someone who called him by name, promising that one "M.N." would give him something (which Descartes took to be a melon from another country). The wind died, and he awoke with a pain in is left side. Turning over, he reflected for some time, slept again, and dreamed of a clap of thunder. Waking, he saw that his room was full of sparks. In the third dream, finally, he found two books, which he discussed with a stranger. The second book, a collection of poems, included one about the choice of a form of life—as well as some copperplate portraits, which seemed familiar.

Waking again and reflecting, Descartes decided that these dreams had been divinely sent. He connected them, both at the time and later, with the discovery of the new method that would ultimately enable him to rebuild philosophy from its foundations. Paradoxically, Descartes, the pre-eminent modern rationalist, took dreams as the basis for his confidence in his new philosophy—a philosophy that supposedly did more than any other to deanimate the world, to convince intellectuals that they lived in a world uninhabited by occult forces, among animals and plants unequipped with souls, where the only ground of certainty lay in the thinking self.

Like Wittgenstein, Descartes enjoys a tribute that modern philosophers rarely offer their predecessors. He is still taken seriously enough to be attacked. Courses in the history of philosophy regularly skip hundreds of years. They ignore whole periods—such as the Renaissance—and genres—such as moral philosophy, since these lack the qualities of rigor, austerity, and explanatory power that win a text or thinker a starring position in the modern philosophical heavens. But Descartes continues to play a major role. In histories of philosophy, he marks the beginning of modernity and seriousness; he is, in fact, the earliest philosopher after ancient times to enjoy canonical status. Students of Descartes can rejoice in the existence of an excellent *Cambridge Companion to Descartes*, edited by John Cottingham, two helpful Descartes dictionaries, and even a brief and breezy *Descartes in Ninety Minutes*—as well as in a jungle of monographs and articles on Descartes's epistemology and ethics, physics and metaphysics, through which only the specialist can find a path. (One standard anthology of modern responses to Descartes's work extends to four thick volumes.) Descartes still provokes.

In a sense, moreover, he provokes more now than he did 20 years ago. In the last generation, developments in a wide range of disciplines—computer and software design, primate research, neurology, psychology—have made the question of how to define human consciousness more urgent, perhaps, than it has ever been. What would show that the computer or an ape thinks as humans do? Can one prove that the measurable physiological phenomena that accompany mental states should be identified with them? How can physical events cause mental ones, and vice versa? And who should settle such questions: philosophers, or scientists, or both in collaboration?

New interdisciplinary programs for the study of consciousness or artificial intelligence provide forums for the debate—which remains fierce—on these and other issues. And the debates are, if anything, becoming fiercer. Successes in solving particular problems—such as the creation of a machine genuinely able to play chess, rather than the man disguised as a machine unmasked by Poe—excite some of the specialists responsible for them to declare victory: if a computer has a mind, then the mind is a computer. Stalwart opponents swat these optimists with rolled-up newspapers, insisting that vast areas of mental and emotional experience—like the pain caused by the rolled-up newspaper—undeniably exist and matter even though they have no counterpart in computer models. From

whatever side they come, a great many of the contributions to these debates start with a reference to, or amount to, a sustained attack on Descartes.

It is not hard to explain why this Frenchman, who has been dead for three and a half centuries, still seems modern enough to interest and irritate philosophers who otherwise feel contempt for most of their predecessors. He felt and wrote exactly the same way about his own predecessors.

Descartes, as is well known, began his career as a philosopher in a state of radical discontent with the resources of the intellectual disciplines. He described this state with unforgettable clarity, moreover, in the autobiography with which he began his most famous text, his *Discourse on the Method* (1637). Born in 1596, Descartes lost his mother as a baby and saw little of his father, a councilor in the *parlement* of Brittany at Rennes. For almost a decade, beginning around the age of 10, he attended the Jesuit college of La Flèche at Anjou. Here, he recalled, he made a comprehensive study of classical literature and science. He read—and wrote—much fine Latin, debated in public, learned how to produce an *explication du texte*. He knew all the clichés that humanists used to defend the classical curriculum, and he recited them with palpable irony: "I knew... that the charm of fables awakens the mind, while memorable deeds told in histories uplift it and help to shape one's judgment if they are read with discretion; that reading good books is like having a conversation with the most distinguished men of past ages."

But all this contact with traditional high culture left Descartes unconvinced. Knowledge of literary traditions and past events might give a young man a certain cosmopolitan gloss, but it could not yield profound and practical knowledge: "For conversing with those of past centuries is much the same as travelling. It is good to know something of the customs of various peoples, so that we may judge our own more soundly and not think that everything contrary to our own ways is ridiculous and irrational, as those who have seen nothing of the world ordinarily do. But one who spends too much time travelling eventually becomes a stranger in his own country; and one who is too curious about the practices of past ages usually remains quite ignorant about those of the present."

The humanists of the Renaissance had praised the Greeks and Romans, who did not waste time trying to define the good but made their readers wish to pursue it with their powerful rhetorical appeal. Descartes recognized fluff when he heard it: "I compared the moral writings of the ancient pagans to very proud and magnificent palaces built only on mud and sand. They extol the virtues, and made them appear more estimable than anything else in the world; but they do not adequately explain how to recognize virtue, and often what they call by this fine name is nothing but a case of callousness, or vanity, or desperation, or parricide." So much for the soft, irrelevant humanities—still a popular view in American and English philosophy departments. Descartes, in other words, was the first, though hardly the last, philosopher to treat his discipline as if it should have the austere rigor of a natural science.

Even the study of mathematics and systematic philosophy, however—at least as Descartes encountered them in his college—had proved unrewarding. The mathematicians had missed "the real use" of their own subject, failing to see that it could be of service outside "the mechanical arts." And the philosophers had created only arguments without end: "[philosophy] has been cultivated for many centuries by the most excellent minds, and yet there is still no point in it which is not disputed and hence doubtful." All previous thinkers, all earlier systems, seemed to Descartes merely confused.

He thought he knew the reason, too. All earlier thinkers had set out to carry on a tradition. They had taken over from their predecessors ideas, terms, and theories, which they tried to fit together, along with some new thoughts of their own, into new structures. Predictably, their results were incoherent: not lucid Renaissance palaces, in which all surface forms manifested the regular and logical structures underneath them, but messy Gothic pastiches of strange shapes and colors randomly assembled over the centuries. Such theories, "made up and put together bit by bit from the opinions of many different people," could never match the coherence of "the simple reasoning which a man of good sense naturally makes concerning whatever he comes across."

Descartes insisted that most of philosophy's traditional tools had no function.

Descartes's "marvellous science" would be, by contrast, all his own work, and it would have the "perfection," as well as the explanatory power, that more traditional philosophies lacked. To revolutionize philosophy, accordingly, Descartes "entirely abandoned the study of letters." He ceased to read the work of others, turned his attention inward, and created an entire philosophical system—and indeed an entire universe—of his own. He hoped that this would make up in clarity and coherence for what it might lack in richness of content. And the first publication of his theories, in the form of the *Discourse* and a group of related texts, made him a controversial celebrity in the world of European thought.

As Wittgenstein, 300 years later, cleared the decks of philosophy by insisting that most of its traditional problems had no meaning, so Descartes insisted that most of philosophy's traditional tools had no function. Like Wittgenstein, he became the idol of dozens of young philosophers, who practiced the opposite of what he preached by taking over bits of his system and combining them with ideas of their own. Unlike Wittgenstein, however, he also became the object of bitter, sometimes vicious criticism, from both Protestant and Catholic thinkers who resented the threat he posed to theological orthodoxy or simply to the established curriculum. No wonder that he, unlike his opponents, remains a hero in the age that has none. What characterizes modernity—so more than one philosopher has argued—is its state of perpetual revolution, its continual effort to produce radically new ideas and institutions. Modern heroes—from Reformation theologians such as Martin Luther to political radicals such as Karl Marx—established their position by insisting that traditional social and intellectual structures that looked as solid and heavy as the Albert Memorial would dissolve and float away when seen from a new and critical point of view. The Descartes who wrote the *Discourse* belongs to this same line of intellectual rebels, and in this sense he is deservedly regarded as the first modern philosopher.

Again like Wittgenstein, Descartes refused to take part in normal or in academic high society. Though he devoted a period at the University of Poitiers to study of the law, he made little effort to follow a career as a lawyer—a path chosen by many intellectuals at the time. Though admired by patrons and intellectuals in France and elsewhere, he took little interest in court or city. He did not spend much time in Paris, where in his lifetime the classic French literary canon was being defined on stage and in the Academy and where the fashionable gossiped brilliantly about literature, history, and sex.

Descartes, who contributed so much to the development of that classic French virtue, clarity, kept aloof from his colleagues in the creation of the modern French language. He lived most contentedly in Holland, sometimes in towns such as Leiden and Deventer but often in the deep country, where he had at most one or two partners in conversation—one was a cobbler with a gift for mathematics—and led an existence undisturbed by great excitements. He only once showed great sorrow, when his illegitimate daughter Francine, who was borne by a serving maid named Hélène in 1635, died as a young child. And he only once departed from his accustomed ways: when he moved to the court of that eager, imperious student of ideas, texts, and religions, Queen Christina of Sweden. There he became mortally ill when she made him rise at four in the frozen northern dawn to give her philosophy lessons. He died at the age of 53, a martyr to intellectual curiosity, in February 1650.

Descartes's "marvellous science" portrayed a whole new universe: one that consisted not, like that of traditional philosophy, of bodies animated by a number of souls intimately connected to them, and related to one another by occult influence, but of hard matter in predictable motion. He cast his ideas not in the traditional form of commentary on ancient texts and ideas, but in the radically antitraditionalist one of systematic treatises that did not cite authorities—other than that of Descartes's own ability to reason. He said that he saw no point in weaving together chains of syllogisms, as the Scholastics of the Middle Ages had, in the vain hope that major and minor premises of unclear validity, drawn at random from old texts and swarming with unexamined assumptions, could somehow yield new and important conclusions. He did not try to protect his weaker arguments from attack by covering them with a thick, brittle armor plating of quotations from ancient and modern sources in the manner of the Renaissance humanists, who saw philology as the mainstay of philosophy.

Descartes, instead, claimed that he could build entirely on his own something new, coherent, and symmetrical. He liked to compare his work to that of the great town planners of his time, who saw the ideal city as a lucid walled polyhedron surrounding a central square, rather than an irregular, picturesque embodiment of centuries of time and change. The "crooked and irregular" streets and varied heights of the buildings in old cities suggested that "it is chance, rather than the will of men using reason, that placed them so," he said. Coherence, uniformity, symmetry attracted him: the Paris of the Place des Vosges rather then the palaces and alleys of the older parts of the city.

Descartes saw mathematics as the model for the new form of intellectual architecture he hoped to create. For he himself, as he discovered later than stereotypes would lead one to expect, was a very gifted mathematician, one of the creators of modern algebra and the inventor of analytical geometry. Like a mathematician, he tried to begin from absolutely hard premises: ideas so "clear and distinct" that he could not even begin to deny them. In these, and only in these, he found a place to stand. Descartes could imagine away the physical world, the value of the classics, and much else. But he could not deny, while thinking, the existence of his thinking self. Cogito, ergo sum.

From this narrow foothold he began to climb. He proved the existence of God in a way that he himself found deeply satisfactory though many others did not: the idea of God includes every perfection, and it is more perfect to exist than not to exist. Hence God must exist—and be the source of the innate faculties and ideas that all humans possess. He worked out the sort of universe that God would have to create. And he devised, over the course of time, a system that embraced everything from the nature of the planets to that of the human mind, from the solution of technical problems in mathematics to the circulation of the blood.

Wherever possible, precise quantitative models showed how Cartesian nature would work in detail: he not only devised laws for the refraction and reflection of light, for example, but also designed a lens-grinding machine that would apply them (and prove their validity). Parts of his system clanked and sputtered. His elaborate cosmology—which interpreted planetary systems as whirlpools, or vortices, of matter in motion—was technically outdated before it appeared. It could not account for the mathematical details of planetary motion established by Tycho Brahe and Johannes Kepler. Nonetheless, the rigor and coherence of his system inspired natural philosophers on the Continent for a century and more after his death.

The reception of Descartes's philosophy was anything but easy or straightforward. At the outset of his career as a published writer, in the *Discourse on the Method*, he invited those who had objections to his work to communicate them to him for reply. He circulated his *Meditations* for comment before he published them in 1641, and printed them along with systematic objections and his own replies. Thomas Hobbes, Marin Mersenne, Pierre Gassendi, and others now known only to specialists pushed him to define his terms and defend his arguments. At the same time, his thought became controversial in wider circles. Descartes long feared this outcome. Both a good Copernican and a good Catholic, he was appalled by the condemnation of Galileo in 1633. This led him both to delay publication of his treatise *The World* and to try to devise a metaphysics that would prove his natural philosophy legitimate.

But once his work reached print, Descartes could not avoid controversy. In 1639, his supporters in the faculty of the University of Utrecht began to praise his new philosophy, holding public debates about his theories. The influential theologian Gisbert Voetius defended traditional theology, not only against Cartesianism but against Descartes, whose beliefs and morality Voetius attacked. Descartes found himself forced to defend himself a series of pamphlets. He lost some sympathizers—such as the scholar Anna Maria van Schurmann, one of a number of women with whom he discussed theological or philosophical issues.

In the 1640s, Descartes's political and legal situation became extremely serious, and his life in the Netherlands increasingly exhausting and disturbing. Nor did he always agree with those who considered themselves his followers. Ironically, if inevitably, Descartes's philosophy mutated into Cartesianism—one more of the philosophical schools whose competing claims had driven the young Descartes to try something completely different. Some academic Cartesians—as Theo Verbeek and others have shown—even used his philosophy along with others in a deliberately eclectic way their master would have condemned.

Nonetheless, until recent years philosophers generally thought they had a clear idea both of what Descartes meant to do and about why he framed his enterprise as he did. The question of consciousness, of the nature of the mind and its relation to the body, provides a good example of how Descartes has generally been read. Earlier philosophers, drawing on and adding to a tradition that went back to Aristotle, explained life and consciousness in a way that varied endlessly in detail but not in substance. A whole series of souls, hierarchically ordered, each of them equipped with particular faculties, accounted for organic life in plants, movement in animals, and consciousness in humans. The number and quality of faculties possessed by each being corresponded to its position in the hierarchical chain of being, which determined the number and kinds of souls that being possessed. And the well-established nature and location of these faculties in the body could be used to show how body and soul were intimately and intricately connected. It made perfectly good sense to assume—as the astrologers, then almost as fashionable as now, regularly did—that celestial influences, acting on the four humors in the body, could affect the mind. No one could establish an easy, clear division between mind and body, man and nature.

Descartes, by contrast, drew a sharp line, here as elsewhere, both between his views and traditional ones and between physical and mental processes. He proved, as he insisted he could, that mind and body were in fact separate. Descartes could imagine that he had no body at all, but he could not imagine that he, the one imagining, did not exist. The mind, in other words, was fundamentally different from the body. Bodies had as their defining properties hardness and extension.

Their other attributes—such as color and texture—were merely superficial, as one could see, for example, by melting a lump of wax. The material world, accordingly, could be measured, divided, cut. The mind, by contrast, was clearly indivisible; when conscious, one always had access to all of it. Descartes divided human beings, accordingly, into two components: a material, extended body, mobile and mortal, and an immaterial, thinking soul, located somewhere within the body but at least potentially immortal. He redefined the struggles between different souls which Saint Augustine had so influentially described in his *Confessions* and of which others regularly spoke as struggles between the body and the soul. These took place, Descartes argued, in a particular organ: the pineal gland, within the brain, the one point where soul and body interacted. He held that animals could not have minds, at least in the sense that human beings do. And the firm distinction he made between the physical plane that humans share with other beings and the mental operations that attest to their existence on more than a physical plane continues to irritate philosophers—just as his sharp distinction between the real world of solid matter in motion and the qualitative, unreal world of perception and passion once enraged T. S. Eliot and Basil Willey, who held him guilty of causing the 17th century's "dissociation of sensibility."

D escartes's position in the history of thought has seemed, in recent years, as easily defined as his innovative contributions to it. By the time he was born, in 1596, intellectual norms that had existed for centuries, even millennia, were being called into question. The discovery of the New World had challenged traditional respect for the cosmology and philosophy of the ancients. The Protestant Reformation had destroyed the unity of Christendom, offering radically new ways of reading the Bible. The Scholastic philosophers who dominated the faculties of theology in the traditional universities, though all of them worked within a common, basically Aristotelian idiom, had come into conflict with one another on many fundamental points, and some humanists claimed that their vast Gothic structures of argument rested on misunderstandings of the Bible and Aristotle.

Some thinkers looked desperately for moorings in this intellectual storm. Justus Lipsius, for example, a very influential scholar and philosopher who taught at both Calvinist Leiden and Catholic Louvain, tried to show that ancient Stoicism, with its firm code of duties, could provide an adequate philosophy for the modern aristocrat and military officer. Others began to think that there were no moorings to be found—and even to accept that fact as welcome, since it undermined the dogmatic pretensions that led to religious revolutions and persecutions. The philosophy of the ancient Skeptics, in particular, offered tools to anyone who wished to deny that philosophers could attain the truth about man, the natural world, or anything else.

Skepticism, as Richard Poplin and Charles Schmitt have shown, interested a few intellectuals in the 15th century, such as Lorenzo Valla. But it first attracted widespread interest during the Reformation. Erasmus, for example, drew on skeptical arguments to show that Luther was wrongly splitting the Catholic Church on issues about which humans could never attain certainty. The major ancient skeptical texts, the works of Sextus Empiricus, appeared in Latin translation late in the 16th century— just as the Wars of Religion between French Calvinists and Catholics were reaching their hottest point. Michel de Montaigne, the great essayist whom Descartes eagerly read and tacitly cited, drew heavily on Greek Skepticism when he mounted his attacks on intellectual intolerance. To some—especially the so-called Politiques, such as Montaigne, who was not only a writer but one of the statesmen who negotiated religious peace in France at the end of the 16th century—Skepticism came as a deeply desirable solution to religious crisis. To others, however—especially to Catholic and Protestant philosophers who still felt the need to show that their religious doctrines not only rested on biblical authority but also corresponded to the best possible human reasoning—Skepticism came as a threat to all intellectual certainties, including the necessary ones.

Descartes tried on principle to doubt everything he knew. (He called his method, eloquently, one of "hyperbolic doubt".) But he found, as we have seen, that there were some things even he could not doubt, and many others found his arguments convincing. Accordingly, Descartes appears in many histories of philosophy above all as one of those who resolved a skeptical crisis by providing a new basis for physics, metaphysics, and morality. Similarly, he appears in many histories of science, alongside Francis Bacon, as one of those who created a whole new method for studying the natural world.

F or the last 20 years or so, however, this view of Descartes's place in the history of thought has begun to undergo scrutiny and criticism. Not only students of consciousness but historians of philosophy and science have begun to raise questions about Descartes's isolation in his own intellectual world. For all his insistence on the novelty of his views and the necessity for a serious thinker to work alone, he always looked for partners in discussion.

And this was only natural. "Even the most radical innovator," write the historians of philosophy Roger Ariew and Marjorie Grene, "has roots; even the most outrageous new beginner belongs to an intellectual community in which opponents have to be refuted and friends won over." Descartes, moreover, not only belonged to a community, as he himself acknowledged; he also drew, as he usually did not like to admit, from a variety of intellectual traditions.

F or example, Stephen Gaukroger, whose intricately detailed new intellectual biography of Descartes elegantly balances close analysis of texts with a rich recreation of context, finds an ancient source for Descartes's apparently novel notion that certain "clear and distinct" ideas compel assent. The core of the Jesuit curriculum Descartes mastered so well was formed by rhetoric, the ancient art of persuasive speech. Quintilian, the Roman author of the most systematic ancient manual of the subject, analyzed extensively the ways in which an orator could "engage the emotions of the audience." To do so, he argued, the orator must "*exhibit* rather than *display* his proofs." He must produce a mental image so vivid and palpable that his hearers cannot deny it: a clear and distinct idea.

Gaukroger admits that Roman orators saw themselves first and foremost as producing such conviction in others, while Descartes saw his first duty as convincing himself. But Gaukroger elegantly points out that classical rhetoric, for all its concern with public utterance, also embodied something like Descartes's concern with the private, with "self-conviction." The orator, as Quintilian clearly said, had to convince himself in order to convince others: "The first essential is that those feelings should prevail with us that we wish to prevail with the judge."

Descartes's doctrine of clear and distinct ideas is usually described as radically new. It turns out, on inspection, to be a diabolically clever adaptation to new ends of the rhetorical five-finger exercises the philosopher had first mastered as a schoolboy. Gaukroger's negative findings are equally intriguing: he interprets Descartes's famous dreams as evidence not of a breakthrough but of a breakdown, and he argues forcefully that Skepticism played virtually no role in Descartes's original formulation of his method and its consequences.

Several other studies have revealed similarly creative uses of tradition in many pockets of Descartes's philosophy. As John Cottingham has shown, Descartes more than once found himself compelled to use traditional philosophical terminology—with all the problematic assumptions it embodied. Despite his dislike of tradition, he also disliked being suspected of radicalism, and claimed at times not to offer a new theory but to revive a long-forgotten ancient one—for example, the "*vera mathesis*" ("true mathematical science") of the ancient mathematicians Pappus and Diophantus. No one denies the substantial novelty of Descartes's intellectual program; but students of his work, like recent students of Wittgenstein, show themselves ever more concerned to trace the complex relations between radicalism and tradition, text and context.

Descartes's dreams—and his autobiographical use of them—play a special role in this revisionist enterprise. His earliest substantial work, composed in the late 1620s but left unfinished, takes the form of *Rules for the Direction of the Mind;* his great philosophical text of 1641 bears the title *Meditations*. In structure as well as substance, both works unmistakably point backward to his formation in a Jesuit college. There he had not only to study the classics and some modern science but to "make" the *Spiritual Exercises* laid down for Jesuits and their pupils by the founder of the Jesuit order, Ignatius Loyola. These consisted of a set of systematic, graded exercises in contemplation, visualization, and meditation. Students—and candidates for membership in the order—had to reconstruct as vividly as they could in their minds the Crucifixion, Hell, and other scenes that could produce profound emotional and spiritual effects in them. These exercises were intended to enable those who did them to discipline their minds and spirits, to identify and rid themselves of their besetting weaknesses, and finally to choose the vocation for which God intended them. Visions—and even mystical experiences—reg-

ularly formed a controlled part of the process, as they had for Ignatius himself. The similarity between these exercises in spiritual self-discipline and Descartes's philosophical self-discipline is no coincidence. Here too Descartes transposed part of the education he thought he had rejected into the fabric of his philosophy.

In seeing visions as a form of divine communication—evidence of a special providence that singled recipients out as the possessors of a Mission—Descartes remained firmly within the Jesuit intellectual tradition. He was, in fact, far from the only product of a good Jesuit education to trace his own development in minute interpretative detail. Consider the case of his near contemporary Athanasius Kircher—another mathematically gifted young man, who studied in Jesuit schools in south Germany before becoming the central intellectual figure in baroque Rome. Kircher's interests were as varied as Descartes's were sharply defined: he spelunked in volcanoes, experimented with magnets, reconstructed the travel of Noah's Ark, and studied languages ranging from Coptic to Chinese, with varying degree of success. But he defined the core of his enterprise with Cartesian precision, if in totally un-Cartesian terms, as an effort to decipher the ancient philosophy encoded in the hieroglyphic inscriptions on Egyptian obelisks. This effort attracted much criticism but also received generous papal support. Ultimately it inspired some of Bernini's most spectacular Roman works of sculpture and architecture, in the Piazza Navona and before the church of Santa Maria sopra Minerva.

Descartes would have found most of Kircher's project risible. Yet they had something vital in common. Kircher, like Descartes, tried to prove the rigor and providential inspiration of his work by writing an autobiography. Kircher's dreams and visions played as large a role in this work as his colorful and sometimes terrifying experiences. Like Descartes, he saw his unconscious experiences as evidence that God had set him on earth to carry out a particular plan. His accidental encounter with a book in which Egyptian hieroglyphs were reproduced and discussed exemplified—he thought in retrospect—the sort of special providences by which God had led him in the right direction. Evidently, then, Cartesian autobiography was actually Jesuit autobiography. Brilliant style, concision, and lucidity set off the beginning of the *Discourse on the Method* from Kircher's Latin treatise. But the enterprises were basically as similar as the larger enterprises they were meant to serve were different. And Descartes's dreams not only make a nice story to adorn the beginning of a lecture but actually shed light on the origins of his central intellectual enterprise.

In effect, then, Descartes has come back to new life in recent years—in two radically different ways. The Descartes who appears in so many studies of the philosophy and physiology of mind—the radical innovator, owing nothing to his predecessors, who devised the brutally simple theory about "the ghost in the machine"—seems hard to reconcile with the Descartes now being reconstructed by historians: the complex, reflective figure, whose relation to tradition took many different forms, and whose system embodied foreign elements even he did not recognize as such. Gaukroger's book marks a first and very rewarding effort to bring the two Descartes together. But the task will be a long one. It may prove impossible to fit Descartes the dreamer into traditional genealogies of modern thought—or to establish a simple relation between his theories of intelligence and current ones. Descartes lives, a troubling ghost in the machine of modern philosophy.

ANTHONY GRAFTON is the Dodge Professor of History at Princeton University. He is the author of *Joseph Scaliger: A Study in the History of Classical Scholarship* (1983–1993), *Forgers and Critics: Creativity and Duplicity in Western Scholarship* (1990), and *Defenders of the Text: The Traditions of Scholarship in an Age of Science, 1450–1800* (1991). His study, *The Tragic Origins of the German Footnote*, appeared in 1997.

From *The Wilson Quarterly*, Autumn 1996, pp. 36-46. © 1996 by Anthony Grafton. Reprinted by permission.

Empires Ancient and Modern

What two eloquent Frenchmen, Voltaire and Montesquieu, had to say in the 18th century about the forces that sustain or shatter great powers remains surprisingly relevant.

PAUL A. RAHE

Three centuries ago, an event took place that is today little remembered and even more rarely remarked upon, though it signaled the beginning of a political and ideological transformation that was arguably no less significant than the one marked in our own time by the fall of the Berlin Wall and the dismemberment of the Soviet Union. In the late spring and summer of 1704, two armies made their way from western to central Europe. The first, led by the Comte de Tallard, marshal of France, sought to upset the balance of power in Europe by establishing Louis XIV's hegemony over the Holy Roman Empire, installing a French nominee on the imperial throne, and securing the acquiescence of the Austrians, the English, the Dutch, and every other European power in a Bourbon succession to the Spanish throne. The second army, led by John Churchill, then Earl, later Duke, of Marlborough, with the assistance of Prince Eugene of Savoy, sought to preserve the existing balance of power, defend Hapsburg control of the Holy Roman Empire, and deprive Louis of his Spanish prize.

At stake, as Louis' opponents asserted and his most fervent admirers presumed, was the establishment of a universal monarchy in Europe and French dominion in the New World. At stake as well for Englishmen, Scots, Irish Protestants, and Britain's colonists in the Americas, were the supremacy of Parliament, the liberties secured by the Glorious Revolution in 1688 and 1689, the Protestant succession to the English crown, and Protestant hegemony in the British Isles and much of the New World.

There was every reason to suppose that Louis XIV would achieve the goal he seems to have sought his entire adult life. After all, on the field of the sword, France was preeminent. The French had occasionally been checked, but on no occasion in the preceding 150 years had a French army suffered a genuinely decisive defeat. Imagine the shock, then, when all of Europe learned that on August 13, 1704, the army commanded by Marlborough and Prince Eugene had captured Tallard and annihilated the French force at the Bavarian village of Blenheim.

Of course, had the Battle of Blenheim been a fluke, as everyone at first assumed, Louis' defeat on this particular occasion would not have much mattered. In the event, however, this great struggle was but the first of a series of French defeats meted out by Marlborough's armies. If we are today astonishingly ill informed about the once-famous battles fought at Ramillies, Oudenarde, Lille, and Malplaquet in the brief span from 1706 to 1709, it is because we have become accustomed to averting our gaze from the fundamental realities of political life. In the United States, despite the leading role in the world our country long ago assumed, not one history department in 20 even offers a course on the conduct and consequences of war.

Yet Winston Churchill was surely right, in his biography of Marlborough, in observing that "battles are the principal milestones in secular history," in rejecting "modern opinion," which "resents this uninspiring truth," and in criticizing historians who so "often treat the decisions in the field as incidents in the dramas of politics and diplomacy." "Great battles," he insisted, whether "won or lost, change the entire course of events, create new standards of values, new moods, new atmospheres, in armies and in nations, to which all must conform."

It would be an exaggeration to say that, in comparison with the Battle of Blenheim, the French Enlightenment and the French Revolution were little more than aftershocks. But there can be no doubt that Marlborough's stirring victories over Louis XIV's France exposed the weakness of the ancien régime, occasioned the first efforts on the part of the philosophes to rethink in radical terms the political trajectory of France, and called into question the assumptions that had for centuries underpinned foreign policy as practiced by all the great powers on the continent of Europe.

■

Events such as the fall of the Berlin Wall and the collapse of the Soviet Union have a way of altering the terms of public debate. Before 1989, Marxist analysis thrived in and outside the academy. After 1991, it seemed, even to many of those who had once been its ardent practitioners, hopelessly anachronistic, at best a relic of an earlier, benighted age. Something similar happened in France after 1713, when the Treaty of Utrecht brought an end to the War of the Spanish Succession. By diplomatic skill and a canny exploitation of the partisan strife that erupted between Whigs and Tories in Marlborough's England,

Louis XIV had managed to preserve his kingdom intact, and even to secure the Spanish throne for his grandson. But the Sun King's great project of European domination proved unattainable. By 1715, it was perfectly clear to anyone with a discerning eye that the French monarchy was bankrupt in more ways than one.

At this point, young Frenchmen began to look elsewhere for workable models. Before the first decade of the 18th century, the French had demonstrated little serious interest in England. The Sun King is said to have once asked an English ambassador whether, in his country, there had ever been any writers of note. Of Shakespeare and Milton, Louis had apparently never heard, and he was by no means peculiar in this regard. To 17th-century Frenchmen, England was nothing more than an object of idle curiosity, if even that. Hardly anyone on the continent of Europe considered England, the English, their language, their literature, their philosophy, their institutions, their mode of conduct, their accomplishments in science, and their way of seeing the world to be proper objects for rumination.

After Marlborough's great victories, however, attitudes changed, and young Frenchmen of penetrating intelligence thought it necessary to read about, and perhaps even visit, the country that had put together, funded, and led the coalition that had inflicted so signal a defeat on the most magnificent of their kings. The first figure of real note to subject England and the English to extended study was an ambitious young poet of bourgeois origin named François Marie Arouet, whom we know best by his pen name, Voltaire.

■

Voltaire spent two and a half years in England, arriving in May 1726 and departing abruptly, under suspicious, perhaps legally awkward, circumstances, in October or November 1728. His sojourn was occasioned by a scrape he had gotten into in Paris, where he insulted a member of the nobility who exacted revenge by luring the poet from a dinner party and having his minions administer a severe cudgeling to the bourgeois upstart. When word got around that Voltaire intended to challenge the noble master of his less-exalted assailants to a duel, a *lettre de cachet* (arrest warrant) was elicited from the authorities and the poet was thrown into the Bastille. He was released on condition that he leave the country, which he did forthwith.

Voltaire had been thinking of visiting England in any case. While there, he dined out, circulating among poets such as Alexander Pope, John Gay, and Jonathan Swift and hobnobbing with both Tories and Whigs. In time, he was presented to King George I, and before he returned to France he dined with George II, then quite recently crowned.

To 17th-century Frenchmen, England was nothing more than an object of idle curiosity.

Voltaire did not limit himself to the world of poets, politicians, and princes. He attended the funeral of Sir Isaac Newton and sought out not long thereafter the great man's niece. He made a point of calling on and becoming acquainted with the dowager Duchess of Marlborough, widow to the warrior and statesman

who, 20 years before, had very nearly brought Louis XIV's France to its knees. Much of the rest of his time Voltaire devoted to mastering the English language. By the time he left Britain, he had published two essays in English, he had begun writing a play in the language, and he had penned in vibrant and compelling English prose more than half the chapters that would make up his celebrated *Letters Concerning the English Nation*.

This last work deserves attention. In London, it appeared in August 1733 to great acclaim, and it was reprinted in English again and again in the course of the 18th century. In April 1734, when a French version was published clandestinely in Rouen under an Amsterdam imprint with the title *Lettres philosophiques* (*Philosophical Letters*), it caused a great stir. To his English audience, Voltaire had offered an elegant satire appreciative of their virtues but by no means devoid of humor and bite. To his compatriots, he presented, by way of invidious comparison, a savage critique of the polity tinder which they lived. As the Marquis de Condorcet would later observe, the *Philosophical Letters* marked in France "the epoch of a revolution." It caused a "taste for English philosophy and literature to be born here." It induced "us to interest ourselves in the mores, the policy, the commercial outlook of this people."

This was all precisely as Voltaire intended. He devoted the first seven of the book's 25 letters to religion, intimating throughout that the great virtue of the English was that their devotion to Mammon rendered them decidedly lukewarm as men of faith. "Go into the Royal-Exchange in London," says Voltaire. It is a "place more venerable than many courts of justice." There, he asserts,

> you will see the representatives of all the nations assembled for the benefit of mankind. There the Jew, the Mahometan, and the Christian transact together as tho' they all profess'd the same religion, and give the name of Infidel to none but bankrupts. There the Presbyterian confides in the Anabaptist, and the Anglican depends on the Quaker's word. At the breaking up of this pacific and free assembly, some withdraw to the synagogue, and others to take a glass. This man goes and is baptiz'd in a great tub, in the name of the Father, Son, and Holy Ghost. That man has his son's foreskin cut off, whilst a set of *Hebrew* words (quite unintelligible to him) are mumbled over his child. Others retire to their churches, and then wait for the inspiration of heaven with their hats on, and all are satisfied.

Voltaire's compatriots can hardly have missed the significance for Catholic France of the lesson he drew in the end: "If one religion only were allowed in England, there would be reason to fear despotism; if there were but two, the people wou'd cut one another's throats; but as there are 30, they all live happy and in peace."

In much the same spirit, Voltaire then examined England's government, tacitly juxtaposing it with the absolute monarchy ruling his native France. Though the English liked to compare themselves to the Romans, he expressed doubts as to whether this was apt. He judged 18th-century Englishmen far superior to the pagans of ancient Rome:

The fruit of the civil wars at Rome was slavery, and that of the troubles of England, liberty. The English are the only people upon earth who have been able to pre-scribe limits to the power of Kings by resisting them; and who, by a series of struggles, have at last estab-lish'd that wise Government, where the Prince is all powerful to do good, and at the same time his hands are tied against doing wrong; where the Nobles are great without insolence and Vassals; and where the People share in the government without confusion.

Voltaire was even willing to celebrate the bourgeois character of English society. "As Trade enrich'd the Citizens in England," he contended, "so it contributed to their Freedom, and this Freedom on the other Side extended their Commerce, whence arose the Grandeur of the State." Commerce enabled a small is-land with little in the way of resources to marshal great fleets and finance great wars. The role the island's commercial classes played in funding the victories of Marlborough and Prince Eu-gene "raises a just Pride in an English Merchant, and makes him presume (not without some Reason) to compare himself to a Roman Citizen." To those among his compatriots inclined to treasure aristocratic birth, Voltaire throws down an unanswer-able challenge: "I cannot say which is most useful to a Nation: a Lord, wellpowder'd, who knows exactly at what a Clock the King rises and goes to bed; and who gives himself Airs of Gran-deur and State, at the same time that he is acting the Slave in the Antechamber of a Minister; or a Merchant, who enriches his Country, dispatches Orders from his Compting-House to Surat and Grand Cairo, and contributes to the Felicity of the World."

■

Needless to say, not everyone in France was as pleased with such bons mots as the author of the *Philosophical Letters*. Upon first reading the book, Abbé Jean-Ber-nard Le Blanc, who was otherwise on excellent terms with Vol-taire, protested in a letter to a common acquaintance that he was "shocked by a tone of contempt which holds sway throughout. This contempt pertains equally to our nation, to our govern-ment, to our ministers, to everything that is highly respect-able—in a word to religion." In his little book, Le Blanc added, Voltaire displayed "an indecency truly horrible."

The authorities were similarly disposed. Paris had recently been in an uproar, in part as a consequence of the ongoing strug-gle within French Catholicism between the Jesuits and the pre-destination-advocating Jansenists, and it was not yet certain that the crisis had passed. Neither party was amused by the antics of a libertine who evidenced a desire to dance in the ashes of both, and the civil magistrate was, for understandable reasons, hyper-sensitive to any criticism of the established order. Within a month of the book's appearance, a *lettre de cachet* was issued ordering the author's arrest. Voltaire's house and that of a friend in Rouen were searched; the printer was arrested; and the re-maining copies of the book were confiscated. Soon thereafter, the *parlement* of Paris, the most prestigious judicial body in France, denounced the *Philosophical Letters* as "scandalous, contrary to religion, good morals, and the respect due to author-ity," and it instructed the public hangman to lacerate and burn

the book with all due ceremony in the courtyard of the Palais de justice—which he did on June 10, 1734.

Voltaire had anticipated the storm. By the time it broke, he was far from Paris, in Champagne, near the border of Lorraine, safely and comfortably ensconced at the chateau of his mistress, the Marquise du Châtelet. There, in a species of exile, he was to spend the better part of the next 15 years.

■

As Voltaire's drama unfolded, another French visitor to England looked on with deep concern. He, too, upon his return from London, had written an ambitious book modest in its dimensions. He had arranged for its publication in Holland, and, now that Voltaire's *Philosophical Letters* had been turned over to the public hangman, he wondered whether it was wise to usher into print some of the more controversial opinions he had very much wanted to convey.

Voltaire was a bomb thrower. Charles Louis de Secondat, Baron de La Brède et de Montesquieu, was nothing of the kind. Montesquieu was trained in the law, a profession inclined to justify decisions by appealing to precedent, and he was respect-ful of the dictates of long experience. When called upon for ad-vice in crises, such as the one that threatened French finances at the death of Louis XIV, he was prudent and tended to opt for modest reform. In no way was he attracted to extremes. But he was no more a traditionalist inclined to subject reason to the dead hand of the past than was his rival Voltaire.

Montesquieu had been born in 1689, Voltaire in 1694. Both had witnessed the War of the Spanish Succession. Both had rec-ognized the significance of Marlborough's victories. And both thought it essential to come to an understanding of the political regime that had so humiliated the nation of their birth. "Ger-many was made to travel in, Italy to sojourn in, ... and France to live in," but England was made "to think in." The sentiment is attributed to Montesquieu, but the words could just as easily have been uttered by Voltaire.

Montesquieu was an aristocrat by birth. As a writer, he had no special need for the passing applause of his contemporaries. He could afford to be patient, and he generally preferred to be indirect, which is why, in the spring of 1734, as he contemplated the fate meted out to the *Philosophical Letters* and visited upon its author, his hapless friend in Rouen, and the book's printer, he chose to censor a volume he had submitted the previous sum-mer to his publisher in Amsterdam, even though the type had al-ready been set.

Voltaire's *Philosophical Letters*, said one observer, displayed "an indecency truly horrible."

On his return to France, in 1731, after a stay of a little more than a year in England, Montesquieu had retreated to his cha-teau in Bordeaux and had devoted two years to writing. In this period of self-imposed solitary confinement, he composed his *Considerations on the Causes of the Greatness of the Romans and Their Decline*. There is no work of comparable length on

Roman history, written before its author's time or since, that is as penetrating.

It is not obvious, however, why Montesquieu thought it worth his while to write this particular book at this time. It barely mentions England, and it has neither a preface nor an introduction to inform us concerning his intentions. Moreover, while it foreshadows in some respects the themes of his most famous work, *The Spirit of Laws*, it evidences little to suggest a pertinence to public policy of the sort that was so central to the concerns that inspired the latter work. It would be tempting to conclude that in the early 1730s Montesquieu was an antiquarian and a philosophical historian, intent on establishing his reputation within the republic of letters by writing a scholarly work on a noble theme.

More can be said, however, for in the quarter of a millennium that has passed since Montesquieu's death in 1755, scholars have gradually become aware that the *Considerations* was but one of three essays that Montesquieu wrote at this time for inclusion within the pages of a single volume. The third of these, which dealt with England, Montesquieu began drafting and then, upon reflection, set aside. In 1748, he inserted in *The Spirit of Laws* a revised version of what he had drafted, giving it the title "The Constitution of England," thereby earning for himself great fame, especially within the English-speaking world.

The second essay, titled *Reflections on Universal Monarchy in Europe*, Montesquieu drafted, polished, and dispatched to his Amsterdam printer in 1733 along with his treatise on the Romans. It was not until after he had received a printed copy of the two that he chose to suppress his little work on universal monarchy, for fear that it would cause him the sort of difficulties that had befallen Voltaire. Fragments of it he subsequently inserted in various places within *The Spirit of Laws*, where they passed virtually unnoticed. The original essay eventually found its way into print in 1891.

Had the Sun King won at Blenheim, Montesquieu wrote, "nothing would have been more fatal to Europe."

These philological details have been known for some time, but to date no one has bothered to join together once again what Montesquieu put asunder. Yet it is obvious that the *Considerations*, the *Reflections*, and the "Constitution of England" form a single work and cannot properly be understood in mutual isolation. When one reassembles the original book, one realizes immediately that this work was intended as a meditation on the larger significance of Marlborough's victory on the battlefield at Blenheim. From perusing Montesquieu's ruminations one gains an unparalleled perspective on the world order emerging in his day and still regnant in our own.

■

"It is a question worth raising," Montesquieu writes in the first sentence of his *Reflections*, "whether, given the condition in which Europe actually subsists, it is possible for a people to maintain over other peoples an unceasing superiority, as the Romans did." For this question, Montesquieu has a ready and unprecedented answer: "a thing like this has become morally impossible."

He gives three reasons. First, "innovations in the art of war," such as the introduction of artillery and firearms, "have equalized the strength of all men and consequently that of all nations." Second, "the *ius gentium* [law of nations] has changed, and under today's laws war is conducted in such a manner that by bankruptcy it ruins above all others those who possess the greatest advantages." "In earlier times," Montesquieu explains, "one would destroy the towns that one had captured, one would sell the lands and, far more important, the inhabitants as well…. The sacking of a town would pay the wages of an army, and a successful campaign would enrich a conqueror. At present, we regard such barbarities with a horror no more than just, and we ruin ourselves by bankruptcy in capturing places which capitulate, which we preserve intact, and which most of the time we return."

Third, Montesquieu argues, because of the changes dictated by technological and moral progress, in modern Europe money has become the sinews of war and the only secure foundation of national strength. Power, once more-or-less fixed, is now subject to "continual variation" in line with the trajectory of the economy of the realm. "To the extent that a state takes a greater or lesser part in commerce and the carrying trade," Montesquieu contends, "its power necessarily grows or diminishes." Under these new conditions, the vast expenditures demanded by war and the disruption it occasions for trade produce economic ruin at home, "while states which remain neutral augment their strength," and even the conquered recover from defeat.

By the 18th century, victory in war often led only to bankruptcy.

It is not difficult to see why Montesquieu judged it imprudent to publish the *Reflections*. In the 17th chapter, with his tongue firmly in cheek, he piously denies the charge that Louis XIV had aimed at universal monarchy—and then he discusses events in a manner suggesting that this had been Louis' aim after all. "Had he succeeded," Montesquieu writes, "nothing would have been more fatal to Europe, to his subjects of old, to himself, to his family. Heaven, which knows what is really advantageous, served him better in his defeats than it would have in victories, and instead of making him the sole king of Europe, it favored him more by making him the most powerful of them all." Had Louis won the Battle of Blenheim, "the famous battle in which he met his first defeat," his "enterprise would have been quite far from achievement": The establishment of a universal monarchy would have required a further "increase in forces and a great expansion in frontiers."

What the Sun King had failed to recognize was that "Europe is nothing more than one nation composed of many," and that the rise of commerce had made his rivals for dominion his partners in trade. "France and England have need of the opulence of Poland and Muscovy," Montesquieu argues, "just as one of their provinces has need of the others, and the state that believes it will increase its power as a consequence of financial ruin visited on a neighboring state ordinarily weakens itself along with its neighbor."

Even in peacetime, Montesquieu insists, the policy pursued by the various powers in Europe is self-destructive. "If conquest on a grand scale is so difficult, so fruitless, so dangerous," he adds, "what can one say of the malady of our own age which dictates that one maintain everywhere a number of troops disproportionate" to one's actual needs? We are not like the Romans, he notes, "who managed to disarm others in the measure to which they armed themselves." In consequence of the arms race taking place in Europe, Montesquieu concludes, "we are poor with all the wealth and commerce of the entire universe, and soon, on account of having soldiers, we shall have nothing but soldiers, and we will become like the Tartars."

■

When examined in light of its original companion piece, *Reflections on Universal Monarchy in Europe*, Montesquieu's *Considerations on the Causes of the Greatness of the Romans and Their Decline* reads like an extended introduction. It was, after all, the image of Roman grandeur that fired the ambition of Europe's greatest monarchs. Had it not been for Caesar's ruthless exploitation of the revolutionary potential inherent in his office as an imperator within the *imperium Romanum*, there never would have been a monarch who styled himself an emperor, a Kaiser, or a czar. In the European imagination, the idea of universal monarchy was inseparable from a longing for imperial greatness on the model of ancient Rome. To find and apply an antidote to "the malady" besetting his own age, Montesquieu had to come to grips with the attraction exerted on his contemporaries by the example of Rome.

In Montesquieu's judgment, there were two reasons for the Romans' success. To begin with, they looked on "war" as "the only art" and devoted "mind entire and all their thoughts to its perfection." In the process, they imposed on themselves burdens and a species of discipline hardly imaginable in modern times. "Never," writes Montesquieu, "has a nation made preparations for war with so much prudence and conducted it with so much audacity."

The image of Roman grandeur fired the ambition of Europe's greatest monarchs.

Of equal importance, in Montesquieu's opinion, was the fact that Roman policy was no less impressive. The Romans employed their allies to defeat the foe, then laid their allies low as well. In the midst of war, they put up with injuries of every sort, waiting for a time suited to retribution. When a people crossed them, they punished the nation, not just its leaders, and on their enemies they inflicted "evils inconceivable." As a consequence, "war was rarely launched against" the Romans, and "they always waged war" at a time and in a manner of their own choosing on those whom they regarded as most "convenient." The statecraft practiced by the Roman senate matched in cunning

and ruthlessness the skill of the generals and soldiers it sent into the field.

Montesquieu's Rome may have been successful, but it was not a benefactor conferring peace and prosperity: It was a predator. It "enchained the universe," and in the process established a "universal sovereignty." But from this sovereignty came no good. Rome's far-flung subjects suffered more from its rule, Montesquieu tells us, than they had from the horrors of their original conquest. And Rome's citizens suffered as well. That they lost their liberty was by no means an accident—it was a natural consequence of their project of conquest: "The greatness of the empire destroyed the republic." Rome's grandeur produced Roman decadence. In subjecting and enchaining "the universe," in achieving "universal sovereignty," the Romans subjected and enchained themselves.

Montesquieu's Rome was not a benefactor conferring peace and prosperity: It was a predator.

"As long as Rome's dominion was restricted to Italy," Montesquieu explains, "the republic could easily be sustained." But once Rome's legions crossed the Alps and passed over the sea, and the republic was obliged to post its warriors abroad for extended periods, the ranks of the army grew through the enrollment of noncitizens, soldiers were no longer soldiers of the republic but loyal instead to the generals who paid them, and "Rome could no longer tell whether the man who headed a provincial army was the city's general or its enemy." At this point, on the horizon despotism loomed.

Montesquieu asks us to contemplate and even admire Roman grandeur: "How many wars do we see undertaken in the course of Roman history," he asks, "how much blood being shed, how many peoples destroyed, how many great actions, how many triumphs, how much policy, how much sagacity, prudence, constancy, and courage!" But, then, after giving classical Rome its due, he asks us to pause and re-examine the trajectory of the imperial republic:

> But how did this project for invading all end—a project so well formed, so well sustained, so well completed—except by appeasing the appetite for contentment of five or six monsters.... [The] senate had caused the disappearance of so many kings only to fall itself into the most abject enslavement to some of its most unworthy citizens, and to exterminate itself by its own judgments! One builds up one's power only to see it the better overthrown! Men work to augment their power only to see it, fallen into more fortunate hands, deployed against themselves!

Gradually, unobtrusively, as Montesquieu weans us from the enticement of Rome, our admiration gives way to horror and disgust. And gradually and unobtrusively, he thereby lays the groundwork for the argument against continental empire that he intended to advance in *Reflections on Universal Monarchy in Europe*.

■

We should not want to imitate the Romans, and in the *Considerations* Montesquieu shows us why. And if for some perverse reason we *wanted* to imitate the Romans, he then demonstrates in the *Reflections* that we could not succeed. After reading the first two parts of Montesquieu's original book, we are left to wonder what alternative to the policy hitherto followed by the states of Europe there might, in fact, be. At this juncture, Montesquieu originally intended to direct our attention to the polity that, as a consequence of the Glorious Revolution of 1688 and 1689, had emerged on the other side of the English Channel.

In his *Considerations*, Montesquieu set the stage for his third essay by drawing the attention of readers to what was apparently the only modern analogue to classical Rome:

> The government of England is one of the wisest in Europe, because there is a body there that examines this government continually and that continually examines itself; and such are this body's errors that they not only do not last long but are useful in arousing in the nation a spirit of vigilance. In a word, a free government, which is to say, a government always agitated, knows no way to sustain itself if it is not capable of self-correction by its own laws.

In the part of this third essay that he managed to draft, Montesquieu then set out to show what it was that occasioned this process of self-correction by discussing in detail the English constitution's institutionalization of a separation of powers, and by exploring the consequences of the rivalries and tensions that this separation introduces within what he elsewhere called "a republic concealed under the form of a monarchy."

When, however, he first began sketching out what came to be called "The Constitution of England," it cannot have been the French philosophe's intention to stop where, apparently, he did. Empire was, after all, the focus of the *Considerations* and the *Reflections*. To finish a work of which these two essays were to form so signal a part, Montesquieu would have had to discuss at some point the imperial policy adopted by the English. He would have had to demonstrate that, by the very nature of its polity, England was committed to a foreign policy that was viable in modern circumstances in a way that the Roman policy followed by the continental powers was not. As it happens, this is one of the issues he addressed in a chapter of *The Spirit of Laws*.

In speaking of the spirit that guides the English polity's conduct abroad, Montesquieu demonstrates that England is free from the malady that so threatens the powers on the Continent with bankruptcy and ruin. He helps us to understand why it is that, in modern times, a well-ordered Carthage, such as England, could defeat Louis XIV's ill-ordered French Rome.

The chief passion of the English is their fondness for liberty, which, Montesquieu says, they "love prodigiously because this liberty is genuine." In defending their freedom, he intimates, they are inclined to be no less resolute than were the citizens of classical Rome. For liberty, this nation is prepared to "sacrifice its goods, its ease, its interests." In a crisis, it will "impose on itself imposts quite harsh, such as the most absolute prince would not dare make his subjects endure." Moreover, possessing as they do "a firm understanding of the necessity of submitting" to these taxes, the English are prepared to "pay them in the well-founded expectation of not having to pay more." The burden they actually shoulder is far heavier than the burden they feel.

England, Montesquieu wrote, has always made its political interest give way to the interests of its commerce.

In this chapter, Montesquieu refrains from observing, as he repeatedly does elsewhere in *The Spirit of Laws*, that the monarchies on the European continent find it well-nigh impossible to inspire the confidence that would allow them to borrow the great sums of money needed to wage war in modern times. It suffices for him pointedly to remark that, given its laws, England has little difficulty sustaining the credit required to cover the costs of war: "For the purpose of preserving its liberty," it will "borrow from its subjects; and its subjects, seeing that its credit would be lost if it was conquered, … have yet another motive for exerting themselves in defense of its liberty."

Though inclined, like Rome, to defend itself with a resoluteness and a vigor that beggar the imagination, England is by no means a nation bent on conquest. The reason why it is so unlike Rome in this particular is simple. Blessed with an island location and a constitution favorable to the freedom of the individual, England is a seat of "peace and liberty." Moreover, once it was liberated from the "destructive prejudices" attendant on religious fervor, England became thoroughly commercial and began to exploit to the limit the capacity of its workers to fashion from its natural resources objects of great price.

Commerce is the distinguishing feature of English life, and Montesquieu's Englishmen conduct it as other nations conduct war. This people has "a prodigious number of petty, particular interests." There are numerous ways in which it can do and receive harm. "It is apt to become sovereignly jealous and to be more distressed by the prosperity of others than to rejoice at its own." Its laws, "in other respects gentle and easy," are "so rigid with regard to commerce and the carrying trade … that it would seem to do business with none but enemies."

In England, commerce is dominant in every sphere. "Other nations," Montesquieu remarks, "have made their commercial interests give way to their political interests; this one has always made its political interests give way to the interests of its commerce." When England sends out colonies far and wide, to places such as North America, it does so "more to extend the reach of its commerce than its sphere of domination." In keeping with its aim, it is generous with such distant colonies, conferring on them "its own form of government, which brings with it prosperity, so that one can see great peoples take shape in the forests which they were sent to inhabit."

Safeguarding its liberty and its commerce does not require an island nation such as Montesquieu's England to spend vast sums on "strongholds, fortresses, and armies on land." But this nation does "have need of an army at sea to guarantee it against invasion, and its navy [is] superior to those of all the other powers, which, needing to employ their finances for war on land [do] not have enough for war at sea." England's supremacy at sea enables it to exercise "a great influence on the affairs of its neighbors." Moreover, because England does "not employ its power for conquest," neighboring states are "more inclined to seek its friendship," and they fear "its hatred more than the inconstancy of its government and its internal agitation would appear to justify." In consequence, although it is "the fate of its executive power almost always to be uneasy at home," this power is nearly always respected abroad.

The simple fact that Great Britain withstood Napoleon proves the prescience of Voltaire and Montesquieu.

Montesquieu was prepared to concede that this England would someday fail. "As all human things have an end," he observed, "the state of which we speak will lose its liberty, it will perish. Rome, Lacedaemon, and Carthage have, indeed, perished." But Montesquieu did not think that England would perish in the foreseeable future. When an Anglo-Irish admirer wrote to express dismay at the licentiousness of his own compatriots and to ask whether Montesquieu thought that England was in any immediate danger of succumbing to corruption and of losing its liberty in the process, the philosophe responded that "in Europe the last sigh of liberty will be heaved by an Englishman," and he drew the attention of his correspondent to the intimate connection between English liberty and the independent citizenry produced and sustained by English commerce. Nowhere did Montesquieu ever suggest that England suffered from a defect comparable to that which felled Rome. Nowhere did he contend that the commercial project on which England had embarked carried within it the seeds of the nation's destruction. Nowhere did he trace a link between English grandeur and English decadence.

∎

Voltaire and Montesquieu had a considerable impact on the thinking of their contemporaries, but in the end they failed fully to persuade their compatriots in France of the superiority of English policy. Perhaps because Voltaire's *Philosophical Letters* was so quickly and thoroughly suppressed, perhaps because the critique Montesquieu directed at imperialism on the Roman model was buried, and thereby rendered inconspicuous, within his *Spirit of Laws,* perhaps because in the 1750s and 1760s Jean-Jacques Rousseau mounted a scathing and rhetorically compelling assault on commercial society, ancient Rome retained its allure. In subsequent generations, the most influential Frenchmen, and those Germans and Russians who looked for inspiration to Paris, rather than to London, failed to take heed. Napoleon tried to establish a universal monarchy in Europe, and, when opportunity knocked, Hitler and Stalin followed suit. Even today, when Europeans appear to have abandoned war as an instrument of foreign policy and frequently speak, and sometimes act, as if Montesquieu was right in suggesting that "Europe is nothing more than one nation composed of many," in some circles the dream of imperial grandeur persists. One need only peruse the book on Napoleon published in February 2001 by Dominique de Villepin, foreign minister of France, and ponder his assertion that, at Waterloo, Europe lost the most splendid opportunity ever to come its way.

The simple fact that Great Britain withstood Napoleon's repeated attempts to extend his dominion over all of Europe proves the prescience of Voltaire and Montesquieu. Despite its diminutive size and limited resources and population, Britain was able to put together, fund, and lead the various coalitions that ultimately inflicted on this would-be Caesar a defeat even more decisive than the one suffered by Louis XIV. Moreover, in 1940, there was once again reason to recall Montesquieu's bold claim that "in Europe the last sigh of liberty will be heaved by an Englishman," for it was Montesquieu's England that stood up to Hitler, and for a time it did so almost entirely alone.

If, in the end, Great Britain did not put together, fund, and lead the coalition that eventually defeated the Nazi colossus, if it did not put together, fund, and lead the alliance that later contained, wore down, and ultimately dismembered the Soviet empire, it was because the British lost their commercial supremacy and came to be overshadowed by another, kindred people, which took shape, as Montesquieu had predicted, "in the forests" of the New World. This great people was endowed by Britain with a "form of government, which brings with it prosperity," and to this people one could aptly apply nearly every word that Voltaire and Montesquieu wrote concerning the England they visited roughly a quarter-century after Marlborough repeatedly demonstrated in battle—at Blenheim, Ramillies, Oudenarde, Lille, and Malplaquet—the superiority of modern to ancient statecraft.

PAUL A. RAHE, a former Wilson Center fellow, is the Jay P. Walker Professor of History at the University of Tulsa. He is the author of *Republics Ancient and Modern: Classical Republicanism and the American Revolution* (1992), and coeditor, with David W. Carrithers and Michael A. Mosher, of *Montesquieu's Science of Politics: Essays on The Spirit of Laws* (2001).

Declaring an Open Season on the Wisdom of the Ages

Under the stewardship of scholars Diderot and d'Alembert, the 18th-century's Encyclopédie championed fact and freedom of the intellect

ROBERT WERNICK

Most everyone in Paris 250 years ago was aware of the band of voluble, enthusiastic men scurrying around town, piling up notes and editing documents for a gigantic publishing enterprise with which they intended to change the world. It was to be called the *Encyclopédie, ou Dictionnaire raisonné des sciences, des arts et des métiers* (Encyclopedia, or Classified Dictionary of Sciences, Arts and Trades), the *Encyclopédie* for short. It took all human knowledge for its province, it took a quarter of a century to complete, it sold enough copies to justify its being called among the very earliest commercial best-sellers of modern times, and it did change the world.

This past winter, a giant exhibition celebrating the opening of new quarters for the Bibliothèque Nationale in Paris, and showcasing library treasures including the *Encyclopédie,* demonstrated just how this was done. The first two volumes of the *Encyclopédie,* which took five years to assemble, appeared in two very handsome and very expensive folio volumes in 1751; the first subscribers had only to open to page 1 to see that something very new was loose in the world. There was the first article, on the letter *A,* starting off quietly enough with a historical summary of the letter and its ancestors, the Greek alpha, the Hebrew aleph. Then the authors of the entry went on to turn the batteries of scorn on previous authorities who had laid down the law on the subject, like the ancient scholar Covaruvias. These authorities had explained that the letter *A* constituted the first sound made by boy babies after being born, it being the first vowel in the syllable *mas,* root of the Latin adjective *masculinus.* Girl babies, the authorities averred, uttered an *e* sound, root of *feminina.* The Encyclopedists (as Diderot and his collaborators have come to be known), disregarding authority, insisted on referring to the behavior of some live babies and reported that they "make different vowel sounds, depending on how wide they open their mouths." A reader of 1997 is unlikely to find anything unusual or objectionable in this observation. But in 1751 it was a war cry of revolt. The Encyclopedists were proclaiming, in an insidiously mocking way, that direct observation of brute fact took precedence over the accumulated pile of ancient wisdom.

Denis Diderot, who wrote most of the *A* article, was never happier than when he could summon up all the ponderous columns of authority that had been tramping down the centuries and blow them away with one gust of rational thought. A few dozen pages after *A,* he found himself dealing with the *Agnus Scythicus,* or Scythian lamb. The names of the authorities roll along like caissons: Scaliger, Kircher, Sigismond, Hesberetein, Hayton the Armenian, Surius, Fortunius Licetus, André Lebarrus, Adam Olearius, Olaus Vormius, "and an infinity of other botanists." All of them had gone on repeating in their learned treatises the same description of this plant growing on the steppes east of the Black Sea. A remarkable plant not only shaped like a sheep but growing a darkish down all over its body, it was said to make excellent garments and also to be the source of a cure for spitting up blood.

It took centuries of solemn repetition before another botanist, named Kempfer, took the trouble to visit the steppes and discover that there was no such thing as an *Agnus Scythicus.* He found only an outsize but otherwise ordinary fern with a kind of dusky fuzz on its leaves. Reflecting on this episode of human folly, said Diderot, will be far more useful to the mind than the Scythian lamb ever was to the lungs. It was open season on the wisdom of the ages.

The *Encyclopédie* was not at all an ambitious project to start with. It had begun back in 1745 when a printer and entrepreneur named André-François Le Breton formed a consortium to finance a French translation of the popular and widely admired *Cyclopaedia* of the Englishman Ephraim Chambers. This was the latest, and in many ways the best, of the compendiums of human knowledge that had been coming out in a more or less steady stream since a scholar in Athens created the form in the second century B.C. Le Breton's was a very modest project, involving a small capital outlay. But the undertaking soon ran into difficulties, partly because the thrifty publishers hired unskilled translators, with the result that no one could understand what they turned out.

They then called in two of the brightest young lights of the Parisian intellectual world, the all-around man of letters Denis Diderot—described in a police report as "a very bright and extremely dangerous fellow"—and the mathematician Jean d'Alembert. These two saw a chance of turning the project into a manifesto of the new age, the new way of thinking.

They never pretended to have invented the new way of thinking, they were only systematizing it, publicizing it, letting it loose to spread its rays of enlightenment and disperse the clouds of ancient superstition. They traced this intellectual revolution back a century and a half to the great Francis Bacon, Lord Chancellor of England. It was Bacon, said d'Alembert, who first recognized the necessity of experimental physics, which is the basis of the modern scientific-technological world. It was Bacon who wrote in his *Novum Organum* (1620) that it was not enough simply to observe nature. It was necessary to put nature to the question, that is to say, to create experiments under controlled conditions, an approach that has since become known as the scientific method.

Bacon could not shake off all the shackles of the old ways of thinking all by himself. He was taken in, like everybody else, by the Scythian lamb. But he was far ahead of his time in insisting that accurate investigation of the phenomena of the world took precedence over ancient officially approved dogma.

Following Baconian principles, the *Encyclopédie* dealt with the random pieces of vulgar reality on the same level as the broad tenets that held them together. You didn't need a witch doctor or the abstract speculations of Aristotle or Thomas Aquinas to tell you how the Universe worked. In the *Encyclopédie* it was all set out in crystal-clear prose and engravings. You could learn how to solve mathematical problems and analyze human emotions, how to construct a coal mine, cast an equestrian statue of Louis XIV, fight a duel, make soap. You could consult an entry on how to perform a bladder operation (restraining your patient first in a special surgical chair) or an article on how to study a flea under a microscope. What was new about the *Encyclopédie's* method was that it mixed the theoretical with the practical. Indeed it had no use for theory without practical application: that was the secret weapon which unleashed the scientific-technological-industrial revolution of modern times.

Everything started with facts, and no fact was beneath the notice of Diderot and d'Alembert. Hence their insistence that the volumes of illustrative plates were as important as the volumes of text. They tried to bring everything up to date, to show just how the world was being run at the very moment. It was this more than anything else that distinguished this encyclopedia from its predecessors.

The editors and authors of the *Encyclopédie* were perfectly willing to devote 20 pages to *lâme,* the soul, in a long account of metaphysical and epistemological speculation. They also devoted 15 pages to the machine manufacture of stockings, one of the principal industrial products of their day, showing in text and engravings all 86 steps in the process.

Previous encyclopedists had aimed to summarize the arts and sciences. But Diderot and company added a significant word to their title—*métiers,* trades and crafts—insisting that no sharp line could be drawn between theory and practice. Such a line had been drawn as a matter of course in the pre-Baconian past, when the idea of treating the human soul and stockings on the same level of seriousness would have seemed obscene. Aristotle and Thomas Aquinas could reason as well as anyone who ever lived, but it would never have occurred to them to reason about the humdrum tools of daily life.

Diderot, as managing editor of the project, kept a strict eye on his collaborators, even when he had to spend four months in jail, to make sure they were accurate and up to date. He had Louis-Jacques Goussier, the superb draftsman who did more than 900 of the plates, spend six weeks in paper mills, six months in ironworks and glassworks, a month watching anchors being made.

It would take more than 20 years to get out the first edition: 71,818 articles arranged alphabetically in 17 volumes, plus 11 volumes containing 2,885 illustrative plates. New editions, revised editions, supplementary editions, rival editions, would go on appearing for another half-century.

There may have been as many as 300 men (and one anonymous woman) who collaborated on writing the articles of the original *Encyclopédie.* They came from different backgrounds; of those whose backgrounds can be identified, 15 percent were doctors, 12 percent were administrative officials, 8 percent were priests, 4 percent were titled nobility, 4 percent were merchants or manufacturers. They included famous scientists and famous writers like Voltaire and Montesquieu.

Diderot, 34 years old when he started the work, was the son of a provincial artisan and wrote more than 5,000 of the articles himself. He got fairly substantial lump-sum payments from the businessmen who were underwriting the project—royalties for authors were unknown in those days—but there were many contributors who worked for no monetary compensation whatever, among them the good-tempered and indefatigable Chevalier Louis de Jaucourt. A learned aristocrat with a noble lineage back to the early Middle Ages, he wrote no less than 17,000 articles.

One of them was the last entry under Z, an article on Zzuéné, or Zzeuene, about which there was nothing to say but that it was a city on the eastern bank of the Nile in upper Egypt not far from Ethiopia. That left the author free to embark on a paean to the completion of the great *Encyclopédie.* In the writer's eyes, this very accomplishment had been foretold by Lord Bacon, who had predicted an assemblage of scholars who would engage in an "admirable conspiracy" to flood with light the world of the arts and sciences. "A time will come," said Bacon, "when philosophers will undertake this effort. Then will arise, from the dark realm of the sophists and the envious, a dark swarm which, seeing these eagles soaring and being unable either to stop or to follow their rapid flight, will try by their vain croakings to belittle their accomplishment and their triumph."

The croakings were not long in coming. The printing of books, at least legally, in France (as was the case in the whole world of the mid-18th century, except for England and Holland) depended like most other aspects of life on what the French called *privilége.* A tight little cartel had the monopoly, and each work they printed had to receive a *privilége* or license, signed by the king, which indicated his gracious permission.

The king could hardly be expected to put his seal of approval on misleading or subversive works. And there was no lack of authorities to point out that the Encyclopedists made many factual errors, often borrowed (some said plagiarized) the work of others and wrote in a tone that was subversive from the word go. After the introduction, a foldout sheet contained a sort of table of contents in the form of an allegorical tree of knowledge, showing how all human understanding flowed up the one trunk of Reason and out into many branches.

This was a perfectly traditional device, except that in traditional books the root of the tree was Revealed Religion, or Theology. In the *Encyclopédie*'s tree, Theology was only one branch of the limb called Metaphysics, and it in turn was divided into twigs labeled Religion, Superstition, Divination and Black Magic. It was higher up on the tree, but no thicker or more handsome than the twigs farther down, such as differential Algebra, Spelling, Heraldry, Hydrostatics, Instrumental Music, Drapery, Syntax, Clock-making, Fireworks.

A Jesuit publication, the *Journal de Trévoux,* accused the Encyclopedists of favoring freedom of thought. Why, it was asked, were there so many articles devoted to obscure pagan deities and so few to kings and saints? Why did Abbé Mallet, the priest who wrote the article on Noah's Ark, spend no time at all on the Ark's spiritual significance and so much time on ignoble calculations of how big the vessel must have been to hold all those animals, how many man-hours Noah and his sons must have spent cleaning out the mountains of daily manure, how many extra sheep and cattle had to be brought aboard to provide food for the wolves and lions? Pope Clement XIII put the *Encyclopédie* on the Index [of prohibited books] in 1759 and ordered all Catholics who owned a copy of the work to have it burned by a priest, or be excommunicated.

The Encyclopedists might face the threat of jail—or hellfire. They were accused of atheism, free thought, political subversion, corruption of morals. Hitherto, said a bishop, "Hell has vomited its venom drop by drop. Today there are torrents of errors and impieties."

The French government, faced with increasing pressure from defenders of traditional values, took a course, common to all governments, of playing both sides of the board. With one hand it condemned. In 1752, the King's Council ordered the first two volumes of the *Encyclopédie* "to be and remain suppressed." In 1759, the government revoked the license that allowed the Encyclopédie to be printed.

With the other hand, it quietly signaled to the Encyclopedists to go on doing just what they were doing. This was possible because the man in charge of suppressing the work was actually devoted to its principles. He was Chrétien-Guillaume de Lamoignon de Malesherbes, a very cultivated and very brave man who 33 years later would again stick his neck way out by undertaking the defense of Louis XVI at the trial that condemned him to death. During the *Encyclopédie*'s early years he was Directeur de la Librairie, the official charged with overseeing the production and distribution of books in France. He was one of the enlightened aristocrats who were convinced that the whole system of *privilèges* and thought control on which the old order was based was both irrational and hopelessly inefficient.

While he acceded to decrees revoking the *Encyclopédie's* permit, he also found time to give Diderot advance warning of a police raid. And Malesherbes offered his own cellar as a safe hiding place for all the thousands of pages of Diderot's notes and drafts until the police were back in their barracks. He found in the arsenal of French government administrators a pleasant little weapon known as *Permission tacite.* This loophole meant that, for instance, while there might be a decree forbidding the printing of the *Encyclopédie* in France, the publishers might, by greasing the palm of a printer in the Swiss city of Neuchâtel arrange a sleight of hand. They could issue the last ten volumes in Paris with fraudulent title pages, stating the printer to be one Samuel Faulche & Compagnie in Switzerland.

Malesherbes realized that the *Encyclopédie,* and all it represented in the way of freedom of thought and experimental physics, formed the wave of the future. So did La Breton and other farsighted, greedy and unscrupulous printer-booksellers, who understood that the new thirst for science and knowledge that was spreading through the world was a potential gold mine. They had stumbled onto a best-seller.

It was a stupendous undertaking. The making and merchandizing of books was still, in the 18th century, a handicraft industry, offering deluxe products to the tiny minority of the population that was both literate and rich. Everything had to be done by hand. The production of paper involved an army of homeless itinerant laborers, who turned ragpickers after the harvest was done, and armies of skilled artisans to turn the rags into paper and then print and bind the volumes.

The quantity of paper needed for the *Encyclopédie* was enormous. Printing only the first volume in the quarto edition called for more than a million pieces of paper, and there were 36 volumes in the quarto edition. There were times when the supply of paper ran low; the work was nearly brought to a halt. Even with a steady supply of paper, it took five months of hard labor by five compositors and 20 pressmen to turn out a volume. A barrel of ink cost as much as a printing press, and a bad walnut crop in the south of France or a revolution in the American Colonies might cause the price of ink to skyrocket.

Very little information has survived of the actual details of book publishing before the 19th century. The *Encyclopédie* is an exception. Prof. Robert Darnton of Princeton discovered about 30 years ago in Switzerland a treasure trove in the form of 50,000 business documents and letters in the archives of the Société typográphique de Neuchâtel, an important publisher of French books in the 18th century. From them he was able to construct, in an admirably thorough and thoroughly enjoyable book called *The Business of Enlightenment,* a full picture of how a work like the *Encyclopédie* was created, manufactured and sold in those years.

It is not a pretty picture. As far as trade practices and merchandising are concerned, it must be admitted that modern publishing houses, so often denounced for their crass commercialism, are paragons of honesty and integrity compared with their forebears of the courtly 18th century. Publishers routinely lied, cheated, swindled, bribed, conspired and spied. They also often mangled and distorted their authors' texts: an article in the *Encyclopédie* might take a different slant depending on whether it was offered for sale in a Catholic or in a Protestant country.

Diderot came to think that his own work, after it had passed through all these dirty hands, was a "monstrosity." When he was asked to collaborate on a revised version of the work, he replied in a few words of colloquial French best translated as "Get lost."

The fact remained that, for all the wrangling and the mendacities and the troubles with the law, the volumes kept coming out—for the very good reason that the bottom line always showed a more than healthy profit. The publishers made money on a scale that had never been seen before in the book business, and that would not be seen again till the arrival of mechanized publishing and cheap pulp paper in the middle of the next century.

By 1789 almost 25,000 sets of authorized folio, quarto and octavo editions printed more or less legally in Paris, Lyon, Geneva, Neuchâtel, Bern, Lausanne, Lucca and Leghorn had been sold throughout Europe. At an average of 30 volumes per set, that makes three quarters of a million books—an extraordinary figure for the time.

The first folio edition was terribly expensive, affordable only by very rich people like government ministers, archbishops, Russian princes, German princelings. But as fiercely competitive publishers poured out less-expensive quarto and octavo editions, the *Encyclopédie* came to be read by more and more thousands of more or less ordinary people. It was still far beyond the reach of most of the population. A skilled locksmith or printer would have had to cough up the equivalent of fifteen and a half weeks' wages for the cheapest octavo edition. If Diderot had to buy it, it would have taken four and a half weeks of his pay for the project. Still, the publishers had judged that there was a huge untapped market for books like this; their profits went up all around.

No one can tell how many people actually read the *Encyclopédie,* but by the standards of the time it was surely very considerable. Everyone in Europe who wanted to keep up with current knowledge and current standards had to read it, or at least say he did.

Apparently few if any copies got to Colonial America. But American revolutionaries had imbibed the 18th-century intellectual discourse that created the *Encyclopédie.* Benjamin Franklin was acting in the spirit of the philosophes when, after sages had been speculating for untold centuries about the nature of lightning, he put a kite up in the sky in an effort to find out.

Jefferson was following the Encyclopedic rules when he heard that pious people were saying that shellfish found at the top of mountains in fossilized form must have been put there by Noah's flood. Jefferson didn't buy the deluge explanation. He took time out to calculate that if all the moisture suspended in the earth's atmosphere were to be condensed into water, the oceans still would not rise halfway up the mountains.

By the time the French Revolution broke out in 1789, Diderot and d'Alembert and many original contributors were dead. However, a new generation had come along to digest the enormous mass of new theoretical and technical knowledge that was piling up year after year. The new Encyclopedists were less philosophical, more technical and more specialized than the old. The new version in 229 volumes that came out between 1781 and 1832 was called the *Encyclopédie Méthodique* (Methodical Encyclopedia). But the Encyclopedists' aims and their methods were in fact basically the same.

Their enemies were quick to proclaim, and have proclaimed ever since, that the Encyclopedists were responsible for the French Revolution, the Reign of Terror, the guillotine and all the horrors of the modern world. Their friends were equally quick to give them credit for the rise of liberty, universal suffrage, freedom of the press and all the progress of the modern world.

The Encyclopedists had no common political program, and their direct influence on political and social events was probably very small. Darnton's analysis of the account books shows that most of the sales went to people very much like the Encyclopedists themselves, upper-class people brought up in a world of privilege and unchallenged authority. An edition that sold 338 copies in the placid provincial town of Besançon, where the population of 28,000 consisted largely of priests, professors, lawyers, officials and landholders, sold only 28 in Lille (pop. 61,000). In that city, the inhabitants were starting to build factories that would change the face of the world, but the people building them were too busy to read anything beyond their balance sheets.

Keenly aware of change, the Encyclopedists had little more prescience than anyone else of how the change was coming. They lived at the dawn of the Industrial Age but could scarcely grasp what would come of it. The technology they admired and illustrated so lovingly was a highly developed handicraft, mostly devoted to luxury goods like stockings and watches. They were not themselves revolutionaries, though their belief in free inquiry and their contempt for irrational authority must have had considerable influence on revolutionaries.

When the revolution in France did come, dismantling the whole vast structure of privilege at one swoop, they had different opinions about it, responded in different ways and had different fates. Some were guillotined, some were pressed into service to make saltpeter and cannon, and to create a rational system of weights and measures. The naturalist Daubenton was asked to dissect a rhinoceros from the former king's menagerie for revolutionary leaders eager to disseminate knowledge.

The great mathematician Condorcet, who had hailed the revolution but had voted against the death penalty for the king, was forced to flee for his life. It was while hiding from the authorities that he wrote his classic demonstration that the progress of knowledge proved that "nature has placed no limit to our hopes" and that the human race was bound to approach ever closer to perfection. Wandering in the country, and starving, he ordered an omelet in a country inn, and when they asked him how many eggs he wanted in it, he faced one of those unexpected practical problems that pop up in times of great social change. He was a marquis by birth, and there would have been no reason for him at any time in his life to see the inside of a kitchen. He answered at random, a dozen, raising doubt as to the reality of his claim to being an unemployed worker. He was thrown into jail and died there, perhaps having swallowed the poison he had hidden in his ring in order to avoid the guillotine.

Most of the surviving Encyclopedists were content to wait out the revolution, and eventually got jobs at universities and government institutes, continuing to amass and channel and analyze the immense flood of knowledge pouring at an ever increasing rate over the earth.

Whatever happened to the individual Encyclopedists, the *Encyclopédie* itself survived. The solemn old volumes may sit unread in libraries, but some of the livelier articles are continually being reprinted in anthologies of 18th-century prose.

Few people today share the Encyclopedists' ingenuous faith that human knowledge could be satisfactorily summarized in 28 volumes or in 229 (as the last *Encyclopédie* numbered) or that greater diffusion of knowledge must lead to greater happiness for mankind.

But in a sense the *Encyclopédie* has been triumphant. The spirit of Lord Bacon, the combination of free curiosity and empirical evidence, roams unchecked over most of the world. When the Catholic Church, which once ordered the *Encyclopédie* to be burned, wished to settle the question of whether the Shroud of Turin really wrapped a crucified man 19 centuries ago or was created by an artist some centuries later, it did not rely on consultation of ancient authorities, as Pope Clement XIII surely would have done. It sent the Shroud to a laboratory. This is just what Diderot would have advised.

A frequent contributor [to] Smithsonian, **ROBERT WERNICK** writes from Paris for part of the year. He reported recently on the restoration of a château in the French countryside.

Thomas Young: The Man Who Knew Everything

Andrew Robinson marvels at the brain power and breadth of knowledge of the 18th-century polymath Thomas Young. He examines his relationship with his contemporaries, particularly with the French Egyptologist Champollion, and how he has been viewed subsequently by historians.

ANDREW ROBINSON

'Fortunate newton, happy childhood of science!' Albert Einstein wrote in 1931 in his foreword to the fourth edition of Newton's influential treatise *Opticks*, originally published in 1704.

> Nature to him was an open book, whose letters he could read without effort. . . . Reflection, refraction, the formation of images by lenses, the mode of operation of the eye, the spectral decomposition and recomposition of the different kinds of light, the invention of the reflecting telescope, the first foundations of colour theory, the elementary theory of the rainbow pass by us in procession, and finally come his observations of the colours of thin films as the origin of the next great theoretical advance, which had to await, over a hundred years, the coming of Thomas Young.

Everyone who studies physics at school is taught that Thomas Young (1773–1829) was the English scientist who first demonstrated—with a candle, a pair of narrow slits and a white screen—that light was a wave, thus disproving Newton's conviction that it consisted of a stream of particles. Equally, anyone who studies ancient Egypt will know that Young was the linguist and antiquarian who 'cracked' the two Egyptian scripts on the Rosetta Stone, which then launched the full decipherment of the Egyptian hieroglyphs by Jean-Francois Champollion in the 1820s. Young was the first to show that demotic (the third script on the Stone, alongside Greek and hieroglyphs) to some extent resembled hieroglyphic visually, hence demotic was derived from hieroglyphic, and demotic was not an alphabet like the Greek alphabet but rather a mixture of phonetic signs and hieroglyphic signs. This thinking led Young to suggest that hieroglyphic, too, might contain some phonetic elements, an 'alphabet', for spelling non-Egyptian names like Ptolemy and Cleopatra.

Less well known is that Young was a physiologist who was the first to explain how the human eye focuses on objects at varying distances; who discovered the phenomenon of astigmatism; and who in 1801 proposed the three-colour theory of vision, confirmed experimentally in 1959.

In addition, Young was a major scholar of ancient Greek; a phenomenal linguist who, after comparing the vocabulary and grammar of some 400 languages, in 1813 introduced the term Indo-European to describe the language family that includes Greek, Latin and Sanskrit; and an extraordinarily prolific and authoritative writer, mainly for the *Encyclopaedia Britannica*, on all manner of other subjects from carpentry and music to life insurance and ocean tides, as well as biographies of eminent scientists and scholars. His professional appointments included: professor of natural philosophy at the newly founded Royal Institution, where in 1802–03 he delivered what is generally regarded as the most far-reaching series of lectures ever given by a scientist; a physician at a major London hospital, St George's, for a quarter of a century; the secretary of the Admiralty's Board of Longitude and superintendent of its vital *Nautical Almanac* from 1818 until his death; and 'inspector of calculations' for a leading life insurance company in the 1820s. In 1794, he was elected a fellow of the Royal Society at the age of barely twenty-one, became its foreign secretary at the age of thirty, and turned down its presidency in his fifties. No wonder, the organizers of an exhibition at London's Science Museum in 1973 stated:

> Young probably had a wider range of creative learning than any other Englishman in history. He made discoveries in nearly every field he studied.

Born to a Quaker family in Somerset, Young was a child prodigy, who later trained as a physician in London, Edinburgh and Göttingen and at Cambridge, where he was known to the students as 'Phenomenon' Young with a mixture of respect and derision. He has never lacked for admirers among great scientists. Just after Young's death, the astronomer Sir John Herschel called him a 'truly original genius' and added that 'to do anything approaching to justice to his reputation … would call for the exercise of powers more nearly allied to his own than I can pretend to boast'. Later in the century, the physicist and physiologist Hermann von Helmholtz stated that Young

> … was one of the most acute men who ever lived, but had the misfortune to be too far in advance of his contemporaries. They looked on him with astonishment, but could not follow his bold speculations, and thus a mass of his important thoughts remained buried and forgotten in the *Transactions* of the Royal Society until a later generation by slow degrees arrived at the rediscovery of his discoveries, and came to appreciate the force of his arguments and the accuracy of his conclusions.

While in 1899, lecturing on the centenary of the Royal Institution, the physicist Lord Rayleigh declared simply: 'it was seldom that [Young] was wrong'. A century later, in 2005, a Nobel laureate in physics, Philip Anderson, summarized Young's achievements as follows:

> He elucidated the optics of the eye, the wave theory of light, the laws of elasticity, the nature of the Egyptian hieroglyphic writing, and Lord knows how many other subjects.

Among non-scientists, Young's position has been less secure. His reputation, like those of Robert Hooke, Benjamin Franklin and Alexander von Humboldt, has suffered from his being a polymath. Polymathy is disturbing, especially to specialists, as historian Alexander Murray noted in connection with Sir William 'Oriental' Jones (1746–94), a polymath of the generation before Young's. Jones is remembered today for being the first person to identify clearly the similarities between Sanskrit, Greek, Latin, Gothic (Germanic), Celtic and Old Persian (the language family which Young then dubbed 'Indo-European')—but Jones worked in many other fields too. An Oxford University symposium on the bicentenary of his death in 1994, edited by Murray, required separate contributions from a Sanskritist and an Arabist, a theologian, a lawyer (Jones was a judge) and an anthropologist, among others. Murray acutely remarked:

> History is unkind to polymaths. No biographer will readily tackle a subject whose range of skills far exceeds his own, while the rest of us, with or without biographies to read, have no mental 'slot' in which to keep a polymath's memory fresh. So the polymath gets forgotten or, at best, squashed into a category we can recognize, in the way Goethe is remembered as a poet, despite his claim to have been a scientist, or Hume as a philosopher, for all the six dumpy volumes of his *History of England*. [Yet,] There are times when a mind of exceptional range, bestriding many conventional disciplines, makes a breakthrough in each because he knows the others, and all of them go on their way, afterwards, without necessarily recognizing what

he did or how he did it. If history is not to be chronically misremembered, it follows that a constant effort must be made—as constant as the mechanism that pulls invisibly in the other direction—to recall those polymathic minds that have made these critical turns.

This applies very well to Young in respect of his research on ancient Egypt—which is probably the part of his work of greatest interest to most historians. Young's ability to decipher the Rosetta Stone and ancient Egyptian papyruses was undoubtedly fed by his powers of mathematical analysis and scientific intuition, by his philological scholarship in ancient Greek and Oriental languages, by his immersion since childhood in the civilizations of the classical world, and by his exceptionally detailed knowledge of the history of ideas in science and medicine, evident in all his publications, especially his greatest work, *A Course of Lectures in Natural Philosophy and the Mechanical Arts,* derived from his Royal Institution lectures and published in 1807, the second volume of which consists of a systematized and annotated catalogue containing 20,000 articles ranging from the ancient Greeks up to 1805. Yet, having said all this, Young's contribution to the hieroglyphic decipherment is frequently underplayed and sometimes even virtually dismissed in favour of Champollion's. Indeed, the dispute between them has become the most notorious in the history of archaeological decipherment, still partly unresolved to this day.

Young stated that Champollion had built his system of reading hieroglyphics on Young's own discoveries and his hieroglyphic 'alphabet', published in various articles and in a major supplement to the *Encyclopaedia Britannica* in 1815–19. While paying generous tribute to Champollion's unrivalled progress from 1822 onwards, Young wanted his early steps recognized. This Champollion was adamantly unwilling to concede. Just weeks before Young's death in 1829, Champollion, writing in the midst of his expedition to ancient Egypt—he was then at Thebes in the Valley of the Kings (a place he had just named)—exulted to his brother:

> So poor Dr Young is incorrigible? Why flog a mummified horse? Thank M. Arago [a French physicist] for the arrows he shot so valiantly in honour of the Franco-Pharaonic alphabet. The Brit can do whatever he wants—it will remain ours: and all of old England will learn from young France how to spell hieroglyphs using an entirely different method … May the doctor continue to agitate about the alphabet while I, having been for six months among the monuments of Egypt, I am startled by what I am reading fluently rather than what my imagination is able to come up with.

The nationalistic overtones—at times evident in Young's writings too—have to some extent bedevilled honest discussion of Young and Champollion ever since. Even Young's friend in physics, Dominique Arago, turned against his work on the hieroglyphs, partly because Champollion was an honoured fellow-countryman. Thus, a recent French book by Robert Solé and the Egyptologist Dominique Valbelle, *The Rosetta Stone: The Story of the Decoding of Hieroglyphics*, deliberately omits the trenchant criticism of Champollion's character written to Young in 1815 by Champollion's former teacher Sylvestre de Sacy (who warned Young that Champollion might plagiarize his work); it also omits other episodes in which Champollion is generally held to have suppressed an erroneous publication of his own and to have failed to acknowledge a crucial inscriptional clue concerning Cleopatra provided by the antiquarian William Bankes.

Egyptologists, who are best placed to understand the intellectual 'nitty-gritty' of the dispute, are drawn to Champollion more than Young because he founded their subject. Even John Ray, a professor of Egyptology at Cambridge University who has done most in recent years to give Young his due, admits:

> ... the suspicion may easily arise, and often has done, that any eulogy of Thomas Young must be intended as a denigration of Champollion. This would be shameful coming from an Egyptologist.

Then there is the cult of genius: many of us prefer to believe in the primacy of unaccountable moments of inspiration over the less glamorous virtues of step-by-step, rational teamwork. Champollion maintained that his advances came almost exclusively out of his own mind, arising from his indubitably passionate devotion to ancient Egypt. He pictured himself for the public as a 'lone genius' who solved the riddle of ancient Egypt's writing single-handedly. The fact that Young was known primarily for his work in fields other than Egyptian studies, and that he published on Egypt anonymously in 1815–19 (to protect his professional reputation as a physician), made Champollion's solitary self-image easily believable for most people. It is a discomforting thought, especially for a specialist, that a non-specialist might enter an academic field, transform it, and then move on to work in an utterly different field.

Lastly, Young and Champollion were highly contrasting personalities. Champollion had tunnel vision ('fortunately for our subject', says Ray); was prone to fits of euphoria and despair; and had personally led an uprising against the French king in Grenoble, for which he was put on trial. The polymath Young, who had a total lack of engagement with party politics, was a man who 'could not bear, in the most common conversation, the slightest degree of exaggeration, or even of colouring' (said his closest friend, the antiquarian and politician Hudson Gurney).

Young never went to Egypt, and never wanted to go. In founding an Egyptian Society in London in 1817, to publish as many ancient inscriptions and manuscripts as possible, so as to aid the decipherment, Young remarked that funds were needed 'for employing some poor Italian or Maltese to scramble over Egypt in search of more.' Champollion, by contrast, had long dreamt of visiting Egypt and doing exactly what Young had depreciated, ever since he saw the hieroglyphs as a boy; and when he finally got there, he was able to pass for a native, given his swarthy complexion and his excellent command of Arabic. In his wonderfully ebullient *Egyptian Diaries*, Champollion describes entering the temple of Rameses the Great at Abu Simbel, blocked by millennia of sand:

> I almost entirely undressed, wearing only my Arab shirt and long underwear, and pressed myself on my stomach through the small aperture of a doorway which, unearthed, would have been at least 25 feet high. It felt as if I was climbing through the heart of a furnace and, gliding completely into the temple, I entered an atmosphere rising to 52 degrees: holding a candle in our hand, Rosellini, Ricci, I and one of our Arabs went through this astonishing cave.

Such a perilous adventure would probably not have appealed to Young, even in his careless youth as an accomplished horseman roughing it in the Scottish Highlands. His motive for deciphering the Egyptian scripts was fundamentally philological and scientific, not aesthetic and cultural (unlike his attitude to the classical literature of Greece and Rome). Many Egyptologists tend not to sympathize with this motive. They also know little about Young's scientific work and his renown as someone who initiated many new areas of scientific enquiry and left others to develop them. As a result, some scholars seriously misjudge him. Not knowing of his fairness in recognizing other scientists' contributions and his fanatical truthfulness in his own scientific work, they jump to the conclusion that Young's attitude to Champollion was chiefly envious. The classicist Maurice Pope (1999) called Young, 'a man with a grievance ... [who] clearly hankered for something with a promise of immortality in it.' The Champollion biographers Lesley and Roy Adkins (2000) are explicit: 'while maintaining civil relations with his rival, Young's jealousy had not ceased to fester.' But such an emotion would have been out of character for Young, and it would have made little sense anyway given his scientific achievements and the fact that these were increasingly recognized from 1816 onwards—to begin with by French scientists. The truth is that for Champollion, the success of his decipherment was a matter of make-or-break as a scholar; for Young, his Egyptian research was essentially yet another fascinating avenue of knowledge to explore for his own amusement.

After 1822–24, when Champollion published his landmark work, Young more or less gave up work on the hieroglyphs. But he continued to work on the second undeciphered Egyptian script found on the Rosetta Stone, which Young called 'enchorial' but which Champollion termed 'demotic'. At this point Champollion, for whatever reason, offered Young access to the swelling collections of demotic manuscripts under his curatorship in the Louvre Museum in Paris. On his deathbed, Young could justifiably write in his final publication, *Rudiments of an Egyptian Dictionary in the Ancient Enchorial Character, Containing All the Words of Which the Sense Has Been Ascertained*, 'thirty years ago, not a single article of the list [of words in the dictionary] existed even in the imagination of the wildest enthusiast: and that within these ten years, a single date only was tolerably ascertained, out of about fifty which are here interpreted, and in many instances ascertained with astronomical precision.' John Ray sums up:

> Young was the first person since the end of the Roman Empire to be able to read a demotic text, and, in spite of a proportion of incorrect guesses, he surely deserves

to be known as the decipherer of demotic. It is no disservice to Champollion to allow him this distinction.

A couple of years before his death, in an autobiographical sketch written for his favourite sister-in-law intended for a future posthumous edition of the *Encyclopaedia Britannica*, Young wrote of himself:

> He might for example, have been styled without impropriety and almost with equal justice, in the middle of a history of his life, a physician, a classical scholar, a linguist, an antiquarian, a biographer, an optician, or a mathematician … Whether the public would have been more benefited by his confining his exertions within narrower limits, is a question of great doubt.

For those of us who feel instinctively drawn to versatility of genius, Young is an inspiration; others whose taste is for genius with a narrow focus (like Champollion's) will regard Young with scepticism. What is undeniable, though, is that his extraordinarily wide learning really does justify our calling him 'the last man who knew everything'—however much he himself would have denied this, for we can safely say, with the endless expansion and bifurcation of knowledge, that no one will be able to stake this awesome claim ever again.

For Further Reading

George Peacock, *Life of Thomas Young, M.D., F.R.S.* (John Murray, 1855, republished by Thoemmes Press, 2003);Andrew Robinson, *The Last Man Who Knew Everything:Thomas Young* (Pi Press, 2006);Thomas Young, *A Course of Lectures on Natural Philosophy and the Mechanical Arts*, 2 vols (Joseph Johnson, 1807, republished in 4 vols by Thoemmes Press, 2002);Thomas Young, *Miscellaneous Works of the Late Thomas Young, M.D., F.R.S.*, 3 vols (John Murray, 1855, republished by Thoemmes Press, 2003).

ANDREW ROBINSON is literary editor of *The Times Higher Education Supplement* and the author of a new biography of Thomas Young, *The Last Man Who Knew Everything*, Pi Press 2006.

The Passion of Antoine Lavoisier

With its revolution, France founded a rational republic and lost a great scientist.

STEPHEN JAY GOULD

Galileo and Lavoisier have more in common than their brilliance. Both men are focal points in a cardinal legend about the life of intellectuals—the conflict of lonely and revolutionary genius with state power. Both stories are apocryphal, however inspiring. Yet they only exaggerate, or encapsulate in the epitome of a bon mot, an essential theme in the history of thinking and its impact upon society.

Galileo, on his knees before the Inquisition, abjures his heretical belief that the earth revolves around a central sun. Yet, as he rises, brave Galileo, faithful to the highest truth of factuality, addresses a stage whisper to the world: *eppur se muove*—nevertheless, it does move. Lavoisier, before the revolutionary tribunal during the Reign of Terror in 1794, accepts the inevitable verdict of death, but asks for a week or two to finish some experiments. Coffinhal, the young judge who has sealed his doom, denies his request, stating, "La république n'a pas besoin de savants" (the Republic does not need scientists).

Coffinhal said no such thing, although the sentiments are not inconsistent with emotions unleashed in those frightening and all too frequent political episodes so well characterized by Marc Antony in his lamentation over Caesar: "O judgment! thou are fled to brutish beasts, And men have lost their reason." Lavoisier, who had been under arrest for months, was engaged in no experiments at the time. Moreover, as we shall see, the charges leading to his execution bore no relationship to his scientific work.

But if Coffinhal's chilling remark is apocryphal, the second most famous quotation surrounding the death of Lavoisier is accurate and well attested. The great mathematician Joseph Louis Lagrange, upon hearing the news about his friend Lavoisier, remarked bitterly: "It took them only an instant to cut off that head, but France may not produce another like it in a century."

I feel some need to participate in the worldwide outpouring of essays to commemorate the 200th anniversary of the French Revolution. Next month, on July 14, unparalleled displays of fireworks will mark the bicentenary of the fall of the Bastille. Nonetheless, and with no desire to put a damper on such pyrotechnics, I must write about the flip side of this initial liberation, the most troubling scientific story of the Revolution—the execution of Antoine Lavoisier in 1794.

The revolution had been born in hope and expansiveness. At the height of enthusiasm for new beginnings, the revolutionary government suppressed the old calendar, and started time all over again, with year I beginning on September 22, 1792, at the founding of the French republic. The months would no longer bear names of Roman gods or emperors, but would record the natural passage of seasons—as in *brumaire* (foggy), *ventose* (windy), *germinal* (budding), and to replace parts of July and August, originally named for two despotic Caesars, *thermidor*. Measures would be rationalized, decimalized, and based on earthly physics, with the meter defined as one ten-millionth of a quarter meridian from pole to equator. The metric system is our enduring legacy of this revolutionary spirit, and Lavoisier himself was the guiding force in devising the new weights and measures.

But initial optimism soon unraveled under the realities of internal dissension and external pressure (the powerful monarchists of Europe were, to say the least, concerned lest republican ideas spread by export or example). Governments tumbled one after the other, and Dr. Guillotin's machine, invented to make execution more humane, became a symbol of terror by sheer frequency of public use. Louis XVI was beheaded in January, 1793 (year one of the republic). Power shifted from the Girondins to the Montagnards, as the Terror reached its height and the war with Austria and Prussia continued. Finally, as so often happens, the architect of the terror, Robespierre himself, paid his visit to Dr. Guillotin's device, and the cycle played itself out. A few years later, in 1804, Napoleon was crowned as emperor, and the First Republic ended. Poor Lavoisier had been caught in the midst of the cycle, dying for his former role as tax collector on May 8, 1794, less than three months before the fall of Robespierre on July 27 (9 Thermidor, year II).

Old ideas often persist in vestigial forms of address and writing, long after their disappearance in practice. I was reminded of this phenomenon when I acquired, a few months ago, a copy of the opening and closing addresses for the course in zoology at the Muséum d'Histoire naturelle of Paris for 1801–2. The democratic fervor of the revolution had faded, and Napoleon had already staged his *coup d'etat* of 18 Brumaire (November 9, 1799), emerging as emperor de facto, although not crowned until 1804. Nonetheless, the author of these addresses, who would soon resume his full name Bernard-Germain-Etienne de la Ville-sur-Illon, comte de Lacépède, is identified on the title page only as C^{en} Lacépède (for *citoyen*, or "citizen"—the democratic form adopted by the revolution to abolish all distinctions of address). The long list of honors and memberships, printed in small type below Lacépède's name, is almost a parody on the ancient forms; for instead of the old affiliations that always included "member of the royal academy of this or that" and "counsellor to the king or count of here or there," Lacépède's titles are rigorously egalitarian—including "one of the professors at the museum of natural history," and member of the society of pharmacists of Paris, and of agriculture of Agen. As for the year of publication, we have to know the history detailed above—for the publisher's date is given, at the bottom, only as "l'an IX de la Rèpublique."

Lacépède was one of the great natural historians in the golden age of French zoology during the late eighteenth and early nineteenth century. His name may be overshadowed in retrospect by the illustrious quartet of Buffon, Lamarck, Saint-Hilaire and Cuvier, but Lacépède—who was chosen by Buffon to complete his life's work, the multivolumed *Histoire naturelle*—deserves a place with these men, for all were *citoyens* of comparable merit. Although Lacépède supported the revolution in its moderate first phases, his noble title bred suspicion and he went into internal exile during the Terror. But the fall of Robespierre prompted his return to Paris, where his former colleagues persuaded the government to establish a special chair for him at the Muséum, as zoologist for reptiles and fishes.

By tradition, his opening and closing addresses for the zoology course at the Muséum were published in pamphlet form each year. The opening address for year IX, "Sur l'histoire des races ou principales variétés de l'espèce humaine" (On the history of races and principal varieties of the human species), is a typical statement of the liberality and optimism of Enlightenment thought. The races, we learn, may differ in current accomplishments, but all are capable of greater and equal achievement, and all can progress.

But the bloom of hope had been withered by the Terror. Progress, Lacépède asserts, is not guaranteed, but is possible only if untrammeled by the dark side of human venality. Memories of dire consequences for unpopular thoughts must have been fresh, for Lacépède cloaked his criticisms of revolutionary excesses in careful speech and foreign attribution. Ostensibly, he was only describing the evils of the Indian caste system in a passage that must be read as a lament about the Reign of Terror:

> Hypocritical ambition,... abusing the credibility of the multitude, has conserved the ferocity of the savage state in the midst of the virtues of civilization.... After having reigned by terror [*regné par la terreur*], submitting even monarchs to their authority, they reserved the domain of science and art to themselves [a reference, no doubt, to the suppression of the independent academies by the revolutionary government in 1793, when Lacépède lost his first post at the Muséum], and surrounded themselves with a veil of mystery that only they could lift.

At the end of his address, Lacépède returns to the familiar theme of political excesses and makes a point, by no means

original of course, that I regard as the central structural tragedy of the nature of any complex system, including organisms and social institutions—the crushing asymmetry between the need for slow and painstaking construction and the potential for almost instantaneous destruction:

> Thus, the passage from the semisavage state to civilization occurs through a great number of insensible stages, and requires an immense amount of time. In moving slowly through these successive stages, man fights painfully against his habits; he also battles with nature as he climbs, with great effort, up the long and perilous path. But it is not the same with the loss of the civilized state; that is almost sudden. In this morbid fall, man is thrown down by all his ancient tendencies; he struggles no longer, he gives up, he does not battle obstacles, he abandons himself to the burdens that surround him. Centuries are needed to nurture the tree of science and make it grow, but one blow from the hatchet of destruction cuts it down.

The chilling final line, a gloss on Lagrange's famous statement about the death of Lavoisier, inspired me to write about the founder of modern chemistry, and to think a bit more about the tragic asymmetry of creation and destruction.

Antoine-Laurent Lavoisier, born in 1743, belonged to the nobility through a title purchased by his father (standard practice for boosting the royal treasury during the *ancien régime*). As a leading liberal and rationalist of the Enlightenment (a movement that attracted much of the nobility, including many wealthy intellectuals who had purchased their titles to rise from the bourgeoisie), Lavoisier fitted an astounding array of social and scientific services into a life cut short by the headsman at age fifty-one.

We know him best today as the chief founder of modern chemistry. The textbook one-liners describe him as the discoverer (or at least the namer) of oxygen, the man who (though anticipated by Henry Cavendish in England) recognized water as a compound of the gases hydrogen and oxygen, and who correctly described combustion, not as the liberation of a hypothetical substance called phlogiston, but as the combination of burning material with oxygen. But we can surely epitomize his contribution more accurately by stating that Lavoisier set the basis for modern chemistry by recognizing the nature of elements and compounds—by finally dethroning the ancient taxonomy of air, water, earth, and fire as indivisible elements; by identifying gas, liquid, and solid as states of aggregation for a single substance subjected to different degrees of heat; and by developing quantitative methods of defining and identifying true elements. Such a brief statement can only rank as a caricature of Lavoisier's scientific achievements, but this essay treats his other life in social service, and I must move on.

Lavoisier, no shrinking violet in the game of self-promotion, openly spoke of his new chemistry as "a revolution." He even published his major manifesto, *Traité élémentaire de chimie*, in 1789, starting date of the other revolution that would seal his fate.

Lavoisier, liberal child of the Enlightenment, was no opponent of the political revolution, at least in its early days. He supported the idea of a constitutional monarchy, and joined the most moderate of the revolutionary societies, the Club of '89. He served as an alternate delegate in the States General, took his turn as a *citoyen* at guard duty, and led several studies and commissions vital to the success of the revolution—including a long stint as *régisseur des poudres* (director of gunpowder, where his brilliant successes produced the best stock in Europe, thus providing substantial help in France's war against Austria and Prussia), work on financing the revolution by *assignats* (paper money backed largely by confiscated church lands), and service on the commission of weights and measures that formulated the metric system. Lavoisier rendered these services to all governments, including the most radical, right to his death, even hoping at the end that his crucial work on weights and measures might save his life. Why, then, did Lavoisier end up in two pieces on the *place de la Révolution* (long ago renamed, in pleasant newspeak, *place de la Concorde*)?

The fateful move had been made in 1768, when Lavoisier joined the infamous Ferme Générale, or Tax Farm. If you regard the IRS as a less than benevolent institution, just consider taxation under the *ancien régime* and count your blessings. Taxation was regressive with a vengeance, as the nobility and clergy were entirely exempt, and poor people supplied the bulk of the royal treasury through tariffs on the movement of goods across provincial boundaries, fees for entering the city of Paris, and taxes on such goods as tobacco and salt. (The hated *gabelle*, or "salt tax," was applied at iniquitously differing rates from region to region, and was levied not on actual consumption but on presumed usage—thus, in effect, forcing each family to buy a certain quantity of taxed salt each year.)

Moreover, the government did not collect taxes directly. They set the rates and then leased (for six-year periods) the privilege of collecting taxes to a private finance company, the Ferme Générale. The Tax Farm operated for profit like any other private business. If they managed to collect more than the government levy, they kept the balance; if they failed to reach the quota, they took the loss. The system was not only oppressive in principle; it was also corrupt. Several shares in the Tax Farm were paid for no work as favors or bribes; many courtiers, even the King himself, were direct beneficiaries. Nonetheless, Lavoisier chose this enterprise for the primary investment of his family fortune, and he became, as members of the firm were called, a *fermier-général*, or "farmer-general."

(Incidentally, since I first read the sad story of Lavoisier some twenty-five years ago, I have been amused by the term farmer-general, for it conjures up a pleasantly rustic image of a country yokel, dressed in his Osh Kosh b'Gosh overalls, and chewing on a stalk of hay while trying to collect the *gabelle*. But I have just learned from the *Oxford English Dictionary* that my image is not only wrong, but entirely backward. A farm, defined as a piece of agricultural land, is a derivative term. In usage dating to Chaucer, a farm, from the medieval Latin *firma*, "fixed payment," is "a fixed yearly sum accepted from a person as a composition for taxes or other moneys which he is empowered to collect." By extension, to farm is to lease anything for a fixed rent. Since most leases applied to land, agricultural plots become "farms," with the first use in this sense traced only to the

sixteenth century; the leasers of such land then became "farmers." Thus, our modern phrase "farming out" records the original use, and has no agricultural connotation. And Lavoisier was a farmer-general in the true sense, with no mitigating image of bucolic innocence.)

I do not understand why Lavoisier chose the Ferme Générale for his investment, and then worked so assiduously in his role as tax farmer. He was surely among the most scrupulous and fair-minded of the farmers, and might be justifiably called a reformer. (He opposed the overwatering of tobacco, a monopoly product of the Ferme, and he did, at least in later years, advocate taxation upon all, including the radical idea that nobles might pay as well.) But he took his profits, and he provoked no extensive campaign for reform as the money rolled in. The standard biographies, all too hagiographical, tend to argue that he regarded the Ferme as an investment that would combine greatest safety and return with minimal expenditure of effort—all done to secure a maximum of time for his beloved scientific work. But I do not see how this explanation can hold. Lavoisier, with his characteristic energy, plunged into the work of the Ferme, traveling all over the country, for example, to inspect the tobacco industry. I rather suspect that Lavoisier, like most modern businessmen, simply jumped at a good and legal investment without asking too many ethical questions.

But the golden calf of one season becomes the shattered idol of another. The farmers-general were roundly hated, in part for genuine corruption and iniquity, in part because tax collectors are always scapegoated, especially when the national treasury is bankrupt and the people are starving. Lavoisier's position was particularly precarious. As a scheme to prevent the loss of taxes from widespread smuggling of goods into Paris, Lavoisier advocated the building of a wall around the city. Much to Lavoisier's distress, the project, financed largely (and involuntarily) through taxes levied upon the people of Paris, became something of a boondoggle, as millions were spent on fancy ornamental gates. Parisians blamed the wall for keeping in fetid air and spreading disease. The militant republican Jean-Paul Marat began a campaign of vilification against Lavoisier that only ended when Charlotte Corday stabbed him to death in his bath. Marat had written several works in science and had hoped for election to the Royal Academy, then run by Lavoisier. But Lavoisier had exposed the emptiness of Marat's work. Marat fumed, bided his time, and waited for the season when patriotism would become a good refuge for scoundrels. In January 1791, he launched his attack in *l'Ami du Peuple* (the Friend of the People):

> I denounce you, Coryphaeus of charlatans, Sieur Lavoisier [coryphaeus, meaning highest, is the leader of the chorus in a classical Greek drama] Farmer-general, Commissioner of Gunpowders.... Just to think that this contemptible little man who enjoys an income of forty thousand livres has no other claim to fame than that of having put Paris in prison with a wall costing the poor thirty millions.... Would to heaven he had been strung up to the nearest lamppost.

The breaching of the wall by the citizens of Paris on July 12, 1789, was the prelude to the fall of the Bastille two days later.

Lavoisier began to worry very early in the cycle. Less than seven months after the fall of the Bastille, he wrote to his old friend Benjamin Franklin:

> After telling you about what is happening in chemistry, it would be well to give you news of our Revolution.... Moderate-minded people, who have kept cool heads during the general excitement, think that events have carried us too far... we greatly regret your absence from France at this time; you would have been our guide and you would have marked out for us the limits beyond which we ought not to go.

But these limits were breached, just as Lavoisier's wall had fallen, and he could read the handwriting on the remnants. The Ferme Générale was suppressed in 1791, and Lavoisier played no further role in the complex sorting out of the farmers' accounts. He tried to keep his nose clean with socially useful work on weights and measures and public education. But time was running out for the farmers-general. The treasury was bankrupt, and many thought (quite incorrectly) that the iniquitously hoarded wealth of the farmers-general could replenish the nation. The farmers were too good a scapegoat to resist; they were arrested en masse in November 1793, commanded to put their accounts in order and to reimburse the nation for any ill-gotten gains.

The presumed offenses of the farmers-general were not capital under revolutionary law, and they hoped initially to win their personal freedom, even though their wealth and possessions might be confiscated. But they had the misfortune to be in the wrong place (jail) at the worst time (as the Terror intensified). Eventually, capital charges of counter-revolutionary activities were drummed up, and in a mock trial lasting only part of a day, the farmers-general were condemned to the guillotine.

Lavoisier's influential friends might have saved him, but none dared (or cared) to speak. The Terror was not so inexorable and efficient as tradition holds. Fourteen of the farmers-general managed to evade arrest, and one was saved as a result of the intervention of Robespierre. Madame Lavoisier, who lived to a ripe old age, marrying and divorcing Count Rumford, and reestablishing one of the liveliest salons in Paris, never allowed any of these men over her doorstep again. One courageous (but uninfluential) group offered brave support in Lavoisier's last hours. A deputation from the Lycée des Arts came to the prison to honor Lavoisier and crown him with a wreath. We read in the minutes of that organization: "Brought to Lavoisier in irons, the consolation of friendship... to crown the head about to go under the ax."

It is a peculiar attribute of human courage that when no option remains but death, criteria of judgment shift to the manner of dying. Chronicles of the revolution are filled with stories about who died with dignity—and who went screaming to the knife. Antoine Lavoisier died well. He wrote a last letter to his cousin, in apparent calm, not without humor, and with an intellectual's faith in the supreme importance of mind.

> I have had a fairly long life, above all a very happy one, and I think that I shall be remembered with some regrets and perhaps leave some reputation behind me. What more could I ask? The events in which I am involved will probably save me from the troubles of old age. I shall die in full possession of my faculties.

Lavoisier's rehabilitation came almost as quickly as his death. In 1795, the Lycée des Arts held a first public memorial service, with Lagrange himself offering the eulogy and unveiling a bust of Lavoisier inscribed with the words: "Victim of tyranny, respected friend of the arts, he continues to live; through genius he still serves humanity." Lavoisier's spirit continued to inspire, but his head, once filled with great thoughts as numerous as the unwritten symphonies of Mozart, lay severed in a common grave.

Many people try to put a happy interpretation upon Lagrange's observation about the asymmetry of painstaking creation and instantaneous destruction. The collapse of systems, they argue, may be a prerequisite to any future episode of creativity—and the antidote, therefore, to stagnation. Taking the longest view, for example, mass extinctions do break up stable ecosystems and provoke episodes of novelty further down the evolutionary road. We would not be here today if the death of dinosaurs had not cleared some space for the burgeoning of mammals.

I have no objection to this argument in its proper temporal perspective. If you choose a telescope and wish to peer into an evolutionary future millions of years away, then a current episode of destruction may be read as an ultimate spur. But if you care for the here and now, which is (after all) the only time we feel and have, then massive extinction is only a sadness and an opportunity lost forever. I have heard people argue that our current wave of extinctions should not inspire concern because the earth will eventually recover, as so oft before, and perhaps with pleasant novelty. But what can a conjecture about ten million years from now possibly mean to our lives—especially since we have the power to blow our planet up long before then, and rather little prospect, in any case, of surviving so long ourselves (since few vertebrate species live for ten million years).

The argument of the "long view" may be correct in some meaninglessly abstract sense, but it represents a fundamental mistake in categories and time scales. Our only legitimate long view extends to our children and our children's children's children—hundreds or a few thousands of years down the road. If we let the slaughter continue, they will share a bleak world with rats, dogs, cockroaches, pigeons, and mosquitoes. A potential recovery millions of years later has no meaning at our appropriate scale. Similarly, others could do the unfinished work of Lavoisier, if not so elegantly; and political revolution did spur science into some interesting channels. But how can this mitigate the tragedy of Lavoisier? He was one of the most brilliant men ever to grace our history, and he died at the height of his powers and health. He had work to do, and he was not guilty.

My title, "The Passion of Antoine Lavoisier," is a double-entendre. The modern meaning of *passion*, "over-mastering zeal or enthusiasm," is a latecomer. The word entered our language from the Latin verb for suffering, particularly for suffering physical pain. The Saint Matthew and Saint John Passions of J. S. Bach are musical dramas about the suffering of Jesus on the cross. This essay, therefore, focuses upon the final and literal passion of Lavoisier. (Anyone who has ever been disappointed in love—that is, all of us—will understand the intimate connection between the two meanings of passion.)

But I also wanted to emphasize Lavoisier's passion in the modern meaning. For this supremely organized man—farmer-general; commissioner of gunpowder; wall builder; reformer of prisons, hospitals, and schools; legislative representative for the nobility of Blois; father of the metric system; servant on a hundred government committees—really had but one passion amidst this burden of activities for a thousand lifetimes. Lavoisier loved science more than anything else. He awoke at six in the morning and worked on science until eight, then again at night from seven until ten. He devoted one full day a week to scientific experiments and called it his *jour de bonheur* (day of happiness). The letters and reports of his last year are painful to read, for Lavoisier never abandoned his passion—his conviction that reason and science must guide any just and effective social order. But those who received his pleas, and held power over him, had heard the different drummer of despotism.

Lavoisier was right in the deepest, almost holy, way. His passion harnessed feeling to the service of reason; another kind of passion was the price. Reason cannot save us and can even persecute us in the wrong hands; but we have no hope of salvation without reason. The world is too complex, too intransigent; we cannot bend it to our simple will. Bernard Lacépède was probably thinking of Lavoisier when he wrote a closing flourish following his passage on the great asymmetry of slow creation and sudden destruction:

> Ah! Never forget that we can only stave off that fatal degradation if we unite the liberal arts, which embody the sacred fire of sensibility, with the sciences and the useful arts, without which the celestial light of reason will disappear.

The Republic needs scientists.

STEPHEN JAY GOULD taught biology, geology, and the history of science at Harvard University.

The First Feminist

In 1792 Mary Wollstonecraft wrote a book to prove that her sex was as intelligent as the other: thus did feminism come into the world. Right on, Ms. Mary!

SHIRLEY TOMKIEVICZ

The first person—male or female—to speak at any length and to any effect about woman's rights was Mary Wollstonecraft. In 1792, when her *Vindication of the Rights of Woman* appeared, Mary was a beautiful spinster of thirty-three who had made a successful career for herself in the publishing world of London. This accomplishment was rare enough for a woman in that day. Her manifesto, at once impassioned and learned, was an achievement of real originality. The book electrified the reading public and made Mary famous. The core of its argument is simple: "I wish to see women neither heroines nor brutes; but reasonable creatures," Mary wrote. This ancestress of the Women's Liberation Movement did not demand day-care centers or an end to women's traditional role as wife and mother, nor did she call anyone a chauvinist pig. The happiest period of Mary's own life was when she was married and awaiting the birth of her second child. And the greatest delight she ever knew was in her first child, an illegitimate daughter. Mary's feminism may not appear today to be the hard-core revolutionary variety, but she did live, for a time, a scandalous and unconventional life—"emancipated," it is called by those who have never tried it. The essence of her thought, however, is simply that a woman's mind is as good as a man's.

Not many intelligent men could be found to dispute this proposition today, at least not in mixed company. In Mary's time, to speak of *anybody's* rights, let alone woman's rights, was a radical act. In England, as in other nations, "rights" were an entity belonging to the government. The common run of mankind had little access to what we now call "human rights." As an example of British justice in the late eighteenth century, the law cited two hundred different capital crimes, among them shoplifting. An accused man was not entitled to counsel. A child could be tried and hanged as soon as an adult. The right to vote existed, certainly, but because of unjust apportionment, it had come to mean little. In the United States some of these abuses had been corrected—but that the rights of man did not extend past the color bar and the masculine gender was intentional. In the land of Washington and Jefferson, as in the land of George III, human rights were a new idea and woman's rights were not even an issue.

In France, in 1792, a Revolution in the name of equality was in full course, and woman's rights had at least been alluded to. The Revolutionary government drew up plans for female education—to the age of eight. "The education of the women should always be relative to the men," Rousseau had written in *Emile*. "To please, to be useful to us, to make us love and esteem them, to educate us when young, and take care of us when grown up, to advise, to console us, to render our lives easy and agreeable; these are the duties of women at all times, and what they should be taught in their infancy." And, less prettily, "Women have, or ought to have, but little liberty."

Rousseau would have found little cause for complaint in eighteenth-century England. An Englishwoman had almost the same civil status as an American slave. Thomas Hardy, a hundred years hence, was to base a novel on the idea of a man casually selling his wife and daughter at public auction. Obviously this was not a common occurrence, but neither is it wholly implausible. In 1792, and later, a woman could not own property, nor keep any earned wages. All that she possessed belonged to her husband. She could not divorce him, but he could divorce her and take her children. There was no law to say she could not grow up illiterate or be beaten every day.

Such was the legal and moral climate in which Mary Wollstonecraft lived. She was born in London in the spring of 1759, the second child and first daughter of Edward Wollstonecraft, a prosperous weaver. Two more daughters and two more sons were eventually born into the family, making six children in all. Before they had all arrived, Mr. Wollstonecraft came into an inheritance and decided to move his family to the country and become a gentleman farmer. But this plan failed. His money dwindled, and he began drinking heavily. His wife turned into a terrified wraith whose only interest was her eldest son, Edward. Only he escaped the beatings and abuse that his father dealt out regularly to every other household member, from Mrs. Wollstonecraft to the family dog. As often happens in large and disordered families, the eldest sister had to assume the role of mother and scullery maid. Mary was a bright, strong child, determined not to be broken, and she undertook her task energetically, defying her father when he was violent and keeping her younger brothers and sisters in hand. Clearly, Mary held the household together, and in so doing forfeited her own child-hood. This experience left her with an everlasting gloomy streak, and was a strong factor in making her a reformer.

At some point in Mary's childhood, another injustice was visited upon her, though so commonplace for the time that she can hardly have felt the sting. Her elder brother was sent away to be educated, and the younger children were left to learn their letters as best they could. The family now frequently changed lodgings, but from her ninth to her fifteenth year Mary went to a day school, where she had the only formal training of her life. Fortunately, this included French and composition, and somewhere Mary learned to read critically and widely. These skills, together with her curiosity and determination, were really all she needed. The *Vindication* is in some parts long-winded, ill-punctuated, and simply full of hot air, but it is the work of a well-informed mind.

Feminists—and Mary would gladly have claimed the title—inevitably, even deservedly, get bad notices. The term calls up an image of relentless battleaxes: "thin college ladies with eye-glasses, no-nonsense features, mouths thin as bologna slicers, a babe in one arm, a hatchet in the other, grey eyes bright with ba-lefire," as Norman Mailer feelingly envisions his antagonists in the Women's Liberation Movement. He has conjured up all the horrid elements: the lips with a cutting edge, the baby immacu-lately conceived (one is forced to conclude), the lethal weapon tightly clutched, the desiccating college degree, the joylessness. Hanging miasmally over the tableau is the suspicion of a de-formed sexuality. Are these girls man-haters, or worse? Mary Wollstonecraft, as the first of her line, has had each of these scarlet letters (except the B.A.) stitched upon her bosom. Yet she conformed very little to the hateful stereotype. In at least one respect, however, she would have chilled Mailer's bones. Having spent her childhood as an adult, Mary reached the age of nineteen in a state of complete joylessness. She was later to quit the role, but for now she wore the garb of a martyr.

Her early twenties were spent in this elderly frame of mind. First she went out as companion to an old lady living at Bath, and was released from this servitude only by a call to nurse the dying Mrs. Wollstonecraft. Then the family broke up entirely, though the younger sisters continued off and on to be dependent on Mary. The family of Mary's dearest friend, Fanny Blood, in-vited her to come and stay with them; the two girls made a small living doing sewing and handicrafts, and Mary dreamed of start-ing a primary school. Eventually, in a pleasant village called Newington Green, this plan materialized and prospered. But Fanny Blood in the meantime had married and moved to Lis-bon. She wanted Mary to come and nurse her through the birth of her first child. Mary reached Lisbon just in time to see her friend die of childbed fever, and returned home just in time to find that her sisters, in whose care the flourishing little school had been left, had lost all but two pupils.

Mary made up her mind to die. "My constitution is impaired, I hope I shan't live long," she wrote to a friend in February, 1786. Under this almost habitual grief, however, Mary was gaining some new sense of herself. Newington Green, apart from offering her a brief success as a schoolmistress, had brought her some acquaintance in the world of letters, most im-portant among them, Joseph Johnson, an intelligent and suc-cessful London publisher in search of new writers. Debt-ridden and penniless, Mary set aside her impaired constitution and wrote her first book, probably in the space of a week. Johnson bought it for ten guineas and published it. Called *Thoughts on the Education of Daughters*, it went unnoticed, and the ten guin-eas was soon spent. Mary had to find work. She accepted a po-sition as governess in the house of Lord and Lady Kingsborough in the north of Ireland.

Mary's letters from Ireland to her sisters and to Joseph Johnson are so filled with Gothic gloom, so stained with tears, that one cannot keep from laughing at them. "I entered the great gates with the same kind of feeling I should have if I was going to the Bastille," she wrote upon entering Kingsborough Castle in the fall of 1786. Mary was now twenty-seven. Her most re-cent biographer, Margaret George, believes that Mary was not really suffering so much as she was having literary fantasies. In private she was furiously at work on a novel entitled, not very artfully, *Mary, A Fiction*. This is the story of a young lady of im-mense sensibilities who closely resembles Mary except that she has wealthy parents, a neglectful bridegroom, and an attractive lover. The title and fantasizing contents are precisely what a scribbler of thirteen might secretly concoct. Somehow Mary was embarking on her adolescence—with all its daydreams—fifteen years after the usual date. Mary's experience in Kings-borough Castle was a fruitful one, for all her complaints. In the summer of 1787 she lost her post as governess and set off for London with her novel. Not only did Johnson accept it for pub-lication, he offered her a regular job as editor and translator and helped her find a place to live.

Thus, aged twenty-eight, Mary put aside her doleful persona as the martyred, set-upon elder sister. How different she is now, jauntily writing from London to her sisters: "Mr. Johnson… as-sures me that if I exert my talents in writing I may support my-self in a comfortable way. I am then going to be the first of a new genus.…" Now Mary discovered the sweetness of financial independence earned by interesting work. She had her own apartment. She was often invited to Mr. Johnson's dinner par-ties, usually as the only female guest among all the most inter-esting men in London: Joseph Priestley, Thomas Paine, Henry Fuseli, William Blake, Thomas Christie, William Godwin—all of them up-and-coming scientists or poets or painters or philos-ophers, bound together by left-wing political views. Moreover, Mary was successful in her own writing as well as in editorial work. Her *Original Stories for Children* went into three editions and was illustrated by Blake. Johnson and his friend Thomas Christie had started a magazine called the *Analytical Review*, to which Mary became a regular contributor.

But—lest anyone imagine an elegantly dressed Mary presid-ing flirtatiously at Johnson's dinner table—her social accom-plishments were rather behind her professional ones. Johnson's circle looked upon her as one of the boys. "Wollstonecraft" is what William Godwin calls her in his diary. One of her later de-tractors reported that she was at this time a "philosophic sloven," in a dreadful old dress and beaver hat, "with her hair hanging lank about her shoulders." Mary had yet to arrive at her final incarnation, but the new identity was imminent, if achieved by an odd route. Edmund Burke had recently published his *Reflections on the Revolution in France*, and the book had enraged Mary. The statesman who so readily supported the quest for liberty in the American colonies had his doubts about events in France.

Mary's reply to Burke, *A Vindication of the Rights of Men*, astounded London, partly because she was hitherto unknown, partly because it was good. Mary proved to be an excellent polemicist, and she had written in anger. She accused Burke, the erstwhile champion of liberty, of being "the champion of property." "Man preys on man," said she, "and you mourn for the idle tapestry that decorated a gothic pile and the dronish bell that summoned the fat priest to prayer." The book sold well. Mary moved into a better apartment and bought some pretty dresses—no farthingales, of course, but some of the revolutionary new "classical" gowns. She put her auburn hair up in a loose knot. Her days as a philosophic sloven were over.

Vindication of the Rights of Woman was her next work. In its current edition it runs to 250-odd pages; Mary wrote it in six weeks. *Vindication* is no prose masterpiece, but it has never failed to arouse its audience, in one way or another. Horace Walpole unintentionally set the style for the book's foes. Writing to his friend Hannah More in August, 1792, he referred to Thomas Paine and to Mary as "philosophizing serpents" and was "glad to hear you have not read the tract of the last mentioned writer. I would not look at it." Neither would many another of Mary's assailants, the most virulent of whom, Ferdinand Lundberg, surfaced at the late date of 1947 with a tract of his own, *Modern Woman, the Lost Sex*. Savagely misogynistic as it is, this book was hailed in its time as "the best book yet to be written about women." Lundberg calls Mary the Karl Marx of the feminist movement, and the *Vindication* a "fateful book," to which "the tenets of feminism, which have undergone no change to our day, may be traced." Very well, but then, recounting Mary's life with the maximum possible number of errors per line, he warns us that she was "an extreme neurotic of a compulsive type" who "wanted to turn on men and injure them." In one respect, at least, Mr. Lundberg hits the mark: he blames Mary for starting women in the pernicious habit of wanting an education. In the nineteenth century, he relates, English and American feminists were hard at work. "Following Mary Wollstonecraft's prescription, they made a considerable point about acquiring a higher education." This is precisely Mary's prescription, and the most dangerous idea in her fateful book.

"Men complain and with reason, of the follies and caprices of our Sex," she writes in Chapter 1. "Behold, I should answer, the natural effect of ignorance." Women, she thinks, are usually so mindless as to be scarcely fit for their roles as wives and mothers. Nevertheless, she believes this state not to be part of the feminine nature, but the result of an equally mindless oppression, as demoralizing for men as for women. If a woman's basic mission is as a wife and mother, need she be an illiterate slave for this?

The heart of the work is Mary's attack on Rousseau. In *Emile* Rousseau had set forth some refreshing new ideas for the education of little boys. But women, he decreed, are tools for pleasure, creatures too base for moral or political or educational privilege. Mary recognized that this view was destined to shut half the human race out of all hope for political freedom. *Vindication* is a plea that the "rights of men" ought to mean the "rights of humanity." The human right that she held highest was the right to have a mind and think with it. Virginia Woolf, who lived through a time of feminist activity, thought that the *Vindication* was a work so true "as to seem to contain nothing new." Its originality, she wrote, rather too optimistically, had become a commonplace.

Vindication went quickly into a second edition. Mary's name was soon known all over Europe. But as she savored her fame—and she did savor it—she found that the edge was wearing off and that she was rather lonely. So far as anyone knows, Mary had reached this point in her life without ever having had a love affair. Johnson was the only man she was close to, and he was, as she wrote him, "A father, or a brother—you have been both to me." Mary was often now in the company of the Swiss painter Henry Fuseli, and suddenly she developed what she thought was a Platonic passion in his direction. He rebuffed her, and in the winter of 1792 she went to Paris, partly to escape her embarrassment but also because she wanted to observe the workings of the Revolution firsthand.

Soon after her arrival, as she collected notes for the history of the Revolution she hoped to write, Mary saw Louis XVI, "sitting in a hackney coach… going to meet death." Back in her room that evening, she wrote to Mr. Johnson of seeing "eyes glare through a glass door opposite my chair and bloody hands shook at me.… I am going to bed and for the first time in my life, I cannot put out the candle." As the weeks went on, Edmund Burke's implacable critic began to lose her faith in the brave new world. "The aristocracy of birth is levelled to the ground, only to make room for that of riches," she wrote. By February France and England were at war, and British subjects classified as enemy aliens.

Though many Englishmen were arrested, Mary and a large English colony stayed on. One day in spring, some friends presented her to an attractive American, newly arrived in Paris, Gilbert Imlay. Probably about four years Mary's senior, Imlay, a former officer in the Continental Army, was an explorer and adventurer. He came to France seeking to finance a scheme for seizing Spanish lands in the Mississippi valley. This "natural and unaffected creature," as Mary was later to describe him, was probably the social lion of the moment, for he was also the author of a best-selling novel called *The Emigrants*, a farfetched account of life and love in the American wilderness. He and Mary soon became lovers. They were a seemingly perfect pair. Imlay must have been pleased with his famous catch, and—dear, liberated girl that she was—Mary did not insist upon marriage. Rather the contrary. But fearing that she was in danger as an Englishwoman, he registered her at the American embassy as his wife.

Blood was literally running in the Paris streets now, so Mary settled down by herself in a cottage at Neuilly. Imlay spent his days in town, working out various plans. The Mississippi expedition came to nothing, and he decided to stay in France and go into the import-export business, part of his imports being gunpowder and other war goods run from Scandinavia through the English blockade. In the evenings he would ride out to the cottage. By now it was summer, and Mary, who spent the days writing, would often stroll up the road to meet him, carrying a basket of freshly gathered grapes.

A note she wrote Imlay that summer shows exactly what her feelings for him were: "You can scarcely imagine with what pleasure I anticipate the day when we are to begin almost to live together; and you would smile to hear how many plans of employment I have in my head, now that I am confident that my heart has found peace...." Soon she was pregnant. She and Imlay moved into Paris. He promised to take her to America, where they would settle down on a farm and raise six children. But business called Imlay to Le Havre, and his stay lengthened ominously into weeks.

Imlay's letters to Mary have not survived, and without them it is hard to gauge what sort of man he was and what he really thought of his adoring mistress. Her biographers like to make him out a cad, a philistine, not half good enough for Mary. Perhaps; yet the two must have had something in common. His novel, unreadable though it is now, shows that he shared her political views, including her feminist ones. He may never have been serious about the farm in America, but he was a miserably long time deciding to leave Mary alone. Though they were separated during the early months of her pregnancy, he finally did bring her to Le Havre, and continued to live with her there until the child was born and for some six months afterward. The baby arrived in May, 1794, a healthy little girl, whom Mary named Fanny after her old friend. Mary was proud that her delivery had been easy and as for Fanny, Mary loved her instantly. "My little Girl," she wrote to a friend, "begins to suck so manfully that her father reckons saucily on her writing the second part of the Rights of Woman." Mary's joy in this child illuminates almost every letter she wrote henceforth.

Fanny's father was the chief recipient of these letters with all the details of the baby's life. To Mary's despair, she and Imlay hardly ever lived together again. A year went by; Imlay was now in London and Mary in France. She offered to break it off, but mysteriously, he could not let go. In the last bitter phase of their involvement, after she had joined him in London at his behest, he even sent her—as "Mrs. Imlay"—on a complicated business errand to the Scandinavian countries. Returning to London, Mary discovered that he was living with another woman. By now half crazy with humiliation, Mary chose a dark night and threw herself in the Thames. She was nearly dead when two rivermen pulled her from the water.

Though this desperate incident was almost the end of Mary, at least it was the end of the Imlay episode. He sent a doctor to care for her, but they rarely met again. Since Mary had no money, she set about providing for herself and Fanny in the way

she knew. The faithful Johnson had already brought out Volume I of her history of the French Revolution. Now she set to work editing and revising her *Letters Written during a Short Residence in Sweden, Norway, and Denmark*, a kind of thoughtful travelogue. The book was well received and widely translated.

And it also revived the memory of Mary Wollstonecraft in the mind of an old acquaintance, William Godwin. As the author of the treatise *Political Justice*, he was now as famous a philosophizing serpent as Mary and was widely admired and hated as a "freethinker." He came to call on Mary. They became friends and then lovers. Early in 1797 Mary was again pregnant. William Godwin was an avowed atheist who had publicly denounced the very institution of marriage. On March 29, 1797, he nevertheless went peaceably to church with Mary and made her his wife.

The Godwins were happy together, however William's theories may have been outraged. He adored his small stepdaughter and took pride in his brilliant wife. Awaiting the birth of her child throughout the summer, Mary worked on a new novel and made plans for a book on "the management of infants"—it would have been the first "Dr. Spock." She expected to have another easy delivery and promised to come downstairs to dinner the day following. But when labor began, on August 30, it proved to be long and agonizing. A daughter, named Mary Wollstonecraft, was born; ten days later, the mother died.

Occasionally, when a gifted writer dies young, one can feel, as in the example of Shelley, that perhaps he had at any rate accomplished his best work. But so recently had Mary come into her full intellectual and emotional growth that her death at the age of thirty-eight is bleak indeed. There is no knowing what Mary might have accomplished now that she enjoyed domestic stability. Perhaps she might have achieved little or nothing further as a writer. But she might have been able to protect her daughters from some part of the sadness that overtook them; for as things turned out, both Fanny and Mary were to sacrifice themselves.

Fanny grew up to be a shy young girl, required to feel grateful for the roof over her head, overshadowed by her prettier half sister, Mary. Godwin in due course married a formidable widow named Mrs. Clairmont, who brought her own daughter into the house—the Claire Clairmont who grew up to become Byron's mistress and the mother of his daughter Allegra. Over the years Godwin turned into a hypocrite and a miser who nevertheless continued to pose as the great liberal of the day. Percy Bysshe Shelley, born the same year that the *Vindication of the Rights of Woman* was published, came to be a devoted admirer of Mary Wollstonecraft's writing. As a young man he therefore came with his wife to call upon Godwin. What he really sought, however, were Mary's daughters—because they were her daughters. First he approached Fanny, but later changed his mind. Mary Godwin was then sixteen, the perfect potential soul mate for a man whose needs for soul mates knew no bounds. They conducted their courtship in the most up-to-the-minute romantic style: beneath a tree near her mother's grave they read aloud to each other from the Vindication. Soon they eloped, having pledged their "troth" in the cemetery. Godwin, the celebrated freethinker, was enraged. To make matters worse, Claire Clairmont had run off to Switzerland with them.

Not long afterward Fanny, too, ran away. She went to an inn in a distant town and drank a fatal dose of laudanum. It has traditionally been said that unrequited love for Shelley drove her to this pass, but there is no evidence one way or the other. One suicide that can more justly be laid at Shelley's door is that of his first wife, which occurred a month after Fanny's and which at any rate left him free to wed his mistress, Mary Godwin. Wife or mistress, she had to endure poverty, ostracism, and Percy's constant infidelities. But now at last her father could, and did, boast to his relations that he was father-in-law to a baronet's son. "Oh, philosophy!" as Mary Godwin Shelley remarked.

If in practice Shelley was merely a womanizer, on paper he was a convinced feminist. He had learned this creed from Mary Wollstonecraft. Through his verse Mary's ideas began to be disseminated. They were one part of that vast tidal wave of political, social, and artistic revolution that arose in the late eighteenth century, the romantic movement. But because of Mary's unconventional way of life, her name fell into disrepute during the nineteenth century, and her book failed to exert its rightful influence on the development of feminism. Emma Willard and other pioneers of the early Victorian period indignantly refused to claim Mary as their forebear. Elizabeth Cady Stanton and Lucretia Mott were mercifully less strait-laced on the subject. In 1889, when Mrs. Stanton and Susan B. Anthony published their *History of Woman Suffrage*, they dedicated the book to Mary. Though Mary Wollstonecraft can in no sense be said to have founded the woman's rights movement, she was, by the late nineteenth century, recognized as its inspiration, and the *Vindication* was vindicated for the highly original work it was, a landmark in the history of society.

From *Horizon*, Spring 1972. © 1972 by Shirley Tomkievicz. Reprinted by permission of the author.

Napoleon: A Classic Dictator?

Laurent Joffrin looks at the paradoxes surrounding a man who has fascinated the French for two hundred years.

LAURENT JOFFRIN

The more closely you look at the myth, the more the paradoxes mount. Napoleon was heir to the Age of the Enlightenment yet held his people in an iron grip; he was the guardian of the Revolution yet founded a dynasty. He was a despot who remains a hero to republican France.

Napoleon regarded the whole world as a theatre in which he was simultaneously playwright, actor, director—even financial backer. To him, Europe was a building site in which he was demolition expert, architect and stonemason. He saw other people as instruments of his visions—and the higher he rose, the greater those visions became.

He was also the epitome of a modern dictator the world over. He showed this in the way he imposed his will on any situation, in his charisma, in his reason, in his conviction, in his brutality, in his firm resolve to tame and to conquer, in his equally fierce determination to build, to transform, to create, in his innate sense of action, in his outrageously grand schemes and in his attention to the tiniest details. Put together, these traits made for tumult on a continental scale, and they resulted both in the fulfilment of some of the grandest ambitions ever seen, and in the most widespread destruction Europe was to experience before the twentieth century.

He was also a model of a good dictator. His despotism was mainly an enlightened one. The Emperor of the French was—at least until the excesses of his final years—a Cartesian, a realist bounded by rules. He believed in order and hard work as the foundations of greatness. He wanted to assert the rule of law, but he dared to write the laws himself. The ends he aimed for were driven by an idea of civilization, but he was often barbaric in the means he employed to achieve them. Had he not had such lofty goals, he would soon have been relegated to history's house of horrors.

Although he deeply compromised the Revolutionaries' ideas of liberty, and although his incessant wars led to the deaths of well over a million French soldiers and civilians, Napoleon Bonaparte remains lodged in French memory as a man with a mission, the man who restored the state and embodied the Enlightenment. As General Bonaparte in the 1790s, he was, and remains, a hero of the Revolution, and as First Consul he still arouses admiration. Had he died before crowning himself Emperor in December 1804, he would be remembered as fondly as George Washington is in the United States. When Napoleon is criticized today, it is as the unhinged despot of his imperial years, the man who introduced the disastrous Continental System and who adopted the garb of monarchy.

The *coup d'etat* of 18 Brumaire (November 9th, 1799) that swept away the weak and corrupt Directory and brought Napoleon to power, might have been a peaceful one. Over the previous years the Revolution had effectively turned from a democratic to an authoritarian regime, albeit its form of authoritarianism operated through constitutional channels made up of new notables, men of the Convention and national worthies. Yet the coup ran into difficulties, and when Napoleon addressed the Council of Five Hundred the following day, he was received so badly he had to be rescued by Murat and his grenadiers who dispersed the deputies. So the political coup became a military one.

The Abbé Sieyès, the Directory member who was Bonaparte's chief associate in Brumaire, devised a new constitution. The victorious general didn't much care what sort of regime it was, just so long as he himself was in charge. During the commission set up to frame its fundamental laws, one of the participants began, 'a good constitution should be brief ...'; Bonaparte finished the sentence for him: '... and obscure'. But the 'obscurity' seemed clear enough to the public. 'What is in the constitution?' people asked. The answer came straight back, 'Napoleon is in it.'

The Directory was replaced with the three-man Consulate with Bonaparte, Sieyes and Roger-Ducos as consuls, but at their first meeting, Bonaparte took the chair. He didn't relinquish it for fifteen years, and made it his throne. Now he began to issue orders, effortlessly and incessantly. His gifts amazed contemporaries. Napoleon was a dictator who spent all his time dictating. On waking at sunrise, he went straight to his bureau, and exhausted his secretaries with his unwavering command, 'Write this!' His orders were methodical, precise, even repetitious, so as to dispel any confusion. They issued from his study, like shot from a cannon, relentless, burning and hard as newly cast metal. At night he could still be found in the same place, hands clasped behind his back, forehead wrinkled, tobacco crushed on his sleeve—but with his mind as clear as it had been at dawn.

In the years of the Consulate (1799–1804), aware of his large areas of ignorance, he decided nothing without first taking advice, interrogating advisers whom he selected for their competence and who gave him their opinions, man to man. But once the decision had been taken, the execution was savage—woe betide any servant who was slow, who forgot to implement or who tried to digress from his orders. Anyone who misinterpreted the will of the master did not last long.

By sheer force of will, in three years he untangled affairs of state that neither the Convention nor the Directory had been able to resolve. He defeated Austria at Marengo in 1800, and made peace with Britain at Amiens in 1802; restored internal order and balanced the budget; the previous year he had found a compromise with the Church, accepting that Catholicism was the religion of the majority of Frenchmen; and overall his administration was efficient and honest. Finally, he effected a slow but indisputable reconciliation between the two halves of the nation divided by the events of 1793; the *émigrés* began to return while the regicides were given assurances for their safety. To achieve all this required exceptional energy and faultless organization.

Yet alongside his extraordinary capacity went implacable methods. First and foremost was the anger, not always feigned, that he felt about insult and injustice, which sometimes led him to behave in a manner more suited to the boxing ring than to the administration of a state. His ministers might find themselves pushed around, even knocked onto a settee; functionaries received dressings-down, and secretaries were deafened by his diatribes. One day, when he dared to contradict the master on a naval matter, Admiral Bruix was threatened with a horse-whip. Pale as death, he took a step back and put his hand on his sword—then an aide intervened.

Napoleon's second technique was repression. Repression of the conquered territories by means of the army—through summary executions, villages burned, opponents imprisoned; and of France itself by means of the new police forces. He loved the police so much that he set up several separate forces, each organized to spy, to manipulate and to inform him about everything from great plots to minor indiscretions. These systematic denunciations became a standard means of government.

The repression was most severe towards the two factions that menaced him—the Jacobins on one side, and the monarchists on the other.

After the failed assassination attempt of December 24th, 1800, when a massive bomb exploded in the rue Saint-Nicaise as Napoleon and Josephine were on their way to the opera, a hundred Jacobins were exiled and the royalist suspects were tortured, and no one doubted who gave the orders for this. After the failure of the second plot to murder him in 1804, the duc d'Enghien, scion of the Condé family, was falsely accused of conspiring with the British to take over France. The duc was seized from across the Rhine, quickly tried and executed, in an episode which horrified much of Europe but reassured the men of the Revolution by placing a corpse between Bonaparte and the Bourbons. In this way methods more suited to war were used in the attempt to establish peace; techniques of arbitrary government practised to re-establish the rule of law.

Napoleon's third means of government was his control of public opinion in a manner that was minutely detailed yet ever-expanding. Bonaparte built up his own image at the same time as he rebuilt France—he kept a close eye on newspapers, theatres and literature, changed the ending of plays, wrote articles himself that were published anonymously, commissioned paintings, statues and monuments to his own glory. 'If there is no good literature in France,' he once wrote to Fouché, minister of police, 'the police department is to blame.' Key to his style of propaganda was a way of attaching falsehoods to truth. He commissioned Baron Gros to paint him at the head of the attack on the bridge at Arcole in Italy in 1796, a moment that established his reputation in the field; when in fact General Augereau actually led the charge. He had David paint him on a rearing horse riding up the Great St Bernard Pass—he had ridden up it on a mule. The campaign in Egypt, though muddled and murderous, was presented as a triumph. The Bulletins of the *Grande Armée* were riddled with falsehoods: 'lying like the Bulletins' became a favourite saying among his soldiers.

Nothing escaped his eagle eye. He silenced actors, exiled writers, sacked journalists, he imprisoned clubleaders. On one occasion when he learned that priests were praising his victories from the pulpit, he issued an immediate ban. 'If I let them comment on my victories, they will comment on my defeats.'

But ultimately, Bonaparte's dictatorship was not like those of Caligula or Timur. Unlike them, he wanted to create new forms of legality, to guarantee the rule of reason, and to establish limits to power. One phrase summed up his thinking, 'It is essential to impose the government that the people desire.' This is not a typical tyrant speaking, and he truly believed he could govern the premier country of Europe just as it most profoundly wished. After enduring revolutionary convulsions far beyond anything that men had imagined or could control, and wracked by tidal waves of bloody violence, France now had to find a point of equilibrium. Napoleon's self-appointed task was to be the one to locate this point and impose it on the country.

He did not ignore the art of compromise, which led him to soften, with a blend of concessions and threats, the great forces jostling for political and social power. The new bourgeoisie, just as much as the old aristocracy, needed to be given jobs and honours. If the people were to enjoy the achievements of 1789, they needed security—the original aim of the Revolution—as well as order.

By adopting both brutality and subtlety to seek this end, liberty was sacrificed. When he wrote his memoirs on St Helena, Napoleon would explain how it happened. We were coming out of a civil war, he said; without an inflexible authority, it would have been impossible to stabilize France, or to avoid a return to terror.

Before he could become a guide for the French nation, he had to be its arbiter. A member of no party but in a position to dominate all parties, he sought a national role and governed from the centre. Thence derived the innumerable civil and religious arrangements that he imposed on the rival factions; thence arose his obsession with restoring the state, with justice, police and administration. Through these instruments he sought to build a new order for a society that had been too rebellious, and he tried to reassure the citizens that political passions once aroused could now be contained, and a proper tranquillity could be established within which the potential of French society could truly flourish.

He did rule arbitrarily, in the sense that he fixed plebiscites, rewrote the constitution at his own discretion and produced his own decrees. But he left his subordinates with a punctilious respect for the law. One day he learned that a general, acting on his own initiative, had decided that he needed no mandate to search the property of some peasants suspected of brigandage. This misdemeanour was met with a vengeful missive from the Emperor, in which he ordered the military to return to barracks and submit immediately to civil authorities. The Emperor himself might act arbitrarily, but others had to obey the law. There was to be a single master of France, but no petty tyrants. The Civil Code, which he introduced in 1804, was his proudest achievement: the foundation of institutions designed to ensure his fondest wish. He was a soldier passionate for civilian business, and if he made war, it was only in order to be able to govern better.

He might have stopped there. But the heir to the Enlightenment was also the embodiment of the excess and the folly of Romanticism. Once crowned Emperor, drunk on his victories, he abandoned his own search for equilibrium. The end of his reign was the era of great mistakes. His propaganda became obsessive, with the change of the calendar—in 1806 he proclaimed the feast of 'Saint Napoleon' on his birthday, August 15th, and he inflicted an imperial catechism on children. Military defeats became a form of butchery, and the utter coldness of his heart left him indifferent to the suffering for which he was responsible. The constitution became ever more authoritarian, and the occasional voices of criticism were snuffed out.

Now he created a new nobility, and succumbed to his dynastic obsession which led him to place members of his family on thrones across Europe. He became entirely intransigent and refused to listen to advice. His daring turned to presumption and his proclamations grew ever more grandiloquent. All this made him appear a despot without restraint. The very qualities that had once brought him resounding successes now, as his fortune began to dwindle, led him to great disasters and cruelty, especially in Spain, Russia and Germany. His dictating now became a kind of delirium, a furious lamentation on a lost greatness. The rational science of strategy was abandoned in the pursuit of a strictly personal adventure.

Now he resembled all dictators at the bloody moment of their nemesis. In the dark days of 1814 the despot had to fight alone, facing the hostility of all those whom he had conquered and humiliated in a search for glory and riches.

His fall restored some restraint to him, and he returned from Elba inspired by the failures of his enemies. When he took up the reins of power again, he adopted the spirit of of compromise in the *Acte Additionnel aux Constitutions de l'Empire*, a balanced adjustment to the constitution constructed with the help of the liberal theorist Benjamin Constant, a man who previously had bitterly resisted Napoleon's appetite for martial glory and arbitrary rule. But it was too late. Europe saw its old nightmare returning, and when the dictator felt it necessary to go on the attack once again, he got no further than the deadly slopes of Mont-Saint-Jean, in front of the village of Waterloo. The Hundred Days, the most fascinating of the whole Napoleonic era for France's incredible switchback of fortune, could not rescue his regime from the disasters of the previous years.

Dictator for sixteen years, Napoleon endures in the French spirit two centuries later. The paradoxes have woven a kind of spell: despite the blood and the death, despite the wars and the repression, his taste for rule and his mania for building have meant that the despot is seen as the favourite dictator of the French republic.

LAURENT JOFFRIN is Editor-in-Chief of the weekly news magazine *Le Nouvel Observateur*. His many historical works include *Mai 68, La Régression Française, Les Batailles de Napoléon* and *La Princesse Oubliée*. This article is translated and adapted from one published in France in *Historia Thematique*, December 2004.

UNIT 3

Industry, Ideology, Nationalism, and Imperialism: The Nineteenth Century

Unit Selections

14. **Slavery and the British**, James Walvin
15. **Victoria**, Lynne Vallone
16. **Bismarck, Prussia, & German Nationalism**, Edgar Feuchtwanger
17. **Napoleon III: 'Hero' or 'Grotesque Mediocrity'?**, Roger Price
18. **The Russians Shall Not Have Constantinople**, Roman Golicz
19. **The Evolution of Charles Darwin**, Frank J. Sulloway
20. **Florence Nightingale as a Social Reformer**, Lynn McDonald
21. **Benjamin Disraeli and the Spirit of England**, T. A. Jenkins
22. **The Incurable Wound**, Lizabeth Peak
23. **Quinine's Feverish Tales and Trails**, Louis Werner

Key Points to Consider

- What were the economic and social reasons for the slave trade?

- How was Queen Victoria important in both government and feminine homelife?

- How did Bismarck create the modern state of Germany in 1871?

- What are some of the differing views about Napoleon III?

- Why did the English call for the Congress of Berlin in 1878?

- Why did Charles Darwin become a supporter of evolution?

- Why should Florence Nightingale be known for more than her work in the Crimean War?

- What were the motivations in the career of Benjamin Disraeli?

- How was rabies viewed and who led to its cure?

Student Web Site

www.mhcls.com/online

Internet References

Further information regarding these Web sites may be found in this book's preface or online.

The Victorian Web
   http://www.victorianweb.org/victorian/victov.html
Historical U.S. Census Data Browser
   http://fisher.lib.virginia.edu/census/
Society for Economic Anthropology Homepage
   http://nautarch.tamu.edu/anth/sea/

The early years of the nineteenth century were marked by two powerful opposite forces. The French Revolution and industrialization provided the impetus for political, economic, and social change in Western Civilization. The ideals of the French Revolution remained alive in France and inspired nationalistic movements in other parts of Europe. Industrialization brought material progress for millions, particularly the burgeoning middle class, but often at the expense of the unskilled workers who were victims of low wages and an impersonal factory system. Shifting demographic patterns created addition pressures for change. It had taken all of European history to reach a population of 180 million in 1800. In the nineteenth century, the European population doubled, casing major migrations on the continent from the country to the city, and sending waves of emigrants to America, Australia, and elsewhere. By 1919 about 200 million Europeans had migrated.

But forces of continuity also lingered on. Notwithstanding the impact of industrialism, much of Europe remained agrarian, dependent upon peasant labor. Christianity remained the dominant religion and the institution of monarchy re-attained the loyalty of those who wanted to preserve an orderly society. In addition, millions of Europeans, having lived through the crises of the French Revolution and Napoleonic eras, were willing to embrace even the most repressive, reactionary regimes if they could guarantee peace and stability.

The interaction of tradition and change raised vital new issues and generated conflicts in politics and thought. By necessity the terms of political dialogue were redefined. The century was an age of ideologies: conservatism, with its distrust of untested innovations and its deep commitment to order and traditions; liberalism, with its faith in reason, technique, and progress; various forms of socialism, from revolutionary to utopian, each with its promise of equality and economic justice for the working class; and nationalism, with its stirring demand, at the same time unifying and divisive, that the nationalities of the world should be autonomous. Even Darwinism was misappropriated for political purposes. Transformed into Social Darwinism, it was used to justify the domination of Western nations over their colonies. Popular misconceptions of evolution reinforced prevailing notions of male supremacy.

In sum, the nineteenth century, for those who enjoyed economic and political status, was the "Golden Age" of human progress. For the rest, many of whom shared the materialist outlook of their "betters," it was a time of struggle to attain their fair share.

Several articles in this unit explore the dynamics of change in the nineteenth century. Important social change is surveyed in "Florence Nightingale as a Social Reformer" and "The Incurable

Wound" discusses how Louis Pasteur made us safer from rabies. Economic forces and related political ideologies are covered in "Slavery and the British." Nation building is the subject of "Bismarck, Prussia & German Nationalism," and "Napoleon III: 'Hero or 'Grotesque Mediocrity'?" And finally, European imperialism in regard to the Ottoman Empire is surveyed in the article, "The Russians Shall Not Have Constantinople."

Slavery and the British

James Walvin reviews current ideas about the vast network of slavery that shaped British and world history for more than two centuries.

JAMES WALVIN

The enforced movement of more than eleven million Africans onto the Atlantic slave ships, and the scattering of over ten million survivors across the colonies of the Americas between the late sixteenth and early nineteenth centuries, transformed the face of the Americas. It also enhanced the material well-being both of European settlers and their homelands. The cost was paid, of course, by Africa: a haemorrhage of humanity from vast reaches of the continent, the exact consequences, even now, unknown. Though they were not its pioneers, by the mid-eighteenth century the British had come to dominate Atlantic slavery, a fact which in turn helped to shape much of Britain's status and power.

Historians have become increasingly interested in the concept of an Atlantic world: a world that embraced the maritime and littoral societies of Europe, Africa and the Americas, and one in which slavery played a crucial role. The Atlantic system developed a gravitational pull that drew to it many more societies than those formally committed to African slavery. Even the economies of Asia were ultimately linked to African slavery. European ships, bound for the slave coast of Africa, brimmed not simply with produce from their home towns, their hinterland and from Europe, but also with goods transhipped from Asia. Firearms from Birmingham, French wines, Indian textiles, cowrie shells from the Maldives, food from Ireland, all were packed into the holds of outbound ships, destined to be exchanged for Africans.

The bartering and trading systems on the coast fed a voracious demand for imported goods that stretched far deeper into the African interior than Europeans had seen or visited. In return, the traders who settled on the coast, and the transient captains, gradually filled the holds of their ships (suitably rearranged for human cargoes) with Africans.

European, American and Brazilian traders flitted nervously up and down the west African coast, always anxious to make a quick exchange and quit the dangers of the region for the welcoming currents that would speed their Atlantic crossing to the expectant markets of the Americas. We have details of some 26,000 voyages throughout the recorded history of the slave trade. Once described as a 'triangular trade', it was in fact a trading system of great geographical complexity, with routes

TO BE SOLD on board the Ship *Bance Island*, on tuesday the 6th of *May* next, at *Ashley Ferry*; a choice cargo of about 250 fine healthy NEGROES, just arrived from the Windward & Rice Coast. —The utmost care has already been taken, and shall be continued, to keep them free from the least danger of being infected with the SMALL-POX, no boat having been on board, and all other communication with people from *Charles-Town* prevented.

Austin, Laurens, & Appleby.

N. B. Full one Half of the above Negroes have had the SMALL-POX in their own Country.

HULTON GETTY

A Boston advertisement for a cargo of slaves, probably from the early eighteenth century.

cutting from Brazil to Africa, from North America to Africa and back, between Europe and the Caribbean—and of direct routes from the slave colonies back to the European heartlands. Ships crisscrossed the north and south Atlantic Caribbean, ferrying Africans and goods needed by all slave societies, finally hauling the vast cargoes of slave-grown produce back to European markets, to sate the appetite of the Western world for tropical and semi-tropical staples. This trading complexity was compounded by commercial transactions with native peoples on the frontiers of European settlement and advancement across the Americas.

This vast network, lubricated by slavery, drew together hugely different peoples from all over the world. Africans in the Caribbean dressed in textiles produced in India, used tools made in Sheffield, and produced rum drunk by indigenous native peoples of the Americas. Tobacco cultivated by slaves in the Chesapeake was widely consumed, from Africa itself to the early penal colonies of Australia.

Though Africans were present in many of the early European settlements in the Americas, the drift towards African slavery was slow. Europeans tried a host of agricultural and social experiments in the Western Hemisphere before the mid- and late-sixteenth-century Brazilian development of sugar cane cultivation. Sugar had long been grown on plantations in the Mediterranean (it came later to the Atlantic islands), before being transplanted into the Americas in the late sixteenth century. But sugar plantations, even in their early form, were labour-intensive, and there was not enough labour available among local peoples, or migrating Europeans. Africa, though, could be made to yield people in abundance. From small-scale, haphazard origins (with Europeans tapping into local slave systems), the demand for labour in the New World spawned violent networks of slave-trading along the African coast and deep into the interior.

By the time the British forged their own early seventeenth-century settlements in the Caribbean and North America, black slavery had already taken root in Spanish, Portuguese and Dutch settlements. Informed by this earlier experience, and able to borrow the technologies of sugar cultivation, backed by Dutch money, and with domestic political support, the British found the commercial opportunities afforded by slavery irresistible. But they, too, tried other systems at first.

Sugar changed all. First in Barbados and the Leewards from the 1630s, then in late seventeenth-century Jamaica, British settlers converted ever more acreage into cane cultivation. In Barbados, sugar cultivation hastened the rise of larger plantations and the decline in the number of smallholdings—and, of course, a growing proportion of the population was black and enslaved. In 1650 there were perhaps 300 plantations on the island, by 1670, some 900. The black population in Barbados stood at about 20,000 in 1655 but less than thirty years later it had risen to over 46,000. In the same period, the white population had declined. The conversion of Barbados to a plantation society based on African slave labour was a pattern repeated across the Caribbean.

In the Chesapeake colonies of Virginia and Maryland, the drift to slavery followed local lines of tobacco cultivation (again on plantations), though they differed in size (and nature) from the sugar plantations of the West Indies. Later, in the early eighteenth century, rice cultivation (also on plantations) in the Carolinas was also driven forward by slavery. Though all depended on imported Africans, each region developed a distinctly different slave system. Plantations varied from crop to crop. Slave demography, social life and culture took different trajectories across the enslaved Americas. But one universal fact remained unflinching: the reduction of African humanity to the status and level (in law, economic and social usage) of property.

From the first, the slave's status clashed with a number of European legal and political practices and conventions. Europeans were turning their backs on bondage in their own continent at the very time they were creating and perfecting African slavery in the Atlantic economy. In turn, the expansion of slavery—British ships carried three million Africans between

1680 and 1807—spawned a confusion of justifications, many of which came to hinge on ideas of race; for what could be the justification for the relegation of humanity to the level of chattel, even when colonial (and imperial) law decreed it so? There consequently evolved a protracted social and political debate about colour and 'race' that entered the intellectual bloodstream of the Western world. By the time the slave systems reached their mature form in the English-speaking colonies in the mid-eighteenth century, to be black was to be enslaved: a piece of chattel. The obvious contradictions in such practices and beliefs were there for all to see. Nonetheless, the political (and legal) tensions generated by the property-status of slaves remained. Ultimately, this ideological core of the slave system was fatally fissured by the seismic impact of the French Revolution of 1789 and the *Declaration of the Rights of Man and the Citizen* passed by the Constituent Assembly in France the same year. And in Britain the assertion of equality encapsulated in the abolitionists' motto 'Am I not a Man and a Brother?', adopted in 1787, would ultimately prove corrosive of slavery.

But slavery and the Atlantic slave trade still continued. Even after 1789, the intellectual or political attachment to black freedom was often overridden by economic considerations. For much of its history, slavery had had its critics. But its basic commercial value served to marginalise whatever criticisms were raised by churchmen, philosophers and even political economists. For a long time the material well-being, visible on both sides of the Atlantic, that slavery brought to so many hushed all protest.

The benefits of slave labour could be seen, initially, in the colonies themselves. Africans and their local-born offspring converted swathes of the settled Americas to profitable agriculture. Though often little more than toe-holds on the American land mass and Caribbean islands, plantations became the means of bringing a luxuriant wilderness into commercial cultivation. Slaves re-ordered the confusions of the natural habitat into fields and fruitful land-holdings, the whole linked by man-made trails and pathways, to local river or coastal docks. Each plantation colony developed its own, often small-scale, urban centres. Towns, cities and ports were both centres of local political power and entrepôts forming a crossroads with the wider world, where goods (and peoples) flowed in from Europe and Africa, and whence produce and profits were dispatched back, across the Atlantic, to Europe.

From the sixteenth to the early nineteenth century, European conflicts were also played out in the Americas, as each emergent colonial power sought to gain advantage over its rival. In the islands, Europeans built massive fortifications to keep other marauding Europeans at bay, and to prevent their own settlements from being destroyed or usurped. The magnificent fortifications that survive along the Caribbean island chain testify to the military threat experienced by each colonising nation, and to the vast expense invested in securing their strongholds. In time, however, the greatest threats came not from other Europeans, but from the enslaved armies toiling reluctantly for their colonial masters. The slave colonies, and the planters in their rural retreats, were permanently embattled against an encircling slave population they vitally needed but never trusted.

Colonial slave societies were held in place not simply by naval and local armed defences, but by ad-hoc federations of militia and armed whites (and by the late eighteenth century even by black troops) marshalled to over-awe and stifle any outburst which might erupt from the slave quarters. Throughout the British slave colonies, violence and resistance among the slaves was endemic (as they were wherever slavery existed). But so too was savage and remorseless repression. Slaves resisted their bondage in a variety of ways. From enslavement in Africa, to life in the squalor of the slave ships, through to the more settled but often brutal life on the plantations, slaves found ways to resist. Most spectacularly in the form of open revolt or rebellion, resistance more commonly took the form of mundane acts of non-compliance: feigning stupidity, failing to do what was required, sabotaging owners' plans and instructions, or simply by presenting the sullen reluctance that whites reported across the slave colonies. There were great dangers here for the slaves: resist too much, too far, and retribution would result in all too predictable a fashion. This was true for healthy young men in the fields (generally the most 'troublesome' group) and for their mothers and sisters working as domestics in white households. How far to go—the boundary between the tolerable and the dangerous—was always an early lesson young slaves had to learn from their elders. Throughout, physical assault, a simple cuff or beating, was an ever-present reality.

Not surprisingly, slaves ran away in all slave societies, though physical circumstances often determined what was possible. Barbados for example—much the same size as the Isle of Wight—offered few obvious escape routes once the island had been fully conquered and put into sugar cultivation. But in other colonies where geography allowed, slaves formed 'maroon' societies: communities of runaways, living beyond the pale of plantation life. Maroons were deeply disliked by planters and military alike. Seen as an obvious goal for potential runaways, they were viewed as a threat in many senses. Yet efforts to destroy them generally failed in the teeth of fierce resistance and the physical difficulties of the local environment (mountains or jungle, ideal country for what were, effectively, guerrilla bands.) Where the British could not bring maroons to heel, they were ultimately forced to [work] with them, conceding their independence, most importantly in return for the handing back of further would-be runaways.

Newspapers throughout the slave colonies were filled with advertisements for slave runaways. Most common was the slave runaway heading for a loved-one. While many were clearly on the run from their plantation or owner most were simply seeking family and friends: a lover or spouse, a child or parent. Runaways might more easily escape notice in urban communities. Curiously, at times, slave owners seemed not to mind when slaves ran away (when food was short, for example, or when the demands of the agricultural year were slack), on condition that they returned—eventually. Always, of course, slaves had to prove their right to roam. Unless they had an obvious task to do, slaves on the move were inevitably suspect, and runaways generally moved furtively, needing the help of other slaves for food or shelter. There were, however, many other slaves with a legitimate reason to be on the move—to and from their own markets, between plantations and the nearest river or port, transporting exports and imports, goods and beasts, along the lines of local (and even international) communication.

Open revolt bloodied the history of the slave colonies. The insurrection of the 1790s in the French colony of Haiti was the only example of slaves in the Americas succeeding in the complete destruction of the system that oppressed them, though not for want of trying elsewhere. African slaves (many with military experience in their African homelands) tended to be more resistant than those born in the New World, with numbers trying, but invariably failing, to escape their bondage by plots, revolt and physical defiance. Failure was measured out in bloody retribution by means of summary executions, dismemberments and exemplary tortures which colonial penal codes (to say nothing of plantocratic instinct) made possible. Nowhere was the 'bloody code' more bloody, and more widely used, than in the slave islands. And each failed slave revolt saw a tightening of plantocratic repression: a vicious cycle of resistance and repression which showed no prospect of change.

One element in the growing British disenchantment with slavery was with the brutality required simply to keep the slaves in their place. What might have gone unquestioned in 1700 had, by the 1820s, become unacceptable. By then there was a changing sensibility about slavery that was partly religious, partly secular but which, when placed in the context of growing economic doubts (was slavery really more efficient than free labour?) helped to undermine the metropolitan attachment to a system that had served Britain so well for two centuries. Moreover, as British missionaries began to win over increasing numbers of slaves to their chapels and churches, they reported back to their British congregations the full nature of slave experience and sufferings, to the growing concern of fellow British worshippers. What kind of system was it that persecuted black Christians, their preachers and their places of worship? By the 1820s few doubted that the British slave system was doomed.

From the late eighteenth century, the adoption of Christianity transformed slave life in the islands. From the first, slaves had evolved distinctive cultures from one colony to another, which blended Africa with local European and colonial life. Belief systems and languages, folk customs (from cooking to health care and dress) and family patterns imported from the slaves' varied African communities, were transformed by the process of enslavement, transportation and settlement in the Americas. Africans in the slave quarters may have sought out their 'own people' (whose language and habits they understood) but they were also forced into the company of other Africans, local-born slaves and Europeans, with whom they had to live and work. The creole cultures that grew from such blendings imposed a distinct style and tone on each and every slave society.

Despite the ubiquitous repression and violence of slavery, slave-owners learned that they secured the best returns on their human capital not by unrelenting pressure, but by allowing free time: breaks at weekends, at high days and holidays. The calendar of the local agricultural year or the Christian Year provided slaves with a breathing space. In those breaks from drudgery, slaves evolved their own particular social activities, investing their breaks with ritual and ceremonies: dressing up in elaborate fashion (in sharp contrast to the everyday dress of the work-place), enjoying particular customs with music, food, drink and elaborate carnival. Equally, the patterns of family and community life—notably birth, marriage and death—evolved their own distinctive patterns and rhythms. Outsiders were often amazed at the vigour and material bounty displayed by slaves in their social life. Where and how did they acquire such elaborate clothing and finery: jewellery and musical instruments, money for lavish food and drink? In fact, they bought such luxuries from the fruits of their own labours. Individual skills (such as music-making, nursing, sewing or craftsmanship) could generate earnings. Gardens and plots, tending animals, cultivating foodstuffs and so on, gave slaves the material wherewithal for barter and trade, for sale and purchase. Such efforts formed the basis of the slave markets which came to characterise the slave islands. All this took place after the normal working day: at evenings, weekends or in other free time. It meant that even in their rare moments of leisure slaves had to toil. Whatever advancement they made (and many clearly did make their lives more comfortable) came from their own sweat and application.

The greatest beneficiaries of slave efforts were of course their owners and their imperial backers. This brings us to the thorny issue of profit and loss. For more than fifty years, historians have squabbled about the economics of the British slave system. What role did slavery play in the transformation of Britain itself? More especially, what was its significance in enabling Britain to become an industrial power from the late eighteenth century onwards? Equally, were Britain's decisions to turn its back first on the slave trade (1807), and then on slavery itself (1834), economically inspired? At one level it is implausible to discount the importance of the Atlantic slave system, it was so massive, its ramifications so ubiquitous, its defenders so tenacious in their attachment to it. In the development of Liverpool, for instance, can we ignore the some 6,000 slave voyages that departed from that port? And can we adequately grasp the nature of Bristol's (or London's) earlier, seventeenth-century involvement in the slave trade and settlement of the slave colonies? Moreover, the accountancy of the system—the facts and figures so carefully researched and teased apart by historians in the past twenty-five years—do not always convey the full social impact of slavery on Britain itself. Whatever the level of profit (or loss) of particular voyages, of specific trading companies and plantations, here was a system that by the mid-eighteenth century had become part of the warp and weft of British life itself. To those at home, slavery was, in general, out of mind and out of sight. Yet its consequences, most obviously the fruits of slave labour (the sugar and rum, the tobacco, rice and coffee) served to transform the social life of Britain (and the West in general.) Africa was obliged to consume vast amounts of Western produce in return for bartered slaves. Plantation societies were kept alive by British imports, from the hats on the slaves' heads, to the hoes in their hands, from equipment in the fields, to the wines on the planters' tables. And a host of British ports, with their immediate economic hinterland, thrived on supplying the whole, filling the ships, plying African markets and the American plantations with vital goods and services: with their manpower (black and white), their finance, firepower and military defences. In the enslaved Atlantic, Britain may have ruled the waves. But even the victorious Royal Navy, hard at its massive task of protecting the British colonies and the sea-lanes from the predatory threats of other Europeans, kept its men at their unenviable tasks by lavish helpings of rum. And who made the rum?

The results of slave labours were inescapable, from the smoke-filled atmosphere (courtesy of Virginian tobacco) of London's myriad coffee houses, to the insatiable appetite of British common people for sugar to take with the tea. Yet the slaves were thousands of miles distant. What gave the slave system a local, British focus was that small band of blacks, living in London, mainly domestics, sometimes slaves, who flit in and out of view; in parish registers, fashionable portraits, as the subject of legal arguments, and often the victims of aggression by employer or owners. They serve as a reminder, however apparently removed from the centre of Atlantic slavery, of other Africans, measured in their millions, whose brutal enslavement and transportation was so fundamental a part of the rise to greatness of eighteenth-century Britain.

For Further Reading

Robin Blackburn, *The Making of New World Slavery* (Verso, 1997); David Eltis, *The Rise of African Slavery in the Americas* (Cambridge University Press, 2000); *The Oxford History of the British Empire: The Eighteenth Century* P.J.Marshall, ed, (Oxford University Press, 1998); James Walvin, *Making the Black Atlantic* (Cassell, 2000).

JAMES WALVIN is Professor of History at the University of York.

This article first appeared in *History Today*, March 2002, pp. 48-54. © 2002 by History Today, Ltd. Reprinted by permission.

Victoria

Lynne Vallone reviews the life of the woman who has occupied the throne longer than any other individual, and considers the tensions between her private and public selves.

LYNNE VALLONE

A s a symbol of domesticity, endurance and Empire, and as a woman holding the highest public office during an age when women (middle-class women, at least) were expected to beautify the home while men dominated the public sphere, Queen Victoria's influence has been enduring. The historian Dorothy Thompson (1990) suggests that the present queen has extended and emphasised the tenets and trends of Victoria's reign to the present day.

The symbolic importance of Victoria's reign (1837–1901) cannot easily be separated from assumptions made by her contemporaries about gender and age. Adjectives such as 'simple', 'modest', 'innocent', 'lovely', commonly applied to Victoria as evidence of her appropriate placement on the throne, would almost certainly not have been used if she had been a man. Similarly, after her death from old age in January, 1901, paeans to the Queen praised her embodiment of traditional feminine virtues rather than acts of bravery, statesmanship, or guardianship. For example, best-selling novelist Marie Corelli, in *The Passing of the Great Queen: A Tribute to the Noble Life of Victoria Regina* (1901), prefers Victoria's model of 'blameless' feminine authority to masculine privilege. Corelli remarks that:

> Personal influence is a far more important factor in the welding together and holding of countries and peoples than is generally taken into account by such of us are superficial observers and who imagine that everything is done by Governments.

Conflicts between the demands of 'masculine' government and 'feminine' home are located within the person of the woman who was from 1837 until her death sixty-three years later, at the head of both. Although she would later express a horror of women's rights, the Queen articulated a clearly-defined sense of women's 'wrongs', the unjust sufferings experienced by many women by virtue of their sex. Victoria's complaint against woman's trials—a minor theme in a number of letters to the Princess Royal beginning in 1860—included her belief that a woman's valuable autonomy is compromised even within a successful marriage:

> All marriage is such a lottery—the happiness always an exchange—though it may be a very happy one— still the poor woman is bodily and molly the husband's slave. That always sticks in my throat.

Victoria could hardly be promoted as a feminist icon for today's young women, yet as Thompson concludes, 'If [Victoria] strengthened the moral authority of women in the family rather than making their presence in public life more immediately acceptable, there must have been ways in which the presence of a woman at the head of the state worked at a deeper level to weaken prejudice and make change more possible in the century following her reign.'

During her long reign, Queen Victoria's particular foibles and gestures—leaning on Albert, recurring pregnancies, mishandling the Prince of Wales, retreating to Balmoral, frowning in formal portraits, to name just a few—were made immediately into caricatures of long-standing effect. Today, she is more widely known for the apocryphal statement 'We are not amused,' due, perhaps, to the dour expression exhibited in almost all extant public photographs, rather than for the private ecstatic professions of joy found in her early journals. 'I was *very much amused indeed*!', Princess Victoria wrote in 1834, just before her fifteenth birthday, after a night at the opera listening to her favourite Giulia Grisi's rendition of Desdemona. Excepting her period of deepest mourning, Queen Victoria was not solemn by nature (notwithstanding her appearance due to the requirements of the early photographic process that encouraged frozen features and the rules governing conduct within public appearances which Victoria held dear), but she *was* serious. As Queen Regnant, Victoria could never separate self from position, her country's interests from her own. From an early age she had been led, often reluctantly, to worship at the shrine of Duty. She never forgot these early lessons, or whose blood ran in her veins, and what was due to her as the Queen of England. From debating issues of supreme political importance such as Home Rule ('those who have spoken and agitated, for the sake of party and to injure their opponents, in a very radical sense must look for another monarch; and she doubts [if] they will find one'), through petty brinksmanship in matters relating to her children's marriages (in 1874 she lambasted Princess Alice who had the temerity to support the idea that Victoria should meet the family of Prince Alfred's intended bride, the Grand Duchess Marie of Russia, on the continent prior to the marriage, '… I do *not* think, dear child, that *you* should tell *me* who have been nearly *twenty years longer* on the throne than the Emperor of Russia and am Doyenne of Sovereigns, and who am a Reigning Sovereign, which the Empress is not, what I ought to do!'), Queen Victoria was ever regal.

The stature that the Queen would claim for herself and attain through her strong personality, determination, and passion for right conduct, could not have been foretold at her accession. At that time the eighteen-year-old Victoria's feminine virtues of sympathy and beauty were proclaimed in doggerel verse to the street ballad-reading public:

The Royal Queen of Britain's isle
Soon will make the people smile.
Her heart none can in the least defile,
Victoria, Queen of England.
Although she is of early years
She is possessed of tender cares
To wipe away the orphan's tears
Now she is Queen of England.
All the flowers in full bloom
Adorn'd with beauty and perfume
The fairest is the rose in June,
Victoria, Queen of England.

Youth and simplicity served Victoria well as she began her long reign. Although she was passionately fond of emotion and melodrama as expressed in romances such as James Fenimore Cooper's *The Bravo* (1831) and in plays, opera and ballet, once William IV's health began to deteriorate for the final time, Princess Victoria readied herself to become queen by turning to a perhaps unlikely source for instruction and guidance: the 'simple' moral tales of her childhood. These earnest, didactic stories written by Maria Edgeworth (1768–1849), an Anglo-Irish novelist and children's author of the previous generation, and published in *The Parent's Assistant* (1796-1800), outlined moral conduct and the rewards of rational behaviour. In her journal, Princess Victoria noted reading these stories on numerous occasions in the months preceding her accession. On March 5th, 1837, she wrote:

Read in 'Simple Susan,' which certainly is the most touching pretty story imaginable, and though the *Parent's Assistant* has been read often by me when a child, I find it far more interesting than many a novel.

At her accession, the diminutive young Queen was often described as pleasingly 'simple' by on-lookers and the press. Indeed, a charming simplicity and modesty of manner, dress, speech and gesture effectively describes the clear-sighted girl who greeted the Archbishop of Canterbury and Lord Conyngham on the morning of June 20th, 1837.

As Britain's 'simple' sweetheart, and thus as unlike her dissolute relations as could be imagined, Victoria at first enjoyed the people's admiration for her freshness and femininity. Yet she expressed her strong will early and often. This characteristic would both support Victoria in times of trial as well as create trouble with her relations. It developed in childhood in part as a response to the political aspirations and machinations of her mother, the Duchess of Kent, and the Duchess's closest advisor, Sir John Conroy. Once she became Queen, Victoria kept the Duchess of Kent at arm's length, while Conroy, after receiving a baronetcy, a payment of £3,000 per year and the Grand Cross of the Order of the Bath, was banished from the Queen's presence, though he continued, until 1839, to haunt Buckingham House like a malcontented fairy. Able to please herself by refusing the attentions of those she did not like, Victoria surrounded herself with her favourites—her prime minister, Lord Melbourne, and her former governess, Baroness Louise Lehzen. The protected young monarch was largely unperturbed by working-class unrest such as expressed in the Chartist movement, or by unrelieved suffering in Ireland and squalid areas of London. Victoria wrote to her half-sister, Princess Feodora:

. . . it is not the splendour of the thing or the being Queen that makes me so happy, it is the pleasant life I lead which causes my peace and happiness.

Yet Victoria was soon roused to outrage when her prime minister was under threat. When Melbourne's Whig government began to fail in May 1939, the Queen faced Melbourne's imminent resignation and the prospect of a (to her mind) disagreeable Tory successor in Sir Robert Peel. Furious at the prospect, Victoria refused to allow the conventional replacement on change of government, of her senior Ladies of the Bedchamber (who were the wives of Whig MPs or peers). The new government was unable to form within this context of sovereign disobedience, and so, to her great satisfaction, though weakened, Melbourne resumed his position. The smug Victoria exulted in a note to Melbourne:

They wanted to deprive me of my Ladies, and I suppose they would deprive me next of my dressers and my housemaids; they wished to treat me like a girl, but I will show them that I am Queen of England.

Although she could not know it at the time, this event marked the beginning and end of Victoria's successfully-waged legislative obstructions. While in the future she (with Prince Albert) maintained an at times needling presence in government decisions, by September 1841, after a general election in which the Conservatives defeated Melbourne's Liberal (Whig) party, Victoria was forced to accept Peel.

The Queen's conduct in the so-called 'Bedchamber Affair' helps to illustrate her fierce loyalty to the many male advisors throughout her life who guided, cajoled and comforted her. The first of these figures was her uncle, King Leopold I of the Belgians (r. 1831–65), the most significant, her husband, Prince Albert, whom she had married on February 10th, 1840. The pain that Victoria felt at the loss of Lord Melbourne (who, following his political demise, suffered a stroke in 1842) as her trusted advisor was eased by the happiness and support she gained through her marriage. After an initial reluctance to consider marriage and a positive dislike of being coerced, Victoria began to lament the lack of young people around her. When Uncle Leopold's choice, her first cousin Prince Albert of Saxe-Coburg-Gotha, and his brother Ernest stopped in England in October, 1839, Victoria, who had found Albert rather dull on their first meeting some three years before, now beheld him with awe: 'Albert is beautiful' she breathed to her journal. Five days later she nervously proposed marriage and was accepted by kisses, embraces and sweet murmurings in German.

Victoria's choice of a young German prince (they were born the same year) was less popular with the press, Tory aristocrats and members of the royal court than with her subjects who gathered to cheer his arrival at Dover a few days before the marriage, and who lined the route of the wedding procession from Buckingham Palace to Windsor Castle where the three-day honeymoon would take place. Cynics insinuated that Albert was a gold-digger. One poet opined:

> He comes the bridegroom of Victoria's choice
> The nominee of Lehzen's Voice;
> He comes to take 'for better or for worse'
> England's fat queen and England's fatter purse.

Although both partners underwent a difficult period of adjustment—Victoria was used to having her own way and lost her temper easily and Albert was homesick and bored with his limited duties and the many official evening events requiring his presence—the marriage was a decided success. The Princess Royal was born within a year of her parents' wedding and eight more children followed; their last child, Princess Beatrice, was born in 1857. Victoria, who suffered from post-natal depression, was not at ease with children—a feeling that had begun as a girl and lasted throughout her life. Less lighthearted in the nursery than her husband, she loved her children, none the less, and greatly preferred their retired familial gatherings and amusements at Osborne House, Balmoral and Windsor Castle, to the exhausting state functions of London life.

During the twenty-year period of Victoria's domestic happiness with Albert, Britain was generally peaceful and increasingly prosperous at home. Victoria's success as Queen was due in large part to the widespread appeal—as both sovereign and 'middle-class' devoted wife and mother embodying the virtues of hard work, charity, practicality and earnestness—she held for a general public also interested in 'home values'. In a long February 1858 letter written to her newly-married eldest daughter, Victoria recounted with pleasure the warm feelings that all classes of people had expressed upon the occasion of Vicky's marriage to Prince Frederick William of Prussia. To the Queen's satisfaction, this kind of support for the Royal Family's affairs demonstrated 'how the people here valued and loved a moral court and a happy domestic home, like, thank God our's has been and is!' The middle classes were energetically elevating trade to respectability and domestic values to a kind of religion. This group, for whom home was a refuge and locus of virtue, were key to this national domestication effort with Victoria at its centre. Victoria was aided to this effect by Albert, of course (whose heightened standing in the government's eyes

was clearly signalled by Parliament's passage of the Regency Bill during the Queen's first pregnancy, naming him as sole Regent) and her Tory and Liberal prime ministers (including, Peel, Russell and Palmerston). On the event of her eighteenth wedding anniversary, Victoria boasted in a letter to King Leopold, that her marriage 'has brought ... universal blessings on this country and Europe!'

The royal family thus stood as a model at the head of a self-satisfied nation that downplayed internal tensions, while external conflict was used as propaganda to underscore Britain's imperialist ideology of national superiority. The mood was epitomised in the Great Exhibition of the Industry of all Nations at the Crystal Palace in 1851. By promoting the superior talents of both Prince Albert and of British technology, art and commerce, the Great Exhibition united the interests of monarchy, industry and people in celebrating the nation's progress. Over six million visitors flocked to Hyde Park; among these was Charlotte Bronte who commented:

> . . . it seems as if only magic could have gathered this mass of wealth from all the ends of the earth.

But in spite of what it represented, the Crystal Palace was a 'magical' place in the midst of quotidian urban despair. The 1850 census revealed that London's population had increased by 21 per cent in ten years and now stood at 2,363,000. The cosmopolitan city of theatres, clubs, fashionable shops and modern transportation contrasted with a London of rampant disease, congestion, squalor, crime and poverty. The passage of the Public Health Act of 1848 began to address some of the worst public health problems. The governing classes were unnerved when, in the same year as revolutions broke out on the Continent, some 150,000 Chartist demonstrators marched from Kennington to Westminster with their petition for political representation for labouring men. The Queen classified all such movements as the highest degree of 'disobedience' imaginable: 'Obedience to the laws & to the Sovereign' she told Lord John Russell in August, 1848, 'is obedience to a higher Power.' Yet, as the Chartists' appeal was ultimately peaceful and any instigators of violence punished, Victoria was well satisfied with her subjects' loyalty. Also in 1848, Albert began to visit the south London slums to indicate the royal family's interest in the plight of the lower classes and support for reform measures.

Ireland, still suffering from the potato blight that had begun in 1845, received less of Victoria's attention than did the poor of England, Scotland and Wales. Victoria visited Ireland only three times—in 1849, 1861 and 1900—and unfavourably compared, as she called them, 'the radical Irish' with the loyal Scots.

The continual agitation in Ireland threatened to disturb, closest to home, an Empire that included territory in India, Canada, Australia, New Zealand and South Africa. However, it was turbulence beyond Great Britain's shores that drew Victoria's gaze away from the homeland and toward the East. Stirred to wage war in the Crimea as part of an alliance that included France and Turkey against Russia, Victoria wrote to Princess Augusta in 1854:

> You will understand it when I assure you that I regret exceedingly not to be a man and to be able to fight in

the war. My heart bleeds for the many fallen, but I consider that there is no finer death for a man than on the battlefield!

The Queen visited sick and wounded British soldiers and commended Florence Nightingale for her effective nursing work on their behalf. Although the death toll of the Crimean War (1853-56) would blunt British appetite for battle, the 'Indian Mutiny' of the following year hardened the hearts of the colonialists against the Hindu and Muslim Indians who rose against the British. From May to mid-July fighting spread over northern-India: British officers and their families were killed by the mutineers, which in turn led to revenge against the Indians. By March 1858, the British had reestablished control. As the stories of massacre and mass executions on both sides of the bloody conflict reached England, Victoria was amazed and horrified. With Albert in agreement, the 'Queen supported Lord Canning, the Governor General, who refused to exact retribution on all Indian people, and sympathised with the religious issues that had, in part, caused native resentment. After the Indian Mutiny, an even greater proportion of India, the 'jewel in Victoria's crown', was under her direct rule (the East India Company having been abolished following the Mutiny), increasing the number of her subjects by almost 200 million people.

A more personal crisis than the violence in India, however, was looming for the Queen at the end of 1861. Exhausted by the behaviour of the wayward Prince of Wales, his extensive commitments at home, and the conflict between the British and the civil war-torn Americans over the Trent incident in November, a pale and depressed Prince Albert fell ill with a feverish cold that November. He was soon diagnosed with typhoid fever and died after a few weeks of illness, at Windsor Castle on December 14th, his wife and five of his children around him. Victoria's sorrow was profound: 'There is no one to call me Victoria now,' she pined.

Victoria's extreme and unrelenting grief defined her existence for years after Albert's death as she shrank from appearing before the public and from living in London. In March 1864, a large poster fastened to railings outside Buckingham Palace satirised the Queen's long absences, underscoring the general resentment they caused by advertising the palace as available 'to be let or sold, in consequence of the late occupant's declining business'. Victoria's ministers had to invent ways to manage their nervous and reclusive sovereign. Benjamin Disraeli (prime minister from February 1868 until the end of that year—returning in 1874) approached the Queen by sending long letters and paying her careful flattery. William Gladstone, whose Liberal government succeeded Disraeli's, and whom Albert had esteemed for his high character, was less successful than Disraeli in his attempts to draw Victoria out of seclusion. The Queen remained in Scotland, attending balls and driving with her blunt and quarrelsome Highland servant, John Brown, whom Victoria called 'so simple, so intelligent, so unlike an ordinary servant …'. At the same time, various achievements of 'High Victorianism'—advances in literature, science, invention and social reform—marched forward, without Victoria's public notice.

The novels of Charles Dickens, along with works by social realists such as George Eliot, Charlotte Bronte, Elizabeth Gaskell, Thomas Hardy and others, offered Victorian readers glimpses of textured fictional lives and highlighted both the evils and inconsistencies of their society and the attitudes and beliefs that could redeem individuals ('pure' marriage, charity, self-sacrifice, hard work). Victoria particularly delighted in Eliot's *Adam Bede* (1859) and 'trac[ed] a likeness to the dear Highlanders' in the virtuous title character. Advancements in still photography allowed greater access to the 'event' of everyday life. Queen Victoria was a great admirer of the process and gave photographers significant access to her family. After his death, photographs became one means for the grieving Queen to recall and memorialise her beloved Albert.

In 1859 Charles Darwin had introduced a 'rupture' in conventional thinking through his theory of 'natural selection' described in *On the Origin of Species*. Darwin's work on the theory of evolution, continued in *The Descent of Man* (1871), contributed to a Victorian crisis of faith. Yet, as Richard D. Altick argues, Darwinism also helped to motivate the Victorian social conscience:

> If historical and dogmatic Christianity could no longer compel belief, ethical Christianity could at least serve as a guide to life. Thus the powers of mind and spirit which in other ages had gone into religious devotion were redirected to social ends, in attempts to fulfill the teaching of the Gospels.

Legislation as well as charitable societies directed toward relieving some social inequalities helped to characterise the Victorian age as one of social activism and reform—much of which was necessary to counteract the effects of a successful Industrial Revolution. The Factory Act of 1844 limited the daily working hours of women and children; the Reform Bill of 1867 completed the general enfranchisement of the middle classes men as well as the majority of male town workers; the Education Act of 1870 acknowledged that the state should support and provide education for children; and the Married Women's Property Bill of 1882 maintained that married women could retain the rights to their property held before or gained during their marriage. In 1897, seventeen different groups formed the National Union of Women's Suffrage Societies (NUWSS) working towards female suffrage as well as other causes pertaining to women's rights.

While social reform was a rallying cry for many Victorians who turned their attentions to the world outside the home in an attempt to create a 'home-like' society, the mourning Queen remained inward-looking. But, while duty to the memory of her husband may have governed her days and distracted her from business, Victoria's grief did not mitigate her formidable nature as 'domestic queen'. She maintained tight control over all her households. Those secretaries, servants, and ministers who were able to flatter, amuse and treat her as a woman as well as a monarch were the most successful with her during this period of protracted grief. An ageing Victoria slowly returned to public view, opening Parliament in 1871 and participating—albeit reluctantly—in a celebration of the popular Prince of Wales's recovery from typhoid fever early in the following year. Though she could no longer function as a symbol of domestic happiness, the Queen now represented the more remote, if well-loved, figure of the suffering and patient woman. Victoria's status as 'Our Mother' had begun.

The golden and diamond jubilees (of 1887 and 1897) were wildly successful for Victoria, securing for her a degree of stature hitherto unimagined. No one, including her cheering subjects, expected the Queen to do much at this point in her life—she was simply to represent Britain. Just as at the beginning of her reign when Victoria both benefited and suffered from the image of the girl Queen and the comparisons it generated with male models of monarchy, the image of the grandmother (which she had become, by 1887, thirty times over)—generally an 'invisible' woman of little social power—had to be reinvented to fit Victoria. Although the aged Queen was strictly bound by tradition and a sense of duty, her true nature was rather unlike the severe caricature often promoted: she loved to laugh, enjoyed theatricals, *tableaux vivants*, and concerts, reading novels and learning some Hindustani from 'the Munshi' (her handsome young Indian servant Abdul Karim). In 1876, the strong-willed Queen, who had pressed for some time for an alteration to her title, was formally declared 'Empress of India'.

Throughout the 1880s, Victoria continued to storm against Gladstone and many of his policies, including Home Rule for Ireland (defeated in 1886), which the Queen felt would damage the union irreparably. In 1886, Victoria would write to a granddaughter that the GOM ('Grand Old Man'), Gladstone, 'behaves abominably. I really think he is cracked.' At the time of her second jubilee, Victoria's name and features were recognisable all over the world; when she died in 1901, few could remember a time when she had not reigned.

If the Victorian age might be judged an era of optimism, Victoria herself was perhaps its greatest optimist. She held an unshakeable belief in the superiority of all things British (particularly British men). When in late 1899 the elderly Queen was given a report of an especially bad week for the British soldiers fighting in the Boer Wars, she was heard to say, 'Please understand that there is no depression in this house; we are not interested in the possibilities of defeat; they do not exist.' Victoria's strongest personal qualities included dedication, persistence, consistency, health, and loyalty. She acceded to the throne an eighteen-year-old girl, rapidly matured into a young wife and mother, spent long years as a widow and, finally, presided as matriarch over an unwieldy family who would marry into the royal houses of Russia, Germany, Greece, Denmark, Romania, Spain and Norway. Certainly the nature of her monarchy over its sixty-three years reflected these personal life stages and changes. Her political legacy is similarly formidable. While Dorothy Thompson has suggested that 'the fact that [Victoria] was a woman certainly helped to strengthen and stabilise the monarchy, and so to prevent the development in Britain of a more rational republican form of government', it can be argued that her reign initiated the modern monarchy. The historian William M. Kuhn states that in the later years of Victoria's reign, a policy of 'democratic royalism' was in place by which the ceremony and rituals of the monarchy were united with the ideals of democracy to great effect:

> Royal spectacles provided evidence that democracy was rooted in a stable and continuous political tradition ... They showed how faith, duty, service, and self-sacrifice were necessary to the success of a political system based on consent, trust and a wide degree of active public participation.

Over time, Queen Victoria the historical figure has become 'Victoria'—a cultural artefact and iconic presence open to changing interpretation and reflective of the protean needs and desires of those attempting to understand the *zeitgeist* of an age through the figure of a powerful woman.

For Further Reading

Richard D. Altick, *Victorian People and Ideas* (W. W. Norton, 1973); Asa Briggs, *Victorian Things* (The University of Chicago Press, 1988); Marie Corelli, *The Passing of the Great Queen: A Tribute to the Noble Life of Victoria Regina* (Dodd, Mead and Company, 1901); Christopher Hibbert, *Queen Victoria: A Personal History* (HarperCollins Publishers, 2000); Christopher Hibbert, *Queen Victoria in Her Letters and Journals* (Viking, 1985); William Kuhn, *Democratic Royalism: The Transformation of the British Monarchy, 1861–1914* (Macmillan Press, 1996); Margaret Lambert, *When Victoria Began to Reign: A Coronation Year Scrapbook* (Faber & Faber, 1937); Dorothy Thompson, *Queen Victoria: The Woman, The Monarchy, and the People* (Pantheon Books, 1990) (Published in Great Britain as *Queen Victoria: Gender and Power*); Lynne Vallone, *Becoming Victoria* (Yale University Press, 2001).

LYNNE VALLONE is Associate Professor of English, Texas A&M University.

Bismarck, Prussia, & German Nationalism

Edgar Feuchtwanger assesses Bismarck's controversial career and legacy.

EDGAR FEUCHTWANGER

'In the beginning there was bismarck'. This is how a leading German historian, Thomas Nipperdey, opens the second volume of his history of Germany from 1806 to 1918. 'In the beginning there was Napoleon' is the sentence opening the first volume. Few would dispute that Napoleon and Bismarck were the two most important personalities in the establishment of a modern German nation state, though it remains a matter of debate how much importance one can attach to single personalities in interpreting major historical events. Ideologies as well as material circumstances have to be part of the interpretation; and both the rise of German nationalism and the coming of industrial society were clearly necessary factors in the unification of Germany. Nevertheless it is paradoxical that Napoleon was not a German, while Bismarck was above all a Prussian, whose relationship with the idea of Germany was far from straightforward. It is the purpose of this article to explain why Bismarck, a member of the pre-industrial Prussian aristocracy, played so central a role in the creation of the modern industrial German state.

Bismarck's Prussian Apprenticeship

Prussia was, like many European countries before the French Revolution, a dynastic state held together by its ruling family, the Hohenzollerns. In the late eighteenth century its population consisted of almost as many Polish as German speakers. On his father's side, Bismarck came from a long line of Junkers, the landowning aristocracy of the Prussian provinces east of the Elbe. The Hohenzollerns, a dynasty originally from South Germany, had from the seventeenth century taken the Junkers into their service, mainly in the army, and had by this and other means built their scattered territories into a major European power. Many of Bismarck's paternal forebears had, besides running their estates, served as generals in the Prussian army. On his mother's side, Bismarck came from a family of leading officials who had filled important positions under Frederick the Great and subsequent Prussian kings.

Bismarck was therefore destined for a career in the Prussian public service, but he was too self-willed and individualistic to fit into a bureaucratic existence. From the age of 24 to 32 he ran one of the family estates in Eastern Pomerania, but the life of a country squire did not satisfy him either. He was a man of exceptional intelligence, who read widely but unsystematically, and who, like many young men of the late Romantic period, modelled himself on the poet Lord Byron. He had a marvellous command of language and might have become a writer. Twice he fell in love with rich and well-connected young Englishwomen travelling on the Continent, but he eventually married another member of the Pomeranian aristocracy. Through her he got religion, having in his youth been a religious sceptic. Bismarck's God was, like his wife, fashioned for his own convenience, to provide comfort and security in his stormy existence as a dominant political figure. He was a man of imperious and domineering temperament, with an unquenchable thirst for power.

Bismarck sprang to prominence in the revolution of 1848 as a man of the extreme right. He and his associates among the Prussian conservatives wanted to defeat the revolution and restore the absolute monarchical regime that had existed in Prussia and most of Europe before 1848. In this they were largely successful, but the defeat of the liberals was not complete or irrevocable. From 1849 onwards Prussia had a semi-constitutional regime under which executive power remained with the King and the ministers appointed by him, but with strictly limited legislative and taxing powers vested in an elected parliament. The elections were held under a restricted three-tier franchise. The voters were divided into three classes, each paying the same amount of tax and having the same amount of voting power. Thus a very small number of men in the first class had as much voting power as the bulk of the population voting in the third class. Essentially this system remained in operation in Prussia until the overthrow of the monarchy at the end of the First World War. When the unification of Germany under Prussia took place in the 1860s, the Prussian system of having an executive minister responsible to the monarch and not dependent on the support of parliament was transferred to the newly created Reich. It was largely the work of Bismarck, when he had risen to the top as Prussian Prime Minister, that so much power remained in the hands of the monarchy in an age when the middle classes and even the masses were increasingly participating in politics. It was a feature that before 1914 distinguished Germany sharply from fully parliamentary states like Britain and France.

Prussia Versus Austria

Bismarck was duly rewarded for the role he had played as one of the leading younger men of the conservative faction in the stormy years from 1848 to 1850. In 1851 he was appointed Prussian envoy to the diet of the German Confederation in Frankfurt. It was a key post in the making of Prussian policy, especially in relation to the future shape of Germany. The attempts to establish either Grossdeutschland (Germany including Austria) or Kleindeutschland (Germany without Austria led by Prussia) had failed during the years of revolution and in 1850 the Confederation of nearly 40 German states called into being in 1815 was simply revived. Austria, as the premier German country, resumed the presidency. In the eight years he spent in Frankfurt between 1851 and 1859 Bismarck began to see clearly that this revived Confederation had no future. It proved impossible to restore the cooperation of the three conservative powers, Austria, Russia and Prussia, which, linked to the personal ascendancy of the Austrian chancellor Metternich, had until 1848 dominated the Confederation and Europe as a whole.

It became Bismarck's overriding preoccupation in Frankfurt to counteract Austria's attempt to continue her leading role in Germany and to assert Prussia's right to equality. He moved away from the views of his conservative Prussian associates who had sponsored his appointment to Frankfurt. They thought the fight against revolution was still the priority and that it required the solidarity of the conservative European powers once enshrined in the Holy Alliance. Although Prussian patriots, they respected the historic role of Austria and her Habsburg rulers in German affairs. They were legitimists, believing in the divine right of monarchs to rule, whether they were Prussian, Austrian or minor German princes. Bismarck, on the other hand, thought that the rivalry of Austria and Prussia might sooner or later have to be resolved by war. To him international relations were a matter of power and not ideology. He tried hard to persuade his mentors in Berlin that Prussia might have to consider an alliance with France, now again under Bonapartist rule. To the Prussian legitimists Napoleon I had been revolution incarnate and his nephew Napoleon III no less so.

Towards the end of his time in Frankfurt Bismarck also began to change his views about German nationalism. He had often in his letters referred to it contemptuously as 'the nationality swindle', but now he thought that the German national movement could be manipulated in the interests of enhancing Prussian power. The middle-class liberals who were the mainstay of the German national movement might become useful allies of the monarchy and the aristocracy. As the events of 1848 had shown, they were as afraid of the masses as the aristocracy. Bismarck's strength was his brutal, cynical realism that made short shrift of all illusions and was sceptical of all idealism; his weakness was that he thought everything and everybody could be manipulated for the purposes of Prussian, and ultimately his own, power.

The 'New Era'

In 1858 Prince William of Prussia, later the German Emperor William I, took over as Regent for his incapacitated brother Frederick William IV. It was the beginning of the 'New Era', when a slightly more liberal regime would prevail, compared with the repressive one installed after the failure of the revolution. Prussia would play a more positive role in reforming the German Confederation and meeting the aspirations of the German national movement. The reputation of being an ultra-reactionary still clung to Bismarck. Frederick William IV had once written against his name: 'to be used only when bayonets rule without restraint'. In the more liberal 'New Era' he was moved from Frankfurt to St. Petersburg, as Prussian ambassador to Russia, a promotion on paper but in fact a relegation. The next three years, 'in cold storage on the Neva', were a period of frustration for him. For years he had been talked about as a possible Prussian foreign minister, but nothing had ever come of it. For all his professions to the contrary, he was greedy for power.

Yet the 'New Era' rested on insecure foundations. The Regent, who became King on the death of his brother in January 1861, was not really prepared to weaken the prerogatives of the Prussian Crown, particularly in regard to its direct power of command over the army. It was through their army that the Hohenzollerns had been able to punch above their weight and make Prussia into a European great power. A constitutional conflict arose over the control of the army between the liberals in the Prussian Lower Chamber and the King. In spite of successive dissolutions of the chamber the number of liberals elected increased and a new and more assertive liberal party, the Progressives (Deutsche Fortschrittspartei), was founded. It wanted further liberalisation at home and progress in the unification of Germany abroad, and it was not prepared to surrender the powers over taxation and expenditure which gave it considerable control even in military affairs. The King thought his military powers were essential to Prussian kingship, which would otherwise become a parliamentary puppet. On the other hand, he was not prepared accept the advice of the reactionaries in his entourage to overturn the constitution by a coup d'etat. This, he feared, would result in civil war and bloodshed. He was on the point of abdicating, which would have brought to the throne his more liberal son, who was married to the daughter of Queen Victoria. Instead he was persuaded to appoint Bismarck prime minister and foreign minister, as the man who would be able to ride out this intractable situation.

Bismarck in Power

Bismarck's appointment was arguably one of the great turning points in history. He now proceeded along the lines he had foreshadowed in the innumerable letters and reports which he had showered upon monarch, ministers and courtiers in Berlin during his time as a diplomat. He, who had once been seen as an unreconstructed Junker reactionary, had begun to look like an unprincipled opportunist ready to make a pact with the devil for the sake of power.

What he now hoped to do was to make progress on the German question through a Prussian policy of strength and thereby to reconcile the Prussian liberals to the uncompromising stand of the King on the question of military control. This was the purpose of the famous 'iron and blood' speech, which he made within a week of taking office. What he meant to say was that if Prussia was to fulfil her role in leading Germany towards greater unity, it could not do so without an efficient army, such as the King's government was seeking to build. But the speech badly misfired, for to most liberal German nationalists such blood-curdling talk from a notorious Junker counter-revolutionary seemed an intolerable provocation. Heinrich von Treitschke, liberal-nationalist historian, later an unqualified admirer of Bismarck, wrote: 'When I hear such a shallow Junker like this Bismarck talk of iron and blood, through which he intends to bring Germany under his yoke, it seems to me not only base, but, even more than that, ridiculous.'

From such inauspicious beginnings Bismarck worked his way, in the next eight years, through masterly diplomacy and the prowess of the Prussian armies, to sensational triumphs. What had triumphed, however, was not German nationalism, let alone liberalism, but the Prussian military monarchy and with it Bismarck himself. Against the odds and in defiance of the spirit of the age, a semi-authoritarian system was perpetuated and foisted on the whole of Germany. But Bismarck was not really a man suited to old-fashioned monarchist absolutism. It was the half-way house that had come into existence after 1848 in Prussia that had given him his chance and it was a similar half-way house that he institutionalised in the constitution of the North German Confederation set up in 1867 and then extended to the German Reich in 1871. It was a complicated balance between monarchical and parliamentary power, between federalism and unitary control, which rendered Bismarck himself virtually indispensable as the only man who could master the system. In foreign affairs, too, he was a man who stood between the old-fashioned cabinet diplomacy that had controlled affairs in the past and the new-fangled intrusion of public opinion and the press, of what has been called the political mass market. The three wars he unleashed in 1864, 1866 and 1870 were limited wars with limited objectives, such as had always been used in the past to adjust European power relations. In the age of modern technology that was just dawning they became impossible to control.

The Bismarckian Paradox

Bismarck remained in power for another 20 years after the establishment of the German Reich. He was such a dominant figure that some historians have called his rule charismatic and bonapartist. As the heroic founder of the empire he had a charisma which no other public figure could match and which he could use to get his way. There is evidence that he was influenced by the way in which Napoleon III, whom he eventually

toppled, ruled in a fast-changing society racked by tensions between bourgeoisie and proletariat. Bismarck included in his constitution for the Reich a parliament (the Reichstag) elected by universal male suffrage, with no control over the executive but with the power to make laws and vote money. It existed alongside the parliament of Prussia, elected on the restricted three-tier franchise, and the parliaments of the other smaller German states. It has been called a system of killing parliamentarism through an excess of parliaments. It was meant to be the half-way house to keep Bismarck in control. In fact the Reichstag, representing the nation as a whole, quickly became the focus of German politics and Bismarck had to resort to increasingly desperate devices to stay on top of the game. He had set out to enhance Prussian power by making it a Greater Prussia which controlled all German land bar Austria. In fact it was the new German Reich that now engaged the loyalty of its population, and much of the old Prussia was swallowed up by the new empire. For this many of Bismarck's former friends among the Prussian Junkers found it hard to forgive him.

The Iron Chancellor, as he was often called, continued to be most successful in foreign affairs. Having taken Prussian power as possible, he declared the new Germany a satisfied power after 1871. He had no wish to make Germany into the predominant country in Europe, so long as her security was safeguarded. Nor was he interested in attaching to the Reich the many Germans, particularly in Eastern Europe, who remained outside the state established in 1870. The desire for hegemony in Europe and for world power were, however, precisely the aims of that strident German nationalism to which the creation of the Bismarckian Reich gave rise.

Lothar Gall, Bismarck's leading modern German biographer, gave the section of his book dealing with the period after 1870 the title 'the sorcerer's apprentice': he remembered the magic formula for bringing forth the flood, but forgot the words for calling it off. The Prussian Junker, who even as Chancellor spent months on end on his country estates, seeking refreshment in a way of life to which he felt he belonged, had laid the foundations of a powerful industrial society, with an ambitious and wealthy middle class and a vast working class milling in its ever expanding cities. Rule by charisma always reaches a limit and it can be disputed that Bismarck's methods were really bonapartist. He never sought to found his own political movement and went out of his way to avoid becoming dependent on any of the parties in the Reichstag. At the end of the day his power depended on retaining the confidence of his monarch, the system of rule in Prussia for generations. The old Emperor William I might complain that it was 'difficult to be emperor under such a chancellor', but the bond between him and his overmighty subject was never broken. Within less than two years of William's death, his grandson, the brash young Kaiser William II, dismissed the chancellor.

Legacy

Even in old age Bismarck's greed for power was such that he spent most of his remaining years seeking revenge. He was his own best propagandist and in his reminiscences he paints a pic-

Timeline

1815	(1 April)	Otto von Bismarck born on family estate of Schonhausen
		Prussia receives Rhine provinces at Congress of Vienna
		German Confederation founded
1840		Frederick William IV becomes King of Prussia
1847		Bismarck elected to the United Diet of Prussia
1848	(March)	revolution breaks out in Berlin
	(December)	after crushing of revolution King imposes a constitution
1849	(April)	Frederick William IV refuses imperial German Crown offered by Frankfurt Parliament
1850	(December)	Punctation of Olmutz ends Prussian attempts to unify Germany
1851	(May)	Bismarck appointed Prussian Envoy to the Diet of the re-established German Confederation in Frankfurt
1854-6		Crimean War
1858	(October)	Prince William of Prussia becomes Regent in place of his incapacitated brother
1859	(January)	Bismarck appointed Prussian Ambassador to Russia
	(July)	Peace of Villafranca ends Franco-Austrian war in Italy
1862	(September)	Bismarck becomes Prime Minister and Foreign Minister of Prussia
1864		Prussia and Austria at war with Denmark over Schleswig-Holstein
1866		War between Prussia and Austria
1867		North German Confederation inaugurated
1870		Franco-Prussian War
1871	(18 January)	German Empire proclaimed at Versailles
1879		Bismarck drops free trade and introduces protective tariffs
1888	(March)	death of William I
	(June)	William II becomes Emperor
1890	(March)	Bismarck forced from office
1898	(30 July)	death of Bismarck

ture of how he single-handedly saved the House of Hohenzollern from descending into the quagmire of constitutional monarchy or even revolution. The disenchantment with his autocratic rule, made rigid by old age, that had enabled the Kaiser to dismiss him, was soon forgotten. More than ever he acquired heroic stature and Bismarck monuments were erected all over Germany.

Yet the Reich founded by him survived his death by only 20 years. The semi-constitutional system of government that he perpetuated proved ill-adapted to the needs of a modern industrial urban society. On the eve of the First World War Germany had the largest socialist party in Europe, which was also the largest party in the Reichstag, yet it was excluded from any share in power. It is just one indication of the extent to which the economic and social development of Germany, which was by contemporary standards very advanced, was out of phase with its political development. Bismarck's sensational success in unifying the country blinded most of his countrymen to the political retardation he had imposed upon them.

Further Readings

Edward Crankshaw, Bismarck (Macmillan, 1981)

Lothar Gall, Bismarck: The White Revolutionary, 2 vols. (Allen & Unwin, 1986)

Werner Richter, Bismarck (Macdonald, 1964)

Bruce Waller, Bismarck (Blackwell, 1997)

D.G. Williamson, Bismarck and Germany 1862–1890 (Longman Seminar Studies, 1998)

Otto Pflanze, Bismarck and the Development of Germany, 3 vols. (Princeton University Press, 1990)

Wolfgang J. Mommsen, Imperial Germany 1867–1918: Politics, Culture and Society in an Authoritarian State (Edward Arnold, 1995)

Hans-Ulrich Wehler, The German Empire 1871–1918 (Berg, 1984)

William Carr, The Origins of the German Wars of Unification (Longman, 1991)

James J. Sheehan, German Liberalism in the Nineteenth Century (Methuen, 1978)

EDGAR FEUCHTWANGER has taught modern German and British history at the University of Southampton. He is the author of Imperial Germany 1850–1918 (Routledge, 2001) and is working on a biography of Bismarck.

Napoleon III: 'Hero' or 'Grotesque Mediocrity'?

Roger Price examines the career of Louis-Napoleon, the nephew of Napoleon Bonaparte, and his position in French historiography.

ROGER PRICE

The Man

Karl Marx, in the 1869 preface to his article on The Eighteenth Brumaire of Louis Bonaparte, a brilliant piece of political journalism written in 1852, described his purpose as being to 'demonstrate how the class struggle in France created circumstances and relations that made it possible for a grotesque mediocrity to play a hero's part'. The 'mediocrity' in question was a certain Louis-Napoleon Bonaparte, born on 20 April 1808, the son of Louis, appointed King of Holland by his brother Napoleon I, and of Hortense de Beauharnais, daughter of the Emperor's first wife Josephine. As a result of the couple's separation and the exile of the Bonaparte family from France, Louis-Napoleon was brought up by his mother at the chateau of Arenenberg in Switzerland, surrounded by memories of Empire. In addition to childhood socialisation, another formative influence on the young prince was to be the unfortunate experience in 1830-31 of joining his elder brother Napoleon-Louis in the disastrous struggle in Italy against Austrian occupation and the temporal power of the Papacy, during which, after both princes contracted measles, the elder died.

Another death, that of Napoleon's son, the so-called Duc de Reichstadt in 1832, left Louis-Napoleon determined to assert his claim to be the great Emperor's heir. As a result of his family background and upbringing he possessed an intense sense of personal destiny and faith in his historical mission. In his determination to become guardian of the Napoleonic tradition he combined the outlook of a romantic mystic with the instincts of a political opportunist. His friend from childhood, Madame Cornu, would describe his 'mission' as a 'devotion first to the Napoleonic dynasty, and then to France ... His duty to his dynasty is to perpetuate it. His duty to France is to give her influence abroad and prosperity at home'. To achieve these objectives he would, of course, first have to gain power.

Otherwise farcical attempts to win the support of the military garrisons at Strasbourg in 1836 and Boulogne in 1840 at least associated him with a powerful popular cult of Napoleonic glory and prosperity. Louis-Napoleon also published his own ideas in a series of pamphlets which enjoyed wide circulation. These included Les Reflections politiques (1832), Les idees napoleoniennes (1839), and L'Extinction du pauperisme (1844). Although the presentation was vague and imprecise and full of contradictions, these writings, reflecting the utopian optimism of the 1830-40s, were to serve as his 'guiding ideas' (Plessis). They were characterised by a determination to eliminate the 'party' divisions which he believed were responsible for political instability. Although sharing with conservatives a determination to safeguard the social order, Louis-Napoleon was distinguished by his apparent commitment to 'social reform' and to 'democracy'. In a restored empire, the Emperor would initiate policy, but periodic plebiscites would be used to approve the regime's general policies, as well as to re-affirm the almost mystical link between the Emperor and 'his' people. The powers of the elected assembly would be reduced to a minimum.

Prince-President of the Republic

Louis-Napoleon's opportunity came as a result of an intense crisis, beginning with poor harvests and agitation for electoral reform and culminating in the revolution of February 1848 which established the Second Republic and 'universal' (i.e. manhood) suffrage. Continued social and political tension characterised by a renewed insurrection in Paris in June, and its brutal military repression by a republican government, ensured that as a result of disappointed expectations, or in the case of conservatives of fear of further revolution, substantial parts of the population were prepared to contemplate the election of a potential 'saviour'. This was the strength of Bonapartism—to be able to appear as 'all things to all men'. One Bonapartist manifesto appealed to 'suffering France' where:

> The unfortunate die of hunger;
> The worker is without work;
> The cultivator is no longer able
> to dispose of his crops;
> The merchant sells nothing;

The proprietor no longer
receives his rent;
The capitalist no longer dares to
invest, lacking security.

It promised that 'The nephew of the great man, with his magic, will give us security, and save us from misery'. Reluctantly supported by conservative politicians, Louis-Napoleon's victory in the presidential election in December 1848 was nevertheless overwhelming. He gained 74.2 per cent of the votes cast (5,534,520). His leading opponent, the republican General Cavaignac, obtained only 19.5 per cent (1,448,302). In Paris the successful candidate gained 58 per cent of the vote, with higher proportions in the popular quartiers for the supposedly 'socialist' author of the Extinction du pauperisme. However, in a still predominantly agrarian country, it was peasant support which would remain the basis of Bonaparte's electoral strength for decades to come.

The Austrian diplomat Apponyi warned conservative political leaders that, in this situation, 'if they believe themselves able … to dominate him, they are badly mistaken'. More dramatically, the journalist Martinelli warned that 'whether you wish it or not',

Bonaparte would be king in
opinion first, and later in reality.
The logic of facts leads there. In a
review some regiments will cry:
Vive I'Empereur! The suburbs will
reply to them and all will be said;
we will be just like Spanish
America, subordinate to the
pleasures of the multitude and
the soldiery. A glorious and
fortunate destiny!

This unique election of a monarchical pretender, of a man with complete faith in his historical 'mission' and, once having gained power, determined to retain it, had made a coup d'etat almost inevitable. This was the point at which the construction of 'the political system of Napoleon III' (Zeldin) might be said to have commenced.

Initially Louis-Napoleon sought collaboration with conservative elites in the re-establishment of social order through increasingly intense repression of the democrate-socialiste left, and with the Roman Catholic Church in the inculcation of 'moral order' through education. Increasingly, however, he also asserted his own independence as head of government by appointing ministers and officials responsible to himself, whilst ignoring protests from deputies in the National Assembly elected in May 1849. Unable to secure the two-thirds majority in the Assembly which would have allowed him to stand for re-election in 1852, the President was well-placed to employ the bureaucracy and army, in which his supporters had already been placed in key positions, to launch a carefully planned coup on 2 December 1851.

In Paris only very limited resistance occurred, due to preventive arrests and to obvious military preparedness. Few workers were prepared to risk a repetition of the bloodbath of June 1848 to defend the rights of a conservative assembly against a President who presented himself as the defender of popular sovereignty and enjoyed the prestige that went with the name Bonaparte. The predominantly conservative deputies who gathered in the town hall of the 10th arrondissement refused to rally to a president who had broken his constitutional oath, but they were unwilling to contemplate more than symbolic resistance to a coup d'etat which promised to establish the strong, authoritarian government which they believed was necessary to end the prospect of a socialist electoral victory in 1852. As the businessman Paul Benoist d'Azy pointed out in a letter to his father:

we are caught between the
regime of the sabre which has
violated the constitution it was
sworn to uphold and the
hideous socialists … We will
support the existing government
… if it can persuade us to forget
its origins by means of energetic
action against the socialists and
vigorous encouragement of
business.

Although easily crushed, more substantial resistance in rural areas of central France, particularly the southeast, was used both to justify the coup and a reign of terror directed at republicans. On 20 December a plebiscite was held to sanction the extension of the Prince-President's authority. The electorate was asked to vote on whether 'the people wish to maintain the authority of Louis-Napoleon and delegate to him the powers necessary to establish a constitution'. This appeal to popular sovereignty was to be a characteristic of the new regime. Louis-Napoleon was determined to secure a large majority as a means of legitimising his actions. It was made clear to all officials, including village mayors, that their continued employment depended on enthusiastic campaigning. The basic theme was the choice between 'civilisation and barbarism, society and chaos'. In place of the era of disorder which had opened in 1848, a new period of order, peace, and prosperity was promised. Nationally 7,500,000 voted 'yes', 640,000 'no', and 1,500,000 abstained.

Ominously, opposition was concentrated in the major cities. Coercion was widespread but primarily the result was due to the immense popularity of the Prince-President. In the countryside he was perceived to be the only safeguard against renewed revolution and, additionally, offered protection against the restoration of the ancient regime. The following November, after a carefully orchestrated campaign, during which Bonaparte promised peace, order and reconciliation and which culminated in a triumphant return to the capital, where he was greeted by enthusiastic crowds and processed to the Tuileries Palace under a succession of triumphal arches, 7,824,000 voters approved the re-establishment of the hereditary empire, which was proclaimed on 2 December 1852, the anniversary of the Battle of Austerlitz.

The Second Empire

The new regime's origins in a coup d'etat, its authoritarian and repressive character, together with its ignominious collapse in the war of 1870, ensured that subsequently it received, and indeed deserved, a bad press. By the 1930s the Second Empire was being described as a precursor of fascism. The system of government established following the coup was certainly constructed with the intention of strengthening the powers of the head of state at the expense of representative institutions. The Emperor appointed ministers and senior officials and assumed responsibility for decision making. The Senate was packed with supporters, the role of the elected lower house—the Corps legislatif—with around 260 members, was initially viewed as essentially consultative, although as its consent was required for legislation, it represented a potential centre of opposition. For this reason its members were selected carefully and every effort was made to determine the outcome of elections through manipulation, coercion and propaganda associating the regime with prosperity and social order.

Nevertheless, the decision to retain manhood suffrage clearly distinguished the Second Empire from previous monarchical regimes. This was a regime which owed its legitimacy not to divine right but to the popular will. In time, as fear of revolution declined and repression eased, the social elites who had been deprived of power by the coup were able to make use of their dominant position in the administration and Corps legislatif to criticise the restrictions on political liberty as well as the Emperor's adventurous foreign policy which had in 1859 led to the collapse of the Papal States and in 1860 to the negotiation of a commercial treaty with Britain. Catholics and protectionists felt betrayed.

Unlike his predecessors, Napoleon was prepared to adapt and to engage in the difficult process of regime liberalisation, in spite of warnings that he risked opening the flood gates. The gradual extension of political liberties, culminating in the establishment of a liberal empire in 1870, represented concession to liberal criticism from the social elite rather than to the growing republican movement. As well as much greater freedom of speech the Emperor accepted that ministers should be responsible to parliament as well as to himself. Yet, as the elect of the people, Napoleon retained considerable personal power, including the right to dissolve parliament and appeal to the people by means of elections or plebiscites, the authority to negotiate treaties and declare war. The new constitution was approved by plebiscite on 8 May 1870 by 7,350,000 votes to 1,538,000. The future of the dynasty appeared to have been assured.

This political liberalisation during the 1860s has, in a more recent 'revisionist' historiography, served to excuse previous authoritarianism. Historians have also focused more on what were perceived to be the regime's positive achievements. Concern with French 'backwardness' and economic stagnation during the inter-war period and with the problems of reconstruction following the Second World War encouraged the search for inspiration in the Imperial regime's 'technocratic' achievements and particularly the reconstruction of Paris, the creation of a modern transportation infrastructure, the reduction of tariff pro-

Timeline

1808	20 April	Louis-Napoleon was born in Paris
1832		Death of Duc de Reichstadt, and hence Louis-Napoleon was now "heir" to the Emperor Napoleon
1836		abortive attempt by Louis-Napoleon to lead rising against the July Monarchy
1840		another failed attempt, leading to his imprisonment
1848	February	revolution in Paris; King Louis Phillippe fled
	June	barricades erected in Paris, revolt suppressed
	December	Louis-Napoleon elected President of the Second Republic
1851	2 December	Louis-Napoleon extended his presidential authority with a coup
	20 December	Plebiscite endorsed the authority of the Prince-President
1852	2 December	Second Empire began
1853		married the Empress Eugénie de Montijo
1859		French victories at Magenta and Sotterino, before peace with Austria made without consulting Piedmont
1860		Cobden-Chevalier free trade treaty with Britian
1870	8 May	new, more liberal constitution approved by plebiscite
	19 July	France declared war on Prussia
	2 September	French defeat at Sedan; Louis-Napoleon captured and imprisoned in Germany
	4 September	Republic proclaimed in Paris
1873		Louis-Napoleon died in Chislehurst, Kent, where he had spent the last two years of his life.

tection and, more broadly, the establishment of the conditions for rapid economic growth, for which the regime had claimed most, and deserved some, of the credit. This revisionism culminated in 1990 in the publication, by the conservative politician Philippe Seguin, of a study entitled Louis-Napoleon le grand and in the inauguration of the Place Napoleon III in Paris by Seguin, flanked by Jacques Chirac—then the city's mayor—and the current Prince Napoleon.

Conclusion

'Revisionism' has probably gone too far. In a perceptive comment in his notebook, Ludovic Halevy, the librettist, who was also responsible for preparing the minutes of the Corps legislatif, wrote following the announcement of the plebiscite results in 1870: 'Too many Yes votes. The Emperor will believe that this is still the France of 1852 and do something stupid'. The decision to go to war against Prussia in July perfectly illustrates the danger of allowing a single individual too much power. In order to avoid loss of face, Napoleon chose to engage in an extremely high risk strategy, although he realised that the French army was not ready. On 28 July, this sick and prematurely aged war-lord, unable to sit on his horse or to concentrate for long periods, left Paris to assume command of his armies. On 2 September an army under his direct command was forced to capitulate at Sedan in eastern France. On the 4th a Republic was again proclaimed in the capital. No one was prepared to defend a regime responsible for such a catastrophic failure.

Assessing the impact of 'historical personalities' is never easy. As Ian Kershaw points out in his study of Adolf Hitler—another political figure supported by conservative leaders who believed they could use him—'Biography ... runs the natural risk of over-personalising complex historical developments, over-emphasising the role of the individual in shaping and determining events, ignoring or playing down the social and political context in which these actions took place'. In Napoleon III's case this context was established by the intense mid-century crisis, culminating in the 1848 Revolution and the counter-revolutionary innovations in government which followed, by the opportunities provided and the strains imposed by accelerating industrialisation and urbanisation, as well as by the growing Prussian threat to the European balance of power. A successful response to such complex and diverse problems required leadership qualities of an extremely high order which very few would have been able to provide.

Further Readings

M. Agulhon, The Republican Experiment, 1848–52 (Cambridge University Press) 1983; S. Hazareesingh, From Subject to Citizen: The Second Empire and the Emergence of Modern French Democracy (Princeton University Press) 1998; J. McMillan, Napoleon III (Longman) 1991; A. Plessis, The Rise and Fall of the Second Empire (Cambridge University Press) 1985; R. Price, The French Second Republic: a social history (Batsford) 1972; R. Price, Napoleon III and the Second Empire (Routledge) 1997; R. Price, The French Second Empire: an anatomy of political power (Cambridge University Press) 2001; W. Smith, Second Empire and Commune: France 1848–71 (Longman) 1985; T. Zeldin, The Political System of Napoleon III (Oxford University Press) 1958.

ROGER PRICE is Professor of History at the University of Wales, Aberystwyth. His books include The French Second Republic: a social history (1972); The Modernization of Rural France: Communication networks and agricultural market structures (1983); A Social History of Nineteenth-Century France (1987); The Revolutions of 1848 (1988); A Concise History of France (1993); Napoleon III and the Second Empire (1997); and The French Second Empire: an anatomy of political power (2001).

The Russians Shall Not Have Constantinople

ROMAN GOLICZ

In the late eighteenth century English politicians began to question what would happen to the Balkans if and when the Ottoman empire disappeared. For as long as the declining Ottoman empire remained in control of the eastern Mediterranean and the Russian empire restricted itself to expansion into Siberia, Britain's naval pre-eminence was unthreatened. However, in the Russo-Turkish war of 1787-92, Russia increased her Black Sea possessions, established a route to the Caspian Sea and expanded into Central Asia. Britain now feared that further Russo-Turkish conflicts might result in the collapse of the Ottoman empire: control of the Black Sea, the Dardanelles, and the Aegean Sea would then fall to Russia who could block Britain's Mediterranean trade and even threaten British waters.

On April 12th, 1791, a cartoon was published in London entitled 'An Imperial Stride!' depicting Catherine the Great as the Giant Bolster of Cornish legend, only with one foot in Russia and the other in Constantinople. The image recalls the empress's epic tour to the Crimea in 1787 when she entered Kherson through an arch inscribed 'The Way to Constantinople'. As Byzantium, this city had been the heart of the eastern Christian empire. After it fell to the Ottomans in 1453, the metropolitanate of Moscow was raised to a patriarchy, making it the spiritual repository of Byzantium until it could be returned to its historical home. This religio-cultural imperative was not to be underestimated but was officially separate from the political aspirations of Russians to reach Constantinople. However, this was not the case with many ultra-nationalists such as the Slavophils, who resented outside interference in Russian affairs, and the Pan-Slavists, who urged a broad political union of all Slav nations; both groups agitated for Russian possession of Constantinople.

The Napoleonic Wars (1803-15) demonstrated that the British navy ruled the waves. But through the nineteenth century this position became less steadfast, and by 1870 Russia possessed the third most powerful navy in the world, after Britain and France. The Ottoman empire, meanwhile, was being maintained as a barely living political entity by the 'balance of power'. Britain had formulated this nebulous policy during the Congress of Vienna (1815) as a means of maintaining European stability principally by denying to any one of the eight signatory powers

advantageous access to 'neutral waters'. But as the century wore on, it was gradually overtaken by a more sell-interested, unilateral stance based on resistance to those who threatened Britain's first ranking position in post-Napoleonic Europe.

Britain therefore rejected as impractical and dangerous a move in 1853 by Tsar Nicholas I for Britain and Russia to dismember Turkey and share the spoils. At the outbreak of the eighth Russo-Turkish ('Crimean') War in 1854 it was not an altruistic sense of a threat to European stability that caused Britain's participation in the conflict against Russia, rather it was the perceived threat of a Russian-engineered destabilisation to British interests in the East.

The ensuing Treaty of Paris of 1856 demanded rectification of the frontier of Bessarabia 'in order more fully to secure the Freedom of the navigation of the Danube'. These cessions were to be annexed by the principality of Moldavia, which with its neighbour Wallachia was placed under the suzerainty of Turkey under the protection of the six other signatory Powers. More importantly, Article XI 'in perpetuity interdicted to the Flag of War' the Black Sea, neutralising it and throwing it open to mercantile vessels of all nations. Thus Constantinople was effectively prevented from becoming a prize worth fighting for, and this was thought to have settled the matter of Russian expansion towards it.

Tsar Alexander II, who had succeeded Nicholas in 1855 and had brought about an early peace, appeared before the world as a liberal autocrat concerned for the welfare of his subjects (he abolished serfdom in 1861) while encouraging a benign foreign policy. In fact the days of an iron-fisted autocracy in Russia when the Tsar's word was absolute were fast disappearing. Although he did not set up representative political institutions, the Tsar effectively introduced accountability to his ministers through a willingness to abandon some of the absolutist autocracy of his predecessors.

This development was not fully appreciated in Britain. Thus when Prince Alexander Gorchakov, the Tsar's influential minister for foreign affairs, audaciously repudiated the Black Sea neutrality clause of the Treaty of Paris in October 1870; he did so with a degree of independence from the Tsar thought impossible in London. In fact, he undoubtedly formulated and initiated the policy, At Westminster it was pointed out that any unilateral violation of the principal treaty by Russia would constitute a *casus belli*. English outrage was exacerbated as Britain had only recently refused to consider a legal revision of the Black Sea clauses as Russia's price for its inclusion (at Britain's invitation) in a European congress following Prussia's war against France.

The signatories of the 1856 Paris Treaty, had to be cautious in their response to Gorchakov's actions: the fledgling Third Republic in France was in turmoil in the period of the Paris Commune; Prussia had not yet a navy to speak of. To all intents and purposes the Eastern Question had become a specifically Anglo-Russian problem. British interests in the Balkans derived from wider economic pursuits in India via the Eastern Mediterranean. In 1858 the British Government had taken direct control over Indian affairs. Since 1869 the Suez Canal had provided it with a direct route to India. Britain needed to secure the shipping routes which passed through areas, like Suez, that were nominally Turkish.

Gorchakov refused to retract. Rejecting a suggestion by the German Chancellor Bismarck for a Black Sea conference at St Petersburg, the British Prime Minister William Gladstone and Foreign Secretary Lord Granville accepted a London date of March 13th, 1871, for the German proposal where representatives from Britain, Austria, France, Germany, Italy, Russia and Turkey agreed that no power could repudiate any part of a multilateral treaty without the full consent of the other signatories. A new article restated the closure of the Dardanelles and the Bosporous to foreign warships but enabled Turkey to open the Straits in peacetime to warships belonging to those nations with whom it was friendly. In practical terms this included British warships and excluded Russian ones.

Alexander's role in Gorchakov's repudiation remains unclear: he had at least approved it by default. The powerful Pan-Slavist movement in Russia that sought Slavic hegemony throughout Eastern Europe and a return to Constantinople ('Tsargrad') was a force against which the Tsar had to struggle with care. Indeed, Pan-Slavists represented by leading military figures such as General Mikhail Chernaev, and Slavophiles with Fedor Dostoevskii as a figurehead, considered Alexander II a suspicious figure overly concerned with Western matters rather than with the rebuilding of Holy Mother Russia according to their medieval view of a vast Russian empire incorporating all Slavic peoples with Constantinople as their spiritual capital.

Meanwhile, Gorchakov's repudiation was allowed to stand simply because Granville felt that Britain was unable to effect a retraction without the support of the other Powers, which was not forthcoming. The London Conference had been a victory on paper only and could affect future treaties but not those ratified in the past. Continued Russian expansion into Central Asia towards Afghanistan and then, according to some, into India was one of the more absurd delusions nurtured by English pundits. But Gladstone's administration (1868-74) was wary of embroiling Britain in a war against Russia. Border issues over Afghanistan were hammered out between Gorchakov and Granville to the satisfaction of both, and Russian occupation of the strategic Uzbeg town of Khiva was accepted on the assurance that this would be temporary. When Khiva was formally annexed in October 1873, the British Government remained impassive.

Many Slavophiles were concerned when in July 1873 it was announced that the Tsar's only daughter would marry Queen Victoria's second son, the Duke of Edinburgh. The match had not been engineered as a political union but it was soon perceived potentially as such both in Russia and Britain. Certainly statements made by the British Press and both Houses of Parliament following the announcements of the engagement and the wedding in January 1874 reveal a regressive nostalgia for an era when nations could secure peace through international marriages. The post-marital euphoria, nevertheless, enabled Alexander to undertake a successful state visit to London in May 1874 in a period that seemed to herald a rapprochement. However, within three years of the royal marriage, Anglo-Russian relations were once more on the rocks.

February 1874 saw Benjamin Disraeli in Downing Street. The new prime minister's politics, rooted in an amoral geopolitical attitude, perfectly suited the mentality of a nation approaching the cusp of Victorian imperial grandeur. In Russia, meanwhile, Slavophiles and Pan-Slavists were increasing pressure for Russian expansion towards Constantinople.

In November 1875, Disraeli purchased all the shares in the Suez Canal owned by the impoverished Khedive of Egypt, and Britain now felt that it had a moral right to consider the canal Anglo-French property. Disraeli also consolidated British prestige through his Royal Titles Bill granting to Queen Victoria the title Empress of India on May 1st, 1876. Regarded by many in England as preposterous, it was meant to demonstrate to the world in general and Russia in particular that India was a British possession of especial significance whose violation would not be tolerated.

The following day, in the town of Panagyurishte in central Bulgaria, Bulgar Slavs rose against their Turkish overlords, prompting severe reprisals and leaving thousands killed. Gladstone made his position clear in his pamphlet *Bulgarian Horrors and the Question of the East,* a denunciation of Turkish misrule fairly representing the Liberal *view* in September 1876. Disraeli responded equally clearly by denying that the atrocities had occurred, since news of them had reached him not through official diplomatic sources but via the popular press, dismissing them as 'coffee-house babble'.

A wider Balkan revolt against Turkish rule was now feared, destabilising the region. A threatening protest drafted in Berlin on May 12th, 1876, by Germany, Russia and Austria-Hungary was delivered to Turkey, demanding an armistice between Turkey and the Balkan insurgents and an agreement to a consular commission set up to oversee internal reforms. The Berlin Memorandum, as this was known, was also intended as a peace proposal between Turkey and the Balkan insurgents to which Britain was expected to assent without becoming involved. Suspicions of Russia's involvement in anything to do with the political future of Turkey, Disraeli persuaded his Cabinet not to take a 'leap in the dark' by assenting. France and Italy had also been expected to assent without involvement, and Disraeli employed this European anomaly to good effect until both France and Italy finally submitted their assent to the Berlin Memoran-

Treaties and Conferences 1871–1918

1871:   **March 13th,** London Conference.

1873:   **October 15th,** Khiva annexed by Russia.

1875:   **July 1st,** uprising of Christians in Herzegovina.

1876:   **May 1st,** uprising of Bulgar Slavs crushed by Turks. May 11th-12th, 'Berlin Memorandum' of Germany, Russia and Austria-Hungary proposing armistice between Turkey and insurgents. Rejected by Disraeli (May 16th).

    July 1st, Serbia declares war on Turkey.

    July 2nd, Montenegro declares war on Turkey.

    September 5th, Gladstone publishes Bulgarian Horrors pamphlet.

    December 23rd, Start of Conference of Constantinople.

1877:   **January 20th,** Turkey rejects proposals for internal reform and extensive Balkan provisions. The Conference dissolves.

    April 24th, Russia declares war on Turkey.

    May 16th, Romania declares war on Turkey.

    June 30th, Mediterranean Fleet sent to Besika Bay.

    December 14th, Serbia restates previous declaration of war against Turkey.

1878:   **January 23rd,** Disraeli orders fleet to Dardanelles.

    January 31st, a defeated Turkey agrees to armistice at Adrianople.

    February 8th, British fleet enters Turkish waters. Russia warns Britain that entry into the Straits would precipitate Russian occupation of Constantinople. British fleet anchors in front of Constantinople. Russia does not carry out its threat.

    February 24th, demonstrations against Russia in Hyde Park end in violence.

    March 3rd, Russia arranges unilateral victorious Pan-Slavist peace treaty with Turkey at San Stefano.

    March 25th, Russia rejects British proposals to lay San Stefano before a European congress.

    March 27th, Disraeli mobilises the Reserves and calls up 7,000 Indian troops to Malta. War with Russia widely anticipated.

    June 12th-July 12th, Congress of Berlin.

1880:   **April 22nd,** Disraeli resigns as leader of the Conservatives after a huge Liberal majority based on Gladstone's pacific and moral judgment during the recent Eastern crisis.

1885-86:   considerable Anglo-Russian tension over the unification of Bulgaria. Further fears of Russian expansion towards Constantinople and also British India.

1914:   **August 2nd,** secret treaty between Turkey and Germany securingTurkish neutrality in the forth coming war. **September 5th,** London Agreement by which no member of the 'Triple entente' (Britain, France, and Russia) may reach separate peace treaties with the Central Powers.

    November 4th, Britain declares war on Turkey after German/Turkish attack on Russian warships.

    November 5th, France declares war on Turkey.

1915:   **March 14th,** Russia, Britain, and France agree to a return of Constantinople and the Bosporous to Russia in the event of victory with full co-operation of Russia.

1918:   **March 3rd,** Bolshevik-German peace treaty of Brest-Litovsk requested by Lenin renders 1915 agreement null and void. When the matter is raised with him, Lenin declares that the 'New Russia' is no longer concerned with Constantinople.

---

dum. Now isolated, Disraeli again demonstrated his prioritising of British above European interests. On May 25th, the Mediterranean Squadron, under the overall command of the Duke of Edinburgh, was mobilised and sent to Besika Bay off the Dardanelles, as a precautionary measure.

Further anti-Turkish revolts by Serbia and Montenegro provoked Russian involvement, in the form of Pan-Slavist propaganda and unsanctioned military intervention. On October 4th, Gorchakov accepted a British proposal for an armistice between Turkey and the Balkan insurgents as a prelude to a major conference, but Turkish unwillingness to co-operate resulted in a Russian retraction. Accordingly, Disraeli, who believed that the Russian retraction from a peace conference concealed further military

expansion southward, proposed to pre-empt a possible Russian occupation of Constantinople by installing a British presence there in the form of the Mediterranean Squadron. Faced with a conflict he had not sought, Alexander II implemented a six-week armistice with Turkey and accepted Britain's proposal for a conference of ambassadors at Constantinople.

On November 10th, Disraeli delivered a careless speech at the Guildhall, which was widely interpreted as bellicose while Alexander spoke in Moscow restating Gorchakov's position—that Russia would take independent action against Turkey if the Sultan's intransigence over Britain's proposal for an armistice failed to settle the matter at the proposed conference. But Disraeli's speech had settled one matter already: Alexander wrote to his daughter proclaiming that he would never forgive Disraeli for his speech, converting (as did his daughter) to a belief in upholding and cultivating the principles of Gladstonian Liberalism in Britain. The Duchess of Edinburgh in fact befriended and supported Gladstone after 1877 and had no further contact with Disraeli.

With the consent of all the powers, the Constantinople Conference opened on December 23rd, 1876. 'I do not want war', the Tsar wrote to his daughter, 'and everyone, and especially myself, will be very happy if the conference … will resolve matters peacefully'. But, as he had feared, Turkish intransigence over Britain's proposal for an armistice made conflict inevitable. The conference collapsed and Russia declared war on Turkey on April 24th, 1877.

Britain announced its neutrality on May 6th, but with the important condition that should Russia threaten her interests in the Persian Gulf, the Suez Canal, the Straits or at Constantinople, such violation would result in the automatic abrogation of neutrality. It was also made clear that Britain would not stand aside indefinitely if Russia did not soon propose equitable peace terms to Turkey.

But the war dragged on, belying British military 'experts' who had predicted Russian occupation of Constantinople within nine weeks. Disraeli's Cabinet was much divided over what action to take. Although it was eventually agreed that any occupation of Constantinople by Russia would be temporary, Disraeli informed Queen Victoria that a unanimous Cabinet had agreed that any occupation of Constantinople would be the *casus belli* for Britain.

The Queen was in accord with her prime minister, five times threatening to abdicate between April 1877 and January 1878 if aggressive measures were not taken, urging 'the importance of the tsar knowing that we will not let him have Constantinople!' News of the fall of Plevna, on the Danube, to Russia after a six-month campaign reached London on December 11th; three days later the Queen visited the prime minister at his private residence, something that she had not done since 1843. 'Some wise persons at home and more abroad … will see in the trip an event pregnant with portentous meaning', noted *The Times*.

Also prompted by the fall of Plevna, against considerable Cabinet opposition, on December 13th, Disraeli succeeded in proposing a war credit of £6 million and an early recall of Parliament to discuss it, having raised the credit from two to five and then six million. However, his suggestion of a recall on January 7th, had to be extended by ten days in order to appear less belligerent, while the confrontational Queen's Speech that he had written with Victoria's approval would have to be toned down. The 'Dictator of Downing Street' often had to be restrained by those within Iris Cabinet who opposed any action that might precipitate a war with Russia, led by lords Carnarvon (Colonial Secretary), Salisbury (India Secretary), and Derby (Foreign Secretary): on October 5th, 1877, Disraeli had proposed British mediation with exclusively Turkish peace terms to be laid before the Tsar; if he rejected them, Britain should consider itself free to intercede on Turkey's behalf. The Cabinet had rejected this astonishing combination of mediation and threat.

On January 16th, 1878, faced with military defeat, Turkey proposed peace terms at Adrianople. An armistice was arranged for January 31st, but Russian forces nonetheless continued to progress towards Constantinople. On February 9th, *The Illustrated London News* announced with relief that 'The war between Russia and Turkey is over'; one week later it was forced to admit that this had been premature: 'There is mystery everywhere … anticipations of today become obsolete on the morrow'.

Disraeli reacted on February 12th by once more ordering the entire Mediterranean Squadron to move from Besika Bay into the Dardanelles, prompting the resignation of two Cabinet colleagues, including Foreign Secretary Lord Derby (who was persuaded to return following certain assurances by Russia and the subsequent withdrawal of half the fleet). With the credit passed on February 7th, part of the remaining fleet entered the Straits and anchored Constantinople. Gorchakov had slated previously that Russia would not attempt a passage through the Straits without British provocation.

Derby believed that sending ships to Constantinople would provide that very provocation and that this was in breech of the agreement by which no foreign vessel of war was permitted to enter these waters while Turkey (which had not given Disraeli permission to act as he had) was at peace. An armistice, it was argued in return, was not a peace treaty. The stage was set for a stalemate.

Many books and pamphlets had already appeared on the most fiercely debated political issue of the century when in January 1878 George William Hunt provided the music-hall singer The Great Macdermott with a 'War Song'. Its chorus would introduce a neologism into the English language and herald unprecedented public participation in the crisis:

> We don't want to fight, but
> by jingo if we do,
>
> We've got the ships, we've
> got the men, and got
> the money too;
>
> We've fought the bear
> before, and while
> we're Britons true,
>
> The Russians shall not have
> Constantinople.

It would be impossible to do justice here to the influence of this inspired piece of popular sabre-rattling and what followed at the height of 'Jingomania' (January to April) in 'Jingoborough' (London) and elsewhere. It is sufficient to record that, as the most outspoken Turcophobe and opponent of any action against Russia, Gladstone's windows were smashed and his carriage turned over in the street as gangs of Jingoes roamed the streets with clubs, chains, and switches shouting 'By Jingo!', the 'party anthem of the warmongers' as Herbert Asquith later recalled it. They disrupted Liberal meetings, carried Turkish diplomatic staff through the streets on their shoulders, made public bonfires out of pacific propaganda topped with effigies of Gladstone, and picketed both the Russian embassy and consulate while hurling abuse at their occupants. The Duchess of Edinburgh had had to leave England by an arrangement agreed between Queen Victoria and Tsar Alexander, and she did not return for almost two years. On February 19th, an accord was reached with Gorchakov whereby no Russian troops would enter Constantinople or Gallipoli in return for Britain not landing troops on either side of the Straits. The protracted stalemate was broken when Russia imposed a Pan-Slavist peace settlement on Turkey at San Stefano on March 3rd, 1878, establishing independence for Montenegro, Serbia, and Romania.

The Treaty also constituted Bulgaria as a tributary principality of Russia; it required a heavy financial indemnity from Turkey; it gave to Russia the right to select a port on the Black Sea; it opened up the Dardanelles and the Bosporous at all times to Russian vessels; it obtained full rights for all Christians remaining under Turkish rule; and it gave Bessarabia to Russia in exchange for the corner of Bulgaria known as Dobruja.

The other European powers were horrified, and Austria-Hungary proposed a complete revision of San Stefano at a full European congress. Disraeli insisted that Britain should be the architect, but Russia rejected his terms on March 25th. War fever erupted once again as Disraeli mobilised the reserves and arranged for the calling up of 7,000 Indian troops to Malta, at which Derby resigned definitively, to be replaced by Lord Salisbury. Hunt wrote a second 'War Song' for Macdermott, and Jingoes in both high and low places sang in their own defence:

Let the scribblers try their wit by
penny paragraph,

And sneer about the 'Jingoes' in
hopes to raise a laugh.

If it's 'Jingo' in love honour then
'Jingoes' sure are we,

If it's 'Jingo' to love England then
'Jingoes' we will be.

The two most highly placed Jingoes in Britain were Disraeli and Victoria. Public criticism of the Queen was not possible, but Disraeli was fair game for his many detractors who found his attitude as unpalatable as it was irresponsible. Graffiti appeared in public, taken from the Book of Genesis: 'Benjamin shall ravin as a wolf, in the morning he shall devour the prey, and at night he shall divide the spoil'. His proposed use of Indian troops—thought unconstitutional and tasteless by Gladstone as they were not British subjects *per se*—prompted a famous rejoinder by Goldwin Smith:

We don't want
to fight, but by
jingo! if
we do,
We'll stay at
home at ease
ourselves,
and send the
mild Hindoo!

The Irish politician Thomas O'Connor, observing the crisis in London, stated bluntly: 'It seemed as if the whole of the country had gone mad'. Disraeli 'represented all that was evil, in his mind and character as well as in politics', while Gladstone 'took on the proportions of the noblest of human figures. Disraeli was Beelzebub against an angel of light'.

This was, after all, a war with Russia in all but name. That it did not actually become one in fact was due to Liberal opposition in England, the intervention of Bismarck, and the acquiescence of Alexander II. By April, he and Gorchakov had agreed in principle to a congress in Berlin in June 1878, to be held under the auspices of Bismarck, and also to the withdrawing of all troops from the vicinity of Constantinople made conditional on Britain withdrawing its warships from the Straits. The madness was at an end.

The Congress of Berlin, which only made formal a number of agreements reached beforehand, was nevertheless seen in Britain as Disraeli's personal triumph. He returned a national hero claiming 'Peace with Honour', or as the Liberal view had it, 'Peace with Honours' after Disraeli accepted the Order of the Garter from his grateful Queen. In reality he had achieved little other than to help set the stage for future Balkan discontent in a treaty that could not have differed more from San Stefano. But how many in England cared for the plight of a Bosnian or Herzegovinan peasant? It was more important that Disraeli had done what Victorian England most welcomed: acquired more territory for the empire, in the shape of Cyprus.

This triumph would be short-lived. A deflated public with nothing to shout about or to deflect attention away from domestic problems rewarded Disraeli with electoral defeat in 1880. Gladstone, campaigning on an ethical foreign policy in contrast to that of his rival, was returned to high office with a huge majority, to the relief of the Tsar who announced to his daughter that he could now work with Britain. Nevertheless, institutional Russophobia in British political circles would die a slow death, and it would be two decades before Salisbury became the first English politician to publicly announce that Britain's support of Turkey against Russia had been the greatest political delusion of the age.

In March 1915, Britain, France and Russia agreed that, in the event of a satisfactory conclusion to the Great War with the full participation of Russia, Constantinople and the Bosporous would be removed from Turkey—now fighting with the Central Powers—and incorporated within the Russian empire.

These two possessions (Constantinople and the Bosporous) over which so much Anglo-Russian tension had been generated for so long would now be made over to Russia as a gift with hardly a raised eyebrow in Britain. However, Russia's inability to participate at Gallipoli and Lenin's early peace terms that contravened the London Agreement of September 1914, by which no member of the 'triple entente' was permitted to reach separate peace terms with the Central Powers, rendered this agreement null and void. Future revolutionary administrations in Russia would not raise the matter; by 1917 the quasi-mystical return to 'Tsargrad' had no more meaning for them than the vanished tsars themselves.

For Further Reading

James Arthur Ransome Marriott, *The Eastern Question: An Historical Study in European Diplomacy* (Oxford, 1917); Robert William Seton-Watson, *Disraeli, Gladstone, and the Eastern Question: A Study in Diplomacy and Party Politics* (Macmillan & Co, 1935); Richard Millman, *Britain and the Eastern Question 1875-1878* (Oxford, 1979); John Charmley, *Splendid Isolation? Britain and the Balance of Power 1874-1914* (Hodder & Stoughton, 1999); Trevor Royle, *Crimea: The Great Crimean War 1854–1856* (Little, Brown and Company, 1999).

ROMAN GOLICZ is an independent researcher.

The Evolution of Charles Darwin

A creationist when he visited the Galápagos Islands, the great naturalist grasped the full significance of the unique wildlife he found there only well after he had returned to London

FRANK J. SULLOWAY

From the nine times I have made the 5,000-mile journey to the Galápagos Islands, to follow in Charles Darwin's footsteps, the most enduring impression I have gained is of life's fragility. The minute a person steps off any of the tourist trails created by the Galápagos National Park Service and heads into the untamed interior of one of these islands, there is the risk of death under the intense, equatorial sun. On Santa Cruz Island, where the Charles Darwin Research Station is located, 17 people have disappeared since 1990. Most were subsequently found alive after having become hopelessly lost in dense underbrush and rugged volcanic terrain. But some perished. One was a young Israeli tourist who lost his way in Santa Cruz's Tortoise Reserve in 1991. A massive, two-month search failed to find him. In fact, some of the searchers themselves became lost and had to be rescued. In the end, fishermen discovered the young man's body. A former Israeli tank commander, he had been in top physical condition, yet had managed to go only six miles before succumbing to the searing heat and lack of fresh water. A sign in the Tortoise Reserve says bluntly: "Stop. Do not go beyond this point. You could die."

Darwin wholeheartedly accepted this theory, which was bolstered by the biblical account in Genesis.

This is the deceptively treacherous world of sun-baked lava, spiny cactus and tangled brushwood into which Charles Darwin stepped in September 1835, when he reached the Galápagos Islands with fellow crew members of the HMS *Beagle*. The *Beagle*'s captain, Robert FitzRoy, described the barren volcanic landscape as "a shore fit for Pandemonium." At 26, Darwin had come to the archipelago, which straddles the Equator some 600 miles west of Ecuador, as part of the *Beagle*'s five-year mission to survey the coast of South America and to conduct a series of longitudinal measurements around the globe. Darwin's five-week visit to these remarkable islands catalyzed the scientific revolution that now bears his name.

Darwin's revolutionary theory was that new species arise naturally, by a process of evolution, rather than having been created—forever immutable—by God. According to the well-established creationist theory of Darwin's day, the exquisite adaptations of many species—such as the hinges of the bivalve shell and the wings and plumes on seeds dispersed by air—were compelling evidence that a "designer" had created each species for its intended place in the economy of nature. Darwin had wholeheartedly accepted this theory, which was bolstered by the biblical account in Genesis, until his experiences in the Galápagos Islands began to undermine this way of thinking about the biological world.

The Galápagos Islands were formed by volcanic eruptions in the recent geological past (the oldest of the islands emerged from the ocean just three million years ago), and Darwin realized that the remote setting must have presented life with a new beginning. "Seeing every height crowned with its crater, and the boundaries of most of the lava-streams still distinct, we are led to believe that within a period, geologically recent, the unbroken ocean was here spread out," he wrote in his *Journal of Researches*. "Hence, both in space and time, we seem to be brought somewhat near to that great fact—that mystery of mysteries—the first appearance of new beings on this earth."

How, Darwin asked himself, had life first come to these islands? "The natural history of these islands," he later pointed out, "is eminently curious, and well deserves attention. Most of the organic productions are aboriginal creations, found nowhere else." Yet all of the creatures showed a marked relationship with those from the American continent. The novel Galápagos species, Darwin reasoned, must have started out as accidental colonists from Central and South America and then diverged from their ancestral stocks after arriving in the Galápagos. As he traveled from island to island, Darwin also encountered tantalizing evidence suggesting that evolution was proceeding independently on each island, producing what appeared to be new species.

Other evidence, from the South American continent, showed that species did not seem to be stable across either geographic space or the deep reaches of paleontological time. But the particularly compelling evidence from the Galápagos Islands catapulted Darwin and life science into the modern age. He subsequently added to his daring endorsement of evolution the crucial insight that species evolve by means of natural selection: variants that are better adapted to their environments are more likely to survive and reproduce. When he finally published *On the Origin of Species by Means of Natural Selection* in 1859, Darwin's revolutionary theories not only recast the study of life but also turned the Galápagos Islands into hallowed scientific ground.

More than three decades ago, I became fascinated by Darwin's life, and especially by his historic voyage around the world. When evolutionary biologist Edward O. Wilson, whose undergraduate course I was taking at Harvard, learned of my interest, he suggested that I go to the Galápagos Islands, and he helped fund a documentary about Darwin's voyage. My first trip, in 1968, was two years before the beginning of organized tourism in the Galápagos. Just getting to the islands was a challenge. Our expedition flew from Guayaquil, Ecuador, in a PBY, an amphibious, twin-engine patrol plane dating back to the World War II era. We sat in seats made of mesh nets. There were numerous holes in the plane's undercarriage, through which I could see all the way to the ocean below. The impression these starkly beautiful islands made upon me was indelible (the volcano that forms the island of Fernandina put on a spectacular eruption during our visit).

Eight expeditions later, I continue to be drawn to these islands in an effort to document their extraordinary impact on Darwin, as well as to study ecological changes since Darwin's day. With the advent of organized tourism, much has changed. Now, two to four passenger planes fly each day to the Galápagos, bringing a total of about 100,000 tourists a year. Puerto Ayora, home to the Charles Darwin Research Station, is a booming tourist stop with a population of about 15,000 people, almost ten times the number that resided there during my first visit. As tourists enjoy their organized cruises around the islands, they are confined to 60 localities, carefully selected by the National Park Service, and are required to stay on clearly marked paths that keep them out of harm's way.

T wo main questions confront the student of Darwin's historic visit: Where did Darwin go, and exactly how did his visit affect his scientific thinking? Answering the first turns out to be easier than one might think, thanks to a rich repository of documentary sources. The British Navy had a penchant for keeping detailed records, and the *Beagle*'s voyage is described in three ship's logs, Captain FitzRoy's personal narrative, a series of excellent maps made by the *Beagle*'s officers, and various watercolors and sketches by crew members. We are also able to draw on Darwin's own extensive record of his dozen or so field trips, which encompasses more than 100 pages of unpublished notes and more than 80 pages of published material.

For five years the *Beagle*'s logs recorded, often on an hourly basis, where the ship was and what it was doing. Two days after the first sighting of land in the Galápagos, on September 15, 1835, the *Beagle* anchored in Stephens Bay on Chatham Island,

now known as San Cristóbal. (All the islands were given Spanish as well as English names by their early visitors, who included Spaniards seeking Inca gold and silver in Peru, and British buccaneers intent on stealing these riches from the Spanish.) From this anchorage, the *Beagle* officers recorded a bearing of N10°E to Kicker Rock, an impressive 470-foot islet about four miles off the shore, and a bearing of N45°E to Finger Hill, a 516-foot tuff crater. When drawn on a map, the place at which these two bearings cross indicates the *Beagle*'s point of anchorage. Using other bearings in the *Beagle*'s logs, together with Darwin's remarks in his diary and scientific notes, it is possible to reconstruct virtually all of Darwin's landing sites and inland treks during his five-week visit. These include many regions that are either in remote or potentially dangerous locations and hence off limits to tourists.

As the *Beagle* sailed from east to west through the archipelago, Darwin visited four of the larger islands, where he landed at nine different sites. On San Cristóbal, Darwin was particularly drawn to a heavily "Craterized district" on the rugged, northeastern coast. "The entire surface of this part of the island," Darwin reported, "seems to have been permeated, like a sieve, by the subterranean vapours: here and there the lava, whilst soft, has been blown into great bubbles; and on other parts, the tops of caverns similarly formed have fallen in, leaving circular pits with steep sides. From the regular form of the many craters, they gave to the country an artificial appearance, which vividly reminded me of those parts of Staffordshire, where the great iron-foundries are most numerous."

As Darwin explored San Cristóbal, he encountered many birds and animals new to him. He marveled at the remarkable tameness of the birds, pushing a curious hawk off a branch with the barrel of his gun, and trying to catch small birds with his hands or in his cap. He also noted the striking dominance of reptiles within these islands, which made the archipelago seem like a journey back in time. On the shoreline were swarms of "hideous-looking" marine iguanas—the world's only oceangoing lizards. On land, the *Beagle* crew encountered large land iguanas, closely allied to their marine cousin; a couple of smaller lizards; a snake; and giant land tortoises, after which the islands are named. (The old Spanish word *galápago* means saddle, which the shape of the tortoise's carapace resembles.)

In the midst of a partly vegetated lava field on San Cristóbal, Darwin came upon two enormous tortoises, each weighing more than 200 pounds. One, he noted, "was eating a piece of cactus, and as I approached it, it stared at me and slowly stalked away; the other gave a deep hiss, and drew in its head. These huge reptiles, surrounded by the black lava, the leafless shrubs, and large cacti, seemed to my fancy like some antediluvian animals." Altogether these giant reptiles contributed dramatically, Darwin thought, to the "strange Cyclopean scene."

Floreana was the next of the four islands Darwin visited. The first settlement in the Galápagos had been established there just three years before, populated by convicts from Ecuador; it collapsed a few years later, after some malcontented prisoners took up arms against the local governor. On Floreana, Darwin remarked in his private diary, "I industriously collected all the animals, plants, insects, & reptiles from this Island"—adding, "It will be very interesting to find from future comparison to what district or 'centre of creation' the organized beings of this archipelago must be attached." Still thinking like a creationist, Darwin was seeking to understand the islands' strange inhabitants within the ruling biological paradigm.

After a brief stop at Tagus Cove, on Isabela, the *Beagle* headed for Santiago. Darwin, three crew members and his servant, Syms Covington, were left for nine days to collect specimens while the *Beagle* returned to San Cristóbal to obtain fresh water. Guided by a settler from Floreana who had been sent to hunt tortoises, Darwin ascended to the highlands twice to collect specimens in the humid zone. There he was able to study, in considerable detail, the habits of the tortoise. These lumbering behemoths, he found, came from all over the island to drink water at several small springs near the summit. Hordes of the giants could be seen coming and going, with necks outstretched, burying their heads in the water, "quite regardless of any spectator," to relieve their thirst. Darwin counted the number of times that the tortoises swallowed in a minute (about ten), determined their average speed (six yards a minute), and studied their diet and mating habits. While in the highlands Darwin and his companions dined exclusively on tortoise meat. He commented that it was very tasty when roasted in the shell or made into soup.

Darwin was a lousy speller. I dated his writings by analyzing changes in misspellings during the voyage.

When he was not collecting specimens, Darwin devoted time to trying to understand the islands' geological features, especially the prominent tuff cones near his campsite at Buccaneer Cove. He was the first geologist to appreciate that such sandstone-like structures, which rise to a height of more than 1,000 feet, owe their peculiar features to submarine eruptions of lava and mud; they mix at high temperatures with seawater, producing tiny particles that shoot into the air and rain down on the land to form huge cinder cones.

On October 17, Darwin and his four Santiago companions reboarded the *Beagle* with their week's haul of specimens. The ship spent the next two days completing a survey of the two northernmost islands and then, 36 days after arriving in the archipelago (during which he spent 19 days on land), the *Beagle* sailed for Tahiti. Although Darwin did not yet fully appreciate it, a revolution in science had begun.

Following in darwin's path, one understands hardships that he overcame that are not readily apparent to readers of his publications. Trekking in the Galápagos, everything is dictated by how much water one can carry, which limits each excursion to about three days—or, for longer excursions, requires stashing food and water along a route.

To Darwin, such logistics would have been even more problematic, as he did not have the lightweight equipment, such as aluminum-frame backpacks and plastic water containers, that we have today. Assisted by his servant, Darwin would have brought his geological hammer, a clinometer for measuring inclines, a shotgun for collecting birds, a compass, plant presses, rodent traps, specimen bottles, spirits of wine for preserving invertebrates, a notebook, a sleeping bag, food and, of course, water. With a characteristic understatement (reflecting perhaps his excellent physical conditioning after extensive fieldwork in South America during the previous four years), Darwin wrote of the 3,000-foot climb to the summit of Santiago merely that the walk was "a long one." During our own climb along this route in 2004, when we were all packing about 70 pounds, one of my expedition companions was so overcome with heat exhaustion that he had to return to our base camp in Buccaneer Cove; another sprained his ankle on the treacherous footing but managed to keep going.

During a previous expedition, I and five companions came to appreciate, much more vividly than we would have liked, Darwin's comparison of Galápagos lava flows to an imagined scene from the "Infernal regions." We were on Santiago, where Darwin had camped for nine days, on our way to a region where tortoises could sometimes be found. Our two guides had suggested a shortcut across a coastal lava flow. What none of us could see from the vantage point of our boat's landing site was that our route involved more than eight miles of almost continuous lava rock—not just the mile or two that our guides had led us to expect. As we began our trek across this perilous field of jagged lava, we had no idea how close to death we would all come. What was supposed to be a 6-hour excursion became a 51-hour nightmare as we climbed over jumbled piles of blocks with razor-sharp edges, and in and out of steep ravines formed by meandering lavas and collapsed lava domes. Such flows, commented Darwin, who ventured onto several smaller ones, were like "a sea petrified in its most boisterous moments." He added, "Nothing can be imagined more rough or horrid."

During our second day on that Santiago lava flow, our water ran out. To make matters worse, our two guides had failed to bring any water of their own and were drinking ours. By the afternoon of the third day we were all severely dehydrated and were forced to abandon most of our equipment. In desperation, our guides hacked off a candelabra cactus branch, and we resorted to drinking the juice, which was so bitter that I retched. Before we finally made it to the coast, where a support vessel was frantically looking for us, one member of the expedition was delirious and close to death. He was subsequently hospitalized for five days, back in the United States, and it took him more than a month to recover.

On another occasion I accompanied Charles Darwin Research Station botanist Alan Tye on a search for the rare *Lecocarpus* shrub, which Darwin had collected in 1835. A member of the daisy family, the plant had not been seen by anyone in a century, causing some botanists to question Darwin's reported locality. The day was unusually hot, and Tye, after a few hours of hiking, felt the onset of heat exhaustion and asked me to take over the lead. Using a machete to help clear our way through the brush, I too became heat exhausted, and began to vomit. Heat exhaustion turned out to be the least of my problems. I had inadvertently cut the branch of an overhanging manzanillo tree, whose apples are poison to humans but beloved by tortoises. Some of the tree's sap had gotten onto a wristband I was wearing and then into both of my eyes. The sting from the sap was almost unbearable, and dousing my eyes with water did nothing to help. For the next seven hours I was nearly blinded and could open my eyes for only a few seconds at a time. As I walked back to our campsite, five hours away, I often had to balance, with my eyes shut, on huge boulders in a dry riverbed, and on the edge of lava ravines. Those were the most painful seven hours I have ever spent. Fortunately, Tye and I did find the rare plant we had been seeking, resolving a century-old mystery and establishing that San Cristóbal has two different members of the same *Lecocarpus* genus.

Darwin personally reported no untoward physical difficulties during his own Galápagos visit, although he and four companions on Santiago did complain about a shortage of fresh water and the oppressive heat, which reached 137 degrees Fahrenheit (the maximum on their thermometer), as measured in the sandy soil outside their tent. Darwin was twice reminded of the potentially lethal outcome of any excursion into the Galápagos wilds. The *Beagle*'s crew encountered one lost soul, from the American whaler *Hydaspy*, who had become stranded on Española, and this stroke of good fortune saved his life. Also, Captain FitzRoy recorded that another sailor from an American whaler had gone missing and that the whaler's crew was out looking for him. One should not be surprised, then, that, while he was engaged in fieldwork, Darwin would have focused his attention substantially on surviving the many hazards of the Galápagos.

Legend has it that Darwin was converted to the theory of evolution, eureka-like, during his visit to the islands. How could he not have been? In retrospect, the evidence for evolution seems so compelling. Darwin tells us in his *Journal of Researches*, first published in 1839, that his fascination with the "mystery of mysteries"—the origin of new species—was first aroused by a chance discussion on Floreana with Nicholas Lawson, the vice governor of the islands. Based in part on differences in the shape of a tortoise's shell, Lawson claimed that "he could at once tell from which island any one was brought." Darwin also noticed that the mockingbirds seemed to be either separate varieties or species on the four islands he visited. If true, he speculated, "such facts would undermine the stability of Species"—the fundamental tenet of creationism, which held that all species had been created in their present, immutable forms.

Darwin's research became so convincing that he did not need the Galápagos evidence to make his case.

Darwin's first reflections about evolution were an afterthought, written during the last leg of the *Beagle* voyage, nine months after his Galápagos visit. (I owe this historical insight to a curious fact—Darwin was a lousy speller. In 1982 was able to date Darwin's earliest and previously undated writings about possible species transformations by analyzing changes in Darwins pattern of misspellings during the voyage.) While in the Galápagos, Darwin was far more interested in the islands' geology than their zoology We know, moreover, from the complete record of his unpublished scientific notes that he was personally dubious about evolution. For nearly a year and a half following his Galápagos visit, he believed that the tortoises and mockingbirds were probably "only varieties," a conclusion that did not threaten creationism, which allowed for animals to differ slightly in response to their environments. According to creationist theory, species were a bit like elastic bands. The environment could induce variation, but the inevitable pull of the immutable "type"—which was thought to be an idea in the mind of God—caused species to revert to their original forms. For the creationist, all variation from the "type" was limited by an impassable barrier between true species.

Darwin's initial failure to appreciate the case for evolution stems in large part from a widely mistaken assumption about the tortoises. Naturalists thought that giant tortoises had been introduced to the Galápagos by buccaneers who had transported them from the Indian Ocean, where similar tortoises are present on several islands. This confusion explains Darwin's astonishing failure to collect even a single specimen for scientific purposes. He and his servant did take back to England, as pets, two baby tortoises. Those juvenile tortoises further misled Darwin, because differences among subspecies are evident only in adults. Not realizing the importance of tortoises for the theory he would eventually develop about the origins and diversity of living things, Darwin and his fellow shipmates ate their way through 48 adult tortoise specimens and threw their shells overboard.

Darwin's famous finches also misled him at first. There are 14 finch species in the Galápagos that have all evolved from a single ancestor over the past few million years. They have become one of the most famous cases of species adapting to different ecological niches. From Darwin's specimen notebooks, it is clear he was fooled into thinking that some of the unusual finch species belonged to the families they have come to mimic through a process called convergent evolution. For example, Darwin thought the cactus finch, whose long, probing beak is specialized for obtaining nectar from cactus flowers (and dodging cactus spines), might be related to birds with long, pointed bills, such as meadowlarks and orioles. He also mistook the warbler finch for a wren. Not realizing that all of the finches were closely related, Darwin had no reason to suppose that they had evolved from a common ancestor, or that they differed from one island to another.

My own discovery, more than 30 years ago, that Darwin had misidentified some of his famous Galápagos finches led me to the Darwin Archive at Cambridge University Library, in England. There I found a manuscript trail that poked further holes in the legend that these birds precipitated an immediate "aha" moment. It was only after Darwin's return to England, when experts in herpetology and ornithology began to correct his Galápagos reports, that he realized the extent of his collecting oversights and misidentifications. In particular, Darwin had failed to label most of his Galápagos birds by island, so he lacked the crucial evidence that would allow him to argue that different finch species had evolved separately while isolated on different islands of the Galápagos group.

Five months after his return to England, in March 1837, Darwin met with ornithologist John Gould. Five years older than Darwin, Gould was just beginning to become known for his beautifully illustrated monographs on birds, which today are highly prized collectors' items. One of my most unexpected discoveries in the Darwin archives was the piece of paper on which Darwin recorded his crucial meeting with Gould. This manuscript clearly shows how Darwin's thinking began to change as a result of Gould's astute insights about the Galápagos birds. Unlike Darwin, Gould had instantly recognized the related nature of the Galápagos finches, and he also persuaded Darwin, who questioned him closely on the subject, that three of his four Galápagos mockingbirds were separate species rather than "only varieties." Gould also informed Darwin that 25 of his 26 land birds from the Galápagos were new to science, as well as unique to those islands.

It is perhaps a question of character. Darwin's uncle once noted Charles was "a man of enlarged curiosity."

Gould's taxonomic judgments finally caused Darwin to embrace the theory of evolution. Stunned by the realization that evolving varieties could break the supposedly fixed barrier that, according to creationism, prevents new species from forming, he quickly sought to rectify his previous collecting oversights by requesting island locality information from the carefully labeled collections of three *Beagle* shipmates. Two of these collections, by Captain FitzRoy and FitzRoy's steward, Harry Fuller, contained 50 Galápagos birds, including more than 20 finches. Even Darwin's servant, Covington, had done what Darwin had not, labeling by island his own personal collection of finches, which were later acquired by a private collector in England. The birth of the Darwinian revolution was a highly collaborative enterprise.

The case for evolution presented by this shared ornithological evidence nevertheless remained debatable for nearly a decade. Darwin was not entirely convinced Gould was right that all the finches were separate species, or even that they were all finches. Darwin also knew that, without specimens in hand, island-to-island differences among the tortoises were contestable, even though a French herpetologist told a delighted Darwin in 1838 that at least two species of tortoise existed in the islands.

In 1845 Darwin's botanist friend Joseph Hooker gave Darwin the definitive evidence he needed to support his theory Hooker analyzed the numerous plants that Darwin had brought back from the Galápagos. Unlike the birds, the plants all had accurate localities attached to them—not because Darwin had collected the plants with evolutionary theory in mind, but because plants have to be preserved in plant presses shortly after being collected. Hence the specimens from each island had all been pressed together, rather than being intermixed. Hooker eventually identified more than 200 species, half of which were unique to the Galápagos. Of these, three-quarters were confined to single islands—yet other islands often possessed closely related forms also found nowhere else on earth. At last, Darwin had the kind of compelling evidence that he felt he could really trust. As he wrote to Hooker: "I cannot tell you how delighted & astonished I am at the results of your examination; how wonderfully they support my assertion on the differences in the animals of the different islands, about which I have always been fearful."

It is certainly testimony to Darwin's intellectual boldness that he had conceived of the theory of evolution some eight years earlier, when he still harbored doubts about how to classify Galápagos tortoises, mockingbirds and finches. To bolster the unorthodox theory, he engaged in an exhaustive, 20-year program of research that ultimately became so convincing that he did not need the inspirational Galápagos evidence to make his case. As a consequence, Darwin devotes only 1 percent of the *Origin of Species* to the Galápagos, barely more than he allotted to the Madeiras Islands or New Zealand.

I have often wondered why Darwin, prior to the publication of *Origin of Species* in 1859, was the only person known to have become an evolutionist based on evidence from the Galápagos—especially after Hooker's compelling botanical study After all, Captain FitzRoy, John Gould, Joseph Hooker and numerous scientific specialists who helped Darwin with the analysis and publication of his voyage findings were flatly aware of the unusual nature of his Galápagos collections. In the end, it is perhaps a question of courageous willingness to consider new and unconventional ways of thinking. When Darwin's uncle, Josiah Wedgwood, was trying to convince Darwin's father that young Charles should be allowed to sail on the *Beagle*, Josiah noted Charles was "a man of enlarged curiosity."

One repeatedly sees the truth of Wedgwood's observation. Charles Darwin's undeniable knack for asking the right questions, bolstered by his five-week visit to an extraordinary workshop of evolution brimming with unasked and unanswered questions, ultimately precipitated the Darwinian revolution. In posing novel questions, Darwin voyaged back to the Galápagos Islands again and again in his mind, reassessing his imperfect evidence in the light of his maturing theory and benefiting from new and better evidence obtained by other researchers.

Although much of what one sees in the Galápagos today appears to be virtually identical to what Darwin described in 1835, the biology and ecology of the islands have been substantially transformed by the introduction of exotic plants, insects and animals. Completely gone from Santiago, for example, are the golden-colored land iguanas, described as so numerous by Darwin in 1835 that "we could not for some time find a spot free from their burrows, on which to pitch our tent." The principal culprits in this extinction, besides *Beagle* crew members and other people who found these iguanas very good eating, were the rats, dogs, cats, goats and pigs introduced by mariners and would-be settlers who left their animals to run wild. Along with visiting whalers, early settlers also hunted the giant land tortoises to extinction on some islands, and they nearly wiped them out on other islands. Recently introduced insects and plants—including fire ants, wasps, parasitic flies and quinine trees—have also become highly invasive and threaten the Galápagos ecosystem.

When I first visited the Galápagos, 37 years ago, quinine was not yet a serious problem, and feral goats, which later invaded Isabela's Volcán Alcedo (home to about 5,000 giant land tortoises), had yet to reach epidemic numbers. But by the 1990s, more than 100,000 goats were devastating the volcano's vegetation. Darwin himself would doubtless have applauded the indefatigable efforts of the Charles Darwin Research Station and the National Park Service to stem the tide of destruction to the fragile ecosystem, and he would also have marveled at some of the occasional success stories, such as the recent eradication of feral pigs from Santiago.

From the many times I have followed in Darwin's footsteps to better understand his voyage of discovery, I have come to believe that the Galápagos continue to epitomize one of the key elements of Darwin's theories. As he argued, over long periods of time natural selection is ultimately responsible for the "endless forms most beautiful and most wonderful" around us. Empowering this evolutionary process on a day-to-day basis is what Darwin termed "the struggle for existence." This evolutionary engine works its slow but unrelenting biological effects primarily through accidents, starvation and death. Perhaps nowhere else is this harsh biological principle more evident than in the strange islands that inspired Darwin's scientific revolution.

For more on **FRANK J. SULLOWAY**, author of *Born to Rebel* and *Freud, Biologist of the Mind.*

Florence Nightingale as a Social Reformer

Lynn McDonald describes the lasting impact of Florence Nightingale on improving public health for the poor.

LYNN MCDONALD

Florence Nightingale (1820–1910), the heroine of the Crimean War, is still best known as the major founder of the modern profession of nursing and as a hospital reformer. Yet her broader contribution to public health care and social reform—notably of a public health care system based on evidence and featuring health promotion and disease prevention—is still scarcely known, although it is recognized by leading experts. With the benefit of hindsight we can see her as a major architect of the modern health care system. Nursing leader Monica Baly referred to Nightingale as the 'greatest Victorian of them all' and observed in *Nursing and Social Change* (1995):

> Had Miss Nightingale's advice on the Poor Law been taken and her plans accepted there might have been a universal health service before 1948.

Nightingale's achievement in introducing professional nursing into the dreaded workhouse infirmaries was one of the greatest contributions of her long life, and it is not possible to imagine a National Health Service without it. Prior to her reforms there were no trained nurses for workhouse patients only 'pauper nurses', or women inmates who were not themselves sick, notorious for stealing their patients' food and gin, no permanent medical staff, only visiting doctors, while shared beds were but one of the santitary defects. Nursing itself, and hospitals as institutions, would have improved without Nightingale, for many people were working on them. But no one else was bold enough to take on the workhouse infirmaries, the 'real hospitals of the sick poor', as they have been called, for they held five people for every one in an ordinary hospital.

Visitors such as Louisa Twining (1820–1912) sought to eliminate abuses in the workhouses and doctors formed an Association for the Improvement of the London Workhouse Infirmaries, which sought various improvements. But Nightingale's vision (shared with her colleague Dr John Sutherland) was much bolder: that the care given in the workhouse infirmaries should be just as good as that in the best nursed civil hospitals in the suburbs. The realization of that vision began in 1865, in the Liverpool Workhouse Infirmary, with nurses and a superintendent, Agnes Jones, who had trained at the Nightingale School at St Thomas' Hospital. It was funded by Christian philanthropist William Rathbone.

Nightingale's strong faith and the 'call to service' she experienced in 1837, at the age of sixteen, is critical to understanding her motivation and the methodology she evolved, which shaped her work. Initially she interpreted her 'call to service' to mean nursing, then not a profession at all but a lower-class and ill-paid occupation. Her family would not permit her to nurse, a source of great frustration, as she tried to act on this call. However, she was allowed to visit hospitals and workhouses, and this she did in her early twenties. A little later she came to understand the call to mean to save lives, for which nursing was but one possibility. Indeed, when she discovered that administrative blunders and bad hospital siting and construction cost so many lives she increasingly directed her attention to these issues.

Nightingale's workhouse visits were to have a great impact. In particular, her tour of the great Marylebone Workhouse in the early 1840s 'broke her heart', as she later wrote. She realized she could do nothing to change the wretched conditions she saw but resolved to do something when she could. The opportunity did not arise until well after her return in 1856 from the Crimean War. She was now feted as a heroine, a status she abhorred, but found useful for getting people's attention and assistance. In January 1864 the Liverpool philanthropist William Rathbone offered to fund a 'lady visitor' at the Liverpool Workhouse Infirmary. Nightingale persuaded Rathbone that skilled nursing was needed, not merely a lady visitor, and nominated Agnes Jones (1832–1868) who had trained at Kaiserwerth and St Thomas' Hospital. Jones became lady superindendent, assisted by a number of Nightingale nurses in April 1865, the first trained nurses in a poor-law institution.

The death of a workhouse inmate from lack of nursing, in November 1864 in the Holborn Union Workhouse, London, prompted an inquiry and press attention. Nightingale seized upon the misfortune to press for reforms in London, telling C.P. Villiers, the President of the Poor Law Board (a Cabinet position), that there was no nursing to speak of in any of the workhouse infirmaries. He responded promptly, visited her and considered fundamental reform, even promising a new bill.

The Liberal government fell in 1866 before Villiers could introduce his reform—although in any case he had some doubts about the radical nature of the changes Nightingale proposed. Nevertheless he continued to support her out of office in his capacity as an MP. In one letter referring to her reforms, he thanked her for the 'peep behind the curtain', but said no one could guess what the 'broth' would be when ready. The fall of the Liberal government also meant the loss in influence of Nightingale's greatest ally, Lord Palmerston.

The new Conservative President of the Poor Law Board was Gathorne Hardy. Nightingale, who did not know Hardy, set about lobbying him. She sent her first letter on July 25th, 1866, enclosing letters from mutual friends to act as an introduction. Hardy proceeded with a less far-reaching set of reforms than Nightingale wanted, that eventually took shape as the Metropolitan Poor Bill, (passed the following year). Asked by Hardy's committee to prepare a brief on cubic space in workhouse infirmaries, Nightingale was not deterred by the narrow terms of reference. Instead, she devoted most of her paper, entitled *Suggestions on the Subject of Providing Training and Organizing Nurses for the Sick Poor in Workhouse Infirmaries*, to what she considered most important.

Nightingale also persuaded key figures such as Edwin Chadwick and J.S. Mill to support the thrust of her reforms. This was some achievement as Chadwick had been a major architect of the punitive amendment to the Poor Law in 1834, and Mill was a newcomer to workhouse reform (and his initial concerns, like Chadwick, were reducing the numbers in workhouses). Both went along with the conventional wisdom, not based on evidence, that the major problem in workhouses was the able-bodied unemployed. Yet a quarter of the workhouse inmates were children, who, Nightingale believed, should not be there at all, while many more were aged and sick.

Nightingale understood that the workhouses held destitute people of many kinds—thrown together by their desperate misfortune, but from quite different causes. In her 'ABC' of workhouse reform, drafted by mid-1865, she made suggestions to revamp the entire system, removing from it all but the small number of able-bodied unemployed, which group itself would be diminished if her proposals for employment stimulation in economic downturns were adopted. Her proposal was:

A. To insist on the great principle of separating the sick, insane, incurable and children from the usual pauper population of the metropolis ...

B. To advocate a general metropolitan rate for this purpose and a central administration.

C. To leave the pauper and casual population and the rating for under the boards of guardians, as at present.

The new system would:

Provide a scheme of suburban hospitals and asylums (1) for sick; (2) for infirm, aged and invalids; (3) for insane and imbeciles; (4) industrial schools for children.

She explained the rationale:

Sickness, madness, imbecility and permanent infirmity are general afflictions affecting the entire community and are not (like pauperism) to be kept down by local knowledge or by hard usage. The sick or infirm or mad pauper ceases to be a pauper when so afflicted and should be chargeable to the community at large, as a fellow-creature in suffering.

There should be 'a general rate for this purpose to be levied over the whole metropolitan area, to be administered by the central authority'. J.S. Mill argued precisely this last point in committee.

The Metropolitan Poor Bill was adopted by Parliament in 1867 and served as the framework from which many further reforms in the system were made. The late Brian Abel-Smith, Professor of Social Administration at the LSE described the Bill as

... an important step in English social history ... the first explicit acknowledgment that it was the duty of the state to provide hospitals for the poor ... an important step towards the National Health Service Act which followed some eighty years later.

The legislation was permissive only, however, so that improvements had to be fought for workhouse by workhouse, which Nightingale, and an increasing number of others did. The broader 'ABC' of reform she had envisaged was not implemented as a system, although many specific improvements were made. The recommendations of the Minority Report of the Poor Law Commission in 1909, advocated by Sidney and Beatrice Webb, were similar. Even then many were only partially enacted, to reappear as recommendations in the Beveridge Report at the end of the Second World War.

That Nightingale obtained the support and assistance of so many high-level medical experts, cabinet ministers and senior officials is a tribute to her careful preparation and attention to detail. People knew they could rely on her and that she did her homework. The best Victorian sanitarians, people like John Sutherland (who for years advised Nightingale, and found data and material for her), statistician William Farr at the General Register Office, engineer and water expert Robert Rawlinson, and many others, were willing to work with her because they shared her vision and respected her methods. Throughout her life Nightingale was able to recruit experts she did not know to her causes.

Although she never used the term, a 'Nightingale methodology' can be identified: read the best information available in print, especially government reports and statistics; interview experts; if the available information is inadequate send out your own questionnaire; test it first at one institution; consult practitioners who use the material; send out draft reports to experts for vetting before publication.

The emphasis Nightingale placed on statistics was bound up with her faith. Not for nothing was she called the 'passionate statistician'. She believed it was 'the plan of God' to teach us 'the laws by which our moral progress is to be attained', or 'the road we must take if we are to discover the laws of God's government of His moral world'. Social reform work, carefully grounded on the best (quantitative) data had a divine mission.

Statistics should be used for making practical decisions. When asked by medical authorities in Staffordshire about the desirability of building a new children's hospital or having a children's ward in a general hospital or carrying on with placing children in adult (normally women's) wards, Nightingale gave what advice she could, based on reports of experienced nurses in the different situations. But, as she noted in a letter of 1876,

> It would be exceedingly interesting to find out the relative rates of mortality and duration of sickness in children's cases, otherwise similar, placed in 'general' or children's wards or hospitals, but unfortunately hospital statistics are not sufficiently well kept to ascertain this.

Keen as she was on scientific method, Nightingale was well aware of the possibility of unintended consequences from the best-intentioned measures, even with the highest religious principles behind them. She urged the monitoring of results from all new programmes. Further, when data showed negative results the intervention should be revised, and the new measures in turn evaluated.

Nightingale's methodology is perhaps best seen in the data collection for the two royal commissions she got appointed after the Crimean War, the first on that war itself and its unnecessarily high mortality rate, and the second on India. Other attempts to use data to fuel and guide reform failed when governments failed to collect the data. For example, Nightingale succeeded in getting the Colonial Office to send out questionnaires she designed (and checked with experts) to colonies on mortality and sickness in their aboriginal hospitals and schools. The data that came back were poor, but enough to show excessive rates. Nightingale's recommendations for improved statistical gathering and ongoing monitoring were not heeded. She gave up on the colonies in general, to concentrate instead on India.

Her methodology also failed, unsurprisingly, when the best available information (previous studies and her own) was not up to the problem at hand. This occurred with her midwifery nurse training programme, which started at King's College Hospital in 1861, but was closed down six years later on account of high maternal mortality from puerperal fever. The cause of this disease was not fully identified until well into the twentieth century, and measures to reduce mortality, beginning with the better use of disinfectants in the 1870s, still left the rates high. It was not until the 1930s, with the introduction of the sulfa drugs, that the rates of maternal mortality were substantially reduced.

Nightingale was well aware that a report was not 'self-executive', as she put it, and that recommendations needed a carefully-devised implementation strategy. In the case of the two royal commissions (influencing not only the terms of reference but the appointment of members) the final reports detailed the changes in administrative structure necessary for implementation.

Nightingale understood the political process well. In a democracy there must be political will to achieve change: questions in the House of Commons, media coverage and the good will of the relevant professionals and opinion leaders. She took pains with both of the royal commissions to get the right people reviewing the reports in the right journals. She knew the circulation of the major periodicals. She understood the importance of getting a story or letter-to-the-editor into *The Times*.

Clearly it was important that able men, committed to the reforms on which Nightingale was working, held key Cabinet posts. On Sidney Herbert's death in 1861 much was lost by the appointment of Sir George Lewis as the new war minister. When he died in 1863 she lobbied furiously for Lord de Grey to get the appointment, for much had been progress had been lost with the 'muff', as she called Lewis, in charge. A telegram to Harriet Martineau famously urged: 'Agitate, agitate, agitate for Lord de Grey to succeed Sir George Lewis.' Martineau did, as did others Nightingale asked. She persuaded Lord Palmerston to read a letter of hers favouring Lord de Grey to Queen Victoria. She even prepared a second letter begging the Queen, which she sent to Sir James Clark (the Queen's physician and a close Nightingale ally) to give her. Clark's son, John Clark, also an ally, prevailed on Nightingale not to proceed, pointing out that her views were well known both to the Queen and Palmerston. He pointed out that if someone else were to get the appointment, he would undoubtedly resent her opposition. When de Grey won the post John Clark congratulated her. The editor of *The Times* also credited Nightingale with the appointment.

Nightingale was born, and died, a Liberal. She even joked that God was a Liberal. As a woman she was not a party member, nor even a voter, but she gave money to her party and (occasionally) wrote campaign letters for its candidates. Of course she had to work with Conservatives when they were in office and she was careful not to be overly partisan in public statements. She was also acutely aware that her own party often let her down. In Nightingale's case the great disappointment was the Liberal failure to take on the cause of India (where, with a population of 150 million in the late 1860s and 1870s, deaths from famine were also counted in the millions). She tried at length to persuade Gladstone to be as liberal on India as he was on Ireland. She failed, or at best got some minor concessions

Nightingale had to protect her time from the many people who wanted it for good reason. She kept her focus on saving lives. When there was an opportunity to intervene she took it. When an influential person might be recruitable to the cause she approached him. In 1880, Indian finance was an urgent issue, when funds for spending on crucial public works (including measures for famine prevention) were cut back for expenditures on war. Henry Fawcett, the 'MP for India', received a forty-four-page letter from Nightingale laying out her case in detail. He must have been surprised to get this tirade, but he replied politely. The point is that the influential Fawcett was open to argument, even if he had taken, in Nightingale's view, the wrong position.

The dominant political theory in Nightingale's time was laissez-faire liberalism, not the interventionist liberalism that later developed, but the belief that social reforms could not work and should not be attempted. To the extreme left of this position was Karl Marx, who also held that social reform would be futile, but who looked to the overthrow of the capitalist system and its replacement with a more humane one. Nightingale represents the great mainstream, reformist middle. As a major liberal reformer Nightingale was a critic of capitalism, like Marx, but with a thoroughly opposing approach to change. Her vision was of a profoundly reformed system, the private sector largely running the economy, but with measures for income security, savings and pensions, employment stimulation in bad economic times, better housing, provision for the disabled, aged and chronically ill, and a whole system of public health care. This can now be seen as an early conceptualization of the welfare state.

It is high time Nightingale is given due credit as a major social reformer, for her vision of a public health care system within a broader system of social welfare, and for offering a method by which these reforms could be achieved.

For Further Reading

E.T. Cook, *The Life of Florence Nightingale* (Macmillan, 1913: the best biography now out of print, but available in libraries); Lynn McDonald, ed., Florence Nightingale on Society and Politics, volume 5 in the *Collected Works of Florence Nightingale* (Wilfrid Laurier University Press, 2003); Florence Nightingale on Public Health Care, volume 6 in the *Collected Works of Florence Nightingale* (Wilfrid Laurier University Press, 2004).

LYNN MCDONALD is professor of sociology at the University of Guelph and director of the *Collected Works of Florence Nightingale*. For details on the project see: www.sociology.uoguelph.ca/fnightingale

Benjamin Disraeli and the Spirit of England

T.A. Jenkins reviews the life and legacy of Benjamin Disraeli, statesman, novelist and man-about-town, on the bicentenary of his birth.

T.A. JENKINS

'Imagination governs mankind'. The force of this observation, made in 1833 in a diary kept by Benjamin Disraeli, who was born two hundred years ago this month, found no better illustration than in the course of his own political career, which involved an extraordinary triumph of imagination over adverse circumstances.

Disraeli was the son of a minor figure in London literary circles, and he did not have the advantage of a public school and university education, gaining much of his knowledge instead from intensive reading in his father's library. As a young man he acquired a modest reputation as a writer of society novels, beginning with *Vivian Grey* (1826) published when he was twenty-two, but he achieved greater notoriety through his flamboyant lifestyle, dressing as a 'dandy' in brightly coloured clothes with lace cuffs and buckled shoes. He was stigmatised, moreover, by the fact that he had been born a Jew (the family name was originally spelt D'Israeli) and only converted to Christianity at the age of twelve because his father thought it would help his social advancement.

Yet this man who appeared so foreign in his physical appearance and ways of thinking, and who was self-consciously an outsider, went on to become leader of the Conservative Party, which was identified with the interests of the aristocratic ruling elite. He served on two occasions as prime minister, and ended his life as the Earl of Beaconsfield and Queen Victoria's personal favourite. Equally remarkable, the myths generated by his career helped to inspire the imaginations of future generations of Conservatives.

Disraeli's character has puzzled historians as much as it did his contemporaries. Until recently, there was a tendency to accept the view of his critics at the time, that Disraeli was a cynical adventurer, a political charlatan, motivated by no consistent principle other than the fulfilment of his personal ambition. However, new insights have suggested a more sophisticated conclusion, that Disraeli did possess a clear set of ideas, derived from his interpretation of history, the insights this provided into England's (it was always England's) national character and des-

tiny, and his belief in his own unique position in relation to them. While undoubtedly an opportunist in his methods, Disraeli's underlying sense of political purpose, and the rhetoric he used to promote his objectives, never changed.

One crucial influence on the development of the young Disraeli's thinking was the work of the German romantic philosophers, notably Kant and Goethe. From his position of relative obscurity, Disraeli became fascinated by the concept of the man of genius whose profound insight into the true meaning of things enabled him to shape the course of events. The impact of this idea is evident in one of Disraeli's occasional jottings, from 1842: *Spirit of the Times. To know it and one'self the secret of success.*

Disraeli's father inspired in his son feelings of reverence for England's historic ruling institutions, the crown, the territorial aristocracy and the established church, which he grew to believe embodied national values and were a vital source of social cohesion. Disraeli's politics were always instinctively Conservative (he often preferred the older label of 'Tory'), and though he flirted for a time with the romantic form of radicalism associated with Sir Francis Burdett, which was itself patriotic and monarchical in character, it was as a Tory romantic that he laid public claim to fill the role of the man of genius, which he had imagined for himself.

In a pamphlet entitled *Vindication of the English Constitution* (1835), and a series of letters to *The Times* in 1836 using the pseudonym 'Runnymede', Disraeli presented an account of six hundred years of history to show how England's laws, liberties and institutions had reached their present state. The villains of his story were the Whig 'oligarchy', who in the eighteenth century had tried to monopolise the government by enslaving the monarchy, whereas the Tories had shown themselves to be a truly 'national party', representing the views of 'nine-tenths of the people'. Although this was obviously an exaggerated view, it was not merely the product of wild fantasy and had some foundation in the work of historical writers like Henry Hallam (it has since found some corroboration from modern scholarship).

The Great Reform Act of 1832, Disraeli's argument continued, was a piece of Whig gerrymandering, designed to rearrange the electoral system so as to perpetuate the dominance of themselves and their allies, the Utilitarian Radicals (whose rationalist philosophy omitted imagination), the Protestant Dissenters and the Irish Nationalists. To this end they were engaged in another destructive campaign to undermine the crown, the House of Lords and the Church of England; the integrity of the Empire and the greatness of England itself was thus imperilled. The country, Disraeli concluded, must look to the revitalised Conservative Party, under Sir Robert Peel, to save it from disaster. Disraeli himself secured election to the House of Commons in 1837, but to his dismay was not considered for office when Peel formed a government in 1841.

As a frustrated backbencher in the early 1840s, Disraeli became the focus for a small group of idealistic young noblemen, including George Smythe and Lord John Manners, who inspired the so-called 'Young England' movement. In a trilogy of novels, *Coningsby or The New Generation* (1844), *Sybil or The Two Nations* (1845) and *Tancred or The New Crusade* (1847), Disraeli sought to disseminate Young England's principles and thereby assert his claim to be recognised as a sage and prophet. He did this indirectly, through the character Sidonia, a mysterious, all-knowing Jewish banker who was in confidential communication with all the great statesmen of Europe. Sidonia was clearly Disraeli's alter ego (the first three letters of his name spell 'Dis'), and his function was to act as an intellectual guide to Coningsby, educating this rather aimless young aristocrat into understanding the responsibility of his class to serve as the leaders and guardians of England's political traditions.

Disraeli used *Sybil* to address current concerns about the 'condition of England', in particular, the problems of poverty and social instability in the rapidly expanding industrial towns. He built upon his interpretation of history, to show how in medieval times the poor had been protected within a hierarchical social structure headed by the aristocracy and the Church. The Whigs were again to blame for what had gone wrong, as it was their ancestors who had plundered the monastic lands, while they themselves had encouraged irresponsible economic individualism and enacted such harsh legislation as the Poor Law of 1834. What was needed was the restoration of a sense of community, through the example set by a paternalistic aristocracy, and a rejuvenated monarchy to inspire the loyalty of the people.

A striking feature of *Tancred*, which dealt with the rediscovery of national faith, is the way that Disraeli reintroduced Sidonia to emphasise the contribution made by the Jewish race to Western civilisation. Indeed, it was argued that Christianity should be seen as completed Judaism (not an altogether unusual view at this time). Disraeli had certainly experienced anti-Semitism in his youth and as he tried to make his way in politics. When he stood for election at Shrewsbury in 1841, for instance, the crowd waved pieces of roast pork on sticks. Far from repudiating or downplaying his Jewish heritage, however, Disraeli boldly celebrated it and used it as a weapon in his fight for political acceptance. He went so far as to assert that his own branch of the Jewish people, the Sephardim, were more aristocratic than the English, in order to demonstrate that he stood on an equal social footing with the English nobility.

The Young England movement accomplished nothing, and its ideology was obviously fanciful, but in calling for the political and spiritual rebirth of the nation, and exhorting the Conservative Party to rediscover its authentic traditions, Disraeli had set himself up as a formidable critic of Peel. Since coming into office, the prime minister had shown a disturbing tendency to emulate the policies of his Whig-Radical opponents, in a bid to attract support from the urban middle-classes. In 1846, Peel's proposal to repeal the Corn Laws, a series of tariffs on imported cereals designed to protect agricultural producers from competition, was the final straw for many Conservatives.

It is at least now possible to understand how Disraeli could, without apparent irony, present himself as the spokesman for an aristocratic and landed order which felt betrayed by its own leader. He launched a series of devastating attacks on Peel, which did much to raise morale on the Conservative backbenches. The key to the effectiveness of his onslaught was that, rather than trying to counter the prime minister with economic theory or trade statistics, he questioned Peel's character and integrity by ridiculing him. Peel was thus described as a mental lightweight, incapable of forming his own opinions:

> . . . he is a burglar of others' intellect . . . there is no statesman who has committed political petty larceny on so great a scale.

Such mockery convulsed the House, and the hapless Peel had no answer to it. Corn Law repeal was forced through, with support from the official opposition, but nearly two-thirds of Conservative MPs voted against Peel and he was forced to resign soon afterwards.

Disraeli's prowess in debate had made him an indispensable asset to the Conservatives, and by 1849 he was effectively the party's leader in the Commons. In keeping with his newly found status, he was set up as a country gentleman through the purchase of Hughenden Manor in Buckinghamshire, with the help of a £25,000 loan from the Bentinck family. Even so, some Conservatives still regarded him with distrust, if not disgust, and he was only tolerated because the Earl of Derby, in the House of Lords, was the party's unquestioned overall leader.

Disraeli's personal triumph was very much a pyrrhic one for the Conservatives, as the Corn Law crisis had fatally split the party and consigned it for a generation to almost permanent opposition. Following Peel's death in 1850 most of his leading disciples, including the man who was to become Disraeli's bitterest rival, William Gladstone, gradually aligned themselves with the Whigs and Radicals in what became known as the Liberal Party. This was to dominate the political scene, and the three brief minority governments formed by Derby, in 1852, 1858–59 and 1866–68, only came about because of temporary divisions among the Liberals. The Liberal policies of free trade and low taxation were quickly established as economic orthodoxy, having apparently laid the foundations for a period of growing prosperity, and by 1852 Derby and Disraeli had abandoned the idea of trying to restore agricultural protection. Nor was much heard of the exotic, socially-reformist Toryism of

Young England, now that it was accepted that state interventionism should be strictly limited. Another problem for the Conservatives was that Lord Palmerston, who became prime minister in 1855, was a moderate Liberal who posed no credible threat to the monarchy or other traditional institutions, while his 'patriotic' conduct of foreign policy made him popular with the country.

In these dispiriting circumstances, Disraeli faced the largely futile and seemingly endless grind of opposition leadership. Given the responsibility of his position, and the more sober front he was expected to present to the world (from 1846 he usually dressed all in black), historians have wondered whether there is any connection at all between the early and later phases of his career. It is possible, though, to detect some intriguing echoes from the past as he finally approached the point of fulfilling his political dreams.

Palmerston's death in 1865 created new opportunities for the Conservatives, and the following year they exploited Liberal divisions over parliamentary reform by joining with dissident moderates to defeat Lord Russell's bill. Russell resigned and Derby formed his third administration. However, far from resisting reform, the Conservatives proceeded to introduce a more extensive measure of their own, which proposed to enfranchise householders in the boroughs.

The 1867 session of Parliament became celebrated for Disraeli's brilliant display of tactical skill, in steering the Reform Bill through the Commons, despite the fact that the government was in a minority. It was essential to prevent the Liberals from uniting behind Gladstone's leadership, and Disraeli was therefore prepared to make concessions on various points, stripping away many of the restrictions in the original bill, in order to secure support from the Radical section of the opposition. This also gave him the personal satisfaction of leaving Gladstone in a beleaguered position. Consequently, the Reform Bill in its final version almost doubled the electorate of England and Wales, to nearly two million, and gave voting rights to many working men.

Although the main reason for carrying the Bill was to give the Conservatives some much-needed credibility, as a constructive party of government, Disraeli used a public speech at Edinburgh, in October 1867, to claim that it had actually been a preconceived plan and was in keeping with the party's eighteenth-century Tory traditions. It proved that the Conservatives were really 'the national party of England', who trusted in the loyalty and political responsibility of the working classes.

Disraeli succeeded the ailing Derby as prime minister in February 1868, but the Conservatives received little reward from the new electorate and suffered a heavy defeat at the general election later that year. The Liberals, now united under Gladstone, returned to power, and his government embarked on a series of ambitious reforms affecting elementary education, the army, public house licensing, the Irish church and Irish land tenure.

For some time Disraeli was obliged to lie low, but by 1872 there were unmistakable signs that the pressures of relentless reforming activity were opening-up fissures within the Liberal ranks. Whereas some feared that Gladstone was going too far too fast, others were disappointed with the legislation on offer. Among the most extreme elements, there were voices criticising the monarchy and the House of Lords, advocating the disestablishment of the Church of England, and demanding that public houses be shut down to promote temperance.

In two notable public speeches, at Manchester in April and the Crystal Palace in June 1872, Disraeli completed the task of re-working his earlier ideas to fit into a changing political context. He condemned what he called the 'cosmopolitan', un-English doctrines of the Liberals, and remarked that Gladstone's was the first government to have been 'avowedly formed on a principle of violence' towards national institutions. There was a remarkable similarity, here, between Disraeli's strictures against the destructive tendencies of Gladstonian Liberalism and his comments about the Whigs in the 1830s. He also accused Gladstone of weakness in the conduct of foreign policy, by failing to uphold the national interest in disputes with Russia and the USA, and alleged that there was a sinister Liberal plan to bring about the disintegration of the Empire.

Disraeli repeated the assertion he had made in 1867, that there was a natural affinity between the Conservatives and the people because they shared the same 'national principles'. The 'working classes', in particular, were 'English to the core' and proud of their country, and they knew that 'the greatness and the Empire of England are to be attributed to the ancient institutions of the land'. In contrast to the Liberals' obsession with attacking these institutions, the Conservatives, according to Disraeli, were interested in carrying social reforms to promote the welfare of the people. He did not specify a programme of measures, but hinted at action in such areas as factory hours and public health. The vision of Young England, it seemed, had not entirely dimmed. Indeed, generations of Conservatives to come would believe that Disraeli had established an enduring platform for his party, based on policies of imperialism and social reform.

At the general election of 1874 the Conservatives finally broke the Liberals' virtual monopoly of government, by recording their first overall majority since Peel's victory in 1841. The party had significantly expanded its support beyond the traditional county strongholds, to include many seats in urban areas, particularly in London and Lancashire. Contemporary observers were agreed that there had been a marked drift of business and suburban middle-class opinion away from the Liberals, as a result of the unease about Gladstone's style of government, which Disraeli had so astutely exploited. Nevertheless, Conservative gains in the boroughs would have been impossible without an appreciable degree of working-class support as well.

Disraeli's social prejudices were apparent in the composition of his government, which was recruited overwhelmingly from members of the 'natural' ruling class. Of the twelve original Cabinet ministers, half were peers, one was the son of a Duke, four others (including Disraeli) were landowners and only one, the Home Secretary R.A. Cross, came from a 'middle class', banking background. Disraeli himself took a peerage in 1876, becoming the Earl of Beaconsfield, as his fragile health was no longer equal to the demands of leading the House of Commons.

The government had no blueprint for social reform and Disraeli, who never cared for the dry detail of administration, left the initiative to other ministers such as Cross. Several useful, and relatively uncontroversial measures were carried, including the Factory Act (1874), which set a maximum fifty-six hour working week for women and children, and the Artisans Dwellings Act (1875), which gave local authorities powers to carry out slum clearance projects. Disraeli attached special importance to the trade union legislation of 1875, which removed the threat of criminal prosecution of strikers and allowed peaceful picketing.

Foreign and imperial affairs were always of greater interest to Disraeli, and it was in this sphere that he made his personal mark, seeking, sometimes through symbolic gestures, to maintain national power and prestige. In 1875, for example, he received plaudits for his secret negotiation to purchase a 44 per cent stake in the Suez Canal Company, thereby registering the country's interest in this strategically and economically important waterway. The following year, at Queen Victoria's request, the Imperial Titles Act elevated her status to that of Empress of India, a move that Disraeli hoped would inspire the imagination and loyalty of the Indians as well as of the electorate at home. He remained convinced of the political value of the monarchy's emotional appeal to the people, and was eager to appropriate it for the Conservative Party.

Disraeli's handling of the 'Eastern Question' (the position of the Turkish Empire in Eastern Europe), in 1876-78, provoked strong passions on both sides of the political debate. Determined to prevent any extension of Russian influence towards the eastern Mediterranean, which he feared might eventually threaten the trade route to India, Disraeli refused to co-operate with international efforts to coerce the Turks, who had brutally suppressed an uprising by Bulgarian Christians. Furthermore, when Russia declared war on the Turks, Disraeli took preparatory steps to threaten the Russians with the possibility of military intervention. Public opinion was sharply divided, with some joining Gladstone in condemning the government's 'immoral', warmongering behaviour, while others expressed violently anti-Russian sentiments, giving rise to the term 'jingoism'. Disraeli's bluff appeared to pay off when he attended a Congress of the European Powers at Berlin, which settled the Eastern crisis and enabled him to return claiming 'peace with honour'.

Thereafter, everything went badly wrong for Disraeli's government. By 1879-80 the economy had sunk into a deep depression, and diminishing tax revenues forced ministers to resort to the shocking expedient of borrowing in order to cover their budget deficit. Worse still, military operations against the Afghans and the Zulus, resulting from actions taken by officials on the spot, suffered embarrassing setbacks for which ministers had to take responsibility. Gladstone brilliantly exploited the mounting public discontent by delivering a blistering moral critique of Disraeli's foreign and financial policies. Disraeli counter-attacked in characteristic fashion, alleging that the Liberals had unscrupulously allied themselves with the resurgent force of Irish nationalism, in a treacherous plot to 'enfeeble our colonies by [a] policy of decomposition'. However, this made little impression on public opinion, and at the general election of 1880 the Liberals were returned to power with a large majority, completely wiping out the Conservative gains of 1874.

At the time of Disraeli's death in April 1881, therefore, it seemed that his vision of the Conservatives as the 'national party' had come to nothing, and that his hated rival, Gladstone, had finally triumphed. But in the event, Disraeli proved to be as great an asset to his party in death as he had ever been when alive. His warning in 1880 about the threat posed by Irish nationalism soon looked remarkably prescient, and resistance to the demand for 'Home Rule' provided the ideological basis for a rejuvenated Conservatism after 1886, when the issue split Gladstone's Liberal Party. Meanwhile, a younger generation of Conservatives, notably Lord Randolph Churchill, hailed Disraeli as the prophet of what was now termed 'Tory Democracy'. An organisation founded in his memory in 1883, the Primrose League (named after his supposedly favourite flower), gave practical expression to this belief in the Conservatives' ability to cultivate support from the working classes, and by 1891 it boasted one million members. Disraeli's reputation as the advocate of 'one nation' politics also made him a hero to many twentieth-century Conservatives, such as Stanley Baldwin and Harold Macmillan. Strange as his ideas may often seem, the power of Disraeli's imagination left a rich legacy to the Conservative Party, and finally made good his claim to be recognised as a masterly exponent of 'English values'.

For Further Reading

Robert Blake, *Disraeli* (Eyre and Spottiswoode, 1966); Richard Shannon, *The Age of Disraeli, 1868–1881* (Longman, 1992); Jane Ridley, *The Young Disraeli* (Sinclair-Stevenson, 1995); Paul Smith, *Disraeli. A Brief Life* (Cambridge University Press, 1996); Charles Richmond and Paul Smith (eds.), *The Self-Fashioning of Disraeli, 1818–1851* (Cambridge University Press, 1998); Todd Endelman and Tony Kushner (eds.), *Disraeli's Jewishness* (Vallentine Mitchell, 2002). See www.historytoday.com for more articles on Disraeli in our online archive.

DR T.A. JENKINS is Senior Research Officer at the History of Parliament, London. He is the author of *Disraeli and Victorian Conservatism* (Macmillan, 1996).

The Incurable Wound

Lizabeth Peak explores the history of the dreaded disease of rabies.

LIZABETH PEAK

Rabies, or hydrophobia, is one of the oldest and most feared afflictions known to humanity. The terror it has inspired throughout the ages is well justified. Its hapless victims may be seized with convulsions or plagued with hallucinations. They become hypersensitive to light, sound and touch. As their throat muscles become paralyzed, they cannot swallow, and appear to foam at the mouth. As their vocal cords go into spasm, they may make guttural sounds as if growling, and become unable to speak. Its effect on the limbic system of the brain causes increased aggressive behavior, and victims may attack other people. Without effective treatment, it is always fatal. In a time when disease was often attributed to sorcery, superstition or sin, such a spectacle would have been a horrifying thing to witness.

What the Ancients Knew

The name rabies is thought to be derived from the ancient Sanskrit word *rahbas*, meaning "to do violence". In the 23rd century BC, the pre-Mosaic Eshunna Code of Babylon described a disease in dogs that was fatal to any person bitten by the dog. The code called for stiff penalties for owners of diseased dogs that caused a death.

The Latin word *rabere*, meaning to rage or rave, is also thought to be derived from the ancient Sanskrit. In first-century-AD Rome, both Aulus Cornelius Celsus and Pliny the Elder wrote extensively on the disease. Both thought it could be successfully treated. Celsus is credited with being the first to thoroughly describe human rabies. His preventive measures included cutting out the bitten area to allow the virus to flow out freely and cauterizing it with a hot iron. He saw no danger in sucking the wound, provided the practitioner had no open sores in his mouth. Pliny had his own unique ideas about how to prevent and treat rabies. "When Sirius rises at dawn, the dog rabies is dangerous to humans . . . a person thus bitten is dying of thirst while abhorring any idea of drinking water." He recommended sheltering dogs for at least 30 days during this time of year while supplementing their food with plenty of fresh hen droppings. His therapies included eating raw dog's liver or applying ashes of the tail hair of the affected dog. Also deemed effective was application of axle grease pounded with lime or ash from the burnt head of the dog, or extracts prepared from "dung of badger, cuckoo, or swallow, or the cast off slough of snakes pounded in wine with a male crab." If one were fresh out of badger dung, snake slough and male crabs, one could try pounded cock's comb, or horse dung sprinkled with vinegar and warmed in a fig. Despite the best efforts of the day, however, those afflicted with the disease had little hope.

The Spread of Rabies

During the Middle Ages, little progress was made in the treatment and prevention of rabies, although there were many outbreaks throughout Europe and the New World. In 1271, groups of rabid wolves in Franconia attacked herds of domestic animals. Emboldened by their disease and rendered unnaturally aggressive, they wandered into towns and villages and were responsible for 30 human deaths. A major scourge hit Paris in 1604.

The first documentation of rabies in the New World was reported in Mexico in 1709 by Fray Jose Gil Ramirez. However, rabies may have been the disease referred to by Petrus Martyr-Anglerius, bishop of the New World, when he wrote in the early 16th century about a disease of madness seen in Spanish soldiers after being bitten by bats. Rabies became more widespread in the Atlantic colonies in the late 18th century as dogs and foxes were imported from Europe for Britishstyle fox hunting. Epidemics were recorded in 1770 and 1771.

Reports of skunk rabies were common in the Western territories in the 19th century, and stories were told of "phobey cats".

Of Vampires and Werewolves

In 1598, in the Jura Mountains of France, a huge rabid wolf descended from the forest and attacked a young boy and girl. The girl was killed immediately, but the boy was able to fend off the wolf with a knife. Unfortunately, he eventually died of his wounds. A hunting party was sent out to find the wolf, but instead they came across Perenette Gandillon, a feeble-minded woman from the district of St. Claude. Because she bore a wound similar to a knife wound, it was assumed by the hunting party that she was the wolf, reverted into her human form. In the village, she was attacked and killed by a mob of peasants. According to Henri Bouget, a French inquisitor notorious for his sadistic methods of torture and execution, "When Perenette Gandillon turned herself into a wolf and killed a child, the creature had no tail and human hands in place of its front paws." Perenette's brother Pierre and nephew Georges were arrested on suspicion of being werewolves. While in captivity, the Gandillon men were said to behave like animals, growling, barking and crawling on all fours. They were eventually burned at the stake for sorcery and "shape-shifting".

Were the Gandillon men simply victims of rabies? Because of the striking similarities between the behavior legend attributes to werewolves and the actual behavior of rabies victims, and because it was so frequently transmitted by rabid wolves, it has been suggested that the disease was at least partially responsible for the rise of werewolf stories in Europe in the Middle Ages. Certainly the bizarre, aggressive behavior of a rabid wolf is far more similar to that folk tales ascribe to werewolves than is the behavior of a healthy animal. Since rabies is also closely associated with bats, the same has been said for the emergence of the vampire legend. Tales of vampirism have often coincided with outbreaks of the disease; one particularly devastating outbreak occurred in Hungary from 1721 to 1728, about the time that vampire stories first began to appear in Europe. The similarities between the two conditions are remarkable. Vampires are active at night and shun daylight. Rabies victims often suffer from insomnia, and are hypersensitive to stimuli such as light and sound. The vampire's aversion to garlic is similar to the rabies victim's intolerance of strong odors. Most vampires of legend are men, as are the great majority of rabies patients. Since both vampirism and rabies are transmitted by biting, it is not outside the realm of possibility that vampire stories could have arisen as a way for ordinary folk to explain the horrifying spectacle of a rabid human being.

The Medicine Men Bite Back

Traditionally efforts to treat and control rabies consisted of little more than modifications of the old methods. Middle Eastern physicians, some of the most learned men of the Middle Ages, also grappled with the disease. In the early ninth century, Jahaiah-Ebn-Serapion of Syria recognized rabies as incurable but still proposed that the patient could be helped by swallowing water enclosed in a capsule of hardened honey. The Arab physician Rhazes wrote of a man who barked like a dog at night and then died, and of another who was seized with trembling and "rigors" whenever he saw water. Avicenna, an Arab physician of the 11th century, directed that bite wounds should be opened and left open for 40 days. He also described rabid people as barking like dogs and trying to bite other people.

In 1546, Italian physician Girolamo Fracastoro of Verona wrote one of the first known treatises dealing exclusively with infectious disease, in which he described the symptoms of rabies in great detail, calling it "the incurable wound":

"The patient can neither stand nor lie down; like a mad man he flings himself hither and thither, tears his flesh with his hands, and feels intolerable thirst. This is the most distressing symptom, for he so shrinks from water and all liquids that he would rather die than drink or be brought near to water. It is then they bite other persons, foam at the mouth, their eyes look twisted, and finally they are exhausted and painfully breathe their last."

Fracastoro recognized that rabies could only be transmitted if blood was drawn, but he wrongly concluded that animals were no longer contagious once they had died. A century before Anton Van Leeuwenhoek (1632–1723), Fracastoro wrote of "germs", or "seeds of disease", with the ability to "propagate and engender what is similar to themselves", a remarkably accurate description of how viruses behave. Unfortunately, in an age when medical thought was still firmly rooted in philosophy, religion and superstition, rather than in clinical observation, Fracastoro's ideas had little influence. Even after Leeuwenhoek's microscopic observations of "animalculae" and the beginnings of the germ theory, little attention was paid to rabies in the face of such scourges as smallpox and plague, which took a much heavier toll in human lives. In addition, even the improved microscopes of the day were not sensitive enough to detect the extremely minute virus, so no causative agent could be identified. Meanwhile, local control efforts usually consisted of the quarantine of suspect animals and destruction of those that became ill.

In England in the late 1700s, a two- to four-shilling bounty was offered for each dog killed, which naturally led to the destruction of many healthy animals. At about the same time, in Madrid, 900 dogs were killed in one day, and in Alexandria, all the dogs in the city were slaughtered.

In the early 19th century, interest in clinical research, direct observation of the patient and animal experimentation began to increase. In 1804, German scientist Georg Gottfried Zinke confirmed the centuries-old theory that rabies was transmitted through saliva by infecting dogs, cats, rabbits and roosters with the saliva of rabid dogs. Nine years later, in a somewhat controversial experiment, Francois Magendie and Gilbert Breschet reversed the process and infected mastiff dogs with the saliva of a human rabies patient. In the latter part of the century, the new profession of veterinary medicine began to provide input into the science of comparative medicine, paving the way for increased use of animal experimentation. In 1879, Pierre Victor Galtier, a professor of veterinary medicine from Lyons, succeeded in transmitting the virus serially through rabbits, a process which was found to attenuate, or weaken, the virus. It was on this foundation that the most significant breakthrough in rabies prevention and treatment would take place.

Mad Dogs and Frenchmen

One year after Galtier's experiments, French physicist and microbiologist Louis Pasteur received a rather unusual gift from a former French Army veterinary surgeon. Though not a gift most people would appreciate, for Pasteur the two rabid dogs sparked the work which would help cement his place in medical history.

Pasteur was born in 1822 in Dole, in the Jura region of France—the province of Gandillon fame. As a child he had witnessed rabies first hand when he watched as a man named Nicole, who had been bitten by a rabid wolf, had his wounds cauterized with a hot iron. Eight other people who had been attacked by the wolf died, but Nicole survived.

Pasteur began his education at the Royal College of Besancon. At 23 he was appointed physics professor at the Tournon High School. Over the next 30 years, Pasteur became a prolific researcher, publishing ground-breaking work on such topics as crystals, transformation of acids, fermentation, diseases of wine and of silkworms and the debunking of the concept of spontaneous generation. Appointments, prizes and honors followed on a regular basis. By the time he received the gift of the rabid dogs, he was already well known among European and American scientific communities. In December 1880, he began his studies of rabies.

After some time experimenting with rabid dogs, Pasteur concluded that saliva transmission was inefficient, unreliable, time-consuming and downright dangerous. Knowing that rabies was mainly a disease of the nervous system, he began using ground-up spinal cord from rabbits who had been clinically infected with the virus. Building on Galtier's earlier work on attenuation, Pasteur induced immunity to rabies in a healthy dog by inoculating it over a 14-day period with successively more virulent spinal cord material. At the end of the two weeks, the treated dog was rendered immune to rabies even when the most virulent cord material was injected directly into its brain.

Having shown that dogs could be vaccinated against rabies, Pasteur now considered the possibility of using his new method to prevent the onset of symptoms in people who had been bitten. He was considerably anxious about testing it in humans; two earlier attempts using different preparations had failed. When his request to try the treatment on convicts was turned down by the French government, Pasteur actually considered infecting himself with rabies. That became unnecessary, however, as the opportunity to test the vaccine on a human literally landed on his doorstep.

On the morning of 4 July 1885, in the town of Meissengott, nine-year-old Joseph Meister was attacked by a rabid dog, sustaining deep bite wounds to his arms and thighs. A bricklayer witnessed the attack and fought off the dog with an iron bar. The dog found its way home, where it was immediately shot and killed by its master. Joseph was taken to the local doctor, who cauterized Joseph's 14 wounds and recommended that he be taken to Pasteur in Paris.

On 6 July, Joseph, his mother and the dog's owner appeared at Pasteur's laboratory. Joseph was in a great deal of pain and could barely walk because of the severity of his wounds. Recalling his earlier failures, Pasteur agonized over the decision of whether or not to treat the boy. After consulting with colleagues, Pasteur became certain that Joseph would die unless something was done. The decision was made, but "not without lively and sore anxiety". That evening, 60 hours after the attack,

Pasteur administered the first of 13 inoculations, given over 10 days. During that time, Pasteur barely slept, plagued with anxiety and nightmares. But 10 days after the final injection, Joseph left Paris for home, completely healthy. (He never forgot his experience with Pasteur. When he grew up, he took a job as a doorman at the Pasteur Institute in Paris, founded in 1888 primarily for research and development of the rabies vaccine. He stayed there until he was 64. When the Nazis invaded Paris in 1940, they ordered Joseph to open Pasteur's crypt. Rather than comply, Joseph chose to take his own life.)

The Aftermath

Pasteur's rabies treatment was initially received with a fair amount of skepticism. Not all patients had as favorable an outcome as Joseph Meister. When a 10-year-old girl died 11 days after her treatment, Pasteur wept openly as he watched her die. The father of another child sued Pasteur, who was criticized in the press, both in France and abroad. Many scientists and physicians felt that the vaccine carried too much inherent risk to justify its use on people. The concept of vaccine-induced "laboratory rabies" was bandied about by Pasteur's critics. Also, the vaccine sometimes caused an inflammation of the brain, which could lead to permanent paralysis.

Work with the vaccine continued, however, and results improved. Records show that between 1880 and 1885, 60 patients died of rabies in Paris hospitals. In the following year, when the vaccine was used, only one treated patient died. In July 1887, Pasteur was appointed permanent Secretary of the Academy of Sciences, the highest honor of his career. In October of that year, Pasteur suffered two devastating strokes a week apart. He died on 28 September 1895, at Marnes la Coquette.

Today, rabies continues to be endemic in many parts of the world, and will probably always be with us. Unlike smallpox, which has been declared eradicated, and polio, which is nearing eradication, rabies can infect almost all warmblooded animals, whereas smallpox and polio are strictly human diseases. Most cases are reported in Asia and Africa. Human cases in Europe and the Americas are now quite rare.

Further Reading

Baer, G.M., J. Nevile, and G.S. Turner. *Rabbis and Rabies: A Pictorial History of Rabies Through the Ages* (Mexico City: Laboratorios Baer, 1996).

Finley, Don. *Mad Dogs: The New Rabies Plague* (College Station, TX: Texas A&M University Press, 1998).

Fleming, George. *Rabies and Hydrophobia* (London: Chapman & Hall, 1872).

Jackson, Alan C., and William H. Wunner. *Rabies* (San Diego: Academic Press, 2002).

From *History Magazine*, October/November 2004, pp. 25-28. Copyright © 2004 by Lizabeth Peak. Reprinted by permission of the author.

Quinine's Feverish Tales and Trails

For centuries, this alkaloid, produced from the bark of an Andean tree, provoked international disputes and intrigue as scientists pursued the cure for malaria.

LOUIS WERNER

Next time you catch inexplicable chill on a hot day in the jungle and an old country doctor prescribes "powders of the countess" ground from "Jesuit's bark" peeled off a "fever tree," you probably have a touch of malaria, and what you will be taking is quinine, which for centuries in one form or another has been the best treatment.

Quinine is the strongest of four fever-fighting alkaloids found in the bark of trees of the genus *Cinchona*, belonging to the Rubiaceae family, of which there are some twenty-three species, all native to South America, growing along the eastern spine of the Andes. While quinine was not isolated in pharmacological form until 1820, cinchona bark had been known by Europeans since the early seventeenth century as a cure for malaria in all its various forms, known then by such archaic names as the *ague, tertiana, quartana*, and double *quartana* fevers.

It is a peculiarity of how scientific knowledge often moves onward—in periodic lags and spurts, in alternating breakthroughs and dead ends—that, for more than one hundred years, cinchona was the well-known bark of an unknown tree that, for more than two hundred years, cured the well-known symptoms of an unknown disease.

Before the discovery of cinchona bark, malaria had no known relief, even though the disease had ravaged the western world for millennia. The ancient Greek physician Dioscorides had first classified malarial fevers as tertian and quartan, that is, recurring cyclically every first and third day or every first and fourth day. His recommended remedy, ingesting either the three-leaf or four-leaf cinquefoil plant, was no more effective than the other leading prescriptions of the day—eating spider webs, wearing amulets containing dogs' teeth, or sleeping with Book 4 of the *Iliad* under one's pillow.

How and when cinchona was first found to relieve malarial fever is unknown, especially given that it is uncertain if people of the pre-1492 Americas suffered from the disease at all, or whether it was an unwanted gift of the Columbian exchange.

That the tree should be called cinchona is due to the legend of its first successfully treated European patient, herself an unwilling participant in this exchange. A subsequent typographical error, made by the Swedish taxonomist Carl Linnaeus when classifying the cinchona tree on the basis of its flower's sexual characteristics, is responsible for its spelling

The countess of Chinchón, wife of the viceroy of Peru and an unhappy resident of the Americas during her husband's ten-year duty there, was said to have taken ill with a debilitating fever in 1635. Word reached the viceregal palace from the northern town of Loja, located in the *audiencia* of Quito, that the bark of a tree there, called *cava-chucchu*, or fever bark, when pulverized and eaten, was known to cure such an ill. So the story was told—the bark was sent for and it cured the *virreina*, whereby the medicine became known under the colloquial name *polvos de la condesa*.

Despite many repetitions of this story through the years, it is probably untrue. The viceroy's personal secretary kept a detailed record of all his mistress's aches and pains while abroad, and in that time all that he noted amiss was one sore throat and one case of mild diarrhea. She did die, however, in Cartagena of undetermined cause, enroute home to Madrid in 1641.

If the countess had known the chronicle of the Augustinian order in Peru, written in Lima by the friar Antonio de la Calancha sometime before her purported malarial bout, she would have read this: "A tree grows which they call the fever tree (*árbol de calenturas*), in the country of Loja, whose bark, of the color of cinnamon, made into a powder amounting to the weight of two small silver coins and given as a beverage, cures the fevers and *tertianas*; it has produced miraculous results in Lima."

How the bark's efficacy against fever first came to light is recounted in other fanciful tales, some related by Charles-Marie de La Condamine, the eighteenth-century French scientist (see *Américas*, January-February 1995). One told of a sick mountain lion that was observed chewing the tree bark and making himself well again—at least La Condamine was skeptical enough to question whether there were in fact feverish lions in South America. Another story concerned a Spanish soldier suffering from a malarial fit, who in his madness drank from a bitter tasting pool of water, fainted, and when revived, found himself cured. Later investigation showed that water's bitterness came from a cinchona, tree that had fallen into the pool.

Jesuits were the first western scientists in Peru, ever curious about its flora and fauna and traveling far afield to collect whatever seemed useful to humankind. Among their finds, based on the help of native informants, was the cough-suppressing syrup of Tolu, the folkloric tonic sarsaparilla, coca leaves, and the febrifugal bark of the so-called Peruvian balsam tree *(Myroxylon pereirae)*, known in Quechua as *quina*, meaning bark, or sometimes as *quinquina*, meaning bark of barks, by which name cinchona bark was often called in error.

Jesuits chewed bark whenever they came upon a new species of tree, and felt that acerbity was the best cure for certain humoral imbalances. The cinchona's bitterness, they were certain, would be good for something that ailed the human race, and thus it came to be known also as "Jesuit's bark."

In 1650, a large shipment of cinchona bark was sent to a Spanish Jesuit in Rome, Cardinal Juan de Lugo, who gave it to the pope's personal physician for testing. A year later, the *Schedula Romana*, a Vatican-issued medical instruction, in its time something like a *Physicians Desk Reference* for Catholics, extolled the benefits of cinchona. Thus the bark's fame was launched in Europe and thereby gained another popular appellation, "powders of the cardinal."

Medical historians shake their heads in disbelief at what happened next. Despite the growing rivalry between the Jesuit-controlled papacy and the Jansenism-influenced courts of northern Europe, in 1652 Archduke Leopold of Austria, suffering from a double-quartan fever, was persuaded to take the Roman cure. It proved a failure, giving him a severe case of heartburn for good measure.

Doctors blamed the Jesuits for their duke's continuing distress, which eventually killed him, and published a nasty diatribe against cinchona entitled "Exposure of the Febrifuge Powder from the American World." This war of medico-theological tract went back and forth for years, with cinchona bizarrely uttered in the same breath as such theological sticking points as predestination and free will.

Who knows how cinchona affected the course of history these early days'? Some think that the Chinese emperor Kang Hsi was cured of his fevers in 1692 by a dose of Jesuit's bark. And one wonders: Had Oliver Cromwell's physician not been so anti-papist, might he have administered the popish powder to his dying patient and thus extended the English Revolution. But as one Protestant physician said, Jesuit doctors "worship the powder and deceive from head to heel."

Not all English doctors were blinded by religion, however. In the 1670s, the entrepreneurial quack Robert Tabor, King Charles II's personal attendant, advertised a secret cure for fe-

ver, "safer" than the Peruvian barks," he called it, in order to avoid the papal taint, and then went to France to sell the secret to King Louis XIV for two thousand louis d'or. The cure was later discovered to be cinchona all along, as the fabulist Jean de la Fontaine wrote in his ode to this newfound remedy, entitled "Le Poeme du Quinquina." "Give thanks to luck, a hundred ships upon the sea bring relief to every soul…. *Quina* has come, a thousand times better a cure than faith and prayer."

Confusion over which species worked best, adulterated potions, and lack of consistency in mixing the powder all played a part in making cinchona more a question mark than a cure. Some patients got better, others had their intestines burn up. An overdose, known as "cinchonism," caused ringing of the ears, temporary deafness, and blurred vision. A widely circulated fraud, cherry bark dipped in aloe, did nothing more than loosen bowels, in 1790, the Spanish crown was forced to establish a monopoly over export charged with quality control, an office first headed by botanist Vicente Rodríguez Olmedo.

Wettness was the major problem facing export. Fresh cinchona bark could contain up to 80 percent of its weight in water—and no wonder, for it grew in the Andean rain shadow, receiving up to two hundred inches per year. Wet bark led to spoilage, fermentation, and loss of active ingredients. Drying at too high a temperature also degraded the drug, as did the indiscriminate mixing of different species within the same batch.

Research meanwhile continued apace. The first scientist to identify the actual cinchona tree in the wild, near Loja, was French botanist Joseph de Jussieu, who accompanied La Condamine on his groundbreaking expedition to the New World. Jussieu's "Description de l'arbre a Quinquina," from 1737, distinguished five different species based on bark color and provided the samples from which Linnaeus made the first taxonomic classification in 1742.

A Spanish botanical expedition led by Hipólito Ruiz and José Antonio Pavón spent the years 1777 to 1787 collecting specimens all over Peru, and their five-volume opus, *Flora Peruviana et Chilensis*, became an essential plant-hunting guide. Ruiz also dabbled in the apothecary's trade, and his supplementary tome, *Quinologia*, praised cinchona's medicinal uses—"cuts simple or complex intermittent fevers, malignant putrefactions, nervous malignancies … cures verminous effects … prevents miscarriage … restores relaxation of the stomach." Modern herbalists make similar claims, tooting the bark's power to heal hemorrhoids, hair loss, leg cramps, alcoholism, and loss of appetite.

When Alexander von Humboldt visited Loja in 1802, he was quite surprised by local people's view of this miracle cure. "Natives there would rather die," he reported, "than have recourse to cinchona bark, which together with opiates they place in the class of poisons exciting mortification. The Indians cure themselves with lemonades, by the oleaginous aromatic peel of the small green wild lemon … and by strong coffee." Although coffee is in the same plant family as cinchona, it is usually thought to cause shakes, not cure them.

In 1820, the quinine alkaloid was isolated from the bark by French pharmacists Pierre Pelletier and Joseph Caventou. Their factory turned out pure quinine pills with measured dosages, quickly becoming a worldwide success. For the first time, it was unnecessary to swallow tree bark to rid oneself of a fever! And just in time for the European imperialist conquest of the tropics.

With the growth of this market came increasing demand for raw materials that Andean collectors could not satisfy. Ruiz had already complained that it took days to find a single tree in the wild and advocated growing them plantation style. The Jesuits had ensured that *cascarilleros*, or bark harvesters, plant five new saplings, aligned in the shape of a cross, for every one they cut down. When they were expelled from Spanish crown territories in 1767, such conservation measures ceased. Ironically, one place where cinchona thrived was in the Galapagos Islands, where the species *Cinchona succiruba* was introduced and now threatens to overrun native plants.

In 1843, just as malarial conditions in North Africa were impeding French colonial designs there, Paris sent their botanist Hugh Weddell to collect cinchona in Bolivia, where the classified the different species based on the bark's quinine content rather than color. His *Histoire Naturelle des Quinquinas*, featuring fine color illustrations, laid out a road map for future plant hunters to zero in on the best species.

And so, just like the heist that rubber smugglers pulled off in 1876—stealing *Hevea brasilensis* trees out of the Amazon to London's Kew Gardens—English and Dutchmen began the mad rush to obtain cinchona saplings and seeds for transplanting in India and Java. In 1852, a Dutch mission led by Justus Hasskarl, traveling under all assumed name to throw off customs inspectors, went to the disputed Caravaya borderlands north of Lake Titicaca. He packed four hundred saplings into bales to resemble wool—but too tightly, for all were dead on arrival in Java.

About the same time, the Englishman Clements Markham—who in later years had a hand in the rubber robbery—sent 237 cinchona trees to India with similarly disappointing results. Insects, climate, and altitude— most cinchona species grow in the wild at altitudes between 4,900 and 9,800 feel—had a part in doing them in.

As an eighteen-year-old Londoner, Charles Ledger had come to Peru to seek his fortune in the alpaca wool trade but spent most of his time botanizing for valuable plants. Thirty, years later, his Indian guide, Manuel Incra Mamami, found a Bolivian species, *Cinchona calisaya*—from the Aymara *cali*, meaning best, and *saya*, meaning bark—which contained a quinine content of 13 percent, more than three times the average. Of the forty pounds of seed he collected, Ledger sold a handful to Dutch planters for twenty pounds sterling.

But blood also paid for that seed. For years, Bolivian woodsmen had been on the lookout, for tree-stealing interlopers. A law forbade their ex-port. Mamani was tortured to death when the news of the Dutch deal was made public. Native bark cutters had been right to worry about their livelihoods. From Ledger's seed, the Dutch grew twelve thousand trees in their Javanese plantations and promptly collapsed the South American market.

To the Eurupeans, a handful of smuggled seeds was no big deal. To the Andean nations, it was ruinous. Fifteen percent of Bolivian tax revenue came from bark-export tariffs. Cinchona had paid for the construction of the La Paz cathedral. The seal on the Peruvian flag featured a cinchona tree as a symbol of national pride. Now it merely symbolized a national rip-off.

Once adapted to Java's climate, the so-called *Cinchona ledgeriana* subspecies developed even higher quinine concentrations. Bark exports from the New World fell from nearly twenty million pounds in 1881 to just under four-and-a-half million in 1884. The price for a pound of quinine sulfate dropped 90 percent in just ten years. The timing of the price drop was perfect, for by the turn of the century the Panama canal workers were taking forty thousand doses a day—a ton a year—to keep the project on schedule.

Javanese plantations handily supplied world demand until the outbreak of World War II, when the Japanese occupation put them off limits. When the war effort in North Africa and the Pacific—where malaria was a bigger enemy than the Axis soldiers—raised demand for quinine to a thousand tons a year, the U.S. army took a new interest in the old South American trees. Military botanists retraced the footsteps of Hipólito Ruiz and La Condamine to secure supplies in the wild, working mostly in Colombia and Ecuador, but were never able to find the quinine-rich *calisaya* groves in Bolivia.

By war's end, twelve million pounds of bark was exported from the Andes, thereby making the tree even more endangered than it had been in the nineteenth century. In an ironic squaring of the circle first begun by the Aymara guide Manuel Incra Mamani eighty years earlier, a bag of *Cinchona ledgeriana* seeds were smuggled out of the Philippines just before the Japanese invasion and planted in Ecuador—too late to produce quinine for the war, but at least a homecoming of sorts for a native plant.

After World War II, synthetic substitutes like chloroquine and mefloquine replaced natural quinine-based tablets, but malaria parasites were quick to develop resistance and doctors scrambled to stay one step ahead of the bugs. Quinine itself was losing out against certain kinds of parasites. As early as 1910, German engineers working on the Madeira-Mamoré Railroad in the Brazilian Amazon could not be cured with the normal tablets. Today, sometimes even intravenous dosages have limited effect.

It is now thought that multi-alkaloid treatments, using a scatter-shot approach rather than a single bullet medicine like pure quinine, may be the best answer to drug-resistant malaria. This sounds a bit like the countess of Chinchon's legendary cure, a powdered bark concoction containing several fever-fighting alkaloids, of which quinine is just one.

Most researchers today put their highest hopes in developing a malaria vaccine, but others remain botanically inclined, looking for a cure in plants like the Chinese herb *qing-hao*, known in the West as *Artemesia annua*, or sweet wormwood. Cinchona, meanwhile, remains in the pharmacopoeia as the basis for quinidine, a drug to treat heart arrhithimias, and as the old standby source for quinine, now used mainly as a food additive. Half of the world's annual seven-thousand-ton bark harvest—cut from Javanese and Sri Lankan plantations—goes into making tonic water, a liter of which contains seventy milligrams of quinine, and various culinary bitters.

Piero Delprete, a Rubiaceae specialist at the New York Botanical Garden, recommends taking a glass of Ferro-China Bisleri, a syrupy digestive made from cinchona (as in the Italian spelling for *quina*, or *china*) to settle the stomach whenever he pushes back from a plate of spaghetti in his native Italy—whether the mosquitoes are biting or not. "Quinine's days as a malaria fighter may be reaching an end," says Delprete, "but it will always be in my liquor cabinet as an after-dinner drink."

LOUIS WERNER is a documentary filmmaker residing in New York City and frequent contributor to *Américas*.

From *Américas,* bimonthly magazine, September/October 2003, pp. 25-31, published by the General Secretariat of the Organization of American States. Copyright © 2003 by the Organization of American States. Reprinted by permission.

UNIT 4

Modernism, Statism, and Total War: The Twentieth Century

Unit Selections

24. **The Divine Sarah**, Joseph A. Harriss
25. **Germany, Britain & the Coming of War in 1914**, Richard Wilkinson
26. **Queen of the Sands**, Kerry Ellis
27. **Art Deco: High Style**, Stanley Meisler
28. **Auschwitz: The Forgotten Evidence**, Taylor Downing
29. **Contemplating Churchill**, Edward Rothstein
30. **The Mystery of Stalin**, Paul Wingrove
31. **Kim Philby had a Remarkable Long Career with British Intelligence—Spying for the Other Side**, Richard K. Munro
32. **The World According to Wells**, Joel Achenbach

Key Points to Consider

- Why is Sarah Bernhardt called the first superstar?

- Who might be the guilty parties in World War I?

- Why was Gertrude Bell so important in Middle Eastern history?

- What are some of the attributes of Art Deco? How did it influence the art world?

- What were the reasons that the Allies did not bomb Auschwitz?

- Why is Winston Churchill one of the most famous statesmen in British history?

- What are some of the interpretations of Stalin's character?

- What was the importance of Kim Philiby, Guy Burgess, Anthony Blunt, and Donald McClean?

Student Web Site

www.mhcls.com/online

Internet References

Further information regarding these Web sites may be found in this book's preface or online.

History Net
   http://www.thehistorynet.com/THNarchives/AmericanHistory/

Inter-American Dialogue (IAD)
   http://www.iadialog.org/

ISN International Relations and Security Network
   http://www.isn.ethz.ch/

Russian and East European Network Information Center/University of Texas at Austin
   http://reenic.utexas.edu/reenic/index.html

Terrorism Research Center
   http://www.terrorism.com/

World History Review/Scott Danford and Jon Larr
   http://members.aol.com/sniper43/index.html

The nineteenth century ended with high hopes for the future of Western civilization. Popular novelists foresaw air travel, television, visual telephones, records, and space travel, and even the construction of a new continent in the Pacific. Technology would liberate those living in this century from most of their burdens, or so argued the futurists of the time. There were skeptics of course: Mark Twain punctured the pious hypocrisies of Westerners who presumed that their Christianity and technology demonstrated their superiority over the heathens of the non-Western world.

Even before this glittering future could be realized, turn-of-the century artists and thinkers brought forth an alternative vision of far greater originality. They set in motion a period of unprecedented cultural innovation and artistic experimentation, out of which emerged modern music, theater, literature, art, and architecture. Never before had there been so many cultural manifestos: Fauvism, Cubism, and Futurism. In "The Divine Sarah" we see the growing fame of a "superstar", while in "Art Deco: High Style," we see how this movement influenced art and architecture around the world. In philosophy it was the age of pragmatism, positivism, and Bergsonism. On the intellectual frontier, Alfred Binet, Ivan Pavlov, and Sigmund Freud reformulated the premises of psychology. Advanced work in experimental science concentrated on radioactivity and the atom, setting the stage for Albert Einstein's abstract theories.

Thus, in the years before World War I, the West was able to point to unrivaled accomplishments. Aristocrats and the middle class were smugly confident of the future because they were eminently satisfied with the present.

In hindsight, all this seems a great illusion. We can now see how such illusions blinded Europeans to the coming war. Millions of lives were lost in World War I, which was a showcase for the destructive forces of European technology. The war dashed the hopes of an entire generation and contributed to revolutions in Russia, Germany, and Austria. The war spurred the breakup of the Ottoman Empire, caused the collapse of the international economy, and was responsible for the emergence of totalitarian dictatorships. These events, in turn, brought on World War II.

Covering the period of the World Wars, we have the article by Richard Wilkinson who asks in " Germany, Britain & the Coming of War in 1914" why the quarrel happened between Germany and Britain which caused World War I, while "Queen of the Sands" details the career of Gertrude Bell and the creation of Iraq at the end of the war. And for World War II, articles describe the world situation concerning atrocities and great political leaders, "Auschwitz: The Forgotten Evidence," "Contemplating Churchill," and "The Mystery of Stalin."

The Divine Sarah

Bewitching her admirers around the world, Sarah Bernhardt dazzled audiences as she pioneered the cult of celebrity.

JOSEPH A. HARRISS

It was the kind of surreal mob scene new york reserves for showbiz celebs, with frenzied fans gathered at the stage door for a glimpse of the famous foreign star. When she finally appeared, late, after 29 curtain calls, they went wild. Everyone was shouting to her, reaching for her. One wild-eyed woman tore a gold brooch from her own coat and nearly knocked her down pinning it on her; another tried to snip a lock of her hair but ended up slicing an ostrich plum from her hat. (After another performance, men thrust out their arms and noisily begged her to autograph their cuffs.) A hysterical girl brandished an autograph book, then realized her pen was out of ink; she plunged her teeth into her own wrist and dipped the instrument in her blood. With the mob out of hand, the frightened star beat a retreat back to the theater. She tore off her hat, veil and chinchilla cloak, put them on her sister and sent her out to impersonate her while she slipped out by another door.

Despite her modest origins, Sarah wasn't very impressed by emperors and their ilk.

It could have been yesterday's rock star event. But it was 1880 and the star was Sarah Bernhardt, The Divine, The Eighth Wonder of the World, and the most celebrated woman of the Victorian era besides—and maybe including—Queen Victoria herself. Arguably the first international entertainment icon, The Bernhardt, as Americans called her, personified stardom carried to mythical proportions; when *Variety* ran a story on the 100 top stars of the 20th century, she was lionized as "the first superstar-diva." It is difficult today to imagine the spell she cast over admirers as various as Sigmund Freud, who purportedly kept a photograph of her in his waiting room, and philosopher William James, who called her "the most race-horsey, high-mettled human being I've ever seen." Mark Twain observed there were five kinds of actresses: bad, fair, good, great— "and then there is Sarah Bernhardt."

Her myth traveled throughout the pre-cinema, pre-television world via paintings, photographs, posters and newspaper stories. One biographer calculates that if pasted end to end, the articles about her during her 62-year career from 1861 to 1923 would stretch around the earth, while a pile of her printed photographs would reach the top of the Eiffel Tower. She promoted that myth with panache, eccentric behavior and in-your-face attitude. She made sure everyone knew that she slept in a coffin. And when a reporter exclaimed during an interview, "Why, New York didn't give Dom Pedro of Brazil such an ovation!" she purred, "Yes, but he was only an emperor."

Despite her modest origins, Madame Sarah wasn't very impressed by emperors and their ilk. Many had been at her feet— and even closer. Britain's Prince of Wales was a very dear friend indeed, and her only child was fathered by Belgian Prince Henri de Ligne. Europe's crowned heads visited her backstage, and she gave command performances in their palaces. Austrian Emperor Franz Joseph placed an antique cameo necklace around her neck, while Archduke Friedrich insisted she stay at one of his palaces while in Vienna. Italy's King Umberto gave her an exquisite Venetian fan, Spain's King Alfonso XII, a diamond brooch, France's Emperor Louis-Napoleon, a magnificent pin with the imperial initials in diamonds. In Saint Petersburg, where they ran a red carpet over the snow to the stage door, Czar Alexander III called on her after a command performance at the Winter Palace. As she was making a deep curtsy, he stopped her: "No, Madame," he ordered, "it is I who must bow to you." And so he did before his entire court.

The Divine continues to fascinate. Earlier this year a New York theater presented *The Divine Trilogy of Sarah Bernhardt*, while Connie Clark, an actress based in North Carolina, has performed her one-woman show, Sarah, tracing Bernhardt's life and career, at the Lincoln Center, universities and in Europe. Paris paid homage to her last winter with a sumptuous exhibition at the ornate old Bibliothèque Nationale, just a short walk down rue de Richelieu from the Comédie Française theater where she starred and stormed.

The show presented paintings, costumes, playbills and photographs recalling her life, loves and many of the 125 plays she acted in. "She was really the first media star of our era," says Noelle Guibert, director of the Bibliothèque Department of Theater Arts, who was the curator of the show. "She incarnated the fantasies of the Belle Epoque. She was the one everybody admired, the one to whom they attributed the wildest passions, eccentricities and perversions."

At a convent school, her tempestuous, headstrong behavior drove the nuns to distraction.

Quite a symbolic load to bear for a pathologically skinny girl whom doctors expected to die before 20. Henriette-Rosine Bernard was born on October 23, 1844, in Paris, the illegitimate daughter of a Dutch-Jewish woman of dubious morals from Amsterdam and an unknown, probably French, father. She was an emotionally unstable, sickly child who seemed to run a constant temperature and frequently spat up blood. Doctors diagnosed a wasting disease like tuberculosis and prescribed snail soup for strength.

Her mother, Julie, a high-flying courtesan, had little time for her. She often left Sarah with a nanny, before sending her to a girls' school in suburban Paris, where she learned to read and write and throw memorable tantrums. After that it was a convent school in Versailles, where her tempestuous, headstrong behavior drove the nuns to distraction. Although she received only six years or so of formal education. She tells us in her memoirs, *My Double Life*, an artful mix of fact and mythmaking, that when she was 9 she adopted her spunky lifelong motto, *"Quand même,"* meaning in spite of everything. She had jumped over a wide ditch on a dare, landing painfully on her face and spraining a wrist. "I'll do it again if they dare me," the willful child screamed through tears at her mother and aunt as they doctored her. "And I'll do whatever I want all my life!" Sighed the aunt prophetically, *"Quelle enfant terrible!"*

At 15 she overheard doctors telling her mother that she had only a few years to live. Death became an obsession, and she acquired a pretty coffin so she could get used to it. (The resulting rosewood and satin model became one of the stage props in her life; countless postcard photographs of her reclining dramatically in the flower-strewn casket were sold in Europe and America.) About this time, too, the influential Duc de Morny, one of Julie's wealthy lovers and Emperor Napoleon III's half brother, advised the family to send the enfant terrible to the Conservatory of Music and Drama in Paris. When Morny got her a box seat at the Comédie Française, France's prestigious national theater, Sarah sobbed uncontrollably at the heroine's plight. That did it: the girl who would become the last of the great Romantic actresses was hooked on the theater.

She threw herself into her lessons at the conservatory, then considered the world's finest drama school, even if she later took the opportunity to mock it in her memoirs. It was solid training, but mostly a bore for Sarah, who always relied on her instincts and raw emotion for effect.

Still, it got her into the august Comédie Française—with a little pull from Morny—at the age of 17. Her first performance on August 11, 1862, was nearly a catastrophe due to a bad case of teeth-chattering stage fright, which would nag her all her life. The critics were indulgent but unimpressed. "Mademoiselle

Bernhardt... is a tall, attractive young woman with a slender waist and most pleasing face," wrote one. "She carries herself well and pronounces her words with perfect clarity. That is all that can be said for the moment." In any case, the high-strung, rebellious young woman felt uncomfortable among the stuffed shirts of the French theater establishment. Within a year she was fired for slapping a leading lady who had been rude to the younger sister Sarah doted on, Régine.

Out of work except for occasional roles, Sarah turned to her mother's trade to make ends meet. It was a time when "actress" was virtually synonymous with courtesan or kept woman, and the dandies expected their favors as a right. One day, for example, the Prince de Joinville, Emperor Louis-Philippe's son, sent a cryptic note to Rachel, one of France's great leading ladies: "Where? When? How much?" She zinged back a succinct, practiced reply: "Your place. This evening. No charge."

In 1864, after a particularly bad performance in a second-rate play, Sarah took off and ended up eventually in Brussels. There she had an affair with Prince Henri de Ligne, got pregnant and gave birth to a son she named Maurice, whom she would adore and indulge for the rest of her life. If anyone had the bad taste to inquire about his paternity, she would assume a pensive pose and reply evenly that she could never make up her mind whether it was French Prime Minister Léon Gambetta, Victor Hugo or perhaps General Georges Boulanger.

Nearly two years later her slow, erratic acting start took a turn for the better when she joined Paris' Left Bank Théatre de l'Odéon. There she honed what would become her trademark technique: authentic, impassioned acting that she reveled in. Favoring improbable, wholehearted, three-hankie drama, she emerged as the consummate tragedienne, running the emotional gamut of tigerish passion, melting seduction, excruciating loss and unbearable sorrow.

Such technique compensated for being no great beauty. Her hair was hopeless, a frizzy, unruly, reddish blonde mop. She hid her low brow beneath a tumble of curls, which also had the advantage of enlarging her small eyes. And in a day when the canons of beauty called for opulent, Rubenesque women, she was not only thin, she was skeletal—"A Madonna's head stuck on a broomstick," as the writer Alexandre Dumas *fils* called her. She never needed an umbrella, boulevard wits said, as she was so skinny she could walk between the raindrops.

It was at the Odéon that a star was born on the evening of January 16, 1872, when she played the love-stricken Queen of Spain in Victor Hugo's *Ruy Blas*. Backstage visitors included the Prince of Wales, who stepped aside respectfully when the white-maned, bewhiskered author, by then a French monument, entered, dropped to one knee, kissed Sarah's hand and murmured *"Merci, merci."* Outside, a cheering crowd filled the streets, while excited students unhitched the horses from her carriage and pulled it themselves shouting "Make way for our Sarah!"

Shortly thereafter the Comédie Française invited her back. Although she was handed some important roles in the House of Molière, she again chafed under rules that rotated leading parts, operated on strict bureaucratic seniority and permitted no stars—a stifling atmosphere for an actress with her temperament. She threw so many tantrums and slammed so many doors that the theater's exasperated director began referring to her as "Mademoiselle Révolte."

But even French bureaucracy could not prevent Madame Sarah's star quality from shining in another Hugo tragedy, *Hernani*, in which she played a Castilian noblewoman who loves the bandit Hernani and takes poison with him at the end. So moved was Hugo this time that he sent her a box with a note in it next day. "Madame," he wrote, "when the public, touched and enchanted by you, applauded, I wept. This tear that you caused me to shed is yours. I place it at your feet." The tear in question was a single perfect diamond on a gold bracelet.

Hugo loved what he termed her golden voice. Not powerful or deep, it was a highly musical voice that writers vied to describe: "As sonorous as pure crystal," wrote Alphonse Daudet, while Jules Lemaitre called it "a caress that strokes you like fingers, so pure, so tender, so harmonious."

But beyond that, the lady could really act. "Acting is all internal, but must be externalized," she said. Sarah built her characters from the inside out and embraced less stylized, more truthful acting than was generally practiced at the time. As a young woman she could transform herself into an 80-year-old crone, simulating blindness by showing only the whites of her eyes. As a 56-year-old grandmother, she could convincingly play the 20-year-old Duke of Reichstadt, Napoleon's consumptive son, dying in the last act "as angels would die if they were allowed to," said one critic. And in *Joan of Arc*, when the judge demanded her age, she invariably brought the house down when she deliberately turned to face the audience, who knew she was 65, and declared triumphantly, "Nineteen!"

Both her memory and stagecraft were the stuff of legends. She could memorize a part merely by reading it through four times, blocking out her moves as she went; after the fifth reading she had it down pat—and performed without a prompter. When playing Cleopatra, she often used a real snake for the final scene. And she captivated audiences at *La Tosca* with her stage business of placing lit candlesticks around the body of Scarpia and a crucifix on his chest after stabbing him, then slowly backing off in horror, her gown's long train trailing along the stage until the curtain fell. It was her acting that inspired Puccini to compose his opera based on the play.

She was said to smoke cigars, take boxing lessons, and dress in men's clothes.

Inevitably, the time came for her to decide whether to stay in safe repertory at the national theater with its stilted acting style or try an independent career. She resigned from the Comédie Française in 1880, formed her own troupe and headed to London's Gaiety Theater to begin her life as an international star. It was the first stop on foreign tours that would, over the next 40 years, take her throughout Europe, from Britain to Greece and Spain to Russia, and to North and South America.

After London, where rumors were rife—she was said to hold a witches' Sabbath certain nights, smoke cigars in the morning, take boxing lessons, even dress in men's clothes—Sarah sailed for New York for a six-month tour. She landed on October 27, 1880, amid all the fanfare her canny impresario for the tour, Edward Jarrett, could muster with spicy advance publicity, perhaps the first deliberate campaign to create an international star. The public was dying to learn more about The Bernhardt.

"I adore this country, she said while visiting America, "where women reign."

Her first New York performance, *Adrienne Lecouvreur* at Booth's Theater, was declared off-limits to children because it dealt with an unmarried actress's affair with a rakish aristocrat. Despite, or perhaps because of, that, she played to a packed house that broke into roaring applause after Adrienne died in the final scene, and went on for 27 curtain calls. It was at Booth's that same month of November 1880 that she created her signature role, Marguerite Gauthier in *La Dame aux Camélias* by Dumas *fils*, that for the next 43 years she would play more than 3,000 times all over the world. On a later U.S. tour, railway magnate William Henry Vanderbilt attended every one of her New York performances of Camille, weeping openly into a large handkerchief. When Sarah returned to France, he gave it to her as a souvenir.

Then it was on to Boston. Proud of its open-minded appreciation of culture, the city welcomed her more warmly than New York. The critics were ecstatic: "Before such perfection, analysis is impossible," wrote one. Sarah returned the feeling. "Boston belongs to women," she declared. "They are in the majority there, they are intelligently puritan, and gracefully independent." The tour comprised 156 appearances in 50 cities and towns from Albany and Pittsburgh to Detroit. After Chicago, she boarded the Sarah Bernhardt Special and rode in her own private Palace Car with walls of inlaid wood, brass gas lamps, Turkish carpeting, lounge area with sofas, piano and potted palms. The dining room table seated ten and was laid with linen and china with her *Quand Même* crest. Two cooks prepared meals. (On another tour, in Louisiana, she bought a small alligator she named Ali-Gaga, which make itself comfortable beneath the bedcovers at night. It finally died, they say, from too much champagne.)

Americans fell in love with Sarah, and vice versa. "I adore this country, where women reign," she said. In at least eight more tours—four billed as "The Farewell Tour of Mme. Sarah Bernhardt"—she crisscrossed the country. She did Camille in huge tents in Missouri and Texas, cornstalk stubble tearing the dresses of women spectators. At one Texas stop a cowboy rode up and asked for a seat. None was available until he pulled his six-shooter. Entering the tent he drawled in passing, "By the way, what does this gal do, sing or dance?"

This was an interesting change of pace for "that anxious, strange, morbid being named Sarah Bernhardt"—her own description. At home in her Paris town house on Boulevard Péreire, her furnishings included a skull on her desk and a skeleton named Lazarus, plus the famous coffin in which she often studied her roles and, gossips said, received her lovers. She liked to welcome other visitors dressed in a long white gown and reclining on a cushion-strewn divan on a platform, canopied with Oriental hangings supported by velvet-covered spears. She kept a menagerie that at various times included her enormous wolfhound Osman, a friendly lynx on a leash, a baby tigress named Minette, and a tame lion, until the beast started smelling too bad. Visitors never knew what to expect. When Alexandre Dumas fils called one day to show Sarah a new play he had just written, a pet puma calmly devoured his straw hat.

None of which deterred her devoted admirers, known as *sarahdoteurs*, from flocking to her. Her court, as she called them collectively, ranged from writers like Hugo, Zola, Dumas, Flaubert and Oscar Wilde, who wrote the play *Salome* especially for her, to statesmen like Gambetta, the Prince of Wales and Theodore Roosevelt. She could be very funny, mimicking some of them wickedly, and regaling them with catty remarks. Of an actress who tried to play the male lead she had made her own in *L'Aiglon*, she said, "The poor dear isn't man enough to make us forget she's a woman, and not woman enough to be appealing."

That wasn't her problem. Sarah played some 25 male parts, from Prince Charming to Cyrano de Bergerac, Judas and Hamlet. She liked men's roles, she said, because they were generally more tormented and intellectual than women's.

When Dreyfus was unjustly sentenced, she helped persuade Zola to write "J'Accuse."

Certainly she had courage enough for several men. When Army Captain Alfred Dreyfus, who was Jewish, was unjustly sentenced to Devil's Island in 1894 on trumped-up, anti-Semitic charges of treason, Sarah took his side against most French popular opinion. Though many of her friends and her son, Maurice, stopped talking to her, she helped persuade Emile Zola to write his famous "J'Accuse" article that turned the tide in Dreyfus'

favor. And when spreading gangrene struck her right leg in 1915, she pleaded with two doctors to amputate it, threatening to shoot herself in the knee if they refused. (She had endured painful problems with her knee for years.) They declined because she was 71 and suffered from chronic uremia. Finally a surgeon agreed, and she hummed the "Marseillaise" as she was wheeled down the hospital corridor. Later, she tried an artificial leg but found it too cumbersome. Also refusing to use a wheelchair, she opted for a specially designed litter chair in Louis XV-style with gilt carving, and was carried around like a Byzantine princess. She altered her stage business so that actors were gathered around her, seated, and kept on acting. For ovations she stood on one leg, held on to a piece of furniture, and gestured with one arm.

Shortly after the amputation, she visited the WWI front lines near Verdun to perform for French troops in mess tents, hospital wards, open marketplaces and ramshackle barns. Propped in a shabby armchair, she recited a patriotic piece to war-dazed men fresh from the trenches. When she ended with a rousing *"Aux armes!"* they rose cheering and sobbing.

Despite failing health, Sarah flung herself into silent movies, making eight in her waning years, including her biggest hit, *Queen Elizabeth*. She was shooting a film on location in her town house for an American producer in the spring of 1923 when she collapsed. She died in the arms of Maurice on March 26 at the age of 78. That evening, all Paris theaters observed two minutes of silence. Parisians lined the streets as her funeral procession wound its way to Père Lachaise cemetery, where Molière and admirers Marcel Proust and Oscar Wilde were buried. There she was interred in the rosewood coffin. In contrast to the famous cemetery's ornate tombs with handsome sculptures and long inscriptions, only two words were deemed worthy to decorate the simple granite tomb of The Divine: Sarah Bernhardt.

JOSEPH A. HARRISS, a frequent contributor, is based in Paris.

Germany, Britain & the Coming of War in 1914

Richard Wilkinson explains what went wrong in Anglo-German relations before the First World War.

RICHARD WILKINSON

Just suppose that, every time a war broke out, all the diplomats and soldiers involved were hanged. Even more fancifully, suppose that diplomats, generals and heads of governments were gifted with second sight. If either of these scenarios had applied in August 1914, there would have been no World War One. The German, Austrian, Russian and Turkish empires would have survived at any rate in the short term, while in the longer term the British and French empires would have escaped the wounds inflicted by that terrible conflict. Millions of young men would have lived, millions of folk at home would have been spared bereavement. As for the economic damage caused by the War, who knows what benefits to mankind might otherwise have accrued?

'If only' must especially apply to Britain's role. Of all the great powers, her involvement seems the most unnecessary. After all, she had kept out of the Franco-Prussian War in 1870. Why not in 1914? This is a good question, as Britain's relations with Germany were mainly cordial. Indeed Joseph Chamberlain had pursued the possibility of an alliance between 1899 and 1901. By the summer of 1914 contentious issues such as the Berlin-Baghdad railway and the Portuguese colonies had been resolved. The royal families were closely connected. When Cecil Rhodes founded his scholarships at Oxford, he decreed that candidates should come from the British Empire, the United States—and Germany. Trade flourished—and while British manufacturers were encountering increasing German competition, no sensible businessman ever wants war.

Wrong Enemy, Wrong Allies?

'How German and how right!' sums up the widespread admiration in Britain for everything German. R.B. Haldane, the War Minister, was not alone in recognising Germany as 'his spiritual home', for many shared his enthusiasm for German culture and philosophy. German secondary and tertiary education was correctly perceived to be decades ahead of Britain, especially in the realm of science and technology. At German universities the seminar prevailed over the absurd one-to-one tutorial in vogue at Oxbridge. Left-wingers admired the German Social Democratic Party as the wealthiest and most influential socialist party in the world. C.P. Scott, the Editor of the Manchester Guardian, spoke for enlightened Britain in opposing the very idea of war against 'our German cousins'. While he attacking the general 'neurosis' with regard to the balance of power, he insisted that if Britain did have a natural enemy, it was Russia. The vast majority of the Liberal Party cordially agreed.

Indeed Britain's relations with both Russia and France had been tense for most of the nineteenth century, and had only recently—and haltingly—improved. Particularly by the British left, Russia was seen as a police state; nor had Bloody Nicholas' suppression of the 1905 revolution been forgiven. As for France, unlike Protestant, hygienic Germany, she had a bad reputation for decadence and corruption, typified by the Dreyfus affaire. Such hostility was cordially reciprocated by both powers. Russia continuously threatened India's north-west frontier, and never forgave Britain's encouragement of Japan in 1904. The French could not forget Britain's seizure of Egypt in 1882 and humiliation of France at Fashoda in 1898. When the colonel of a Breton regiment was congratulated by a British staff officer for its gallant assault on the German lines in 1915, he replied, 'I've told them that they are attacking the English!'

So why the quarrel between Britain and Germany? What went wrong? Who were the Guilty Men in 1914? This article considers the role of the Kaiser, pilloried at the end of the war as a war-criminal. It looks critically at the Anglo-German naval rivalry, considered by most historians to be the prime cause of hostility between the 'two white races' (to quote the toast proposed by the Kaiser at the Kiel naval review in 1909). First, however, Britain's responsibility must be assessed as against Germany's. After all, Britain declared war on Germany, and not the other way round.

British War Guilt?

Anti-German forces certainly existed in British government and society. The most strident were Foreign Office mandarins such as Nicolson, Hardinge and Eyre Crowe who allegedly 'captured' the Foreign Secretary, Sir Edward Grey. Soldiers such as the francophile Henry Wilson and admirals such as the pugnacious Jacky Fisher almost welcomed war with Germany. The Kaiser's latest biographer, Giles MacDonagh, criticises the British establishment for its unsympathetic, supercilious attitude towards his hero. In the crisis of July-August 1914 Bonar Law and Lansdowne on behalf of the Conservative Party urged Asquith to declare war on Germany. Why? Perhaps they wished to demonstrate to the world Britain's great power status, having failed to do so during the humiliations of the Boer War. Perhaps they appreciated the inevitable problems which a Liberal government would experience in the management of a major war-to the certain benefit of the Conservatives. Perhaps here too there was visceral hatred of Germany.

More puzzling is the Liberal cabinet's decision to go to war—with only John Burns and John Morley in opposition. Here the finger of accusation points at Grey, the Foreign Secretary. He is blamed for his rigid adherence to the ententes with France and Russia, and for misleading both cabinet and Commons with regard to Britain's commitments. If he was not exactly germanophobe, he certainly listened to his professional advisers. Would he have deterred Germany if he had converted the entente into an alliance? Churchill observed: 'We have all the disadvantages of an alliance without its advantages'. John Charmley has criticised Grey for writing out blank cheques which he wrongly hoped would never be cashed. All one can say here is that these criticisms were not expressed at the time; nor does Grey, the gentle fisherman and bird-watcher, really convince as a war-monger. He was in an awkward position, desperately wanting to reassure his French friends but unable to take steps which would be disowned by his cabinet colleagues. And the Germans were consistently bellicose and aggressive, touchy and suspicious. As we shall see, they made the running in the final crisis of July-August 1914.

Perhaps indeed the plain truth is that Britain was more sinned against than sinning. Granted that Article 231 of the Versailles Treaty, which put the responsibility for the War on Germany and her allies, may have been 'victors' justice'. But the case against Germany has been put most cogently by a German. In 1962 Fritz Fischer rocked West Germany's academic establishment with his Germany's Aims in the First World War. According to Fischer there was little to choose between the foreign policies of the Second and the Third Reichs. The cynical and ruthless leaders of the Kaiser's political, military and business establishments anticipated Hitler's imperialist aggression. Bethmann-Hollweg's description of Britain's treaty obligations to Belgium as 'a scrap of paper' would have come appropriately from von Ribbentrop, while the exploitation of defeated Russia at Brest-Litovsk in March 1918 amounted to the acquisition of lebensraum on a scale of which the Führer would have approved. Fischer's arguments have been widely attacked. Yet mitteleuropa (a huge area of exploitation in the centre of Europe) still looks a convincing explanation of German aggression leading up to war—and of her treatment of defeated Russia.

The Kaiser

Even if Fischer's thesis is fully accepted, it is hard to see how Britain was affected, at any rate in 1914. British admiration for Germany was reciprocated. German friendliness towards Britain was widespread. It was expressed formally by her' ambassadors to the Court of St. James, first Metternich, then briefly Marshall and finally the urbane and reasonable Lichnowsky. When the British sailed away from the Kiel naval review in July 1914, a German warship signalled, 'Friends in the past, friends for ever'. The Kaiser personified German admiration for the British way of life. 'I adore England', he told Theodore Roosevelt. When he arrived in Holland as an exile, his first request was for 'a cup of real good English tea'. He corresponded with Tsar Nicholas in fluent English and read P.G. Wodehouse aloud to his entourage, glaring at them when they failed to laugh. He even appreciated critical cartoons of himself in Punch—'a good likeness, do you not agree?' When he asked a British businessman what the man-in-the-street thought of him, he was fobbed off with a story about two 'Tommies' watching a parade in Berlin; one explained to the other that senior generals had two clean shirts a day, whereas the Kaiser's day consisted of 'shirt on, shirt off, shirt on, shirt off the whole time'. Wilhelm laughed uproariously.

Unfortunately the Kaiser was inconsistent. It has been remarked that 'he approached every question with an open mouth'. His notorious telegram in which he congratulated the Boer premier Paul Kruger on his defeat of the Jameson raid in 1895 caused deep offence in Britain. His frosty relationship with his uncle Edward VII was well-known. Nor was his description of British cabinet ministers as 'unmitigated noodles' appreciated. Yet the Kaiser meant well. He acquired genuine and widespread popularity in Britain when Queen Victoria died in his arms.

How much impact had Wilhelm on the outcome of events? Modern historians question the Kaiser's direct influence on policy. We are told that at the most he interfered, gratifying his own desire to show off. As a Berlin society-lady remarked, 'The trouble with the Kaiser is that he wants to be the bride at every wedding and the corpse at every funeral'. But the most indisputable area where the Kaiser did indeed affect policy and also damaged Anglo-German relations was in the creation of the German navy. This is an instructive story in which admiration of all things British combined with the Kaiser's typically German touchiness and nationalistic aggression.

Two points, however, need stressing. First, there was never any German ambition to take on the Royal Navy. Admiral Tirpitz, who master-minded the whole project, was like his master an admirer of Britain. He too spoke fluent English, he enjoyed English literature and he sent his daughter to Cheltenham Ladies' College. His intention was to prevent Britain entering a future war against Germany by confronting her with the prospect of a naval war in which she would encounter unacceptable losses. But the point was that it would not happen. The deterrent would deter. Of course it did not turn out like that. Bismarck and the elder Moltke were right. Both had been adamant that British friendship followed from Germany's disinterest in seapower. Unfortunately Tirpitz could not match Bismarck's perspicacity. Like the Kaiser, he was a snob, rather than a statesman. Germany needed a fleet 'to be well-born'. It was just for show.

Secondly, the Kaiser, who loved big ships and personally designed a battleship which would do everything except float, adopted the irrational, emotional approach of the rabid enthusiast. He was a military sentimentalist. So when it came to actually using the fleet, he had a purely sentimental scenario in view, as his Chancellor Bulow observed:

> 'What William II most desired was to see himself at the head of a glorious German fleet, starting out on a peaceful visit to England. The English sovereign with his fleet would meet the German Kaiser in Portsmouth. The two fleets would file past each other, the two monarchs each wearing the naval uniform of the other's country would then stand on the bridge of their flagships. Then after they had embraced in the prescribed manner, a gala dinner with lovely speeches would be held in Cowes.'

'Not much harm in that', one might retort—though it was certainly an expensive way of gratifying the Kaiser's hobby.

Unfortunately it did do harm. For in practice things were not always so amiable. The British could be forgiven for suspecting more sinister objectives when in June 1911 the Germans sent the gunboat Panther to Agadir on the Atlantic coast of Morocco—a handy coaling station for forays into the Atlantic. Nor did the Germans take kindly to Winston Churchill's description of the German navy as 'a luxury', in contrast to Britain's navy on which her lifeblood depended. Nevertheless the same Winston Churchill, never the most pacific of characters, was apparently sincere when he commented on the naval rivalry with Germany: 'I deeply deplore the situation, for I have never had any but friendly feelings toward that great nation and her illustrious sovereign & I regard the antagonism which has developed as insensate. Anything in my power to terminate it I would gladly do'. And in fact the antagonism caused by the naval rivalry had subsided by the summer of 1914. Britain had demonstrated her determination to maintain her lead in battleships which Germany had come to respect.

The tragic and, for Britain, highly disconcerting war at sea which eventually materialised may well have invested the pre-war naval race with greater significance than it possessed at the time. The Germans soon showed their teeth. Early in the War German battle-cruisers raided east coast towns. The bombardment of Scarborough at 8 a.m. on 16 December 1914 was especially shocking. The town was full of wealthy holiday-makers and boarding-school children departing for Christmas. Mass panic ensued. Men in pyjamas stampeded onto trains leaving the town, and crowds streamed down the road to York shouting 'the Germans are coming!' After 29 people of all ages and sexes had been killed, the commander of the battle-cruisers, Admiral

Hipper, was christened 'the Baby-killer' while 'Remember Scarborough!' featured on recruitment posters.

The naval war emphatically demonstrated German technological superiority. When the German fleet was eventually cornered at Jutland on 31 May 1916, British losses exceeded German to such an extent that sailors coming ashore at Rosyth after the battle were booed by angry crowds. Even more humiliating was the effectiveness of Germany's U-boats. In January 1914 Admiral Jackie Fisher accurately predicted the nature of submarine warfare: 'There is nothing else the submarine can do except sink her capture and therefore, however inhuman and barbarous it may appear, the submarine menace is a truly terrible one for British commerce'. Asquith was so shocked that he refused to circulate Fisher's paper, while Churchill minuted 'I do not believe that this would ever be done by a civilized power'. The sinking of the Lusitania in May 1915 when 1,201 people drowned and the unrestricted U-boat warfare introduced in January 1917 which brought Britain to her knees proved Fisher right, Asquith and Churchill wrong.

July Crisis

While these horrors were in the future—only a very few visionaries guessed what war would be like either on land or sea—Germany's actions in July and August 1914 brought Britain into the war. Whether Fischer's arguments are accepted or not, Germany's support for Austria-Hungary in delivering the unacceptable ultimatum to Serbia, her declaration of war on Russia and France and, above all, her implementation of the Schlieffen Plan cannot be denied. Even if Fischer's indictment is rejected, criminal stupidity must be laid at Germany's door. For the Schlieffen Plan was the wrong plan. The Kaiser realised that attacking France through Belgium did not answer the actual crisis which emerged after the assassination of Franz Ferdinand. Germany had no quarrel with France. The right answer therefore was to avoid any provocation in the west and deliver an all-out attack on Serbia's ally, Russia. But no such alternative plan existed.

Might-have-beens are not normally the historian's province. But it is impossible not to speculate with regard to Britain's involvement in the First World War. All the evidence suggests that France's pacific left-wing government would have remained neutral if Germany had attacked Russia, and not France. In which case there was no way that Britain would have intervened. Indeed Britain would probably have stayed out if Belgium's neutrality had been respected even if France had been attacked. Grey would then have resigned. The Tories would have made Asquith's position very difficult. But Britain would have stayed on the touchline—at any rate for the time being. In the event Germany's rigid adherence to the wrong plan solved the Liberal government's problems. The invasion of Belgium contravened the treaty of London (1839). Intervention on Belgium's behalf enabled the Liberal government to occupy the moral high ground. Significantly the 'horrible hun' stories subsequently invented by British propaganda portrayed the raping of Belgian women and the hanging of Belgian monks. It was left to the Labour leader Ramsay MacDonald to protest that the threat to Belgium did not justify the disruption of European peace.

Thus it was that Germany demolished centuries of friendship between 'the two white races'. George V's famous defence to the U.S. ambassador—'My God, Mr. Page, what else could we have done?'—oversimplifies a complex situation. Yet Britain's response was at least understandable, however fraught with disastrous consequences. Germany was primarily responsible for the breakdown of the concert of Europe. For a whole century this concert had kept the peace. Apart from the Crimean War explosive issues had been solved by diplomacy ever since Waterloo. The last occasion on which this concert worked was at the end of the first Balkan War in December 1912 when Edward Grey presided over a peace conference in London. His efforts to convene another such conference in July 1914 failed. Why? Some historians have adopted determinist explanations—economic rivalry, the violence of nationalism, the impact of technological change and so forth. But the fact was that Germany opted for war. Her armies were poised, the Kiel Canal had just been widened. The railway timetables were perfected down to the last wagon—and so the troop-trains headed for Belgium. Next stop, Armageddon.

The Responsibility

Yet the pity of it! No German welcomed war with Britain. 'The dead Edward is stronger than the living I', fatuously bleated the Kaiser, attributing Germany's 'encirclement' to his machiavellian uncle. Why could men not behave sensibly, for instance by accepting Grey's conference invitation? V. R. Berghahn has applied the term 'autism' to the perpetual inability of the two armed camps to think rationally about the intentions of the other side a term originally used in the context of the Cold War. Just occasionally common sense broke through. When Edward Grey told Count Metternich that the terms of the Franco-Russian alliance did not provide for revanche, the German ambassador smiled grimly: 'Yes, we know very well that it does not'. Yet sadly such honest admission of the truth was unusual.

MacDonagh blames the Kaiser for the failure of German diplomacy in which he longed to play a prominent part. For in the final crisis the politicians and the diplomats—who opposed war—were swept aside by the generals who believed that 'war now' was in Germany's interests. Here the comparison with the Cold War is especially instructive—for its contrasts rather than its parallels. For in the 1950s and 1960s the nuclear deterrent really deterred. Dr. Strangelove remained fictional, the Cuba missiles crisis—certainly nail-biting but resolved peacefully—was factual. In 1914 the arms race in conventional weapons led to the launching of a European war by the leaders of the German general staff because they were not deterred by their enemies' arsenal. On the contrary, they believed that Germany' interests were best served by war as soon as possible.

Timeline

1894	Dual Alliance between Russia and France
1898	Tirpitz's first Navy Law
1901	Joseph Chamberlain pursues alliance with Germany
1904	Anglo-French Entente
1907	Anglo-Russian Entente
1911	Agadir crisis
1912–3	Balkan wars settled by London conference
1914	(28 June) Assassination of Franz Ferdinand at Sarajevo
	(23 July) Austria-Hungary's ultimatum to Serbia
	(1 August) Germany declares war on Russia
	(3 August) Germany declares war on France and invades Belgium
	(4 August) Britain declares war on Germany

Meanwhile the politicians from the Kaiser downwards failed to control the generals. Again the Cold War springs to mind. President Truman's dismissal of General MacArthur when he advocated 'nuking' Communist China contrasts with Bethmann-Hollweg's weak acquiescence in the Schlieffen Plan. Grey's devious misleading of cabinet and parliament has been called 'the failure of the democratic process'. So it may have been, but in the Kaiser's reich there was no democratic process at all. 'The officer strode the land like a god, the reserve-officer like a demi-god'. When Berchtold, Austria-Hungary's cynical foreign minister, was restrained by Germany's politicians but urged on by her generals, he minuted: 'What a laugh—who rules in Berlin?' The appalling answer was that the long-dead Schlieffen called the shots both in Berlin and in London.

Further Reading

Giles MacDonagh, *The Last Kaiser* (Weidenfeld and Nicolson, 2000)

V.R. Berghahn, *Germany and the Approach of War in 1914* (Macmillan, 1993)

Richard Hough, *Former Naval Person* (Weidenfeld and Nicolson, 1985)

Richard Langhorne, *The Collapse of the Concert of Europe* (Macmillan, 1981)

John Charmley, *Splendid Isolation?* (Hodder and Stoughton, 1999)

John Lowe and Robert Pearce, *Rivalry and Accord: International Relations, 1870–1914* (Hodder and Stoughton, 2nd edition, 2002)

RICHARD WILKINSON has taught History at Marlborough College.

This article first appeared in *History Today*, March 2002. Copyright © 2002 by History Today, Ltd. Reprinted by permission.

Queen of the Sands

Gertrude Bell pioneered Middle Eastern archaeology.

KERRY ELLIS

In April 2003, reports concerning the looting of Baghdad Museum reached the West and provoked outrage from academics and laymen alike. While the argument still rages over whether the looting was in fact as widespread or as malicious as first reported, one fact remains. Gertrude would have been furious.

Gertrude Bell (1868-1926), granddaughter of renowned scientist, industrialist and ironmaster Isaac Lowthian Bell, was the first woman to graduate from Oxford with a First in Modern History. Her acumen was matched by her determination, and Gertrude was determined to travel. Her uncle, Frank Lascalles, had been appointed British envoy to the Shahanshah of Persia, and a visit was arranged.

Gertrude arrived in Teheran in May 1892 with her aunt. Her first letter home was jubilant. 'Oh the desert around Tehran!' she wrote:

> … miles and miles of it with nothing, nothing growing; tinged in with bleak bare mountains snow crowned and furrowed with the deep courses of torrents. I never knew what desert was till I came here …

The following years were spent mountaineering in the Alps and travelling the world. However, Gertrude was captivated by the desert and its people, and in 1900 she returned. Around a hundred miles north-east of Jerusalem, and dressed like a Bedouin man, she rode out into the Hauran plain in search of the Druze.

The Druze, a secretive militant Muslim sect living in territory uncharted by Westerners, had been fighting the ruling Ottoman Turks for two hundred years. Cleverly evading the Turkish authorities, Gertrude reached the Jebel Druze mountains and was taken to Yahya Beg, the Druze king. She was impressed with him ('a great big man, very handsome and with the most exquisite manners …') and they ate and talked together—Gertrude being fluent in Arabic, along with French, German, Italian, Persian and Turkish—and earned each other's friendship and respect. Weeks later, Yahya Beg asked a visitor: 'Have you seen a queen travelling?'

The following year Gertrude was studying under the French archaeologist Saloman Reinach, who urged her to study Roman and Byzantine ruins in the Middle East in order to ascertain the impact of these civilisations upon the region. Gertrude agreed,

and planned to make a more thorough study of the Bedouin and the Druze. In January 1905, she went back to the Middle East.

No ruin or individual was too inconsequential to be recorded in her diary. She lunched in the tents of both the Druze and their sworn enemies, the Beni Sakhr, and met with the sheiks of various Bedouin tribes. Her observations, grasp of the inadequacies of Ottoman rule, eye for detail and exhaustive descriptions would not only benefit her book The Desert and the Sown (1907) but, ultimately, the British government.

In March 1907, Gertrude journeyed to Turkey to work with the archaeologist William Ramsey, a venture that resulted in a joint book, A Thousand and One Churches (1909), about their excavations and which secured Gertrude's reputation as a serious archaeologist.

It may seem ironic that an independent traveller and scholar like Gertrude would also have been active in the anti-suffrage movement. In fact, many other eminent women were opposed to giving women the vote, not least Queen Victoria herself, who as far back as 1870 had written 'This mad, wicked Folly of Women's Rights … a subject which makes the Queen so furious that she cannot contain herself.' Gertrude, as honorary secretary of the Women's Anti-Suffrage League, believed herself all equal of any man, but certainly did not think the same could be said of all other women.

But the struggle over suffrage in Britain would not hold her attention for long. Gertrude planned another book and, in January 1909, left for Mesopotamia where she intended to map the uncharted wastes.

This time, she visited the ancient Hittite city of Carchemish and recorded countless inscriptions there, then stumbled upon the spectacular yet undocumented fortress ruin of Ukhaidir where she set about taking photographs and drawing precise plans. Next came Babylon: 'an extraordinary place … I have seldom felt the ancient world come so close,' then Najav, the holy Shi'ite city of pilgrimage. Returning to Carchemish, she found two young British archaeologists nervously awaiting her arrival. Observing Their excavations, she declared their methods 'prehistoric' and proceeded to instruct them in the modern techniques of digging. In a last-gasp attempt to impress her, the two, Campbell and Lawrence—'an interesting boy, he is going to make a traveller'—seated Gertrude for dinner and proceeded to entertain her with knowledgeable and lively conversation. She warmed to them. It was the first—but not the last—time she would advise the future 'Lawrence of Arabia'.

The Ottoman government, crippled by financial strife, had lost its grip on its Balkan provinces in the later nineteenth century and in the Balkan wars of 1912; the fate of Ottoman interests in Syria, Mesopotamia and Arabia was now in the balance. In the early years of the century the Germans had financed a railway from Berlin to Baghdad, and had become increasingly close to the Ottoman Turks. This unnerved the British, who in 1912 signed for a major share in the Anglo-Persian Oil Company after Winston Churchill, the First Lord of the Admiralty, had decreed that the nation's battleships convert their coal-burning engines to oil. The British were keen to know who among the Arab tribes in the Ottoman provinces would be dependable allies should war break out.

In June 1914 Archduke Franz Ferdinand, heir to the Austrian-Hungarian throne, was assassinated, starting a chain of events that would plunge Britain into war. The Turks allied themselves with the Germans in a secret treaty on August 2nd and Gertrude was called upon by the director of Military Operations in Cairo to submit a report on everything she had gleaned from her visits to Syria, Mesopotamia and Arabia.

Having seen the Ottomans lose influence over the Arab tribes, she was confident that Britain could benefit from the situation and recommended the Arabs be organised by British agents to revolt against the Turks. Gertrude asked to be posted in the Middle East, but her request was denied; it was considered too dangerous for a woman. Frustrated, she journeyed to France to volunteer with the Red Cross.

In November 1915, she was summoned to Cairo to the Arab Bureau: a small espionage branch that occupied three rooms at the Savoy Hotel. Also present were archaeologists T.E. Lawrence and Leonard Woolley who had been recruited to make maps, write geological reports and manage press releases. All were under the supervision of General Gilbert Clayton, a passionate believer in the Arab revolt. Success, however, depended upon Military Intelligence winning the confidence of the strong leaders among the Arabs. But first, they would need to discern who those leaders were.

Gertrude was not offered an official position but worked at length, cataloguing the Arab tribes in detail. Her amazing memory proved invaluable as she remembered lineages, water sources, terrain and each sheik's areas of influence. In the meantime, the British had been in the process of negotiating terms of an alliance with Sharif Hussein of Mecca, one of the three most powerful men in Arabia along with Ibn Saud and Ibn Rashid. His territory extended over a vast area that included the holy sites of Mecca and Medina and therefore, as a descendant of the Prophet Mohammed, the Sharif was the most religiously important of the three.

For ultimate success against the Ottomans, though, Britain needed Mesopotamia. Its grain supplies would feed her army, its oil would fuel her navy and its strategic location would impede the Turks. Gertrude was sent to persuade Mesopotamia to co-operate. On March 3rd, 1916, she arrived in Basra. An Anglo-Indian force had captured the strategically important city in

November 1914, and the province of 33,000 Arabs was now British Occupied Territory and under military rule. Chief Political Officer, Percy Cox, overseer of the new administration in Mesopotamia, already believed the General Command in London to be incompetent and was not reassured when they chose to send a woman to Basra. But Gertrude soon proved her worth.

In the early spring of 1916 British forces were struggling towards Baghdad. They were suffering from the heat and shortage of food; before them lay unmapped deserts and swamps, a sizable Turkish force and the threat of ambush from Arab tribes. In March the local commander of the India Expeditionary Force invited Gertrude to dinner and desperately asked her advice.

Gertrude knew the importance of personal ties to the Arabs. Indeed, she knew many of the sheiks of the region by name, and had dined in their tents. With her help, she argued, the Arabs could be convinced to aid the British. Further, she would draw maps so that the army could reach Baghdad without mishap. That afternoon, Gertrude and her maps were removed from previously cramped working conditions onto a great veranda and she was given the title Liaison Officer, Correspondent to Cairo. Major Miss Bell was the sole female Political Officer in the British forces.

On March 10th, 1917, the British army finally took Baghdad and, a few days later, Percy Cox, now Civil Commissioner, summoned Gertrude to the city and presented her with the title of Oriental Secretary. She was charged by her work. 'It's amazing,' she wrote to her father. 'It's the making of a new world.' She admired Percy Cox and thrived under his leadership. She was somewhat distressed when, towards the end of summer, she learned that he was departing to watch over the situation in Persia, leaving A.T. Wilson as Acting Civil Commissioner.

During the summer of 1916, tribes in Arabia who had been age-old enemies now united behind Faisal, the third son of Sharif Hussein who defeated the Turkish garrison in Media in June. A strong and shrewd leader, Faisal, with T.E. Lawrence acting as his political officer, led the Arab army to victory after victory against the Turks in the Hejaz, Palestine and Syria campaigns of 1917-18. The success they enjoyed was in no small part thanks to the reports written by Gertrude in Cairo in 1915 but, like Lawrence, she eschewed any notion of fame and even rebuked her parents for talking to journalists about her.

Malaria landed Gertrude in bed for much of the autumn of 1918, but she was cheered when news arrived that General Allenby and the Arab army had taken Damascus. On October 1st, Faisal, accompanied by several hundred mounted Arab soldiers, entered the city and within three days, with the assistance of T.E. Lawrence, an Arab government was put in place in Syria with Faisal at its head. On October 31st, Gertrude received news that the Allies had made peace with Turkey then, eleven days later, with Germany also. 'It's almost more than one can believe.'

The Ottoman Empire had collapsed and was in chaos. A secret agreement had been made in 1916, between the French and the British, to determine spheres of influence for the two nations in the region, and when the Anglo-French declaration of November 8th, 1918, announced the 'final liberation of the populations living under the Turkish yoke and the setting up of national governments chosen by the people themselves', the

Arab world was thrown into further confusion—nowhere more so than in Iraq.

In Baghdad, which fell within the British-controlled area, most of the people wanted an Arab emir, but could not decide upon whom. The Kurds in the north sought independence, and the Shi'ites and Sunnis both wanted their religious leaders to preside over them. The Jewish community disliked the idea of being ruled by Arabs so intensely that they were clamouring for British citizenship, while Turkish sympathisers newly returned to Baghdad were themselves stirring up unrest in an anti-British campaign.

In London too, the question of who should lead Iraq was also unresolved, and in late January 1919 Gertrude was asked for a report. She was wildly excited by the prospect of helping to rebuild Iraq. 'I feel at times like the Creator about the middle of the week. He must have wondered what it was going to be like, as I do.'

It took her ten months to compile the report, which contained everything from Zionism to Arab nationalist factions. But most importantly, it contained a change of heart. She had previously believed that the Arabs could never govern themselves, but having visited Damascus where Faisal's government had been in place for a year, she was not only convinced that they could, but must:

> An Arab State in Mesopotamia ... within a short period of years is a possibility, and ... the recognition or creation of a logical scheme of government on those lines, in supercession of those on which we are now working on Mesopotamia, would be practical and popular.

Gertrude's notion of an Arabruled Mesopotamia so angered her superior A.T. Wilson that he made sure the report reached London with a covering letter stating that he felt her assumptions were 'erroneous' and indignantly turned the Political Officers against her. Ostracised and miserable, Gertrude buried herself in her work.

At Whitehall, Mesopotamia was still an object of heated debate. Many thought it too costly to maintain a presence, but Gertrude argued against withdrawal:

> If Mesopotamia goes, Persia goes inevitably, and then India. And the place which we leave empty will be occupied by seven devils a good deal worse than any which existed before we came.

Finally, on April 25th, 1920, Britain and France came to an agreement regarding the Arabic lands. Arabia would remain independent but under the guidance of the British, Syria would be mandated by the League of Nations to France and Mesopotamia to Britain until they 'could stand on their own', and both France and Britain would share in the production of oil in Mesopotamia.

However, eighteen months after the expulsion of the Ottomans there was still no Arab government in place, and a rebellion started by the Euphrates tribes was in full swing. A.T. Wilson's punishment of those responsible was swift and brutal, but only served to fuel the insurrection. Meanwhile in Syria where Faisal had proclaimed himself king, France refused to recognise him and sent an army from Beirut to Damascus carrying an ultimatum that demanded acceptance of France's rule

over the Arab forces, the railroads and the economy. Faisal abdicated and left Damascus. Gertrude commented:

> We have made an immense failure here. The system must have been far more at fault than anyone suspected ... I suppose we have underestimated the fact that this country is really an inchoate mass of tribes which can't as yet be reduced to any system. The Turks didn't govern and we have tried to govern ... and failed.

By late autumn 1920, the rebellion in Mesopotamia had cooled, but not before claiming the lives of 10,000 Arabs and several hundred Britons.

On October 11th, 1920, Percy Cox returned to Baghdad. He was welcomed by a cheering crowd and an overjoyed Gertrude. Cox asked her to continue as Oriental Secretary—for liaising between the High Commissioner and the new Arab government—when it was in place—meant she could keep an eye on both.

It was finally decided that the Naqib—the Sunni holy man of Baghdad—was the best candidate to be prime minister. Respected by the Sunnis and Shi'ites alike, his religious and social standing commanded respect and raised him above suspicion. However, Iraq still needed a king, and for Gertrude, there was only one choice. Faisal, with his military and administrative experience, his diplomatic flair and charisma made him the perfect choice, and Gertrude would do everything in her power to make him king.

A few weeks later, Churchill, now Colonial Secretary, summoned a group of Orientalists to Egypt to determine the future of Mesopotamia, Transjordan and Palestine. Amid the forty official delegates, Gertrude was the only woman. She and T.E. Lawrence outlined a plan for bringing Faisal to Iraq so that he might gain popularity before the vote for a leader was put to the Iraqis; it was vital—though it would not be easy—to convince the Iraqis that Faisal was their choice rather than the choice of the British.

In June 1921, Faisal arrived in Basra, and journeyed on to the holy cities of Kerbala and Najav to emphasise his religious worth as a descendant of the prophet. After cool receptions in both cities, he arrived in Baghdad to a warm welcome from a large crowd of dignitaries. Having not set foot in Iraq before, Faisal knew little of its people and history, and even spoke a different dialect of Arabic. Gertrude took it upon herself to advise him in everything from tribal geography to the best way to deal with Baghdadi businessmen; the two soon became friends.

Faisal won acceptance from almost all, and when the vote went out to the general public, their decision was nearly unanimous. On August 23rd, 1921, he was crowned King of Iraq. Delighting in her triumph, Gertrude supervised the appointment of the rest of Iraq's government and formulated grand plans for the country, which prompted Britons and Arabs alike to refer to her as 'the Uncrowned Queen of Iraq.' Indeed, no one seemed closer to Faisal, nor wielded as much influence over him.

A treaty of alliance between Britain and Iraq was still to be signed. Faisal considered that signing the treaty would make Iraq a sovereign state, the equal of Britain, as he expected the treaty to supersede the League of Nations Mandate. Britain, though, presented the King with a choice: to reject both the treaty and the underlying Mandate (and with it Britain's aid), or to accept them both. Gertrude explained to a friend:

> From the beginning the King told us with complete frankness that he would fight the Mandate to the death. His reason is obvious. He wants to prove to the world of Islam which is bitterly anti-British dial in accepting the British help he has not sacrificed the independence of an Arab state.

Finally a pledge arrived from Churchill stating that, if the treaty was signed, he would do everything he could to have Iraq accepted into the League of Nations. Faisal agreed.

On May 1st, 1923, Sir Percy Cox retired and left Iraq. It was a poignant moment lot Gertrude. 'I think no Englishman has inspired more confidence in the East,' she lamented. But with Cox's departure, Gertrude's duties also waned and it wasn't long before melancholy descended. 'I want to feel savage and independent again,' she declared, and drove out into the desert.

Arriving at what was once the Sumerian city of Uruk, she discovered the ancient mound crawling with natives hunting for treasure. Rounding them up, she demanded to know if they had any enticas and offered to pay baksheesh for anything they had found. A cylinder and a seal were produced and Gertrude paid for them and left, taking the objects directly to her new museum of Iraqi antiquities.

The museum, temporarily housed within the royal palace in Baghdad, now became Gertrude's new focus. Supervising digs and personally examining even the tiniest of finds, Gertrude worked to bring the fragments of ancient Iraq together beneath one roof where she could identify and catalogue them.

But Gertrude felt lonely and depressed. Most of her friends had left Baghdad, and as Iraq stabilised, she began to feel redundant. She spent an 'infernal' fifty-sixth birthday in ill health, and by the end of August was bedridden. She returned home briefly in 1925, but her childhood home had become a cheerless place. Due to the wider economic circumstances, the Bell family fortune was slipping away. Her parents had no choice but to abandon their home. As the house was being emptied around her, Gertrude again left for the Middle East:

> I don't care to be in London much … I like Baghdad, and I like Iraq. It's the real East, and it's stirring; things are happening here, and the romances it all touches me and absorbs me.

Soon after her return, she developed pleurisy. She recovered, only to learn a month later that her brother Hugo had succumbed to typhoid and died. Over come with grief, Gertrude nevertheless reflected that he'd 'had a complete life. His perfect marriage and the joy of his children.' Two things Gertrude had long desired.

June 1926 brought respite in the way of celebration. After the gathering of over 3,000 items, Gertrude's new Baghdad archaeological museum was officially opened. Furthermore, a treaty was signed with the Turks, ceding the city of Mosul to Iraq. At the state banquet in honour of the treaty, Faisal gave thanks to the representatives of the British government for all they had done for Iraq. Now Gertrude truly realised her work was done. Her power and influence had diminished, the family fortune had disappeared, she was in poor health, and despite a small number of passionate but ill-fated affairs, she was still—and more significantly than all else—alone.

On the evening of Sunday July 11th, 1926, Gertrude retired to bed, took an extra dose of sleeping pills and fell asleep for the last time.

Under King Faisal's direction, Iraq was admitted to the League of Nations in 1932, signifying the country's independence. One year later, however, Faisal died unexpectedly on holiday in Switzerland.

Ghazi, his twenty-one year old son succeeded him, and while his intentions were good, he lacked his father's ability to rule. After six years, King Ghazi was killed—perhaps intentionally—in a road accident,

The kingdom was left in the hands of his four-year-old son Faisal II with his maternal uncle, Prince Abd al-Ilah, acting as regent. Faisal was enthroned in 1953, reigning for five years before a military coup overthrew the monarchy and Iraq was declared a republic. The regime that Gertrude had worked to establish lasted only thirty-seven years before falling to the revolutionaries.

'The real difficulty here,' she once wrote, 'is that we don't know exactly what we intend to do in this country … it's not the immediate war problems here I think of most; it's the problems after the war, and I don't know what sort of hand we shall be able to take in sorting them.'

Such insight would have been invaluable today.

For Further Reading

Gertrude Bell, The Desert and the Sown (Heinemann, 1907, Beacon Press, 1987); Amurath to Amurath (Heinemann, 1911); Gertrude Bell and Sir William Ramsey, The Thousand and One Churches (Hodder and Stoughton, 1909); Janet Wallach, Desert Queen (Phoenix, 1999); Susan Goodman. Gertrude Bell (Berg, 1985); A.J. Barker, The Neglected War—Mesopotamia 1914-1918 (Faber & Faber, 1967); John Charmley, Lord Lloyd George and the Decline of the British Empire (St. Martin's Press, 1987); David Garnett, Letters of T.E. Lawrence (Spring books, 1964); Bruce Westrate, The Arab Bureau: British Policy in the Middle East 1916-1920 (Pennsylvania UP, 1992); Billie Melman, Women's Orients: English Women and the Middle East, 1718-1818 (Ann Arbor, University of Michigan Press, 1992).

KERRY ELLIS is an independent writer and researcher.

Art Deco: High Style

The glamorous look marked skylines from New York to Shanghai and streamlined everything from film and fashion to jewelry and automobiles.

STANLEY MEISLER

As a child in New York City in the 1930s, I grew up with Art Deco all around me. I never knew it was Art Deco; it was simply the world I lived in. The wondrous skyscrapers like the Empire State Building and the Chrysler Building, Radio City Music Hall, where my mother took me at Christmas, and my junior high school in the Bronx—all Art Deco. Many of the sumptuous sets in the movies I saw on Saturdays were Art Deco; even the Marx Brothers crossed the Atlantic on ocean liners decked out in Art Deco. At age 15, I worked at a flower shop in the majestic Art Deco Rockefeller Center, a virtual museum of the style, with more than 100 Deco paintings and reliefs in its buildings. And the New York World's Fair of 1939 and '40—in some respects Art Deco's culmination—was for me an attraction greater than any Xanadu.

Art Deco was the name given, long after the fact, to the brazenly commercial, streamlined style that emerged in Europe, primarily Paris, prior to World War I. Spreading around the globe, it dominated architecture and decorative arts during the 1920s and '30s. Whereas worshipers of Art Nouveau— the previous stylistic rage—were obsessed with nature and decadent symbolism and filled their designs with arabesques, whiplash curves, tendrils and images of seductive women, Art Deco designers embraced machinery and power. Using modern materials such as plastic and chrome, opulent fabrics and precious gems, their designs were replete with geometric patterns—circles, zigzags, squares—classical motifs, bright colors and just about anything that hinted of speed. There is pizazz and energy in Art Deco, as well as glamour and luxury

By the end of World War II, Art Deco had come to be seen as too frivolous for a world in shock from death and destruction. But in the past quarter century, critics and scholars have taken up the style and preservationists have saved its buildings from the wrecking ball. Prices for Art Deco furniture and objects have soared. In 2003, Paris-based fashion designer Karl Lagerfeld sold his collection of Art Deco furniture, rugs, lamps and ceramics at auction in Paris for $8 million, nearly three times the expected price.

Perhaps the most comprehensive exhibition ever of Art Deco artifacts and images is on view at the Museum of Fine Arts, Boston, through January 9. First mounted last year by the Victoria & Albert Museum (V&A) in London, the show features more than 240 works: diamond and onyx jewelry from Cartier, a 1935 Auburn 851 Speedster, evening gowns by a host of French couturiers, travel posters by the Ukrainian-born French designer known as Cassandre and furnishings from the lavishly decorated grand salon of the 1925 world's fair of design in Paris.

It is from that fair—the Exposition Internationale des Arts Décoratifs et Industriels Modernes—that Art Deco takes its name. Mounted on 55 acres in the heart of Paris, it hosted pavilions displaying the decorative arts of some 20 countries, including Austria, Poland, Sweden, Czechoslovakia, the USSR and Italy. (The United States declined to take part because, according to the office of then Secretary of Commerce Herbert Hoover, "there was no modern design in America.") But the fair's main intent was to promote the work of new French designers. More than 16 million people visited over the six months it was on view.

Although the Swiss architect Charles-Édouard Jeanneret, better known as Le Corbusier, had designed a pavilion sponsored by *L'Esprit Nouveau*, a decorative arts magazine he had founded, he disdained most of the works in the exposition. In a series of articles he wrote for the magazine, he called them too decorative, too luxurious and too expensive, mocking them as mere "*arts déco*," from the title of the fair. But Le Corbusier's coinage did not catch on at first.

Over the years, the style acquired several names. Some called it "Jazz Modern" or "Zig-Zag Modern." Others referred to it as "Moderne." When critics, historians and curators began to take renewed interest in the style in the late 1960s, they focused on the 1925 Paris fair as its launchpad. Some picked up Le Corbusier's "arts déco" to describe the style—this time admiringly. British art historian Bevis Hillier dropped Le Corbusier's "s" for his 1968 book, *Art Deco of the 20s and 30s*, and the Minneapolis Institute of Art followed in 1971 with an exhibition called "The World of Art Deco." "The genie was out of the bottle," says Ghislaine Wood, curator of the V&A show. The name stuck.

Art Deco made its mark in many fields, from architecture to fashion, film to furniture, graphic arts to dishware, even in the design of trains, planes, automobiles and ocean liners. Such va-

Lanvin made ten years later, "the streamlining has [itself] *become* the decoration."

Art Deco is associated in particular with two expatriates living in Paris: Josephine Baker and Tamara de Lempicka. Baker, a 19-year-old, St. Louis-born African-American dancer, enthralled Paris as the star of the 1925 La Revue Négre. One print of her by her lover, the French artist Paul Colin, depicts her dancing at the Folies-Bergère in nothing but a skirt made of bananas. Polish-born artist Tamara de Lempicka also burst upon the scene in 1925 when a German fashion magazine put her self-portrait on its cover; wearing leather gloves, a pilot's helmet and a flowing beige scarf, Lempicka sat grandly behind the wheel of a green Bugatti. Her distinctive painting style featured elongated, sexually charged geometric figures. (Not surprisingly, perhaps, the singer Madonna collects Lempicka paintings.)

On this side of the ocean, the novelist F. Scott Fitzgerald wove Art Deco accouterments through his chronicles of the high jinks and illusory dreams of the young veterans and flappers who chased after life with devil-may-care abandon. It was during the close of the Jazz Age, as Fitzgerald called those years after World War I, that New York City sprouted what may be the greatest monuments to the Art Deco aesthetic: skyscrapers. Since the 792-foot-high Woolworth Building had been completed on Broadway in 1913, no developer had tried to top the world's tallest structure until Walter P. Chrysler, the automobile magnate, and architect William Van Alen teamed up in 1928. Their Chrysler Building was in the final stages of construction in 1930 when they learned it was about to be trumped by two feet by another new skyscraper, the Bank of Manhattan at 40 Wall Street. Van Alen, it seemed, had lost out to his former partner H. Craig Severance, architect of the Bank of Manhattan building. Soon after, workmen at the Chrysler Building assembled an enormous, 27-ton steel spike (secretly brought into the building in sections) and pushed it through the skyscraper's crown to make it 1,046 feet tall, outdoing 40 Wall Street by 119 feet.

With its colored frieze of automobile hubcaps at the 31st floor, steel gargoyles shaped like eagles on the 59th, and a magnificent, seven-story crown of stainless steel arches and triangular windows topped by its surreptitious spike, the Chrysler Building remains the most spectacular Art Deco skyscraper. But its title as the world's tallest held for only 11 months, until the 1,250-foot-high Empire State Building opened on May 1, 1931. By then, however, the boom was over. Wags joked that the tallest building in the world ought to be renamed "the Empty State Building." A *New Yorker* cartoon of the time shows a clerk poking out of a Chrysler Building Window, peering through a telescope at the Empire State Building and telling his boss, "They haven't got a single tenant on the fifty-fourth floor yet, Mr. Chrysler."

What the great skyscrapers did have, especially during the Depression, was cachet. In the Bronx, the six-story Herman Ridder Junior High School, my alma mater, was completed in 1931 and named after the patriarch of the family that now runs the Knight-Ridder newspaper chain. It paid homage to skyscraper design with setbacks and vertical window strips. "Modernism in architecture has reached the schools," the *New York Times* wrote of the facility in 1929. Citing it as the first Art Deco

riety makes the style hard to define. But there is one key element. "In Art Deco," Wood says, "decoration is more important than anything else."

Art Deco designers also liked exotic themes and materials, elongated figures, artificial light and repetitive patterns of geometric and abstract forms. They drew inspiration from the cultures of ancient Egypt, Mesoamerica, East Asia and sub-Saharan Africa. And in the movement's later years, they incorporated the era's fascination with speed and began to streamline their work, making everything look as if it were in motion, even when the object—like a 1925 Ronson cigarette lighter in the exhibition—did not move at all.

At first glance, a sleek, streamlined object may seem less decorative than the elaborate works shown at the 1925 Paris fair. But, says Wood, comparing an ornate 1925 evening dress designed by Jeanne Paquin with an unadorned gown by Jeanne

school building in New York City, the city's preservation commission designated Ridder as a landmark in 1990.

It was Hollywood that beamed Art Deco to the world. "The backdrops for this exploration of contemporary dreams and aspirations were fantastic Deco-styled hotels, night-clubs, ocean liners, offices, apartments and skyscrapers," V&A curator Wood writes. During the darkest days of the Depression, some 60 million to 75 million Americans-out of the nation's 125 million people—went to the movies each week, often in lavish Deco movie palaces.

Busby Berkeley choreographed scores of synchronized dancers on enormous mechanical Art Deco sets for musicals such as *Gold Diggers of Broadway* (1933). Fred Astaire and Ginger Rogers whirled against a background of soaring columns and smoky-glass fixtures in Deco hotels and nightclubs in *Flying Down to Rio* (1933), *Top Hat* (1935) and *Shall We Dance* (1937). And Greta Garbo, John Barrymore and Joan Crawford cavorted gloomily in the Academy Award-winning *Grand Hotel* (1932), with its Deco chrome-and-glass-fitted lobby and streamlined French furniture.

The gleaming symbol of the 1939 New York World's Fair was a 700-foot-high Art Deco Trylon (a triangular-shaped pylon) and a 200-foot-diameter Perisphere (a massive round ball). Art Deco industrial designers such as Raymond Loewy and Norman Bel Geddes created some of the fair's most memorable exhibitions. I was barely 8 years old at the time, but I still vividly remember riding through a model landscape of cities, highways and farms in Bel Geddes' Futurama exhibit in the General Motors complex while a disembodied voice described the wonderful world in store in faraway 1960: slumless, pristine cities linked by cars speeding down 14-1ane highways. After the ride, I proudly wore on my jacket a pin that read: "I have seen the future."

But Art Deco's moment had already passed, if only because, as Wood says, "the idea of chic luxury was seen as inappropriate after World War II." It was fun while it lasted.

Washington-based author **STANLEY MEISLER** is a frequent contributor to [the Smithsonian]. He wrote about Maya art in the July [2004] issue.

Auschwitz: The Forgotten Evidence

Sixty years ago, on January 27th, 1945, the Red Army liberated what was left of the Auschwitz extermination camp. Taylor Downing reveals extraordinary aerial photographs of the camp taken during the summer of 1944, which pose awkward questions about why the Allies did not act to stop the killing.

TAYLOR DOWNING

On august 23rd, 1944 a Mosquito aircraft of the 60th Photo Reconnaissance Squadron loaded up with camera and film to fly a long 1,200 mile mission over southern Poland. The aircraft was based at the recently captured Foggia airfield in south-east Italy and the use of this airfield enabled Allied photo-reconnaissance flights to cover much more of occupied Europe than had previously been possible. The mission of this flight was to photograph the I.G. Farben chemical plant near a town called Monowitz, near Krakow in southern Poland. Allied intelligence had picked up evidence that this chemical plant was being expanded in order to produce synthetic oil. As access to the oilfields and refineries of south-eastern Europe was being lost to the Germans, the production of synthetic oil was now crucial for the Nazi war machine. And destroying this petrochemical industry was becoming a priority for the Allies.

That day the skies over southern Poland were clear, and when the Mosquito was over the Monowitz area the pilot activated his camera. As was usual, the camera took a run of fifty exposures as the plane flew at 30,000 feet and at about 400 mph. The pilot barely looked down to see what he was photographing. He was more concerned with encountering German fighters this deep into occupied territory. Unarmed, the only possibility of escape if attacked rested on the speed of his aircraft, which was faster than all German fighters in the pre-jet era.

When the Mosquito returned to Foggia the photos were developed and printed. They told the photo-interpreters a great deal about the I.G.Farben plant at Monowitz and the site of the factory was declared a target for the heavy bombers to destroy. What the photo-interpreters failed to examine was a large complex of barrack-styled huts less than five miles from the industrial complex at Monowitz, also recorded in the fifty exposures taken on this mission. Europe was covered with labour camps and the photo-interpreters, enormously skilled in analysing industrial sites, had no instructions to analyse labour camps. They simply filed away the photographs. Subsequent photo-reconnaissance missions over Monowitz, which enabled the interpreters to understand the full workings of the

chemical plant and even to predict with accuracy the output of the plant, also recorded the complex of huts a few miles away.

What no one realised at the time was that these photographs taken by accident recorded the workings of the most notorious Nazi extermination centre of them all, at Auschwitz. Here, in remarkable and chilling detail, the camp known as Auschwitz I can be seen, where the Germans had systematically murdered hundreds of thousands of Soviet prisoners-of-war, gypsies, homosexuals and political opponents. And only a few miles away the photographs also show with astonishing clarity the second and largest of the three Auschwitz camps, Auschwitz-Birkenau, which had been built specifically to kill Jews.

Construction of Auschwitz-Birkenau had begun in late 1941 and was conceived on an industrial scale. The photographs show that the camp consisted of some 250 barrack blocks, along with nearly a hundred support buildings. On the photographs the four large gas chambers and crematoria that were built to exterminate as many as 12,000 prisoners a day, can clearly be seen. The photos even capture the moment when a train is arriving at the camp. The ritual going on in these photographs had been repeated hundreds of times before. The prisoners are being disembarked from cattle wagons after a hellish journey lasting several days. On arrival the SS guards ordered everyone off the train and all arrivals would go through a process of 'selection'. All the very young and the old, most of the family groups, the ill and the weak, are sent to the left and went straight to the gas chambers. On these photos a group can be [seen] walking along a ramp towards Gas Chamber II whose gate is open. Probably 80–85 per cent of all the arrivals were regularly stripped of their clothes and belongings and taken straight to the gas chambers. The remainder, the fittest-looking of the new arrivals, were sent to the right where they were tattooed with a number and became inmates of the labour camp.

During the summer of 1944 this vast killing machine was operating at maximum capacity as 750,000 Jews living in Hungary, newly incorporated into the Third Reich, began to be rounded up and sent to Auschwitz. Such were the numbers arriving at the camp that even the four crematoria could not cope with disposing of the number of corpses. It was recorded that bodies were burnt in open pits at the edge of the camp. In one of the very few records of this, the aerial photographs clearly show smoke rising from pits at the edge of the camp.

The Auschwitz complex of camps was photographed several times during the summer and autumn of 1944 as Allied photo-interpreters gathered more and more evidence of the activity at the I.G. Farben petro-chemical plant at Monowitz. (Prisoners not only worked here, but helped to build the complex, and some were housed in the Monowitz camp known as Auschwitz III.) All the photographs of the extermination camp were ignored, however, and filed away. They were not 'discovered' until 1979 when two CIA photoanalysts, Dino Brugioni and Robert Poirier, came across them while researching aerial images of Poland.

The existence of these photographs today prompts uncomfortable questions. If the camp could be photographed so clearly from the air why could it not be bombed? Why were the gas chambers not destroyed and the killing stopped? Are the Allies to be blamed for a terrible moral lapse in not acting to stop one of the most barbaric acts in all of history, the Nazi genocide of the Jews?

And indeed requests to bomb the camps did come to the Allied governments during the summer of 1944, when the extent of evidence about the Nazi extermination policy, the 'Final Solution', became overwhelming. Today an understanding of what is called the Holocaust, the vast Nazi killing machine that murdered 6 million Jews, is a vital part of our understanding of the horror of the Second World War. But at the time, the evidence about the killing was fragmentary and confusing. And many officials faced with trying to understand what was going on in occupied Europe, found the evidence, literally, beyond comprehension. It simply seemed inconceivable that the Germans were killing such huge numbers of civilians as was being reported.

It was essential for the Nazi killing machine to keep the existence of the camps and details of what was happening in them secret. To exterminate vast numbers, the Nazis needed the civilians rounded up across the whole of occupied Europe to get on the deportation trains in the belief that they were being sent to resettlement camps 'in the East'. Or, at least, to think they were going off to work for the German Reich somewhere. They needed people on arrival to disembark from the trains and to go to the gas chambers believing what they were told—that they were going into showers before starting work. If information about the existence of the death camps became known to the Allies and if they broadcast this to the people of occupied Europe then the dreadful process of killing could easily break down.

The first evidence picked up by Allied intelligence about the development of the death camps was in late 1941 and 1942 through decrypts of Enigma messages sent by the police and by the SS. This suggested that the Nazi rule of terror in the occupied East featured regular atrocities. The numbers of deaths being reported in these messages shocked the intelligence officers but they failed to realise that this added up to a full-scale extermination policy. Rumours of the horrors of the camps filtered through Jewish groups and the Polish underground, back to London and Washington. In August 1942 a telegram from Gerhart Riegner of the World Jewish Congress arrived in London.

Based on reports smuggled out of Germany it was the first evidence of a co-ordinated Nazi plan to annihilate the entire Jewish population of the Occupied territories. But still, officials were sceptical of the idea that vast death camps had been constructed somewhere in the East.

In the spring of 1944 a set of reports arrived in the west from inmates who had escaped from Auschwitz. The first of these reports was written by Rudolf Vrba and Alfred Wetzler, two young Slovakian Jews who had tricked the SS guards and managed to escape to Zilina. From here the underground Jewish network smuggled out Vrba's report. Later in the year Vrba took part in the Slovakian Uprising. Whilst at Auschwitz he had for some months been assigned to working on the selection process as new arrivals came in off the trains. He had an almost photographic memory and brought out from Auschwitz details of literally hundreds of deportation trains that had arrived at the camp. He had memorised not only where the trains had come from, but also the approximate numbers of prisoners on each train. Furthermore, he had memorised roughly the number from each train that had been admitted to the camp and how many had been sent straight to the gas chambers. When Vrba and Wetzler were de-briefed by the Jewish authorities in Bratislava their story was at first not believed—until the details of their evidence was tied up with the existence of actual deportation trains that had made the journeys as reported by the escapees. This report eventually reached Jewish groups in Switzerland who passed it on to London, Washington and to the Vatican.

At the beginning of July 1944, Chaim Weizmann, President of the Jewish Agency, made a formal request to the British and American governments to bomb the camps or the railways leading up to them, to prevent further killing from taking place. This began a debate in Whitehall and Washington, and within their respective air forces, about what could be done. Churchill was told of the request by Foreign Secretary Anthony Eden and immediately committed himself to it, scribbling in the margin 'Get anything you can out of the Air Force. Invoke me if necessary'.

It was quickly decided that the use of heavy four-engined bombers would be counter-productive. With the accuracy of bombing techniques at this point of the war, a bombing raid led by, say, American B-17 Flying Fortresses would run the risk of destroying the entire camp and killing tens of thousands of inmates. No Allied commander wanted to take this risk.

More time was spent considering the option of sending precision fighter-bombers to attack the gas chambers. British Mosquito squadrons, for instance, had been trained in high-precision raids. Attacks on the Gestapo headquarters in Copenhagen and on the Amiens prison had proved a great success. But it was soon pointed out that these raids were over short distances. The possibility of re-locating these specially trained squadrons from English airfields to southern Italy, then for them to fly massive long-range 1,200 mile missions and to find and destroy gas chambers that were roughly the size of tennis courts, seemed an impossible task. Furthermore, it was felt that bombing the railways would only be a temporary measure. The Germans were good at repairing railways in hours or at the most days and the only way to ensure permanent destruction was by repeated bombing, which would take up too many Allied air resources.

Part of a letter from Anthony Eden to Winston Churchill, July 6th, 1944

PRIME MINISTER

I have had another appeal from Dr Weizmann that we should do something to mitigate the appalling slaughter of Jews in Hungary. Sixty thousand a day according to the Jewish Agency's information are being gassed and burnt at the death camp of Birkenou. This may well be an exaggeration.

Dr Weizmann recognized that there was little His Majesty's Government could do, but made the following suggestions:

(a) Something might be done to stop the operation of this death camp
    (i) by bombing the railway lines leading to it (and to similar comps) and also
    (ii) by bombing the camps themselves so as to destroy the plant used for the gassing and cremation.
    I told Dr Weizmann that we had already considered (ii) [sic], but that I would now re-examine it and the further suggestion of bombing the camps themselves. I am in favour of acting on both these suggestions.

(b) Dr Weizmann suggested that a greater impression might be made upon the obduracy of the Hungarians if a warning couched in the strongest terms were addressed to the Hungarian Government by Marshal Stalin. I told Dr Weizmann that I would consider this suggestion. I am in favour of it. You will remember that the Soviet Government joined His Majesty's Government and the United States Government in 1942 in a declaration condemning similar atrocities and pledging themselves to exact retribution. The most appropriate form of approach would, I think, be a message from yourself to Marshal Stalin. Would you be willing to do this?...

Above all, the Allied military planners knew they were at a critical stage of the war in both the Pacific and in Europe. The battle for Normandy was at its height. The V-bomb campaign against England had begun, and it was felt that the limited numbers of trained precision attack aircrews were needed to hunt down and destroy the V-bomb launch sites. The strongest argument of all was that the best way to save the people of occupied Europe was to defeat the Nazi war machine and that all Allied military efforts should be directed to this end. Only with the defeat of Hitler's regime would the Jews of Europe be truly saved, it was argued.

And so, when the Allied air planners reported back in the autumn of 1944, it was decided to do nothing to bomb the death camps. This has become one of the most controversial decisions of the war. Surviving inmates have said several times that, convinced they were all going to die in the camps, they would much rather have died from Allied bombs than from Nazi torture. More than anything else, even an attempted air raid on the death camps would have been a gesture, a sign to the Nazis that the Allies knew what was going on and would seek retribution against those guilty of committing these appalling crimes when the war was over.

Sixty years later, it is difficult to see how action against the killing was avoided. Certainly the practical difficulties were immense. But the moral case was also overwhelming. Between the time when the first formal request to bomb the camps was received, and the point at which the SS dismantled the Auschwitz camps in the wake of the advancing Soviet Army, it is estimated that about 150,000 Jews were exterminated at Auschwitz. Not to have lifted a finger to have stopped this mass murder now seems an appalling lapse on behalf of the Allies. Of course, there is another dimension to this whole argument: Auschwitz was in the Soviet zone and it was the Red Army that eventually liberated the camp in January 1945. Blaming the western Allies is one thing, but Stalin also did nothing to stop the killing of Jews.

There are many ironies relating to the discovery of the aerial photographs. The pictures that were taken of the Monowitz petro-chemical works on the same missions that accidentally photographed Auschwitz, did prompt action. The I.G. Farben plant was bombed on September 13th, 1944, by American Liberator bombers of the 55th Bomb Wing. Nine bombers were lost on this mission and another fifty-five were damaged. One of the B-24 bombers had a camera in its bomb bay photographing the bombs it dropped. One of these photographs shows the bombs targeting I.G. Farben, which they hit, actually dropping over the gas chambers of Auschwitz-Birkenau. This extraordinary image is a frustrating reminder of what might have been done had the Allied air forces decided to act to prevent further deaths. And during this raid bombs did fall on Auschwitz I, though by accident, hitting several barrack blocks and killing forty inmates and fifteen SS guards. Never has photographic evidence come so near to showing what might have been done had the Allies decided to try to stop the horrors of the killing at Auschwitz in the summer of 1944.

For Further Reading

Michael J. Neufeld and Michael Berenbaum (eds), *The Bombing of Auschwitz* (University Press of Kansas in association with the US Holocaust Memorial Museum, 2003); William D. Rubinstein, *The Myth of Rescue* (Routledge, 1997); Martin Gilbert, *Auschwitz and the Allies* (Michael Joseph, 1981); Rudolf Vrba, *I Escaped from Auschwitz* (Barricade, 2002); 'The Holocaust Revisited' by Dino Brugioni and Robert Poirier. See http://www.globalsecurity.org/intell/library/imint/holocaust.htm

TAYLOR DOWNING is the producer of *Auschwitz: The Forgotten Evidence* which has been shown on Channel 4, and will be screened on The History Channel on January 27th.

Contemplating Churchill

On the 40th anniversary of the wartime leader's death, historians are reassessing the complex figure who carried Britain through its darkest hour.

EDWARD ROTHSTEIN

Chartwell must have been a heady place to be in exile. Standing on the manor's back lawn on a misty autumn day, buffeted by brisk, sweet winds, it is easy to imagine the appeal these panoramic views of the Weald of Kent must have had for Winston Churchill, luring him away from London's political battlegrounds. During much of the 1930s, Churchill, who had been denied cabinet position and governmental power by his own Conservative Party, was stubbornly locking horns with both sides of Parliament's aisle. Chartwell was his refuge. And he cultivated the landscape with the same meticulous obsession he gave to his speeches, his hands restlessly probing, meddling, tinkering. There is a photograph of Churchill, wrapped in a muffler and overcoat, some 70 years ago, tiling a cottage roof on his estate. Similar Churchillian handiwork still remains evident in the garden wall of brick he painstakingly laid, and in the artificial lakes he designed and excavated. One of his own paintings (he was a talented amateur) hangs in the dining room of the rambling, oddly cramped house—now a museum run by the National Trust; it shows a gathering for afternoon tea, the seated figures pausing in midsentence. Except that Churchill is turned away from the others—justly confident that the conversation will wait until he is prepared to turn back.

Chartwell was also, at times, a burden—its repairs and staff devoured Churchill's income as fast as his epic writing projects and fecund journalism could replenish it—but the estate grounded him in the English past, perhaps even reminding him of the legacies his parents had so cavalierly squandered. He even established a kind of informal government in exile at Chartwell. It became a place where his devoted friends and counselors shared information and assessed prospects, his country seat, particularly during those "wilderness years" (as they have been called), when there seemed little chance of his ever wielding power again and little reason to hope for it. After all, by the mid-1930s Churchill was entering his 60s. He had served in Parliament for nearly 30 years, had switched party allegiances twice, had been chancellor of the exchequer, and first lord of the admiralty, and had held ministerial posts ranging from home secretary to colonial secretary. But he was beginning to seem out of step even with the conservatives in his party,

opposing, for example, any hints of independence for India, saying he was nauseated by the "fakir" Gandhi. One of his biographers, Robert Rhodes James, writes: By the end of 1933 Churchill was widely regarded as a failed politician, in whom no real trust could be reasonably placed; by June 1935, these opinions had been fortified further." If he had ended his career here—puttering around Chartwell and making an occasional appearance in Parliament—few would have missed or mourned him.

But what also isolated Churchill during those years was his sharp, unrelenting focus on the growing Nazi German threat. And as it turned out, that preoccupation—considered to be "scaremongering," militaristic and dangerous during much of the decade—eventually brought him back to power and helped ensure his enduring reputation. In fact, Churchill's foresight, his independent stand, his unwavering attention—and later, his wartime leadership—granted him a stature in Britain that no American wartime leader, other than Lincoln, has ever achieved in the United States. Franklin Delano Roosevelt may have guided America through the Depression and led it to the brink of victory in World War II, but his personal triumph was not as mythic or startling as Churchill's; the risks of wartime defeat were not so great; and the effect of a single man's talents not so evident. Churchill was voted the greatest Briton who ever lived, in a recent BBC poll. He touched some fundamental nerve that still vibrates. The historian John Lukacs says that Churchill's reputation may now be at a peak. It is testimony to Churchill's continued importance that the backlash against him may be at a crest as well. One British historian, David Cannadine, recently asserted that Churchill, at his worst, was a "bombastic and histrionic vulgarian," while others have attacked "the cult of Churchill" that seeks to recruit him as an ally in the war on terrorism. In recent years, particularly since 9/11, his very reputation can seem up for grabs, as his statements and actions are heatedly invoked in debates about the nature of enmity, the causes of hatred, the dangers of appeasement and the risks of engagement.

SO IT IS A PROPITIOUS MOMENT for a new Churchill Museum to open in London, which it did last month to mark the 40th anniversary of Churchill's death at age 90, January 24,

1965. World War II lies at the heart of the museum, since it is actually a 9,000-square-foot extension of the Cabinet War Rooms—the reconstructed underground bunker from which a good part of England's war was directed, and which itself has become something of a shrine honoring Churchill's wartime leadership. But the museum is the first major British attempt to tell the story of Churchill's life, surveying its achievements and controversies. Phil Reed, the director of the Cabinet War Rooms, has shepherded the new Churchill Museum exhibition through its $11.2 million fundraising campaign and guided design in consultation with scholars.

But the challenge is daunting, even in recounting Churchill's World War II triumphs. The broad narrative has become familiar and has endured despite challenges and modifications. Reed suggests it will also shape the museum's account. During the 1930s, most of Britain, along with its leaders, believed that negotiation would be effective in controlling Hitler. After all, it was argued, Germany was still recovering from harsh penalties imposed after World War I, so its restlessness was understandable. Besides, after the horrors of that war, no one could imagine embarking on another. Churchill's ultimate position—that negotiation and appeasement were doomed to fail and that war postponed would be more bloody than strength displayed—was considered irresponsible; his warnings wild, paranoid, extreme. So he stood, with just a few allies, nearly alone, and spoke out with a foresight that is now difficult to comprehend.

But the details of that foresight, some of which will emerge in the new exhibits, are extraordinary. As early as 1930, Churchill, attending a dinner party at the German Embassy in London, had expressed concern about the dangers latent in a rabble-rouser named Adolf Hitler; Churchill's warning was considered novel enough to be forwarded to Berlin. In 1934, when the Nazis were in power and were stirring the German populace, Churchill told Parliament "there is not an hour to lose" in preparing to build up British armaments (armaments that he had, a decade earlier, helped reduce). Germany, he said, was "arming fast and no one is going to stop her." That same year, six years before the blitz, he predicted there could come a time when "the crash of bombs exploding in London and cataracts of masonry and fire and smoke will apprise us of any inadequacy which has been permitted in our aerial defenses." Hitler knew enough to be wary of Churchill, but on native grounds, Churchill's passion was generally mocked as hysteria. He seemed to have been cursed like Cassandra: to speak the truth but not to be believed. In 1935, before Hitler's plans had become clear, Churchill, in dismay, saw "Germany arming at breakneck speed, England lost in a pacifist dream, France corrupt and torn by dissension, America remote and indifferent."

At Chartwell, during his time in exile (while he also produced 11 volumes of history and memoir and more than 400 articles for the world's newspapers), his judgments became more informed and certainly more astute than those of the government. He would be fed detailed intelligence about German rearmament by trusted visitors and gain support from a small group of like-minded friends. Then he would head to the House of Commons to duel with the successive governments of Stanley Baldwin and Neville Chamberlain, who saw little to be so exercised about. In March 1938, after Hitler had already fortified his army, built the *Luftwaffe*, militarized the Rhineland, absorbed Austria and threatened Czechoslovakia, Churchill chastised Parliament: "For five years I have talked to the House on these matters—not with very great success. I have watched this famous island descending incontinently, fecklessly, the stairway which leads to a dark gulf." He made one final urgent appeal: "Now is the time at last to rouse the nation."

But John Maynard Keynes, writing in the *New Statesman*, was urging the Czechs to negotiate with Hitler. And so, it seems, was everybody else. The newspapers ignored Churchill's speech, reporting instead Chamberlain's remark that the situation in Europe had greatly relaxed. And the day after the speech, one of Churchill's major journalistic contracts, with the *Evening Standard*, was cancelled because of his "views on foreign affairs."

When Churchill was finally brought back into the cabinet in 1939 as first lord of the admiralty, and then, in 1940, when he became prime minister in the midst of war, his challenge was not to instill fear but to keep it under control. On June 18, 1940, Churchill said that if England could stand up to Hitler, "all Europe may be free, and the life of the world may move forward into broad, sunlit uplands; but if we fail, then the whole world, including the United States, and all that we have known and cared for, will sink into the abyss of a new dark age." In the House of Commons on October 8, 1940, Churchill's jeremiads turned biblically somber: "Death and sorrow will be the companions of our journey; hardship our garment; constancy and valour our only shield." Six days later, No. 10 Downing Street, the prime minister's residence, was damaged by German bombs. Chartwell had already been closed down—it was too obvious a target.

Because of the blitz, the government's war cabinet regularly met underground, in a low-ceilinged, sandbagged basement in the Office of Works opposite St. James's Park, where chemical toilets and rudimentary sleeping quarters formed the setting for discussions of England's strategy (more than 115 war cabinet meetings were held there, a tenth of the war's total). Those secret corridors—the Cabinet War Rooms—were opened by the Imperial War Museum in 1984 and are now a pilgrimage site for 300,000 visitors a year. What was at stake in those rooms is made clear in an entrance-hall exhibit. In Hitler's bombing of England, 60,595 civilians died, 29,890 in London alone. When invasion seemed imminent and the appearance of German soldiers and officers in Piccadilly Circus likely, the government distributed a leaflet: "Enemy Uniforms at a Glance." The leaflets turned out to be unnecessary, partly because of what happened in these spare, windowless rooms, their walls hung with maps dotted with pushpins, their tables covered with paper pads and ashtrays, their basement infrastructure offering clanking pipes and poor plumbing.

That primitive setting makes the museum's point: so much was done by so few with so little. But visitors will also be able to pass from the War Rooms into the new Churchill Museum, where so much is being done by so many to shed light on a single man. It promises the kind of technological flash that original users of the War Rooms could hardly have imagined, including state-of-the-art multimedia displays and a 50-foot-long electronic "Lifeline": a complete timeline of Churchill's life, with 1,500 documents and 1,000 photographs that appear in response to a visitor's touch. The exhibition room is less about objects than about ideas and information. But it contains documents and artifacts from Chartwell, the Imperial War Museum, the Churchill Archives Centre at Churchill College, Cambridge, and private collections, including Churchill's baby rattle and a pistol he used in his escape from a prison camp in the Boer War. There is even a red velvet, one-piece zip-up suit Churchill liked to wear (inadvertently demonstrating an area where he showed questionable taste). Because viewers enter the new space directly from the War Rooms, its biographical narrative actually begins in 1940 and then proceeds to Churchill's death before leading back to Churchill's birth.

By beginning with the war, of course, the new museum exhibit necessarily gives Churchill's life a heroic cast. But when I toured the new museum with Reed, he emphasized one point: "We wanted to avoid accusations of hagiography." Of course, he continued, "we have accepted Churchill as a great leader and a great man. But we want to see what greatness meant in his life. Great people are not great all of the time."

In fact, it is impossible to recount Churchill's life without incorporating its controversies, failures and falterings. Even when the war's victory neared, there were reasons for melancholy: Churchill's increasing awareness of England's decline, his failure to convince Roosevelt and then Truman of Stalin's political intentions; and the Conservatives' resounding defeat in the 1945 election that tossed Churchill out of office just as the war was ending. Then came increasing physical frailties and frustrations when he again became prime minister in 1951 and persistently tried to arrange summit meetings that might temper the growing cold war. Some of the controversies in Churchill's earlier life, Reed points out, include the disastrous 1915 Dardanelles campaign he advocated as lord of the admiralty in World War I, a campaign that led to his resignation and a lifetime of recriminations and blame (unjustly so, a government report once affirmed and some historians now argue).

Churchill, it must be said, thought too much of himself to bother hiding his flaws. He did not have much interest in other people's opinions; he was self-indulgent and intolerant; late in World War II, he was often accused of coming to meetings without having read the basic documents. Alan Brooke, chief of the imperial general staff, famously wrote, "Winston had ten ideas every day, only one of which was good, and he did not know which it was." He could also be intemperate: after nearly winning a war against Nazism and its evils, it could not have helped his election prospects to have argued in a 1945 radio broadcast that the opposition Labor Party's socialist policies would lead to a "sort of Gestapo."

But the heroic foundation has remained remarkably sturdy. Churchill's stature has been shored up not just by popular perception but by the sheer accumulation of detail in eight volumes of the "authorized biography," begun by his son, Randolph, and brought to a conclusion by Martin Gilbert, along with the splendid, popularly written two volumes of the late William Manchester's biography *The Last Lion* (the third volume will be completed by another author). Churchill also once boasted that he would ensure his place in history by writing the history himself, which he did: his six-volume account of World War II helped win him the Nobel Prize in Literature in 1953 but does not pretend to be a scrupulously objective history. Churchill also deliberately cultivated the aura of heroism; he courted its charms, welcomed its dangers. He must have been dismayed at the War Rooms' bunker; he preferred to climb to rooftops to watch the German bombs fall, just as at the end of the 19th century, when fighting in Sudan, he would casually stand exposed to enemy fire. There is something childish, even foolish in such dares, and Churchill really did have an almost perverse attraction to warfare (while still being sober about its purposes and horrors). But heroism requires some foolishness: it shuns carefully reasoned second-guesses. And sometimes such actions turn out not to be self-indulgence but sacrificial accomplishment; there were hints of both in Churchill's acts.

THERE HAVE, HOWEVER, been important challenges to the main outline of the heroic narrative, some of them far more radical than any the Churchill Museum could fully countenance. Robert Rhodes James' 1970 book on Churchill's wilderness years, for example, was subtitled *A Study in Failure*. It argued that given how unreliable Churchill had proved himself before the 1930s, it is no surprise he was discounted when it came to his warnings about Hitler. John Charmley's 1993 *Churchill: The End of the Glory* went even further, pinning on Churchill major responsibility for the disintegration of the British Empire. He and others have also suggested that there might well have been a way to reach an agreement with Hitler without going to war. This was the very subject of cabinet discussions extending over several days in May 1940, soon after Churchill became prime minister. The foreign secretary, Lord Halifax, whom many, including the king, would have preferred to see in Churchill's place, argued that compromise with Hitler would still be preferable to a war in which many would die and England could lose. These views, of course, also required a more genteel understanding of Hitler's long-term goals and methods than that which Churchill had gotten from reading *Mein Kampf* and watching Hitler at work. Other revisionist views of Churchill include skepticism about the very idea of there being such a thing as a "great man," let alone one who might actually lead a nation in a Tolkienesque battle between good and evil. The historian A.J.P Taylor, for example, in his *Origins of the Second World War*, argues that even Hitler had been misunderstood; some of his acts were the result of misinterpretations or misjudgments. "This is a story without heroes," Taylor wrote of World War II, "and perhaps even without villains." A doubtful proposition on one count, which makes it also doubtful on the other.

More recently, though, attempts to dampen Churchill's heroic stature have cited views now considered beyond the political pale. Churchill had a Victorian, racialist view of the world. He held unattractive views of blacks and, at times, Jews. He even signed onto the premises of the eugenics movement in the early years of the century, worrying over the population growth of the "feeble-minded and insane classes." He was a believer in the importance of the British Empire (a position that once would not have inspired the automatic recriminations it does now). He was even known to have praised the character of such tyrants as Mussolini—"a really great man"—and Stalin—"a great and good man." (Was there a bit of job envy in his compliments?)

Yet at every turn in such criticisms, complexities abound and contexts are missing. Churchill may have been inflexibly opposed to ending the Raj and granting India independence, for example, but his predictions about massacres of millions once the British pulled out proved fatefully prophetic. He may have been overly obsequious to Stalin in some wartime meetings, but he also understood, better than Roosevelt, why it might be important to get American troops into Prague sooner rather than later.

But these are not just historical debates about the nature of this particular man or academic disagreements about historical judgments. They are also debates about what sort of an example Churchill provides the 21st century. If he is considered a vulgarian warmonger, then his stance against appeasement is seen as just another one of his militant poses that, like a stopped clock, happens to be right twice a day. If he is a visionary who understood the nature of war and national interest, then his positions take on more resonance. If he held no position that could now be deemed morally justified, he becomes a historical monster, a figure who simply happened to play the right role at the right time. If his positions are understood as more nuanced, affected by his time and place, but transcending narrow preoccupations—if, that is, they were part of a larger vision—then he becomes a figure more deserving of his reputation.

So battles over Churchill's relevance are battles over his virtue and value. And a wave of such conflicts began soon after 9/11. At a time of danger and imminent conflict, Churchill was invoked as an icon of leadership, foresight and courage. After the attacks, President Bush, predicting a long and difficult war, deliberately echoed Churchill's rhetoric: "We will not waver, we will not tire, we will not falter, and we will not fail." Britain's prime minister, Tony Blair, quoted Churchill. Defense Secretary Donald H. Rumsfeld invoked him as well. And New York mayor Rudolph W. Giuliani read the British politician Roy Jenkins' recent biography. Jenkins returned the compliment; he was quoted in *Time*: "What Giuliani succeeded in doing is what Churchill succeeded in doing in the dreadful summer of 1940: he managed to create an illusion that we were bound to win." In a new book about Churchill's posthumous reputation, *Man of the Century*, the historian John Ramsden cites a cartoon in a Texas newspaper that ran after 9/11, showing New Yorkers looking at a photograph of Churchill: "They say he was a Giuliani-esque leader," one says.

Other analogies have been made not just to Churchill's character but to historical circumstance. Because Islamist terrorism has been a growing problem for well over a decade, the failure to adequately respond to previous, smaller attacks—such as the first bombing of the World Trade Center or the bombing of U.S. embassies abroad—has been compared to the failure to adequately respond to Hitler's first tentative violations of the Versailles Treaty, such as his remilitarization of the Rhineland. And last year, Spain's decision to remove its troops from Iraq after

the terrorist bombing in Madrid was compared to the appeasement of Hitler, an attempt to assuage an enemy or protect oneself by granting what was being threateningly demanded.

Yet when complications in Iraq mounted, such Churchillian invocations, with their implicit praise, were attacked for their naiveté. Churchill was even criticized for being partly responsible for contemporary problems in the Middle East; it was he, after all, who as colonial secretary in 1921 had helped draw the borders of current-day Iraq. And in polemics that attracted widespread attention last spring in *The Nation* and *The Spectator*, the American journalist Michael Lind argued that Churchill was being ritualistically invoked by a "neocon cult" that is both unduly supportive of Israel and seeking to extend American war interests; Lind also suggested that worship of Churchill is itself perverse, since it can be accomplished only by sanitizing him, ignoring his racism and ruthlessness.

Even in Britain, contemporary political positions may be chipping away at Churchill's once regnant reputation. In November, for example, "the first large-scale survey of British academic experts in British politics and/or modern British history" rated Clement Atlee, the Labour prime minister from 1945 to 1951, above Churchill as the most successful 20th-century prime minister. Churchill was considered a unifying figure because of his leadership of an embattled England; now it seems his reputation is becoming associated with political conservativism.

These are questionable judgments, seeming to magnify the unimportant and shrink the essential, but as memories of World War II fade and as current political debates evolve, assessments of Churchill's stature are bound to shift. The heroic image may start to erode. There are times, of course, when even an admirer of the man might welcome some restraint. The War Rooms can overdo it in their attempts to re-create his time and presence. The museum's current entrance, for example, is not the one that was used during the war; so sandbags are there not because they were used in 1940, but in order to evoke wartime danger; they are props. The furniture in Churchill's underground quarters is more authentic—it is meant to resemble the furniture shown in photographs—but neither is most of it original; it came from flea shops and attics. More props. And in one of the small basement rooms, a plaster figure of Churchill, supposedly speaking on a secure phone line to Roosevelt, seems positively cultic.

But that is also part of the point. There are theatrics in such a museum, because it is attempting to dramatize, to bring a particular historical moment back to life, to reconstruct a particular set of experiences and ways of thinking. It is meant to restore something to contemporary awareness, to rescue the past from the pressures of contemporary perspective. And that requires more than just the portrayal of a place. After all, the main cabinet room, in which Churchill and his select group of ministers and officers would hear reports and determine strategy, is little more than a nondescript meeting room with pads and pencils set at every place and maps on the wall. The clock reads 2 minutes before 5, the date is October 15, 1940, and a mannequin of a British officer, papers in hand, is obviously setting things in place before a meeting. It would seem just a Madame Tussaud period piece if one hadn't already gotten a sense of Britain's danger at the time and didn't also know that No. 10 Downing Street had been damaged by shrapnel the night before.

When Reed leads me into the room—which can ordinarily be viewed only through a window—the mundane scale of these objects does indeed make the immense dangers of the outside world more palpable.

Reed also points to the marks on the ends of the arms of Churchill's wooden chair, from which he ran the meetings through a haze of cigar smoke; near the end of each armrest, the furniture finish is worn away in thin lines. These narrow gashes were created, Reed explains, by the tapping of Churchill's signet ring and the nervous drumming of his fingernails. Given what was being discussed at these meetings—where the German bombs were falling, what kind of assistance the United States might give, how to deal with ships of French allies suddenly becoming part of Vichy's navy—the tapping and drumming make perfect sense. In these worn lines there are also signs of heroism, but heroism of the human, traces of a man, not a monument, tapping and scratching with frustration, excitement, anticipation, worry. On a card placed in front of Churchill's seat is a quotation from Queen Victoria from the Boer War: "Please understand there is no depression in this house and we are not interested in the possibilities of defeat—they do not exist." This message now seems obvious, unsubtle. But then, in that setting, when alternatives were not only possible, but actively considered, Churchill's signal accomplishment becomes clear.

Another thing that makes his heroism seem so extraordinarily human is that he had no illusions, only ideals. The goal was kept intact, even if the reality would fall far short; that meant constant vigilance was required. He recognized this even in his youth. In his 1899 book, *The River War*, he wrote: "All great movements, every vigorous impulse that a community may feel, become perverted and distorted as time passes, and the atmosphere of the earth seems fatal to the noble aspirations of its peoples. A wide humanitarian sympathy in a nation easily degenerates into hysteria. A military spirit tends towards brutality. Liberty leads to license, restraint to tyranny."

One of the reasons why Churchill later said that if he had to relive any year of his life it would be 1940 is that at the beginning of that life-or-death struggle, the path was clear, the goals undistorted. He actually became more and more depressed as victory neared, because he saw that the "sunlit uplands" he had promised at the war's beginning were now clouded by unforeseen events. Nor was he so content with the compromises he had to make in the midst of war—he agonized, for example, over the bombing of German cities. In fact, his triumph coincided with Britain's decline—and his own.

And no sooner had one cataclysmic conflict ended than others loomed. Before Churchill delivered his famous 1946 "Iron Curtain" speech in Fulton, Missouri, he had watched as Stalin tightened his grip on Eastern Europe: "From Stettin in the Baltic to Trieste in the Adriatic, an iron curtain has descended across the Continent," he said. "Behind that line lie all the capitals of the ancient states of Central and Eastern Europe." His speech was, in part, a warning that the war may have ended, but that struggle could not. There would be no pastoral retreat.

"It is necessary," he argued, "that constancy of mind, persistency of purpose and the grand simplicity of decision shall rule and guide the conduct of the English-speaking peoples in peace as they did in war." Constancy of mind and persistency of purpose—those are familiar Churchillian virtues: they led him out of the wilderness and England out of darkness.

But "the grand simplicity of decision" is something else. It is a recognition that in the midst of a complex world, any act or decision will have a "grand simplicity" about it. Decision necessarily omits, rejects, determines. It could be grand, perhaps magnificent, and possibly necessary. But it may also seem too simple, imperfect and flawed, narrow and restrictive. And it will have consequences that cannot be foreseen. It will be, that is, human. Acting forthrightly with that kind of understanding in the face of Britain's greatest danger—that may be Churchill's greatest claim to heroism.

EDWARD ROTHSTEIN, who writes frequently about history and the arts, is cultural critic-at-large for the *New York Times*.

The Mystery of Stalin

Paul Wingrove examines the starkly different interpretations that seek to explain the career of Joseph Stalin, who died fifty years ago this month.

PAUL WINGROVE

Among twentieth-century statesmen perhaps none was so self-contained, enigmatic, mysterious and unapproachable as the Soviet leader Joseph Stalin. To his closest comrades-in-arms and to foreign statesmen and diplomats he was a man of few words, reticent, patient and imperturbable, pacing or smoking quietly while he worked his way through a problem. His calm, thoughtful demeanour convinced even Franklin Roosevelt and Winston Churchill that they could work with him and, to a degree, take him at his word. In the Soviet Union and in the Communist Bloc created after First World War, by coercion or as a voluntary act of allegiance, Stalin was the wise, omniscient, certainly unchallengeable, leader. His portrait appeared everywhere; the slogans praised his genius; and the history books told only of Stalin and his unerring capacity to be right. His was the steady, purposeful hand which, however dreadful the sacrifices, would guide the masses on the arduous path to Communism.

Such an unreal representation was, of course, achieved through Stalin's extraordinary personal self-control, and through absolute state control of every public—and private—source of information. By such means was established, in Nikita Khrushchev's phrase when he denounced Stalin at the Twentieth Party Congress in 1956, the 'cult of personality'. This is an odd, evasive phrase. In fact it was used by Khrushchev as a criticism of the system of arbitrary one-man rule established by Stalin, rather than of any 'personality' which engendered and maintained that system. One-man rule was simply anti-Leninist, contravening the ideal of rule by the party of the working class; and hence the act of criticising this allowed Khrushchev to re-assert the validity of a Leninist system which, in this view, had been perverted by Stalin. Nor, interestingly, did Khrushchev dig too deeply into the 'personality' of Stalin since that would have opened up all sorts of embarrassing questions about morality and personal responsibility, perhaps even touching on the moral responsibility of such people as Khrushchev himself. Of course, Khrushchev intended not to open up Stalinism for historical examination, but quietly to bury the more odious and unsettling parts as quickly as possible and re-assert some sort of normality and governing capacity in a Soviet Communist party which had been largely destroyed by its own leader.

For Western historians, however, Stalin's creation of his own myth and the concealment and distortion of truth at all levels has always been a stumbling block to understanding. There were, of course, accounts by exiles and defectors (including, not least, by Svetlana, Stalin's own daughter), or by the disaffected, but only enough of this sort of material to allow historians to scratch the surface of the history of the Stalin era and obtain some limited understanding of the nature of a ruthless tyranny. But now, fifty years after the death of Stalin in March 1953, knowledge and understanding of the man and his era are growing, fuelled particularly by access to Soviet-era archives, although those archives are only partly open, with much of the most sensitive material strictly off limits.

Of course, even if the archives were freely open we might find that crucial evidence does not, in fact, exist. Thus, while we now have records of Stalin's engagements—those whom he saw, and for how long—and even some of his early letters, as far as we know he never kept a diary; and similarly, many of those who ruled alongside him did not record their memories or have, for obvious reasons, sanitised them. Furthermore, many records have simply been destroyed, either deliberately or as a result of war. Nonetheless, even limited access to the archives has begun to establish some of the truth of those times, to make historical sallies behind the palisade of the myths and distortions. Paradoxically, as we shall see, this has engendered a considerable argument over the real meaning of what we know about Stalin.

There are many discrete parts of the history which have now been exposed. In external relations, to choose some arbitrary examples, we know that Stalin encouraged Kim Ilsung to attack south Korea; we know that Stalin treated his supposed ally Mao Zedong in the most offhand manner when he visited Moscow in December 1949; and we know that Stalin almost certainly planned to assassinate another quondam ally, Tito, in a plan described as 'some kind of active measure against Tito personally' in the document discovered by Russian historian Dmitri Volkogonov. We also know of Soviet guilt for the Katyn massacres in eastern Poland in 1940.

As for the bloody infighting and the purges of the Bolshevik party leadership in the 1930s, J. Arch Getty notes (in Getty and Manning, Stalinist Terror) that we have

> ... an abundance of gruesome new details. We know that there is human blood splattered on Marshal Tukhachevskii's 'confession.' We know that Zinoviev denounced Kamenev, that Ezhov would not permit Piatakov to execute his own wife, and that M. Riutin never capitulated to his interrogators. In addition ... [w]e know ... that [Stalin] personally edited the lists of defendants and their statements for the 1936 and 1937 show trials.

We also have conclusive evidence that Stalin's signature appears on lists of individuals named for execution which often ran into thousands.

Yet the arresting details of the conflict at the apex of the party are in some ways less interesting than what we learn about the dynamics of party in the hands of Joseph Stalin, especially during the purge of many of his former colleagues on a conveyor belt of arrest, imprisonment, torture, confession to imaginary political crimes, show trial and—finally—execution, in the second half of the 1930s. The 'iron discipline' of the party of Lenin, which in large part explains how that process could be carried out, was supported, even urged, by some of those who were later to be its victims. Hence Bukharin, one of the last of the Old Bolsheviks to be cut down by Stalin, declared in 1930 that he would 'always march in step with the party'. Shkiriatov, in 1933, called for 'iron, Bolshevik discipline in the party ... when there aren't any members in the party who are not in agreement with the party line'. Rudzutak, at the same party plenum, noted that 'you won't find a single instance where Comrade Stalin has hesitated or retreated. That is why we are with him. Yes, he vigorously chops off that which is rotten ... if he didn't do this he would not be a Leninist.' Such sentiments, such unstinted support, provided the medium and mechanism for the growth and survival of Stalinism. There was no room for difference with the party, no place for nuance or individual opinion. As Trotsky said, it had to be 'my party, right or wrong'.

In this atmosphere a Bolshevik such as Yenukidze had to protect himself even when he failed to 'draw the appropriate conclusion from the report given to me ... to the effect that a certain cleaning woman was engaged in counter-revolutionary conversation'. This is almost laughable and yet, of course, the Old Bolsheviks, and many others, were executed or sent to die in the camps not because they had been insufficiently alert to trivial instances of counter-revolution or (more likely in this case) simple below stairs grumbling, but on charges that did not contain even that grain of truth: that they had been Trotskyists, wreckers, spies for foreign powers, or that they had plotted the death of Stalin. Nearly all such charges laid against the Old Bolsheviks and against countless thousands of others were without the slightest foundation and rested on nothing more substantial than on confessions extracted by torture.

The difficulty of opposing the party, and Stalin, once its course was set, is evident from the despairing speeches of Bukharin and Rykov to a party Central Committee of 1937 which had by now labelled them anti-party and anti-Stalin. Bukharin first:

> I've been guilty of many things, but I protest with all the strength of my soul against being charged with such things as treason to my homeland, sabotage, terrorism ... The whole tragedy of my situation lies in this, that Piatakov and others like him so poisoned the atmosphere, such an atmosphere arose that no one believes human feelings—not emotions, not the impulses of the heart, not tears. (Laughter)

Then Rykov:

> Oh my Lord, be it your will, it's all too clear. I was never a part of any bloc. I never belonged to any rightist center. I never engaged in any wrecking, espionage, sabotage, terrorism, or any other vile deeds. And I will continue to assert this as long as I am alive.

Despite their pleas, members of the central Committee one by one called for their expulsion from the party, to be followed by investigation by organs of state security. Neither man, old comrades of Lenin though they were, survived the Stalinist meat grinder. Another part of the battle of understanding is over the statistics—how many suffered and died under Stalin?—but here there is no easy agreement, and may never be. There are too many arenas of oppression, too many assumptions to be made, too few hard statistics and too many inconsistencies in what is available. Perhaps there was more slave labour than once we thought, and perhaps fewer executions, although Getty and others give figures of more than 300,000 executions in each of the years 1937 and 1938, horrific by any standards. But the estimates for deaths due to the character and policies of the regime vary from several millions to as many as twenty millions, with the variation explained as much by assumptions of authors as by hard statistics.

Even if the figures cannot delimit the Stalin regime precisely, the terrible suffering of the Stalin years cannot be denied, and much of it is now well documented: the attacks on, and deportations of, the peasants in the drive to collectivise agriculture; the devastating and partly man-made famine of the early 1930s which killed hundreds of thousands; the extensive use of slave labour (on canals, in logging, in gold and uranium mining); the arrests, tortures, confessions and executions which characterised the show trials of leading party members; the arrests of families of the accused (including children) almost as a matter of course; the extensive system of camps (the gulag) in which so many perished; the purge of the Red Army; the shooting of thousands of Polish officers at Katyn; the wholesale deportations of national groups during and after the war; the arrest and execution of foreign communists resident in the USSR; the suppression of the church, of free thought, music and literature, and of freedom itself.

Death, suffering and oppression were at the core of Stalinism. In this context, numbers matter, but only to a degree—quantity, as it were, should not overwhelm quality.

However patchy and insubstantial some of the evidence may still be, the fall of the Soviet Union in 1991 and the subsequent outflow of documentation has necessarily established a more empirical approach to the study of Stalinism; and from this empiricism there arises the spectre of 'revisionism', a term which Getty—often seen as the leading 'revisionist'—does not much care for, but let us use it nevertheless.

Revisionists explain Stalinism in terms of a system of interests, of social attitudes, of party discipline, of bureaucratic conflicts, of nervous leaders seeking security in a dangerous time, of smaller men following the twists and turns of policy to save their own skins, creating and colluding with a system, and thereby colluding with Stalin. As these other factors enter the equation so does the image of the cunning, cruel, plotting 'Man of Steel' diminish. Thus Getty, in his Origins of the Great Purges (based mainly on the captured Smolensk archive rather than newer sources), can find no Stalinist 'master plan' and therefore, presumably, no master planner: 'There is no doubt that he [Stalin] had chief responsibility for political leadership, but the [account given here] has more than once failed to conclude that the events were part of a coherent plan'. In his later work, The Road to Terror (from which come many of my documentary citations above), Getty still maintains that 'there is precious little evidence of a plan for terror'. He now gives greater emphasis to the anxieties of the ruling elite:

> Their fears of losing control, even of losing power, led them into a series of steps to protect their position and manage the situation: sanctioning and building a unifying cult around Stalin, stifling even the hint of dissent within the elite by closing ranks around a rigid notion of party discipline, and embarking on a programme of centralisation in everything from administration to culture.

So Stalinism becomes a version of bureaucratic politics, while Stalin is no longer the master manipulator. His guilt, his cruelty, his paranoia—these appear as diminuendo themes buried in a flurry of factions, local and bureaucratic interests and power-plays.

Robert W. Thurston takes this line even further in his Life and Terror in Stalin's Russia. He argues that Stalin '… was not guilty of mass first degree murder and did not plan or carry out a systematic campaign to crush the nation … this fear-ridden man reacted, and over-reacted, to events'. Compare this interpretation with that of Robert Conquest, who writes that as a result of the terror of 1936-38 '… the country had been silenced and broken'; and it is clear who broke it. For Conquest and others, such as Roy Medvedev, the explanation of these years is also empirical, but it is in addition clearly an act of remembrance, a documentation of the evil that was perpetrated, and a determination of moral culpability. Their explanation is in terms of the psychotic, paranoid personality of Joseph Stalin.

In the past year a novitiate historian has joined the battle. Martin Amis, the novelist, turning his hand to history in Koba the Dread, writes with biting passion to remind us of what happened under Stalin—or rather, to warn us never to forget or find excuses. Not only does he anathematise Stalin, he turns his fire on others who must bear some of the guilt by purporting to see good in the USSR and turning a blind eye to the cruelties. Included in this group is Amis's old friend Christopher Hitchens, but Amis also takes a sideswipe at the 'revisionist' historian Getty, who is dismissed in a scornful footnote: 'If Getty goes on revising at his current rate, he will eventually be telling us that only two people died in the Great Terror, and that one very rich peasant was slightly hurt during Collectivisation.'

Novelists, as opposed to academic historians, can say things like that. Amis was understandably influenced by his friendship with writers and scholars such as Robert Conquest, who opened the historical charge sheet on Stalinism with The Great Terror, and with Tibor Szamuely, sent to the camps for eight years for being heard to call Soviet Prime Minister Malenkov a 'fat pig', though afterwards managing to flee to the West. Martin Amis speaks for them and for a tradition within Stalin studies which contests with the new empiricism. However, the field is not simply dominated by Getty and those who take a different view. From the new materials scholars such as Davies, Viola, Roberts, Khlevniuk are deepening our understanding of ordinary life under Stalin, of agricultural collectivisation, of foreign policy, of the operations of Stalin's politburo. This fiftieth anniversary will see many more studies appearing. By such work we will come to a more rounded appreciation of Stalin and the system he made or, conversely, the system that made him.

PAUL WINGROVE lectures in the Department of History and Politics at the University of Greenwich.

Kim Philby Had a Remarkably Long Career with British Intelligence— Spying for the Other Side

RICHARD K. MUNRO

Among the master spies of the 20th century, Kim Philby was also a master traitor. Philby betrayed his wives, his colleagues, his friends, his country and the entire Western world in the secret service of the Soviet Union. The tale of this Napoleon of moles is a morality tale—character matters.

Harold Adrian Russell Philby was born in India on New Year's Day 1912. His father was a famous explorer of Arabia and his mother was the toast of the Cavalry Brigade at Rawalpindi and cousin to then-Lieutenant Bernard Law Montgomery. Neglected by his parents, Philby grew up in the kitchen among Punjabi-speaking servants. One day the father overheard his son speaking like Kim—Rudyard Kipling's fictional young hero of intrigue—hence H.A.R. Philby's life long moniker.

During World War I, Philby senior served on the staff of Sir Percy Cox in British Intelligence in Mesopotamia. In 1925, however, the elder Philby resigned from the civil service, left his family in London, traveled to Riyadh and quite literally "went native" in Arabia. He abandoned his wife, assumed the name Abdullah, and partook of the harem of his newfound companion and co-religionist, King Ibn Saud.

Meanwhile Kim grew to manhood and entered Cambridge in 1929. He became friends with one Guy Burgess, who in turn introduced Kim to Anthony Blunt. Soon all three men were members of the Apostles, a secret Cambridge society. Hedonistic and devoid of religious faith, the Apostles became strongly Marxist and, in the case of four of their members—Philby, Burgess, Blunt and Donald Maclean—strongly pro-Stalin.

At the same time, Philby became alienated from the ineffectual Labour Party of Ramsey MacDonald. In 1933, Philby graduated from Trinity College, Cambridge, and with a 14-pound sterling prize bought the complete works of Karl Marx. A well known instructor at Cambridge, Maurice Dodd, had done much to make communism seem intellectually respectable to undergraduates and it was he who introduced Philby to Communist organizations in Europe. Philby became romantically involved with a Jewish Communist named Alice "Litzi" Friedmann. They both became embroiled in the violent disturbances be-

tween the rising Nazi party and the Communists in Vienna. The police were closing in on Litzi, so he married her to give her the protection of a British passport. Soon afterward they went to England where Philby underwent a transformation—on orders from Moscow—to establish a right-wing reputation. He joined the Anglo-German Fellowship, which included many prominent Britons.

When the Spanish Civil War began in July 1936, Philby arranged to become a journalist covering the Nationalist side. Once in Spain he solidified his Nazi facade by taking a right-wing mistress—the sexy Frances "Bunny" Doble, aka Lady Lindsay-Hogg. But Philby's career almost ended before it began when Walter Krivitsky defected from the Soviet Union in 1937 and revealed that the Soviets had a young Englishman in their employ in Spain, using journalism as a cover. British Intelligence, however, did not follow up on that lead, which it dismissed as "insignificant." Philby recounted the time, while carrying Soviet codes, that he barely escaped exposure when questioned by Spanish Loyalist Guardias Civiles. Then, on December 31, 1937, while driving from Zaragosa to Teruel with a party of journalists, his car was struck by artillery. Three of the passengers eventually died, but Philby escaped with minor injuries. That incident proved of great importance to the budding spy.

The following March, Philby was decorated by Generalissmo Francisco Franco Bahamonde. Willie Gallacher, the Scottish Communist MP, then denounced Philby on the floor of Parliament—although even that may have been a clever Communist ruse. In any case, from that time on, Philby became known as "the Englishman decorated by Franco." As Philby himself said, that distinction opened "all sorts of doors."

Philby left Spain in August 1939 with his left-wing tendencies cleverly papered over. He also took up with another woman, Aileen Furse. Philby began World War II as a journalist, but his shadowy contacts arranged an interview for him with the code and cypher school at Bletchley Park. Philby was turned down, but then Guy Burgess helped arrange an interview with MI/5 British Intelligence. Mysteriously, the background checks on Philby came up "NRA" (nothing reported against); a fire had destroyed the security files three weeks before his application, and the microfilm backups were deemed illegible. An old friend of his father's vouched for Philby, and the new mole was placed ever nearer to Winston Churchill's spymaster, Stewart Menzies.

Philby was assigned to Section D of the Secret Intelligence Service (SIS), his job being to aid the anti-Nazi resistance in Europe. He trained agents and spread disinformation behind German lines, and soon was promoted to counter intelligence. Between 1941 and 1944, an unknown number of non-Communist resistance fighters met their death because of Philby's betrayal. Lists were compiled of the Catholic opposition in Germany who could help the Allies establish an anti Communist government there after the war. By 1945, almost everyone on the lists had been liquidated, either by the Nazis or by Soviet forces. Philby is believed to have passed the names to his Soviet controller.

In the winter of 1945-46, Philby visited France, Germany, Sweden, Italy and Greece. His task was to recruit agents in order to establish a broad anti-Communist network. Needless to say, Philby saw to it that those agents and their contacts ended up in the gulag. They were the lucky ones. Countless Albanians, Latvians, Germans and Poles who were recruited by the SIS or the American Office of Strategic Services (OSS) died lonely, anonymous deaths after being caught by Communist secret police agents. Philby himself said, "I have always put politics first." His star was rising with a little help from fellow moles, but the sudden defection of two Soviet agents threatened to end his bloody, two-faced game.

William Stephenson, a Canadian who was head of the British Security Coordination in New York during the war, helped Igor Grouzenko defect. Grouzenko brought invaluable information as to the true identities of Soviet spies working in the West—but Philby was not among those identified. The other defector Konstantin Volkov, offered to reveal the names of three Soviet agents working in Britain in return for money and a safe passage for himself and his wife to Cyprus. Incredibly, Philby, through luck and intrigue, was assigned to investigate his own case. He nonchalantly delayed the operation, taking time to cruise the Aegean and booze it up with the British ambassador while Volkov was rooted out. One of the British agents involved, John Reed, angrily complained that the whole Volkov affair was bungled, but Philby brushed his complaints aside. Reed became convinced that Philby was either totally incompetent or a traitor. Reed tried to pass the information to American agents in Ankara, Turkey, but at that time the OSS was in the process of dissolution, and its successor, the Central Intelligence Agency (CIA), had not yet been organized. Philby had escaped detection once again.

In 1946, Philby was made a Commander of the Most Excellent Order of the British Empire (CBE). He divorced Litzi and married Aileen in September 1946. In February 1947, Philby was sent to Turkey, where Turkish police noted that he seemed to spend a lot of time with "students" from Communist Balkan states. One of Philby's tasks was to infiltrate Western agents into Soviet Georgia. Needless to say, the Soviet Union proved

"impenetrable"—one of Philby's agents was shot dead within minutes of crossing the frontier.

In the spring of 1948, Philby's old chum from Cambridge, Guy Burgess, visited him. On the surface, they spent their time boozing, but in reality Philby was preparing for his next assignment: the British Embassy in Washington D.C. By the time the Korean War broke out on June 25, 1950, the old triumvirate of Burgess, Maclean and Philby was set to pass British and American secrets to the Communists. As the war dragged on, General Douglas MacArthur wrote that his strategic movements were being leaked to the enemy. General James M. Gavin said: "I have no doubt that the Chinese were…well-informed. All of MacArthur's plans flowed into the hands of the Communists through the British Foreign Office." In consequence, one can only guess how many American, South Korean and United Nations units were cut to pieces by Chinese soldiers led by the wily and well-informed Peng Dehuai between November 1950 and January 1951. One thing that saved American soldiers in the field was their ability to respond autonomously to catastrophe—as at the Chosin Reservoir, where the U.S. Marines' very isolation saved them from betrayal by the perfidious Philby gang.

Yet time was running out for the treacherous trio. The Federal Bureau of Investigation was closing in on a Soviet spy code-named "Homer." Homer was Donald Maclean, whom Philby had succeeded. Philby was then the liaison officer between the CIA and the SIS. In retrospect, Burgess' alcoholic lapses and perverse behavior may have been part of the moles' cover, but on May 24,1951, the SIS, Foreign Service and MI/5 decided that it was time to interrogate Maclean. Philby was due to be reassigned. Burgess, meanwhile, continued his obnoxious behavior to the point that he had to be sent back to London—which, of course, was just what Philby wanted. On May 25, both Burgess and Maclean defected to the Soviet Union. It is possible that Burgess did so to deflect suspicion from Philby himself.

On June 12, 1951, Philby left Washington. Coincidentally, the U.N. forces engaged in a vigorous counterattack, inflicting well over 100,000 casualties on Communist forces in late May and June. On June 23, 1951, the Soviet delegate to the U.N. proposed a cease-fire. Neither side launched major offensives after that date, though the Korean War sputtered on until an armistice was finally signed on July 27, 1953.

Although FBI agents such as Robert Lamphere were convinced that Philby was a Soviet mole, others with impeccable anti Communist credentials, such as Malcolm Muggeridge, defended Philby against the hysteria of"McCarthyite suspicions." Philby, ever the astute tactician, offered his resignation to the Foreign Service. He was investigated by MI/5 and seemed doomed to be either convicted for treason or left in the cold by both sides. Yet luck saved him again.

J. Edgar Hoover, acting on a tip from Vladimir Petrov, a Soviet defector, made it known that Philby had helped Burgess and Maclean escape. On October 23, 1955, the New York *Sunday News* named Philby as the third man. The Philby case became a matter of lively controversy in the House of Commons. But Hoover had misjudged the anti-MacCarthy feeling in England. No hard evidence against Philby existed except "guilt by association." On November 7, Foreign Minister Harold Macmillan announced to the Commons, "I have no reason to conclude that Mr. Philby has at any time betrayed...this country." Philby responded immediately by holding a live television press conference the next day; it was a public relations triumph.

By 1956, Philby was once again on the payroll of the SIS, his cover being that of a journalist for the *Observer* in Beirut. He spent five years in Lebanon, perhaps pretending to be a double agent, while the SIS told the CIA that he was no longer with them.

Philby's career as a mole came to an implausible end. Aora Solomon, a pro-Israeli friend, was angered by Philby's remarks, publicly and privately, in support of Egyptian president Gamel Abdel Nasser and the Palestinians. She told Lord Rothschild that Philby was a Communist, and that the *Observer* and MI/5 should know about it. In 1962, an SIS agent, Nicholas Elliot, interrogated Philby in Beirut. Either the SIS wanted to force Philby to escape so as to show his guilt, or they wanted to nab

him while he tried to escape. Whatever the case, on January 23, 1963, Philby excused himself for a moment from a dinner party. Six months later he surfaced in Moscow.

Philby spent the rest of his life in the Soviet empire, living a life of luxury and seeing himself become a legend. Philby, or a thinly disguised fictional counterpart, still stalks through many modern spy novels. Lucky to the end, he died in November 1988—just in time to receive full state honors. Two years later, the Soviet government, the only thing he ever served with any loyalty, was gone.

Some people can draw strange morals from morality tales, though. In February 2001, the FBI arrested one of its own members, Robert P. Hanssen, on charges of spying for the Soviet and later Russian intelligence services between 1985 and 2000. Besides money, Hanssen claimed he betrayed the Bureau, the State Department and his country for the thrill of outwitting his colleagues. His role model, since age 14, had been Kim Philby.

The World According to Wells

Best-known for sci-fi classics like *The Time Machine* and *The War of the Worlds*, H.G. Wells became one of the most prolific, and controversial, writers of his day.

JOEL ACHENBACH

H. G. Wells did not invent the future, but he tried. He foresaw, decades in advance, the invention of the atomic bomb and its use to obliterate cities during a world war. He dreamed up the armored vehicle we call the tank. In 1895 he dabbled with the notion that time is inextricably linked to space—that it is a fourth dimension. Ten years later Einstein said pretty much the same thing, albeit in a more complete and scientific form, in his special theory of relativity.

Wells said that there would come a day when cars would entirely replace horse-drawn carriages. Trucks would carry freight on paved roads from one city to another. Corporations would move their headquarters to the suburbs, and their factories overseas.

He warned that someday biologists might use advanced technologies to engineer new life-forms. (He did not foresee that investors would bid up the stocks of biotech firms.)

He imagined that all the world's knowledge would be available in a single location, what he called the World Brain. (We've got something like that now, and we call it the Internet.)

Wells foresaw a sexual revolution. Women would be liberated, more marriages would end in divorce and people would embrace the idea of free love. Scandalously, he put his theories into practice.

And, finally—not incidentally—he pretty much invented the genre of modern science fiction.

Although we know Wells best as the author of such novels as *The Time Machine* and *The War of the Worlds*, few people realize the breadth of his literary output or the extent of his influence. When not writing his classic "scientific romances," he cranked out nonfiction tomes on human destiny and thick, Dickensian novels about ordinary people trapped by the class structure of England.

He befriended, and feuded with, the leading intellectuals of his day. In the 1930s he had private meetings with both Roosevelt and Stalin. During World War II, in his final years, he wrote the first draft of what would become the Universal Declaration of Human Rights. He was, according to the Dictionary of Literary Biography, "the most serious of the popular writers and the most popular of the serious writers of his time."

I began thinking about H. G. Wells while working on a book of my own about our fascination with extraterrestrial life. (Wells, as one scholar told me, "was the first person to create a really *alien* alien.") I was struck, reading *The War of the Worlds*, by its intellectual ambition, its muscular discussion of English culture, of the construction and destruction of the social order. The author wasn't just writing about marauding Martians with deadly heat rays; he was writing about human civilization.

It seemed quite appropriate that I mark this "turn of the century" by learning more about the great sage of the last. I read his books, retraced his steps and tried to see his world beneath the modern varnish.

If only he'd show up! He could pop out of a time machine, look around, and deliver his own profound assessment of what we'd done to the planet. My guess is that even H. G. Wells—in his day the most future-obsessed man on Earth—would be shocked by what he beheld.

Herbert George Wells was born in a time when people never went very far in life—literally. They died where they were born, or within a league or two. The widow on the throne had been there for decades and would be there for decades more. The empire was an immutable fact. The universe was static. Wells, according to society's master plan, would grow up to be a shopkeeper or a servant.

He was born in 1866 in a shabby bug-infested home in the High Street in the village of Bromely, in what is now a suburb of London. It wasn't the absolute bottom of the social ladder, but it was close.

The front room of the house was a store, run by his father, Joseph, that sold crockery and cricket bats on the odd occasion that a customer would appear. His mother, Sarah, had worked as a servant at Uppark, one of the great country mansions. Now, in Bromley, she was little more than a slave in her own home. "Every night and morning and sometimes during the day she prayed to Our Father and Our Saviour for a little money, for a little leisure, for a little kindness, to make Joe better and less negligent," Wells wrote in his autobiography. "It was like writing to an absconding debtor for all the answer she got."

In general, Wells cared less about the specifics of technology than about the prospects for humanity.

His mother scraped together enough money to put him in a small private academy, giving him a better education than most of the children in his social class. But when the family's financial misfortunes forced Sarah Wells to return to Uppark as a housekeeper, she arranged to have "Bertie," then 14, leave school as well, and become apprenticed to a draper. Only after threatening suicide did the lad escape the apprenticeship and take a job as a student teacher at a grammar school. An elder teacher noted that Wells was gifted. A scholarship came: Wells would attend the prestigious Normal School of Science, in South Kensington, London.

Imagine the dazzling change of fortune: the shopkeeper's son, seemingly destined for a dreary and limited life as a draper, suddenly was in the most important city in the world, learning the most revolutionary of theories. His professor was none other than T. H. Huxley, the man so ferocious in his advocacy of evolution that he became known as "Darwin's bulldog." Darwinian evolution inspired Wells' writings forever after.

After leaving college, Wells became a science teacher, and even managed, in 1893, to write a biology textbook. Otherwise, his life was rather miserable. He'd smashed himself up playing football, enduring a crushed kidney, and was an invalid on and off for the next decade. Worse, in a state of sexual infatuation, he'd fallen in love with his pretty cousin Isabel Wells and, in 1891, married her. The sensual fever soon broke. Wells felt trapped, that sensation he most intensely loathed. His eye wandered. He became embroiled in an affair with a student, Amy Catherine Robbins, and Isabel found out. Later, in his semiautobiographical novel *TonoBungay*, Wells would re-create the pain of the revelation, the negotiation and the divorce, while putting it in a cosmic perspective: "Every wrong done has a certain justice in it, and every good deed has dregs of evil."

He married Miss Robbins, and—his belief in women's independence notwithstanding—unilaterally decided she needed a new name. He called her Jane. She stabilized his life, gave it order, gave him a home and, eventually, two loving sons, all the comforts of traditional English domesticity. And she typed! Wells had found the perfect partner: someone infinitely tolerant of his escapades and capable of cleaning up a manuscript.

Wells had been jotting down stories his entire life and, in the early 1890s, turned to writing full-time. He wrote some theatrical reviews and scientific essays, and kept reworking a short story he'd started back in the 1880s, while still a student. It was called "The Chronic Argonauts." In 1895 he finally published it as a finished novel—*The Time Machine*. It was an instant, stunning success.

Other writers had transported characters backward or forward in time, a la Rip Van Winkle, tens or even hundreds of years. But Wells' Time Traveller (he has no other name in the novel) voyages 800,000 years into the future, at the controls of a machine. He discovers a time in which the class divisions of Victorian England have led, disastrously, to two distinct human species: the childlike, incompetent Eloi, and the monstrous, subterranean Morlocks (who occasionally come out at night and eat the Eloi). Not a cheery tale, this one.

Wells believed in evolution as a process, but—like his teacher Huxley—did not have any confidence that it was progressive, that it would make us better creatures in a happier world. Evolving toward what? That was Wells' question.

His Time Traveller keeps moving, peeking ahead into the farthest realm of time, when humans have disappeared entirely and primitive crablike creatures crawl sluggishly on the shore of a dismal sea, all prefiguring the extinction of life itself.

Unlike Jules Verne and other writers of fantastic tales who'd come before, Wells focused on the possibilities of science, without worrying terribly about the current state of knowledge. In general, he cared less about the specifics of technology than about the prospects for humanity. All great science fiction today follows the same general rule—it's not the gadget that matters, but the characters and their culture.

The Time Machine proved transformational. Intellectuals sought Wells' company. He found himself at fashionable parties—a traumatic experience, as Wells remained dreadfully conscious of his servant-class background.

"I see you like caviar," someone commented at a party, as Wells piled the foreign stuff onto a plate.

"Love it," he lied.

Despite some slight discomforts, these were the best years of Wells' literary life. He became the intimate friend and debating partner of such literary lights as Joseph Conrad, Ford Madox Ford, Stephen Crane and Henry James. He churned out novel after novel, each a future classic of science fiction—and each dealing, in its own way, with human hubris. In *The Island of Doctor Moreau* (1896), an exiled scientist plays God by creating humanlike animals, and ultimately pays with his life. *The Invisible Man* (1897) was another cautionary tale of science gone awry. And in *The War of the Worlds* (1898), Wells reminded his countrymen, guilty of their own imperialist conquests, that there might someday be a power greater than the British empire. (The Martian attack, not coincidentally, is focused solely on England.)

In 1900, with almost a dozen books to his credit, Wells finally had enough money to build himself a proper home. Spade House, as it was called, sat on a hilltop in Sandgate, with a view of the sea.

There, and then, Wells found himself in the perfect place at the perfect time. He was stunningly successful, had his health back, and was brimming with ideas. He was poised at the dawn of a new century, a citizen of the world's greatest empire, riding a wave of expanding literacy in a time when radio and television remained several decades in the future. People read novels. They read H. G. Wells.

And then he made a fateful decision. He would try his hand again at nonfiction. In 1901 he produced a provocative little book called *Anticipations of the Reaction of Mechanical and Scientific Progress Upon Human Life and Thought*.

It was another fabulous commercial success. Wells could do it all! In a matter of months he was giving a lecture to the Royal

Institution, grandiosely titled "The Discovery of the Future." He had a squeaky voice, and tended to mumble through his mustache, but still his words were treated as the most precious wisdom.

All of a sudden, Wells wasn't just some poor kid who'd become a writer. He was a prophet. "Among other people who were excited by *Anticipations*," he wrote in his autobiography, "was myself. I became my own first disciple. … "His artistry, some would argue, never recovered.

In *Anticipations* and later works, Wells developed his vision of the future. He believed that, for mankind to survive, there would have to be a new world order. It would be conceived and governed by a scientific, technologically trained elite, who would outlaw war, abolish the nation-state, install a world government. Democracy would be carefully reined in, to prevent the uneducated masses from being manipulated by demagogues. Resources would be distributed equitably. Traditional institutions would fall away; the government would now become the preeminent guardian of children. Religion would fade. Marriage would be less restrictive. The monarchy, needless to say, had to go.

Anticipations drew the attention of Beatrice and Sidney Webb, leaders of the Fabian Society, the most prestigious and well-heeled band of socialists in England. Wells joined, and helped bring young people into the Fabian fold. But he also came to view the established Fabians as too stodgy, a drag on the revolution. The most famous Fabian, playwright George Bernard Shaw, considered Wells an "egotist" and a "spoiled brat."

Then things got really nasty. Wells had by this time begun tapping into new possibilities for erotic adventure. "'Thou shalt not,'" he wrote, was a phrase he accepted "with extreme reluctance and a sustained protest."

He initiated an affair with Rosamund Bland, daughter of a prominent Fabian. Her father, she said, was showing incestuous interest in her, so Wells charged to the rescue "by absorbing her" himself. When that ended, amid much outrage, he began a relationship with Amber Reeves, also a daughter of prominent Fabians. Though Wells merely wanted "an incidental refreshment," Reeves eventually bore him a daughter. When her father found out about the affair, he vowed to shoot Wells.

All this was much more exciting than arguing politics.

Wells resigned from the Fabians in 1908 and fictionalized the contretemps in a scandalous novel, *Ann Veronica*. Jane stood by her husband throughout—"She had always regarded my sexual imaginitiveness as a sort of constitutional disease, " Wells wrote.

Next came the young English writer Rebecca West, 19 when they met, beautiful and brilliant. She had reviewed a novel by Wells, unfavorably, and he'd invited her to lunch. What ensued was a stormy ten-year relationship, which produced a son, Anthony. West hated Jane Wells; she demanded that Wells divorce his wife and marry her. He refused.

"You set out in life to be a free woman," Wells reminded her.

"But is it my fault," she countered, "that I have to be a free mother?"

(Years later, while still involved with West, Wells would find an answer with a new paramour, birth control advocate Margaret Sanger.)

Meanwhile, Wells had epic literary feuds. For years he squabbled, in the most formal of tones, with Henry James. They differed drastically over the mission of "the novel" James believed in art for its own sake. His literature did not lecture. He was content to describe the world as it was, letting the details speak for themselves. Wells could never be so complacent. For him, art was a means to an end, the end being nothing less than a radically revised civilization.

"He did the worst thing possible," Wells scholar Patrick Parrinder told me. "He not only had no interest in writing a novel like Henry James, he had the cheek to tell Henry James he had no interest."

Finally, Wells did the unthinkable, explicitly attacking James in print. In his 1915 novel Boon, Wells famously compared James' style to a "magnificent but painful hippopotamus resolved at any cost, even at the cost of its dignity, upon picking up a pea which has got into a corner of its den."

Wells soon apologized in a letter to James, but James would hear none of it. They'd never see each other again; James died the next year. Wells kept up the argument on his end for years to come, but the literary establishment was clearly on the other side. Wells' style of fiction—as Virginia Woolf pointed out publicly in the early 1920s—was becoming woefully outdated. But that did not stop Wells, who—though never fully abandoning fiction—had gradually transformed himself from a serious literary novelist into a full-time didact.

In the years since *Anticipations*, Wells had written a number of successful novels—many autobiographical, most comic—about the role of class and the plight of the "little man" in English society. Later, he would reflect that his role "has always been that of a propagandist, direct or indirect, for world socialism." That role would become more explicit with the onset of World War I. Credited with the phrase "The war that will end war," Wells published a book by that title in 1914, and with it, entered the arena of international affairs. He lobbied for a league of nations and, after the war, became frustrated with the one that emerged.

For a few years, he turned his attention to the modest goal of educating mankind. "Human history," he determined, "becomes more and more a race between education and catastrophe." He convened experts, mined their knowledge and wrote, in 1919, *The Outline of History*. To find a piece of writing as broad in scope you'd have to go back to Genesis. He begins with the formation of the sun, and takes it from there. At the height of its popularity, the two-volume *Outline* outsold every other book by a living author. Wells then teamed up with Julian Huxley, the scientist grandson of T. H. Huxley, and with his own son George, to write another wide-ranging, influential textbook, *The Science of Life,* published in 1931. All the while, he was turning out novels and prophetic tomes, addressing the nation on the BBC, dabbling in Hollywood movies and publishing essays widely.

The central library in Bromley keeps a Wells archive, a dizzying, groaning oeuvre, including innumerable fat novels that only serious Wellsians have ever heard of. Wells produced more than 100 books, plus countless essays and newspaper articles, throughout a writing career that spanned five decades. You have to wonder: Did the man ever write a sentence that he didn't publish? At his best, Wells was a marvelous writer. At his worst, he was unreadable. In his autobiography he admitted that "much of my work has been slovenly, haggard and irritated, most of it hurried and inadequately revised, and some of it as white and pasty in its texture as a starch-fed nun."

By the end of his life, Wells was considered something of a crank, rambling on about world government and human rights.

"He became obsessed with his idea of a world-state," John Partington tells me. Partington is the 27-year-old editor of The Wellsian, the journal of the H. G. Wells Society. Fans of H. G. Wells aren't as numerous as Jamesians or Conradians or Woolfians, but they're dedicated, and a bit resentful.

"Most people have heard of him, but don't read him," Partington says flatly. (The sad, unspoken truth is that were it not for Orson Welles' historic, panic-inspiring 1938 radio adaptation of *The War of the Worlds*, or countless other popularizations of Wells' science fiction since, many people might not know of him at all.)

Partington agreed to accompany me on a jaunt to the English countryside to visit sites associated with Wells. We headed southeast, along the M20, a freeway slicing across the pastures of Kent. Those fields would soon explode in golden hues as the rapeseed plants blossomed—a normally sanguine event marred, this particular year, by public consternation over the accidental use of a small percentage of genetically modified seeds. This was a story breaking on the very morning of our trip, and I kept thinking: What would Wells say?

When you read a lot of Wells, and see the range of his mind and the confidence of his intellect, you realize he would have had a sage opinion on almost anything to do with science, technology, marriage, politics, war and the general destiny of the species.

The very existence of the motorway, allowing us to speed to the Channel, might have thrilled Wells, but he would have been even more taken with the incredible tunnel that allows trains to travel from England to France or back again with a mere 20 minutes of darkness. The geographical obstacle that stopped Hitler in Wells' final years had vanished in a feat of engineering—one that, Partington points out, Wells had presaged in 1905 in *A Modern Utopia*. Were he with us, I think Wells would quickly opine that the next step should be the obliteration of the political boundaries. Everything connects to the world-state, if you think about it.

We reached Sandgate, a sleepy beach town. Spade House, a century old, remains in fine condition. A couple of plaques on an exterior wall identify the place as the former home of Wells. It's now a home for the elderly. The proprietors, Don Faulkner and Nina Morgan, agreed to show us around.

Inside, there wasn't the slightest hint of H. G. Wells, his obscure wife or their two sons. His furniture was gone. We stood in the room where Wells had played floor games with his children, but there wasn't so much as a solitary, residual tin soldier.

Faulkner took us to a small outbuilding. Maybe Wells had written here, he said. But he wasn't sure. The most basic facts of Wells' occupation have faded. Where did he write?

Before we left town, Partington and I stopped at the local library. We asked the librarian if she had any books by Wells. She had one: a once controversial, now utterly unread novel called *The New Machiavelli*.

"He's very dated now, isn't he," the librarian whispered.

We drove to Rye and climbed some cobbled streets to the summit of the village. There, just a few steps from a tenderly maintained 12th-century church, is Lamb House, the fabled home of Henry James. It is owned by the National Trust. It contains his furniture and his books. Lamb House is everything that Spade House is not: a monument to literary genius, preserved for posterity.

The lesson? Maybe it's simply that James was the greater talent. But I think it also shows that Wells lost that literary argument. The things that last are not the predictions of the future, no matter how prescient some may be. Characters last. Beautiful writing lasts. A compelling narrative lasts. Art survives long after ideas go extinct—particularly if the art is exceptionally good, and the ideas, less consistently so.

By the early 1940s, it appeared that Wells, in his passion for government over individuals, was on the wrong side of history—that his scientific utopia, led by a powerful elite, bore an uneasy relationship to the totalitarian horrors of Nazi Germany and the Soviet Union. Already, in the early 1930s, while one grandson of T. H. Huxley was collaborating with Wells, another—Aldous—was writing a spoof of Wells' ideas in his satirical novel, *Brave New World*. In 1941 George Orwell, who had grown up adoring the writings of Wells, said in a withering essay that Nazi Germany was what Wells had been lobbying for all his life.

It didn't help that Wells had flirted with eugenics in *Anticipations*, raising the possibility that the elites of the future will kill off the diseased, ill-formed or unintelligent members of the human race.

By the end of his life, Wells had backed off from eugenics, and was widely championing the cause of human rights. But he was also despairing. He spent World War II living in London, even during the V-2 rocket attacks. One of his final books, *Mind at the End of its Tether*, published in 1945, is an almost incomprehensible moan of pessimism. "The end of every thing we call life is close at hand and cannot be evaded," he wrote.

He died in 1946, infinitely frustrated. His world-state had not come about—and he'd lost his audience.

Today, in Wells' hometown of Bromley, the closest thing to a monument to the writer is a three-story mural that features a portrait of Wells and scenes from his more popular novels. A block away, a small, blue plaque marks the spot where Wells was born. But his childhood home is long gone. In its place is a huge department store, overflowing with the spiked shoes and leather jackets and all the consumer desirables of a churning capitalist civilization—one that has entered a new, boisterous era of globalization.

Wells foresaw advances in communications and transportation that would make nation-states irrelevant. Today, our planet is surrounded by communications satellites. We are hooked up globally via the Internet. Financiers and politicians and medical authorities convene in Switzerland to discuss emerging pathogens and free trade. Europe, shattered by wars, has come together to form a Union. The United Nations has endured, if imperfectly, as have multinational strategic partnerships like NATO. Most significantly, perhaps, corporations have gone multinational—functioning in many ways as their own world government, relatively free of local control.

It isn't quite what H. G. had in mind. But it isn't so far off, either. In Wells' more confident, big-picture moments, says Patrick Parrinder, he might well view our present world as a scattered path to the same end—Wells' ultimate dream of a worldstate. But, adds Parrinder, "no doubt he'd be frustrated that it was taking us so long."

Washington Post writer **JOEL ACHENBACH'S** latest book is *It Looks Like a President Only Smaller,* from Simon & Schuster.

From *Smithsonian*, April 2001, pp. 111-124. Copyright © 2001 by Joel Achenbach. Reprinted with permission of the author. Joel Achenbach is a reporter for The Washington Post.

UNIT 5

Conclusion: The New Millennium and the Human Perspective

Unit Selections

33. **Beloved and Brave**, Kenneth L. Woodward
34. **The Rise and Fall of Empires: The Role of Surplus Extraction**, Harold Perkin
35. **The Maestro of Time**, Patricia Fara
36. **'You Say You Want a Revolution'**, Mikhail Safonov
37. **Europe's Mosque Hysteria**, Martin Walker
38. **Folly & Failure in the Balkans**, Tom Gallagher
39. **The End**, Michael D. Lemonick
40. **Why We Study Western Civ**, Steven Ozment

Key Points to Consider

- Why would John Paul II be considered a very important pope?

- How did Albert Einstein's theories change the world?

- What are the problems involved in the Balkan situation?

- Is there anything that can be done to stop global warming?

- Why is the study of Western Civilization important?

Student Web Site

www.mhcls.com/online

Internet References

Further information regarding these Web sites may be found in this book's preface or online.

Center for Middle Eastern Students/University of Texas/
http://menic.utexas.edu/menic/Society_and_Culture/Religion_and_Spirituality/

Europa: European Union
http://europa.eu.int/

The North-South Institute
http://www.nsi-ins.ca/ensi/index.html

Organization for Economic Co-operation and Development/FDI Statistics
http://www.oecd.org/home/

U.S. Agency for International Development
http://www.info.usaid.gov/

World Bank
http://www.worldbank.org/

World Wide Web Virtual Library: International Affairs Resources
http://www.etown.edu/vl/

Looking at the future, from the vantage point of the recent Millennium celebrations, the West contemplates the twenty-first century. This time the prospects for disillusionment seem real, for there is little optimism about the current or future prospects of Western civilization. Indeed, with the development and spread of weapons of mass destruction in the non-Western world, we are forced to consider the possibility that our civilization might destroy itself in an instant, as evidenced by the terrifying events of September 11, 2001. Of course, like our ancestors a century ago, we can point to continued progress in science, medicine, and technology.

Our ambivalence about technology is paralleled by our growing recognition that we can no longer depend upon an unlimited upward spiral of economic growth, as seen in the recent erratic swings of the stock markets and national economies around the world. In the course of the last century, other visions have eluded us, including the hope that we could create a just and equal society through drastic and rapid social reorganization. Most of the great revolutionary promises of the age have not been met. Nor do we see that elimination of repressive social and moral taboos will produce an era of freedom and self-realization. By now most areas of human conduct have been demystified; confusion rather than liberation seems to be the immediate result. Finally, modernism, that great artistic and intellectual movement of the century's early years, has exhausted itself. For decades avant-garde experimentation had challenged established styles and structures in art, music, architecture, and literature, creating an ever-changing "tradition of the new," to borrow Harold Rosenberg's phrase. Avant-gardeism presumed the existence of cultural norms to be tested, but now we find ourselves in the so-called postmodern condition, "a kind of unregulated marketplace of realities, in which all manner of belief systems are offered for public consumption." Old beliefs and new are in a continuous process of redefinition.

These developments have contributed to an uncommon degree of self-consciousness in our culture. Seldom in any era have people been so apprehensive about the future of civilization and the prospects for humanity. The articles in this concluding section convey some current optimistic or pessimistic concerns. "Europe's Mosque Hysteria" ponders troubled Western relations with Islam, while "The Tipping Point" describes serious global warming and what we can do to stop it. Yet at the same time the world has hope for the future with men such as Pope John Paul II ("Beloved and Brave") and Albert Einstein (The Maestro of Time").

Beloved and Brave

Priest, evangelist, poet. Protector of the poor and defender of the faith. John Paul II's legend and legacy.

KENNETH L. WOODWARD

H ere and there, faint prayers were heard, but most of the faithful moved their lips soundlessly. In the vast silence of St. Peter's Square, parents whispered in their children's ears. Couples hugged each other for reassurance. Many men and women stood transfixed, looking at the lighted windows where the pope lay dying. When the word finally came, on Saturday night, it was a quiet, almost modest announcement. A handful of black-clad prelates assembled on the steps of St. Peter's, off to the side as if they didn't want to attract too much attention. "I have something very sad to tell you," said Archbishop Leonardo Sandri, the Vatican's under secretary of State. "The Holy Father has returned to the house of the Father." There was no audible cry, but a wave of grief rolled through the crowd of thousands. Then the prelates began reciting the rosary. And a single bell began to toll.

Last Thursday, with a raging fever, the 84-year-old pontiff had gone into septic shock and his blood pressure had dropped dramatically, triggering a worldwide vigil that lasted almost 48 hours. Before dawn on Friday, he summoned his immense and legendary personal strength, and joined as best he could in the recitation of mass. An aide read the Stations of the Cross, recounting the sufferings of Christ from condemnation to crucifixion to burial.

"When the moment of our definitive 'passage' comes," John Paul II wrote a few years ago, "grant that we may face it with serenity, without regret for what we shall leave behind. For in meeting You, after having sought You for so long, we shall find once more every authentic good which we have known here on earth, in the company of all who have gone before us marked with the sign of faith and hope." When the pope died, at 9:37 p.m. on Saturday, he was surrounded by about a dozen people: physicians, nuns, staff, friends. All were praying.

John Paul II held the chair of Saint Peter for more than 26 years—leading his flock longer than almost any other pope. For nearly a decade, he persevered in office despite a slow and painfully public deterioration from Parkinson's disease. This avid outdoor athlete who spent many a papal vacation skiing and hiking in the mountains, this former actor who made all the world his stage, this relentless global traveler who bent and kissed the tarmac in tiny countries never before visited by a pope, aged,

suffered and physically declined before our eyes. And so we watched as he lost the ability to walk, as he slurred when he tried to talk, as his head dropped and saliva fell from his lips during church ceremonies. Those who follow Christ must welcome suffering, he firmly believed, and he would not hide his own from public view.

Future historians seem certain to record that John Paul personalized the papacy in ways that none of the cardinals who elected him (with 103 of 109 votes after 10 ballots) could have foreseen. He transformed the See of Peter into a fulcrum of world politics—his politics. The papal voice—his voice—was heard and often heeded in major capitals like Moscow and Washington. Above all, he took the papacy—which only a century earlier was locked inside the ecclesiastical confines of Vatican City—on the road. He visited Africa four times, Latin America five, managing altogether an astounding 104 pilgrimages to 129 countries around the globe. In doing so, he transformed the figure of the pope from distant icon to familiar face. His face.

John Paul was the most photographed public figure of his era, a man seen in person by more people than even evangelist Billy Graham. Of all the images he leaves behind, four stand out as markers of a remarkable papacy: the defiant new pope, summoning the allegiance of millions of fellow Poles during his triumphant first pilgrimage to his communist-run homeland in 1979; the magnanimous pope, forgiving the deranged Turk who shot him, Mehmet Ali Agca; the stern pope, admonishing the kneeling Father Ernesto Cardenal, the Sandinista Culture minister, in Nicaragua, and the contrite pope, placing a handwritten acknowledgment of Christian sins against the Jewish people in a crevice of the Western Wall in Jerusalem.

I n person, as in public, John Paul was a figure of striking contrasts. As a young man he was a quarry worker, but also a published poet and playwright. As a priest he was a pastor to Polish youth, but also a philosopher of world-class rank. As bishop he outfoxed communist officials, but wanted nothing more than to become a monk. As pope he championed clerical celibacy, yet preached a series of rapturous sermons extolling the beauty of conjugal love. The most authoritarian pope since Pius

XII, he was nonetheless the first pope to drop the papal "we" and to write books under his own given name, Karol Wojtyla. A consummate politician, he nonetheless forbade priests in Latin America from joining political movements and those in the United States from holding elective office. Though he repeatedly mentioned the Shoah, he reminded the world again and again of the Christians who were also martyred under the Nazis. And despite enormous efforts to unify and purify the church, Roman Catholics were still divided at the close of his reign—and more scandal-ridden than at any time in centuries.

History helps unravel these seeming paradoxes. Growing up under Nazism and then communism, Wojtyla saw firsthand what totalitarian ideologies can do to enslave a subject population. He saw, too, that a unified Catholic Church, with its deep roots in Polish history and culture, was the only institution that stood up to a totalitarian state. Yuri Andropov, head of the Soviet secret police—the KGB—was right when he warned Polish leaders in 1979 that they had made a big mistake in allowing the Polish pope to return to his homeland.

Wojtyla's concept of "solidarity" became the banner under which the Polish workers rallied and eventually wrested power from communist overlords. By awakening the latent "Pan-Slavism" of Eastern Europe, "this Slav pope," as he called himself, boldly challenged the legitimacy of communist governments. Ten years later the Soviet Empire disappeared without war. Like his American contemporary (and fellow actor) Ronald Reagan, Wojtyla successfully confronted his adversaries face to face. Little wonder, then, that the only major countries that barred their doors to a papal visit were China, North Korea, Vietnam and post-communist Russia.

One of the effects of the fall of communism in Europe was to project John Paul II as geopolitician of the first rank. As head of a transnational organization second only to the United Nations in scope (but much more coherent in policy), the pope transformed the Vatican into a major port of call for presidents and prime ministers. Every American president from Jimmy Carter to George W. Bush appeared at his doorstep. So did former Soviet prime minister Mikhail Gorbachev, who hastened to establish warm personal ties with the Polish pope. Under John Paul, the Holy See gained more political clout and diplomatic recognition than it had enjoyed since the Renaissance. In 1980, Queen Elizabeth II became the first British monarch to visit a pope at the Vatican; two years later Britain appointed its first ambassador to the Holy See since King Henry VIII had broken with Rome 450 years earlier. A month later the Protestant countries of Denmark, Norway and Sweden followed suit. In 1984, the United States established full diplomatic relations with the Vatican. By 1990, Russia, Mexico, Israel and Jordan, plus most of the former communist countries in Eastern Europe, had joined the list. Compared with 1939, the eve of World War II, the number of nations with formal representatives to the Vatican tripled during the reign of John Paul II.

Wojtyla's image as a world leader obscured for a time the role he chose for himself. Although a pope is by definition the chief teacher, pastor and administrator of the Roman Catholic Church, John Paul II saw himself primarily as an evangelist. From his first appearance on the balcony of St. Peter's Basilica, he proclaimed to a worldwide audience that "Christ, Christ is the answer." Among the first to notice this new evangelical emphasis in papal preaching was another evangelist, Billy Graham, who called John Paul "the moral conscience of the West."

As a young man he was a quarry worker but also a published poet and playright. As a priest he was a pastor to youth but also a world-class writer and thinker.

Unlike Graham, however, John Paul vigorously pursued what he called "the evangelization of culture"—and urged his fellow bishops to do the same. For Wojtyla, Christ was not only the revelation of God to man but also the revelation of what it means to be truly human. Translating this Christian humanism into the language of political philosophy, he challenged governments to recognize the freedom and dignity of every individual as the object of God's love. His major social encyclicals were sharply critical of both socialist and capitalist systems—the first for inhibiting individual freedom and development, the second for neglecting social responsibilities. His first, "On the Dignity of Labor" (1983), offered a new gospel of work based on "he priority of labor over capital," and gave qualified support to the nationalization of industries in Eastern Europe. Inspired, Catholic bishops in the United States and Western Europe issued pastoral letters sharply questioning the economic priorities of their own governments.

But after communism collapsed in Europe and socialism no longer seemed a viable option anywhere, John Paul modified his views. In his 1991 encyclical, "One Hundred Years," he offered one-and-a-half cheers for free-market capitalism. "On the level of individual nations and international relations," he acknowledged, "the free market is the most efficient instrument for utilizing resources and effectively responding to needs." He even went so far as to recognize "the legitimate role of profit as an indication that a business is functioning well"—thus using the dreaded P word that his predecessors had usually avoided. Still, the pope was no convert to pure capitalism, and chafed at media stories claiming that he was. He found ample room for the state in ensuring social justice, and pointedly warned the emerging Central European democracies of the soullessness of consumerism.

Like his immediate predecessors, John Paul used his bully pulpit to give powerful voice to the cause of world peace. He publicly opposed both the 1991 gulf war and the 2003 American invasion of Iraq, and, appearing in person at the United Nations, he twice appealed for an end to war in international affairs. Though not a pacifist, he extended his opposition to violence of all kinds by personally and emphatically changing Catholic teaching, declaring that capital punishment is both unnecessary and, in all but extreme cases, immoral.

History will show, of course, that his appeals went unheeded. But it will also show that he was more effective in reducing tensions among religious faiths. Astonishingly enough, he did this by personally asking forgiveness as head of the Catholic Church. To that end, he issued a series of unprecedented papal apologies—to Jews for centuries of Christian anti-Semitism, to Protestants for the Catholic Church's role in the post-Reformation wars of religion and to the world at large for ecclesiastical arrogance like the church's disciplining of Galileo. Indeed, the pope's *mea culpa*s were a source of embarrassment to some of his own cardinals, who believed that the church was owed a few apologies as well. But few were forthcoming.

John Paul took the papacy on the road. He was the most photographed public figure of his era, seen in person by more people than even the evangelist Billy Graham.

Healing relations with Jews was one of John Paul's keenest concerns. In 1986 he became the first pope to visit Rome's ancient synagogue, and in 1993 he established diplomatic relations between the Vatican and Israel. On a personal level, he maintained close relationships with Jewish friends with whom he had played soccer in his youth. He made a point of meeting with representatives of Jewish communities wherever they existed. His moving pilgrimage to Israel in 2000 was one of his greatest personal triumphs. Four years later, Israel's chief rabbis repaid him by calling on John Paul at the Vatican.

The pope's efforts at Christian unity met with less success—but included some innovative gestures. Recognizing that the papacy itself is a major obstacle to the reunion of Christians, John Paul issued a public letter inviting other Christian bodies to consider how the See of Peter might function in a reunited church. Others were slow to take up his offer. Again, as part of the church's millennium celebration, he instructed his bishops to help him create a list of all the Christians—Protestant and Orthodox included—who had died as martyrs under the Nazis, the communists and other anti-Christian tyrannies during the 20th century. "Perhaps the most convincing form of ecumenism," he declared, "is the ecumenism of the saints and martyrs."

Even so, he failed to move Christian churches closer to reunion. The Orthodox churches, recovering from decades of communist repression, were too weak to consider rapprochement with Rome. The Russian Orthodox Church, in particular, repeatedly refused the pope's efforts to make a post-Soviet visit to their country, despite former president Boris Yeltsin's desire to host Wojtyla in Moscow. Although Protestant and Catholic representatives reached agreement on a number of important theological issues, the role of women in the church, especially as bishops, further separated Rome from the Anglican and other traditions. The pope was marginally more successful in reaching out to Muslims: in Africa and the Middle East he repeatedly appealed for reduced tensions between the church and Islam, but there was no one single Muslim group or authority with whom he could establish sustained relations. At Assisi, where he hosted an unprecedented international worship service involving religious leaders, Hindu holy men and assorted tribal

shamans in 1986, he sat side by side with the only other "His Holiness" in this spiritual firmament—the Dalai Lama.

As chief teacher and leader of the world's 1 billion Roman Catholics, Wojtyla left his fingerprints on every aspect of the church. His predecessor, the affable Albino Luciani, had taken the name John Paul I, signaling his readiness to continue the spirit of Pope John XXIII, who convened Vatican Council II, and Paul VI, who presided over its completion. After just 33 days in office, however, Luciani died of a coronary embolism. Wojtyla had played an important but initially unrecognized role in the council's deliberations, and when he chose John Paul II as his name he seemed to indicate that he would continue the council's reformist bent. But as Catholics soon discovered, this new pope who traveled the world, kissing lifted babies, who sang along at festivals where millions of Catholic youth chanted "John Paul Two, we love you," who put non-Catholic leaders at ease and hosted intellectuals and scientists each year at his summer residence, was a stern disciplinarian bent on curbing what he saw as a dangerous leftward drift in Catholic theology and practice.

One of his first projects was the revision of the church's code of canon law, an enormous task left unfinished by Pope Paul VI. Wojtyla astonished his aides in the Roman Curia by re-viewing the entire code line by line, making his corrections in the margins. The general effect was to limit the council's democratic impulse to give greater authority to local conferences of bishops and to strengthen the role of the Curia, the church's central administration. Thereafter, papal nuncios played a much greater role than local hierarchies in the selection of bishops. As a result, most of today's bishops are conservative men of his choosing, as are most of the cardinals who will elect his successor.

John Paul's most decisive early act was to reaffirm the discipline of priestly celibacy. Under Paul VI, the Vatican had allowed an average of 2,000 priests a year to resign from the ministry—most of them to marry. Wojtyla reduced this flood to a trickle. Although polls in the United States and Europe showed that most Catholics supported making celibacy optional for priests, the pope extolled it as a precious gift to the church, and opposed a married clergy. Polls also showed wide support for opening the priesthood to women, but in 1995 he issued an apostolic letter, "Ordinatio Sacerdotalis," declaring that the church has no power to ordain women, since Jesus had chosen only male Apostles. Moreover, he declared, "this judgment is to be held by all the Catholic faithful"—an effort to bind his papal successors to his position. The effect of these decisions was the creation of a new test of "orthodoxy" in the church. Priests who supported such liberal causes had no chance of becoming bishops, and bishops who showed sympathy to these reformist ideas were reprimanded, marginalized and left to languish in minor posts.

The new orthodoxy was felt by Catholic theologians as well. Under the direction of Cardinal Joseph Ratzinger, the Vatican's Congregation for the Doctrine of the Faith tightened the limits of tolerable dissent. Those suspected of undermining the faith were called to Rome for questioning, and a dozen or so, such as the

Swiss-born Hans Kueng, a liberal intellectual hero of Vatican II, were declared no longer fit to teach Catholic students. Others were ordered to revise their books. Liberation theology, a politically charged mix of the Gospel and Marxist social analysis, was suppressed in Latin America where, the pope believed, it had been used to foment class warfare. A further intellectual chill was felt in Catholic higher education when the Vatican declared that all Catholic theologians must sign a "mandatum" declaring their readiness to uphold the magisterium, or "teaching authority," of the pope. In the United States, which has more Catholic colleges and universities than the rest of the world combined, this would require bishops to approve academic appointments—something most bishops have neither the background nor the desire to do—and would raise serious questions of academic freedom.

All these disciplinary measures, it should be said, were rather mild compared with the silencings and outright excommunications meted out by previous popes. But in 1981 John Paul took a step that few of his predecessors would have dared try. He suspended the constitution of the Society of Jesus (the Jesuits), and placed a man of his own choosing as temporary head of the church's largest religious order of men. The Jesuits, he charged, had caused "concern to the church" by some of their teachings, especially involving liberation theology. Within two years the Jesuits' self-governance was restored, but John Paul had shown his hand. Conservative lay and clerical movements like the Communione e Liberazione, the Legionnaires of Christ and especially the secretive Opus Dei would find in him a powerful patron.

A major mark of the new orthodoxy was the pope's emphasis on sexual morality. Although the church had long opposed abortion, contraception and euthanasia, John Paul was alarmed at the rapid acceptance of these practices in the West, even among many Catholics. Post-communist Poland, for example, was reporting more abortions than live births. Against this rising "culture of death," John Paul the evangelist called on Catholics and others to foster a "culture of life." To that end he formed coalitions with Muslim countries to counter American-led efforts to make contraception and abortion primary tools in U.N. programs to reduce population growth in Third World counties. These bold moves stiffened Catholic opposition to abortion in most countries, but did not decrease Catholic acceptance of contraception.

Inevitably, the pope's declining years were the least active or successful of his papacy. At the start of Christianity's third millennium, he called for a "new evangelization" that he hoped would energize the entire church in its witness to what he called "the splendor of truth." Instead, he was confronted with one of the church"s greatest scandals: revelations of widespread child sex abuse by Catholic priests in the United States, Ireland and other parts of Europe. Although the abuses were committed by a small percentage of priests, the number of victims was in the thousands. Moreover, the cover-ups by some bishops—notably Cardinal Bernard Law of Boston—enraged lay Catholics and sparked demands for greater transparency in church governance. Amid rumors that he could no longer put in a full day's work, the pope did not seem to grasp the disgrace that had engulfed the church. Like other popes whose lives outlasted their effectiveness, he had long since ceded the daily administration of the church to subordinates who divided the Vatican into fiefdoms.

It will be decades before scholars can begin to assess the full impact of Wojtyla on the church. His output of speeches and writings runs to more than 150 thick volumes. In an institution that looks constantly to tradition for guidance, this prodigious lode of papal teachings is certain to influence more than one successor. Despite critics, John Paul managed to bring a new clarity to basic church doctrine—in part by producing a new catechism for the church and in part by listenin's calendar of saints, beatifying and canonizing more than all of his predecessors combined.

As head of a transnational organization second only to the U.N. in scope, he transformed the Vatican into a major port of call for presidents and prime ministers.

Was Wojtyla himself a saint? Fellow Catholics were his sharpest critics. But even those who think his decisions on balance hindered progress in the church readily separate the singer from the song. Certainly Wojtyla was a man of deep prayer as well as a man of deep thought and bold action. Meditation came to him naturally: he could slip into contemplative repose in the middle of a public gathering. Despite his grueling schedule, he spent hours every day in prayer—usually on his knees, sometimes flat on the floor. Those who knew him in the full vigor of middle age were shocked to see him bent and seemingly broken in the last years of his life. But his ailments only accentuated his evident inner strength. His decisions, political and ecclesiastical, may have at times been faulty—papal infallibility is no protection against errors in judgment. He most certainly failed to return once Christian Europe to its spiritual roots. But Karol Wojtyla was a tireless evangelist, challenging a recalcitrant world to join him in "crossing the threshold of hope." Last Saturday, after he slipped away from this world, the bereaved faithful outside his windows in Rome found solace in the words that had shaped his life from his boyhood in Poland to his remarkable reign as the Vicar of Christ on Earth. Repeating the Hail Mary, the mourning crowd murmured: "Holy Mary, Mother of God, pray for us sinners, now and at the hour of our death." Then they sang the Magnificat, the words Mary said after Gabriel told her she was to bear the Christ child: "My soul doth magnify the Lord, and my spirit hath rejoiced in God my Savior"—a fitting benediction for a pope whose spirit so long rejoiced in prayer and in expectation.

With **CHRISTOPHER DICKEY, EDWARD PENTIN** and **BARBIE NADEAU** in Rome.

The Rise and Fall of Empires

The Role of Surplus Extraction

HAROLD PERKIN

Global history has taken a boost from the current conflicts, protests and riots against corporate globalisation, and the threat of worldwide terrorism against the West. These events fit into a global pattern of the rise and fall of societies, that can be traced back to ancient times. True of all the ancient empires we know, the cycle of rise and decline appears to be accelerating. The twentieth century saw the collapse of seven great empires—Mandarin China, Germany, Austria-Hungary, Ottoman Turkey, Japan, the British empire, and twice over in the case of Tsarist and Soviet Russia. Since the events of September 11th, 2001, the twenty-first century seems likely to threaten the sole remaining superpower, the United States, with nemesis.

The key to the formation, survival and decline of all historical societies is their use of surplus income and resources. Without the extraction, by an elite, of products surplus to immediate requirements—in the form of food, arms, luxuries and other goods and services produced by farmers, craftsmen, traders and servants—no society, beyond the most primitive, would be able to afford the protection, law and order, administration, defence, spiritual advice, personal services, cultural production and so on essential to its existence. This is so obvious that it scarcely needs expressing, yet we know little about the way it arose out of the chaos of pre-civilised experience. The rise is shaded in pre-history, since the formation of a society cannot be known until it has acquired the tools—written language or a reliable oral tradition—to express it.

The few traditional sources that look back to the time of state formation, are mostly so tainted by accumulated myth that they confuse more than they inform. In the eighth century BC, Homer looked back some five hundred years: but even in that epoch kings of small island and city communities already existed and the process was substantially complete. Priam's Troy was already a rich state worth plundering, with gold as well as plentiful food, equipment and weapons. Though the Greeks who attacked it were thugs and pirates, they too were 'civilised' in the sense of being resourced by a home population that could provide them with the means of subsistence and warfare.

The Hebrew Testament, which was compiled over a period of more than a thousand years, tells the story of the formation of the Jewish nation from Semitic desert tribes united by the myth that they were descended from a common ancestor with a personal relation to God, and and that in the fifteenth century BC they escaped from slavery in one of the most famous civilised societies—one which was itself already a couple of millennia old. The Hebrew account is detailed and persuasive, but it does not address the problem of how such societies arose, and indeed shrouds it in assumptions of prior state formation in both Egypt and Canaan.

It also shows how the various groups who extract surplus from the producers can compete between themselves: in this case the prophets and priests, who claimed to speak for God and demanded offerings in His name, were in competition with warrior kings whom the priests created at the people's demand and yet still, if ineffectively, controlled.

That competition illustrates two of the three main ways in which the extraction may be practised, by warriors, priests, bureaucrats or capitalist merchants, that is, via politics, professional service, or economics.

The origins of other civilised societies are so embedded in myths and miracles that it is almost impossible to guess at the underlying reality. The Chinese emperor was the Son of Heaven and essential to producing a good harvest (the main source of the extractable surplus), but we know little of how he persuaded his subjects to accept his semi-magical role and material extraction rights. The Japanese emperor was descended from the Sun God, Amaterasu, but whether he achieved his surplus income by charisma, spiritual aura, or force, we can only guess. When Buddha sat under the Bhodi tree, Hindu society was already a thousand years old, and he was not concerned with organising society—except perhaps for the monks of the Sangha—but with escape from the cycle of life and human existence. The Mayans, Incas and Aztecs all have had their creation myths, but these tell us equally little about how their societies actually came into being.

In the absence of reliable sources, we can only guess at the process of societal formation. No society, though, could avoid extracting surplus from the producers for the use of the organisers. Even the most primitive hunting and gathering bands had their chiefs and matriarchs, weapon and tool makers, and shamans or witch doctors who had to be supported, and their part-time services needed subsidy by the rest. No doubt the dominant elite emerged from among these specialists, especially when settled agriculture produced a larger surplus, but the process is beyond modern knowledge. It is as mysterious as Archdeacon William Paley's analogy of the pigeons (in *Principles of Morals and Political Philosophy*, 1785), where, to explain the institution of property, he compared human society to a flock in which one pigeon sits back while the rest bring him the bulk of their gathered corn with no payment in return. (Offending his own superior extractors, 'Pigeon Paley' thereby lost his hope of a bishopric.)

There are three major means by which surplus income and resources are extracted. A good analogy is a three-sided pyramid. Its sides represent different ways of extracting surplus from the producers, by three different sorts of elite. The three faces can, after Max Weber, be labelled Power, Class and Status; or the political/military, economic/ commercial, and socio-cultural means of extraction. The three extracting elites are strong men (warriors, conquerors, home-grown mafia); profit takers (merchants, industrialists, capitalists); and professionals (charismatics, priests, bureaucrats, lawyers). Which of them succeeds in dominating a particular society and establishing the right to priority extraction depends on its specific history and what the elite have to offer in exchange: internal protection and external defence, a share in increased wealth and income, or religious, personal or administrative services.

Once the system is inaugurated and surplus income flows freely, however, those who control the flow ensure that they absorb benefits from the other two faces. Military conquerors quickly turn their political/military power into status and income: their *ad hoc* campaign leadership roles (duke, baron, knight) rapidly become permanent titles of honour, and their tribute, taxation, or control of the scarce resource, the land itself (i.e. the right to labour service, crops or money rent from it) also ensure income and accumulated wealth. Merchants who come to dominate a society, like the commercial oligarchies of Renaissance Italy or the Netherlands, swiftly acquire civic honour and military power as well as profit and property.

Interestingly, priests and bureaucrats, like the Roman Church, Buddhist monks, or the Chinese mandarinate, have special advantage. While conquerors and profit makers are often resented and only reluctantly obeyed, priests and bureaucrats operate by persuasion and extract voluntary contributions from the faithful or visibly necessary taxes from the beneficiaries of their administration. The keys of heaven and hell gave the Papacy a means of selling eternal life to the believers, who bought it so avidly that at times almost a third of the land of medieval England, for example, ended up in the hands of the Church, a process which had to be limited by the Statute of Mortmain, 1279.

The Lamas of Tibet maintained the loyalty and voluntary contributions of their followers through repeated Chinese occupations, and still do. The imperial Chinese bureaucrats were less beloved but were recognised, with the emperor, as the guarantors of the harvest and masters of the flood control system. Even the Bolsheviks in 1917 persuaded the Russian peasants that only they had the bureaucratic expertise to provide bread and land.

Every elite knew that persuasion was more efficient than force or purchasing power in maintaining the loyalty and obedience of the population and took steps to propagandise to that end. Public relations are cheaper and more seductive than naked violence or the manipulated price of labour and commodities, and all governments saw reason to preach their own ideology as the best means of retaining power. Religious, tribal or nationalistic unity held elite and people together, especially if the community was threatened from outside. We know from the insights of Benedict Anderson and Linda Colley how 'imagined communities' can convince themselves of common interests, notably against external enemies, which often contradict their material advantages.

It is amazing how long some communities have held together in the face of extraction rates that amount to exploitation or predation. The Aztecs taking their daily human sacrifices and facing their temples with skulls, the Romans increasing taxation and the weight of slavery in an empire threatened by barbarians, the medieval Papal crusades against internal heretics like the Cathars of southern France, or the Tsarist Russians expanding serfdom while Western Europe was reducing it, all show how the most oppressive of societies can survive for long periods. Propaganda and brute force can hold societies together provided that exploitation is not seen to be unbearably excessive. This gives a hint of the ordering of priorities between the three forms of elite extraction. It is usually assumed that conquest by external warriors or internal dominance by mafia-type strong men is the norm, and that their main competitors, as in Marxist theory, are the merchant-capitalists of the towns. To the contrary, it may be that the non-violent, non-commercial professionals came first.

Before conquerors can take over a society it must already be organised, and at a level of material production to make it worth the effort. Traders and profit-makers need an organised society with laws governing property, contracts and exchange before they can operate successfully except at the margins, which means that the economic face necessarily waits upon the establishment of reasonably settled communities.

Since humans fear the unknown, death, disease, and perdition more than they fear their mortal enemies, men and women probably ran to shamans and wise women long before they settled in villages and towns. Priests, seers and prophets, witches and medicine men were in a strong position to inaugurate their own system of extraction. The power of priests in a fearful age extends over the warrior kings themselves, and over the traders whose portable wealth is subject to its own vulnerability. It was not for nothing that warrior kings called on the priests to bless them before battle and pray to their gods to bring them victory. And merchants, far from being sceptics, were often the agents of religious fervour and proselytism on the shifting trade routes between civilisations. Most major religions, like early Christianity, Buddhism and Islam, migrated along the trade routes with the cargoes of merchants and the backpacks of missionaries.

One ancient source demonstrates how the agents of God emerged before the warrior kings and then imposed on them. The history of Israel as a nation begins with the priestly Moses, who led his people out of bondage. Thereafter, the 'chosen people' are led by priests and prophets who regularly bring them back after multiple apostacies to the true God, but exercise tight control over their conduct, especially towards the priests and their rights.

This model of voluntary surplus extraction set the pattern for all sacerdotal societies. In exchange for spiritual services and mediation with God, the priests and prophets lived handsomely, with the best cuts from the burnt offerings, gold embroidered clothes, and prime accommodation in and around the temples. Their first duty was to prove their authenticity by out-competing the priests of rival faiths. They could then turn their efforts to controlling the morals and rites of the tribes in order to propitiate their God. In doing so, they increased their own control over the nation and reinforced their right to surplus extraction. They did not do so without struggle. The Israelites rebelled against them whenever they were absent, as Moses found in Mount Sinai when Aaron made the golden calf; but Moses and the Levites always managed to persuade them back into the fold.

Even more telling was their control of the warrior leaders. The prophets could not themselves fight and used warriors like Joshua and David in battle, who turned out to be models of belief and obedience. But the priests' supreme test came with the people's demand for a king to defend them against their neighbours. The prophet Samuel's anointing Saul as king is the paradigm of this transition from priestly to royal surplus extraction. When the Israelites asked for a king to lead them against the Philistines, Samuel warned them that he would become a tyrant. The people persisted, so Samuel called down a thunderstorm on the harvest and threatened them with starvation. He finally relented on condition that they and their king obeyed the Lord—that is, continued to obey God's will as ordered by Samuel and his sons, the priestly judges.

King Saul and his successors David and Solomon did exactly as Samuel foretold. They built a vast palace and a magnificent temple, brought hundreds of young men and maidens into their personal service, and even stole their wives and daughters, as in the case of David and Bathsheba. They triumphed in battle and slaughtered their enemies, but never thoroughly enough for the priests. When God through Samuel ordered Saul to destroy the Amalekites, every man, woman, and child and all their flocks, and the king slew only the people, Samuel sent him back to slaughter the animals and to hew the captured King Agag into pieces.

In other words, while the priests were willing to give up a share of their surplus extraction to mollify the people and defeat their enemies, they made sure it was on their own terms and they kept overall control of the king. That struggle between these two faces of the pyramid, the military/political elite and the professional/sacerdotal, has continued throughout Western history and is the main source of the unique pluralism of European civilisation. The upside of this rivalry is that when exploiters fall out, exploitees sometimes come into their own again. The limited freedom of intellectuals in medieval universities, the great source of dissident and innovative thinking in the modern West, owes much to the division between church and state which began with Samuel and Saul and continued into Christian Europe.

In the end, all elites face the temptation to turn extraction into exploitation. Once a system of extraction is in place, the elite are tempted to take more and more and to think that unlimited power, wealth and comfort are theirs by right. Concentra-

tions of wealth begin to appear far beyond the real needs of the elite and more than the society can reasonably afford. These concentrations may, for example, be royal palaces and aristocratic houses full of luxuries and servants, great estates privatised out of the common pool of land for private hunting and enjoyment, access to unlimited personal service, private transport, and bodyguards. The palaces of the Roman, Chinese or Russian emperors at Capri and Agrigento, the Forbidden City and Summer Palace, and the Hermitage and Tsarskoe-Selo, far removed from their public functions, are one symptom of excess. Even in the twentieth century, the private rations, special shops, accommodation, dachas, social clubs, hunting estates and brothels of the Soviet *nomenklatura*, and the gated and guarded housing compounds of the American corporate rich, were evidence of excess extraction—not to mention the steel barriers and armed police guarding the WTO, IMF, World Bank and G8 leaders at their annual summits.

In the public sphere, great public buildings, monuments, temples and mausoleums are a sign of excess. The Parthenon marks the excesses of 'democratic' but imperialist Athens in its golden-age exploitation of the colonies of the Delian League. The Persian and Egyptian temples and palaces were a tempting invitation to Alexander's Macedonians and the later Romans, Mamluks, Arabs and Turks, which the subject populace did not too eagerly defend. The palaces and mosques of the Mughal emperors, Muslim symbols of oppression over the Hindu population, marked the decline of their rule and their vulnerability to intruders. Even the enigmatic stone gods of Easter Island represent an extraction of labour from a servile population that ended, to judge from the archeological evidence, in revolt and the extermination of the ruling elite.

The building of St Peter's in Rome and its accompanying art works were, through the selling of indulgences to pay for them and the Papacy's lavish life style, the immediate cause of the Reformation. Even the puritan Oliver Cromwell succumbed to the temptations of easy riches and emulated Charles I in his courtly extravagance and the ostentation of his daughter's wedding.

The Faberge eggs and jewels of the Romanovs were, along with the fabulous art works of the Hermitage, an expression of Russian autarchy and foretold its ultimate collapse. Latterly, the multi-million dollar extractions of the Marcoses in the Philippines, the Sukarno and Suharto families in Indonesia, Nkrumah in Ghana, Idi Amin in Uganda, Daniel Arap Moi in Kenya, Milosovic in Serbia, and Mugabe in Zimbabwe are examples of the inability of dictators to keep their hands out of the public till.

The main objection to predatory extraction is not merely injustice. It is the threat to societal survival which this excess entails. Marx wrote about the contradictions of capitalism, resulting from the inability of the producers to buy their own products, and the consequent cycle of economic depression and decline which inevitably follows. In truth, the same contradictions apply to all historical societies where the elite takes more than a reasonable share of the available resources. If the elite takes too much, the general populace is unable to consume the products of its own industry. In theory, the elite can, as Malthus argued, spend their gains on luxury goods and services and still support the economy, but in practice they never spend enough on the mass consumer goods that drive the economic cycle. As Keynes suggested, they hold much of their wealth in liquid form (in modern terms, in Swiss bank accounts), which stultifies production. The result is increasing depression and discontent and, ultimately, economic implosion.

The problem is exacerbated when the elite are of a different ethnic group or religion from the main population.

Even before implosion occurs, discontent can take moral and political forms which threaten the stability of the state. Long before depression becomes a direct threat, morale sinks to perceptible lows, to show itself in the form of increased crime, alcoholism, drug dealing, foot-dragging and absenteeism at work, and low levels of productivity, and the defence of an alienated government is viewed with indifference or hostility. In the late Western Roman empire the increased weight of slavery in the countryside and heavy taxation in the towns made the populace indifferent to the survival of the state, and defence was left to German mercenaries who eventually overran the government and usurped the emperor's power.

The problem is exacerbated when the elite are of a different ethnic group or religion from the main population. In the exploitation of China by Genghis Khan's Yuan dynasty the peasants rallied against the Mongols to Zhu Yuanzhang, the peasant warlord who threw them out and founded the Ming dynasty in 1368. The Muslim Mughals were always fearful of their Hindu subjects and could not rely on them to fight against European rivals, notably the British. In reverse mode, the Indian rulers of East Kashmir are violently resented by their Muslim subjects. Even the Popes protected themselves against their co-religionists with a Swiss Protestant bodyguard.

Although not technically alien, the Russian Tsars and *pomeshchiki* were so aloof from their subjects that they spoke French rather than Russian and lived in a Western rather than Slavonic culture. Having paradoxically extended their extraction rate when they abolished serfdom at the cost of heavy redemption dues, the landed aristocracy saw their legitimacy challenged by the peasants who thought them an alien burden and declared in the 1905 Duma that 'We are yours but the land is ours'. Even without, or before, revolution or foreign invasion, states can decline of their own inanition.

So, while we know little about how societies were first organised for surplus extraction, we know a great deal about how they survive and eventually decline. The larger the society, the greater the opportunity to extract surplus from an immense territory and population. That is why great empires decline and fall—eventually—faster and further the more they exploit.

Paul Kennedy has shown how superpowers decline through external causes, specifically 'imperial overstretch' when the military costs of expansion and defence exceed the fiscal capacity of the state. This is undoubtedly an ancillary cause of economic and political decline, but it is really a byproduct of the internal problem, the failure of surplus extraction to match the rulers' ambitions. It reflects the comparative size of the resource base and the rising cost of military and economic power in an increasingly competitive world. No European power acting alone can compete on the scale needed for superpower status at the turn of the twentieth and twenty-first centuries. The cost of projecting power escalates exponentially with the cost of modern weaponry, and the resource base required to qualify as a superpower expands with it.

Only two super-states survived the Second World War with a sufficient extraction base, and one of them has since collapsed. But the decline of both superpowers, through excessive surplus extraction from their 'spheres of influence' if not at home, has lessons for the current state of the world and its sole remaining superpower, the United States.

The question now is, what lesson does this hold for the current hegemonic power? Is the United States any more immune to decline than previous ones? Or is 'the end of history', so confidently forecast by Francis Fukuyama, able to halt the direction of change and continue 'the American century' far into the new millennium? Despite the lightning success in Afghanistan, the inability of the United States to impose its will on such insignificant powers as Somalia, Iran, Iraq, Serbia, North Korea or East Timor—or to guarantee its citizens at home or abroad immunity from suicidal Al-Qaida terrorists—suggests that the empire is not invincible. It cannot bring itself, it seems, to rein in the multi-national corporations that now manipulate the global economy for their own profit and force genetically modified crops, polluting industries, and monopolistic services on other countries. Global warming, disproportionately caused by the US, is already backfiring on America with disasters like Midwest and Texan floods, Californian forest fires, Atlantic coast hurricanes, and encephalitis-carrying mosquitos in New York.

Earlier empires declined because the elites took more than their share of income and resources and paid the price in internal malaise, depression, rebellion or external conquest. The American is the first empire in which the whole home population, though very unequally, shares in the exploitation of the whole world. Will the rest of the world accept this unequal balance? Or will it revolt against being dragged down into economic and climatic chaos?

Surplus extraction, without which civilisation and decent human life are impossible, can too easily slip into exploitation and so lead to self-destruction. The best hope of avoiding this pessimistic finale is to recognise the danger and find the means to avoid it. The first requisite is to end the excess and seek a balance between reasonable extraction and reckless exploitation. This has the advantage of also producing a more egalitarian and socially just society, not only for the sake of the many but for the salvation of the few, the elites themselves who have most to lose from decline. The ancient Greeks had a solution, though even they failed to implement it, as the excessively costly Parthenon built on colonial exploitation demonstrates. It was the golden mean: 'Nothing in excess'. With the world's population just passing the 6 billion mark, more than a third of it living in poverty, it is surely time to practise moderation.

For Further Reading

S. Amin, I Wallenstein et al., *Transforming the Revolution: Social Movements and the World System* (New York Monthly Review Press 1990); Benedict Anderson, *Imagined Communities: Reflections on the Origin and Spread of Nationalism* (Verso 1991); Linda Colley, *Britons: Forging the Nation* (Yale UP 1992); Andre Gunder Frank and Barry Gills, eds, *The World System: 500 Years or 5,000?* (Routledge, 1993); Francis Fukuyama, *The End of History and the Last Man* (Penguin 1992); Paul Kennedy, *The Rise and Fall of the Great Power* (Random House 1987); William H. McNeill *The Pursuit of Power since AD 1000* (University of Chicago Press, 1982); Harold Perkin, *The Third Revolution: Professional Elites in the Modern World* (Routledge 1996); Harold Perkin 'The Tyranny of the Moral Majority' in *Cultural Values* (Lancaster University, special issue on Religious Fundamentalism worldwide, April 1999).

HAROLD PERKIN is Professor Emeritus, Northwestern and Lancaster Universities; Honorary Professor, Cardiff University.

The Maestro of Time

Patricia Fara marks two significant Einstein anniversaries and points out some contradictions in the reputation of this great scientific hero.

Patricia Fara

Albert Einstein (1879–1955) relished explaining how his theory of relativity had revolutionized time. 'An hour sitting with a pretty girl on a park bench passes like a minute,' he quipped, 'but a minute sitting on a hot stove seems like an hour.' As an enthusiastic self-publicist, he would have agreed that exactly the right amount of time has now passed to justify some celebrations: it is fifty years since Einstein died, and a hundred years since his so-called *annus mirabilis*, 1905, when he published not one but three world-changing papers.

Einstein liked to think of himself as Newton's successor in the pantheon of scientific geniuses, as if some numinous power could be passed on from one to another. Scientific icons are often worshipped as other-worldly beings who float above the realities of daily life, yet Einstein's career demonstrates how even the most abstract thinkers do not match such visions. Einstein's theories were rooted in practical problems of clock co-ordination. And being a scientific figurehead posed political dilemmas: the pacifist became a Zionist and a target for antisemitic activists, and was persuaded to encourage research into the atomic bomb.

'Why is it,' Einstein asked a *New York Times* journalist in 1944, 'that nobody understands me and everybody likes me?' He was not, of course, expecting an answer, but it is an intriguing question. How did the obscure creator of an arcane cosmological theory become world-famous? Until he was forty years old, few outside a small circle of mathematical physicists had heard of him. He hit the headlines in 1919, when an expedition to investigate a solar eclipse confirmed his General Theory of Relativity. Although the *New York Times* evidently failed to recognize the significance of the event, since they sent their golfing correspondent to cover the story, within a few years Einstein's trade mark Brillopad hair and droopy moustache immediately identified the hero who had challenged Isaac Newton—and won.

Like Newton and his apple tree, Einstein himself originated some of the tales that have boosted his fame. He maintained that he was only a child when he made one of his first important discoveries: toes make holes in socks. After concluding that time spent darning was time wasted, he wore his shoes over bare feet, a life-long habit which contributed to his reputation of eccentricity. He cultivated this image of affable genius by dressing shabbily, proclaiming his passions for sail-boats and violins, and producing pithy aphorisms—his deceptively throw-away remark that 'God is subtle but not malicious' is now carved above a fireplace at Princeton University.

But Einstein could not control every aspect of his influence. To his disgust, cocktail parties buzzed with the catch-phrase 'Everything is relative', a mockery of his attempt to redefine that elusive concept known as time. His fascination with time was shared by artists, musicians and writers who also wanted to find new ways of representing the world, and who claimed to be stimulated by his physics. Among the early literary tributes was William Carlos Williams' poem 'St Francis Einstein of the Daffodils', inspired by Einstein's first visit to the United States in 1921. Williams hailed the physicist as a holy savior in the spring-time of his career; Einstein had, he wrote, liberated the New World from the stifling shackles of old knowledge:

> *April Einstein*
> *through the blossomy waters*
>   *rebellious, laughing*
> *under liberty's dead arm*
>   *has come among the daffodils*
> *shouting*
> *that flowers and men were created*
> *relatively equal.*
>   *Oldfashioned knowledge is*
> *dead under the blossoming*
>   *peachtrees.*

Einstein insisted that relativity was more complicated than this, but his protest only reinforced the notion that he was a genius who had created a theory incomprehensible to normal mortals.

On the cover of *Time* magazine for July 1st, 1946, almost a year after two nuclear bombs were dropped on Japan, 'Cosmoclast Einstein', the iconoclastic cosmologist, looks weary and disillusioned—as if aware of being reviled as an alchemical Frankenstein who had wantonly unleashed the hidden forces of nature. Behind him, a fleet of tiny warships is dwarfed by a dark mushroom cloud branded with his famous equation, $E=mc^2$. Paradoxically, the same formula also symbolized the optimistic surge of faith—expressed by Williams—that the new science would bring freedom and equality to a war-wracked world. Einstein was an ardent pacifist who was surprised when the destructive possibilities of a nuclear chain reaction were first explained to him—'I never thought of that!' he exclaimed.

In reality, Einstein was no child genius. By the time he was nine, his teachers in Munich had given up hope for his future. He hated school, left under dubious circumstances and went to the Polytechnic in Zurich, over the border from his native Germany. Looking back, Einstein asserted that he was sixteen when he first imagined what would happen if he rode on the back of a light beam, the question that led to his Special Theory. But he was a rebellious, awkward student who found it hard to get a job; eventually friends pulled strings, and in 1902 he became a patent officer.

Only three years later, Einstein published three outstanding papers on physics. The first provided a new way of thinking about the movement of atoms and molecules in liquids. The second, more ambitious, dealt with the fact that some metals produce an electric current when light shines on them; Einstein explained this 'photo-electric effect' by arguing that light is quintile—its energy can sometimes be described as grouped into packages, even if in other circumstances it should be considered as travelling in a continuous wave. Nothing to do with relativity, this itself revolutionized basic concepts in physics and laid the foundations for quantum physics, the mathematical tools now used for describing the subatomic world.

In the same year, he produced his first outline of relativity. Even the article itself looks strange: this 9,000-word essay lacks conventional scientific references and footnotes, almost like a patent application written by an inventor claiming utter originality. It completely reversed the common-sense ways of thinking about time and space which had been established by Newton three centuries earlier. For Newton, space was fixed and time flowed inexorably at a steady rate; for Einstein, time depends on where you are and how fast you are moving: it only makes sense to define your own personal time with respect to—or relative to—something else. In Einstein's cosmos, only one quantity appears identical to everybody: the speed of light.

Einstein is celebrated as an intellectual whizzkid, but—like many famous scientists—he was also a technological wizard. Research rarely takes place on some theoretical plane divorced from reality. Relativity did involve abstract thought, but it sprang from contemporary worries about the very practical problem of coordinating time across the globe. The world is now divided into time zones, but it took many decades of negotiation before different countries finally agreed in 1884 to adopt a zero line through Greenwich. The American historian Peter Galison has explained how Einstein's colleagues were obsessed with the technical problems of linking clocks in Zurich with those in America as well as Europe. International collaboration was essential to ensure that trains would not collide and that telegraph systems could communicate.

Scientific heroes are also often commemorated as lone explorers, isolated from their peers and blessed with superior insight. Einstein provides an example of how such images are created retrospectively. His relativity theory did not cause an immediate revolution in physics: it was developed over many

years after 1905 and some aspects were not experimentally confirmed for half a century. For many people, relativity is summed up by the equation $E=mc^2$, which ties together energy, mass and the speed of light, and implies that a small amount of mass can be converted into a large amount of energy. Einstein only deduced this relationship after introducing the basic theory: it is a consequence, not a founding tenet.

When Einstein introduced the Special Theory, he focused on what it means to say that two events occur simultaneously. Imagine you are standing on a station platform, exactly halfway along a stationary train. Now suppose that you see two torch flashes, one from a passenger at the front of the train, and one from the back. Because all three of you are stationary, you know that the two passengers sent their light signals at exactly the same time. However, now imagine that the train is moving past you at a steady speed. If the two people on the train flashed their torches at what they thought was the same time as each other, you would see the one from the front later than the one from the back, because the light signal would have to travel further to reach you. In other words, events that seem simultaneous to the passengers appear to take place at different times for you. This effect is negligible under normal circumstances, but becomes important when particles are moving extremely fast. The General Theory takes account of acceleration, when the two systems—the two trains—are not moving at a uniform speed relative to each other. Unfortunately, science starts to seem incomprehensible: talking about the curvature of four-dimensional space-time makes sense mathematically but has little to do with everyday experience. However, one of the theory's most important consequences is clearer: when light travels past a heavy object such as the sun, it no longer travels in straight lines but is curved by gravity.

Satirists latched on to the bizarre implications. A *Punch* cartoon showed policemen trapping a burglar with torches whose rays bent round corners, while a poet coined this limerick:

> *There was a young lady named*
> > *Bright,*
> *Who traveled much faster than light.*
> *She started one day*
> *In the relative way,*
> *And returned on the previous night.*

There are, though, several perversions of relativity theory in this verse: Ms Bright would greatly increase in mass as she approached the speed of light; nothing can travel faster than light; and the order of events cannot be changed, only the interval between them.

The jokes helped make Einstein a household name. But with hindsight it seems less clear that he deserved all such accolades. For one thing, as he developed his theories, Einstein relied heavily on the work of other mathematicians. Even the first influential description of a four-dimensional space-time universe, now seen as a fundamental component of relativity, was made in 1908 by his former lecturer in Zurich, Hermann Minkowski.

The Australian historian Richard Staley argues that Einstein's iconic status suited the German mathematical community. Although science supposedly transcends national boundaries, German scientists were ostracized during the First World War; and to counterbalance Britain's Newton and Italy's Galileo, they placed Einstein within a scientific Germanic lineage going back to Copernicus and Kepler.

On November 7th, 1919, Berlin traffic ground to a halt as political activists celebrated the second anniversary of the Russian Revolution. On the same day Einstein, also in Berlin, woke to find himself a media star. The President of London's Royal Society had just announced that the General Theory had been experimentally confirmed. All over the world, headlines proclaimed that Einstein had summed up the cosmos. Einstein sold his photographs for charity and set off on an international publicity campaign.

British physicists were deluged by worried inquiries about the defeat of their national hero, Newton—even though the experimental expedition to prove Einstein's theory had been led by a Cambridge astronomer, Arthur Eddington. The planning for this had started a couple of years earlier, when Eddington was searching for a way to avoid detention as a conscientious objector during the war. To justify the expenditure on a nonmilitary project, Eddington was committed in advance to proving that Einstein was right—hardly the spirit of neutral enquiry that scientists like to boast about. Einstein himself took little notice of Eddington's endeavors, because he was confident that he was right. So much for the idea that scientists test their hypotheses with careful experiments!

Eddington made the trial sound simple. Newton saw space as uniform, but according to General Relativity theory, light is bent as it travels past a massive body. This means that, if the Sun is almost in the line of sight for a star, astronomers would see it in a different place in the sky than if the Sun were far away and the starlight travelling in a straight line. If Eddington could measure a star's position near the Sun during an eclipse, and compare it with other recordings when it was in distant parts of the sky, he could see if the results matched up to Einstein's or to Newton's prediction.

To do this was highly complicated in practice. No stars were conveniently close to the Sun during the period of the eclipse of November 1919. This meant choosing a star that placed heavy demands on accurate measurement: Eddington faced a task equivalent to measuring a small coin from a mile away. There were technical difficulties associated with temperature and light fluctuations, to say nothing of the errors introduced by transporting delicate equipment to Principe off the west coast of Africa. When the big day arrived, the weather was cloudy.

When the results proved inconclusive, Eddington massaged the data, discarding photographs that failed to confirm his views and suppressing contradictory evidence from other eclipse teams. Many scientists were already converted to Einstein's ideas, and Eddington drew on his influential contacts to convince them that his expedition demonstrated the outcome they wanted to hear. Perhaps he was responsible for this anecdote:

Interviewer: 'Professor Eddington, you must be one of the three people in the world who understands General Relativity.'

Eddington (after a long pause): 'I'm still trying to think who the third person might be.'

Nevertheless, some experts remained skeptical and for several years opposed recommendations to award Einstein the Nobel prize, insisting that General Relativity had not yet been definitively proved and did not constitute a useful discovery as stipulated in the Prize regulations. In 1922 he did eventually receive the Physics prize, not for relativity but for his 1905 work on the photoelectric effect. When Einstein had suggested that light and electricity are transmitted in little energy parcels called *quanta* (the Latin plural of *quantum*), other scientists were at last able to explain some perplexing observations. Within a few years, additional equations were developed to account for quantum effects and the relationships between atoms, wave shapes and energy.

But herein lies another paradox: Einstein initiated quantum mechanics but never accepted this form of physics. According to later quantum theories about the subatomic world, the familiar rules of cause and effect no longer apply because it is impossible to pin particles down with absolute certainty. Einstein could never accept that God would have created a universe dominated by chance. 'I am convinced,' he declared, 'that He does not play dice.'

It might seem strange that Einstein should justify his theories by appealing to God. Science and religion are traditionally said to be at war with one another. Einstein would have none of that; in yet another snappy saying, he declared that 'Science without religion is lame, religion without science is blind'. He felt that they complemented rather than opposed each other.

Although active in Jewish politics, Einstein came to reject monotheism and life after death. Instead, he coined the term 'cosmic religion' to describe his faith in the divine nature of the world itself. The universe is, he believed, an orderly system characterized by mathematical simplicity, an ideal often perceived as a type of beauty. Reality can be grasped by the mind, he taught, but experience is the ultimate test of truth—and the search demands courage, persistence and imagination. One scientist remarked that, like Socrates, Einstein knew that we know nothing.

Einstein was already forty when he was recruited by the Zionist movement. He had scarcely been aware of his Jewishness as a young man, and he instinctively mistrusted a nationalist organization whose aims might contravene his long-held pacifist principles. But once he had capitulated, he displayed the enthusiasm of a late convert. In February 1923 he went on an American lecture tour and then visited Palestine, where he gave the inaugural address at the Hebrew University, for which he had helped to raise money. 'I consider this the greatest day of my life,' he proclaimed as he encouraged the Jewish people 'to make themselves recognized as a force in the world.'

One reason for Einstein's movement towards Zionism in the 1920s was the anti-Semitism he was experiencing in Berlin. The attacks were led by Philipp Lenard, an expert on Einstein's photo-electric effect who had won a Nobel prize in 1905. As well as vilifying Einstein personally, Lenard and his colleagues organized public lectures denouncing relativity as part of a giant Jewish plot that was corrupting the soul of Germany. Naively,

Einstein struck back in the press with an article called 'My Answer to the Anti-Relativity Theory Company Ltd.' He later confessed that this had been a 'sacrifice at the altar of stupidity', but the controversy rapidly escalated until Lenard and Einstein confronted each other directly in a packed lecture theatre guarded by armed policemen.

Lenard and other German physicists continued to hurl abuse at what they called the Jewish science of relativity, but Einstein only renounced Germany, leaving Europe for America, in October 1933. In some ways, his fame worked against him. Once he visibly supported the Zionist cause, all his acts of generosity towards other Jews could be misinterpreted—and publicized—as favoritism. Although Lenard had at first stirred up only fringe extremists, as the National Socialists gained strength Einstein became a potent symbol for inciting antisemitic hatred. He was painted as the originator of a crazy theory and the evil representative of a Jewish conspiracy to dominate the world.

In 1939, now at Princeton, Einstein learnt that German scientists might be developing an atomic bomb, and this ardent pacifist became convinced that the best way to prevent war was for America to develop its own bomb. Aware of his influence, Einstein wrote to President Roosevelt warning him about the German interest in uranium and recommending immediate action. In 1941 a full-scale American research programme, the Manhattan Project, was launched. Einstein always regretted having written that letter: 'Had I known that the Germans would not succeed in producing an atomic bomb', he wrote later, 'I would not have lifted a finger.'

During the last two decades of his life, Einstein embarked on a solitary, unsuccessful quest to find one single unifying theory for modeling the universe. Although he thereby set himself apart from mainstream physics, Einstein remained Princeton's most distinguished scientist. His ideas remained incomprehensible to most people, but his powerful reputation made him an invaluable mascot for political campaigns. In 1952, aged seventy-three, he was invited to become President of Israel, but despite being promised he 'could continue with his scientific work without interruption', he declined the offer.

After Einstein's death, experts found new ways to take advantage of his iconic status. Neuroscientists sliced away slivers of his brain which had been preserved in small sections, hoping to validate their pet theories relating physiology and psychology. Feminist historians trawled through archives seeking information about his first wife, Mileva Maric, claiming that Einstein could not have created relativity without her. 'When you're my dear little wife,' he told her affectionately during their engagement, 'we'll diligently work on science together.' A tempting promise, but there is no hard evidence of any serious collaboration after they were married.

Einstein would have appreciated the festivities being organized in his honor this year. In 1927, when scientists converged on a Lincolnshire town to commemorate the anniversary of Newton's death, Einstein sent them a message. 'You have now assembled in Grantham,' he wrote, 'in order to stretch out a hand to transcendent genius across the chasm of time.' His letter arrived late—even the maestro of time could not control delays.

For Further Reading

Brian Denis, *Einstein: A Life*, (John Wiley, 1996); Ronald Clark, *Einstein: The Life and Times* (Hodder and Stoughton, 1973); Alan Friedman and Carol Donley, *Einstein as Myth and Muse* (Cambridge University Press, 1985); Peter Galison, *Einstein's Clocks, Poincaré's Maps* (Sceptre, 2003); Jeff Hughes, *The Manhattan Project: Science and the Atom Bomb* (Icon, 2002).

PATRICIA FARA is a Fellow of Clare College, Cambridge. She is the author of *Newton: The Making of Genius* (Macmillan, 2002).

'You Say You Want a Revolution'

Mikhail Safonov argues that the Beatles did more for the breakup of totalitarianism in the USSR than Alexander Solzhenitsyn and Andrei Sakharov.

MIKHAIL SAFONOV

During a chess competition between Anatoly Karpov and Gary Kasparov in the 1980s, the two grandmasters were each asked to name their favourite composer. The orthodox Communist Karpov replied: 'Alexander Pakhmutov, Laureate of the Lenin Komsomol Award'. The freethinking Georgian Kasparov, though, answered, 'John Lennon'.

No-one would claim that Kasparov won the world chess championship simply because he was a Beatles fan. However, Kasparov has won the sympathies of people far beyond the game of chess, and his musical preference reflects his particular character—one that was not afraid to declare out loud the name of a person who could never, ever have become Laureate of the Lenin Komsomol Award.

A few years ago Russian television screened a film on Mark Chapman, the man who assassinated John Lennon in 1980. The advance publicity suggested the story was comparable to that of Salieri and Mozart, but the film highlighted a rather different theme. The murderer, on setting off from his New York hotel room to do the deed, left a copy of the Bible, open on a page on which was printed 'The Gospel According to St John'. Chapman had amended it so that the text read 'The Gospel According to John Lennon'. After the assassination he made no attempt to hide, and when the police arrived he was quietly reading J.D. Salinger's *The Catcher in the Rye*, whose young hero Holden Caulfield is shocked by the falsehoods of the adult world. Chapman associated with Caulfield. He considered that Lennon preached one message but lived by a quite different set of commandments. Lennon therefore was a liar and a cheat. He must die.

The name of Chapman has become linked with that of Lennon—as other murderers are connected to their victims: Brutus and Caesar, Charlotte Corday and Jean-Paul Marat, Lee Harvey Oswald and John Kennedy. Paradoxically, Lennon himself can be linked with the name of the Soviet Union in just the same manner. It was Lennon that murdered the USSR.

Lennon did not live to see the collapse of the USSR, and could not have predicted that the Beatles would cultivate a generation of freedom-loving people throughout this country that covered one-sixth of the Earth's surface. Without that love of freedom the fall of totalitarianism would have been impossible, however bankrupt economically the Communist regime may have been. Lennon himself would probably be very surprised to

read such words. But it is so. I will begin with my personal memories; trying to give order to what I saw and heard and to what I myself was witness.

I first heard of the group at the start of 1965. An article about some unknown 'Beatles' was published in the journal *Krokodil*. The name grated on the ear, perhaps due to its phonetic content, associated in my mind with whipped cream (*vzbeetiye slivki*) and biscuits (*beeskvit*).

The article described how a BBC announcer had told the world that Ringo Starr had had his tonsils removed—but had pronounced tonsils so indistinctly that listeners thought the drummer had had his toenails removed, and how the Liverpool postal service had to work over time due to the number of letters requesting the toenails in question.

The first song I heard was on Leningrad Radio. It was 'A Hard Day's Night', and the presenter added the comment, 'in pursuit of money'. I didn't like it: it seemed monotonous, and I doubted if it was worth all those 'toenail' requests. Then a collection of songs was released in the German Democratic Republic, taken from the first album. Initially I listened, not because I particularly liked the songs, but it was impossible *not* to listen when all anyone was talking about was the Beatles. Then someone gave me recordings of 'A Hard Day's Night' and 'Help', which had been brought from France: the cover read '*Quatre garcons chantent et dansent*'. For many Russians, Beatlemania began here.

It is worth recalling what it was like to listen to music in those days. At home we had a radio-tape recorder, the Minia-2, a big wooden panelled box which dominated our small flat. Cassettes didn't exist back then so it was a reel-to-reel system. If you wanted to move forward or back through the tape you needed to have assistance, as the tape kept on tearing, and we had to stick it with home-made glue, which gave off a pungent smell. The rewind often failed, so we had to do it by hand. The sound was scratchy mono. But the music itself came to us from an unknown, incomprehensible world, and it bewitched us. In his 1930s novel *The Master and Margarita*, Mikhail Bulagakov says that love fell upon the heroes like a mugger with a knife from a side street. Something similar happened to the souls of our 'teenagers' (a word we learned thanks to the Beatles).

Beatlemania took a variety of forms in Russia. There could not be the same fan hysteria of the kind that we would see on our television screens years later. In the West the governments encouraged Beatlemania, and even tried to use it for their own purposes. In the USSR the Beatles were proscribed, and 'well-brought up' boys dreaming of a successful career were forced to hide their worship of the group.

In the early days, infatuation with anything to do with the Beatles implied an unconscious oppositional stance, more curious than serious, and not at all threatening to the foundations of a socialist society.

A few instances: during an astronomy lesson in our tenth-year class, my schoolmate was given the assignment of giving a talk about one of the planets in the solar system. Having recited everything that he had religiously copied from a journal, he made his own addition: 'And now the latest discovery of four English astronomers—George Harrison, Ringo Starr (and the two others)—the orbit of such and such planet is approaching the Earth, and in the near future there may well be a collision.'

Astronomy was taught as a kind of additional burden and the physics teacher barely knew more than we did about the planets. So she listened to this talk of 'a possible collision' unsuspecting. She had not heard of these 'astronomers'. She hadn't even heard of the Beatles. Similarly, once when she told us that the Soviet scientists Basov and Prokhorov had been awarded a Nobel prize, someone in the class shouted, 'The Beatles were given the prize!' (not long before, the group had been awarded the Order of the British Empire). The teacher replied, 'Don't shout: I didn't say that foreign scientists hadn't been awarded the prize, all I am saying is that Soviet scientists have been awarded the prize as well.' In our teenage adulation for the pop stars, even the merest mention of their names was a minor victory.

My classmates formulated their love for the Beatles in the following manner: 'I would have learnt English in its entirety, exclusively from the things that Lennon spoke about.' This was a paraphrase of the words of Mayakovsky inscribed on a stand in the literature classroom: 'I would have learnt Russian in its entirety, exclusively from the things that Lenin spoke about'. In the 1960s you could not actually be imprisoned for changing the name of Lenin to that of Lennon, but trouble awaited anyone who blasphemed against the name of the immortal leader: problems dished out by the Komsomol (Communist Union of Youth) could wreck your career. And so, bit by bit, we Lennon fans became ensnared in doubting the values that the system was trying to inculcate.

To make the slogan about the English language come literally true would have been impossible, as we were learning in a class of forty pupils and had just two hours of foreign language teaching per week. We wrote down the texts of the English songs using Russian letters. Many of us didn't understand their meanings, but sang them all the same. One lad gave a rendition of 'Can't Buy Me Love' with his guitar. It sounded like *'Ken pomyeloo, oo'*.

There was a fashion to have Beatles hairstyles. Young people, 'hairies' as the old people called them, were stopped on the street and had their hair cut for them in police stations.

I myself completed my schooling with a grade that qualified me for a silver medal. But, with my own Beatles-inspired haircut, I would never be awarded my medal—I needed a 'state hairstyle', with my hair brushed back and washed in a sugar solution. After the leavers' evening, at which I was solemnly awarded my

school-leaver's certificate (though not the medal, which would be awarded on another occasion), I was walking out of the Palace of Culture when I was seized by police officers and pushed into their pillbox—all because of my haircut. I said to the officers, 'What are you doing? Do you want to spoil the best day in my life? I have just been awarded a medal and you push me into a pillbox.' The policemen began to laugh at me. 'A hairy hippy has been awarded a medal—what a laugh!' Although I didn't have the medal itself yet, I showed the policemen my certificate. They let me go because I had humoured them so ...

One of the Leningrad schools staged a show trial against the Beatles. A mock public prosecutor was appointed, and the proceedings were broadcast on the radio. The schoolchildren proclaimed themselves outraged by all that the Beatles had done. The verdict of the trial was that the Beatles were guilty of anti-social behaviour. All this reeked of 1937. But even in Stalin's time show trials were not held for famous foreigners of this kind, who had become almost an integral part of the way of life of the Russian people.

Yet the more the authorities fought the corrupting influence of the Beatles—or 'Bugs' as they were nicknamed by the Soviet media (the word has negative connotations in Russian)—the more we resented this authority, and questioned the official ideology that had been drummed into us from childhood. I remember a broadcast from a late 1960s concert of some high Komsomol event: it wasn't a Party Congress nor an anniversary of the establishment of the Leninist Young Communist League of the Soviet Union, but something of the sort. Two artists in incredible wigs, with guitars in hand, walked around the stage back to back, hitting one another and making a dreadful cacophony with their instruments. They sang a parody of a Beatles tune: 'We have been surrounded by women saying you are our idols, saying even from behind I look like a Beatle! Shake shake!!! Here we don't play to the end, there we sing too much. Shake shake!!!'

The Komsomol members raved wildly at this caricature, even more than real English fans raved at true Beatles' concerts. They raved not because they enjoyed this absurd parody, but rather because they all needed to demonstrate to their colleagues—and most importantly to the leadership—that they approved of how the Beatles were being pilloried. Yet everyone knew that those same Komsomol functionaries listened to the Beatles every day: it was through them (and also through ocean-going sailors) that we found out about all new rock bands. These loyal and duplicitous shows of enthusiasm by Komsomol workers are some of the most negative memories of my teenage years.

Similarly, during a broadcast from a Komsomol Congress, Brezhnev had made a speech, and the Komsomol members had had to be given a dressing-down for the way in which they had interrupted the General Secretary's speech with rapturous ovations. Brezhnev had problems with his speech: certain words stuck in his throat, and he needed to rest after each short phrase. It was revolting to watch young people doing all they could to show their enthusiasm short of climbing up the walls, all shouting, 'Lenin is with us! Lenin is with us!' Even the General Secretary seemed to grow tired of them towards the end.

The government tried to persecute the Beatles and nailed their fans to the pillar of shame. But the history of the Beatles' persecution in the Soviet Union is the history of the self-exposure of the idiocy of Brezhnev's rule. The more they persecuted something the whole world had already fallen in love with, the more they exposed the falsehood and hypocrisy of Soviet ideology. Despite gloomy forecasts of the imminent collapse of the Bugs, no collapse transpired. Instead the Beatles became more and more of a phenomenon in the cultural life of the entire planet, something impossible to ignore. So the original blanket condemnations changed as the bans were gradually removed. The form that this recovery took was fantastical. The first song to be released in the USSR was 'Girl', which was included in a collection of foreign popular music. I will never forget when I first got hold of this recording, looking down the titles, scarcely believing a Beatles song could be released in our country. And indeed, there were no Beatles listed. I searched for the title 'Girl'. It was not there either. At the end of the list was '*Dyevushka* [Russian for 'girl']: An English folk song'.

To think of it, the music was of the people—in a sense it *was* folk—and the words were too. But it was not possible to put the names of Lennon and McCartney on the record after all the dirt that had been poured over them. In the 1970s, after the break-up of the group, records with just four Beatles songs appeared in the USSR. All the songs were named correctly, but they were credited to 'a vocal-instrumental group'—rather as if *A Hero of our Time* were published in England, but instead of M.Y. Lermontov's name the publisher put simply 'a writer'.

Machiavelli was right to contend that people are willing to forgive big insults, but small ones are impossible to forgive. The Soviet authorities committed so many sins against their people that these musical 'misunderstandings' seem to be childish prattle. But it was these 'misunderstandings' that sometimes hurt the most, forcing people to feel in these small details the full extent of the inhumanity of the regime.

Why did the Communists persecute the Beatles to such an extent? It would be a huge simplification to argue that they saw in the pop industry a reflection of the rotting culture of bourgeois capitalism. This, though, was how it was officially branded. Deep down, the Communists felt (though no-one expressed it openly) that the Beatles were a concealed and potent threat to the their regime. And they were right.

Andrei Tarkovsky's film *The Mirror* (1974) opens with a boy undergoing a doctor's examination. The doctor skilfully encourages him to lower his defences and a flood of confession starts. The creativity of the Beatles can be compared to such a flood from which all barriers have been removed. There was a definite kinship between Tarkovsky and Lennon. (It wasn't by chance that the Communists so despised the film director. Tarkovsky wanted to make a film of Bulgakov's *The Master and Margarita* and to use Lennon's music for the soundtrack.) This flood washed into the collective consciousness. Becoming swept away by it, Soviet citizens started to be aware that the individual is highly valuable, and individuality is in itself one of the most important values of life. This was in such contradiction to the socialist message of the primacy of the collective that, when a person had educated himself in the culture of the Beatles, he found he could no longer live in lies and hypocrisy.

Beatlemania washed away the foundations of Soviet society because a person brought up with the world of the Beatles, with its images and message of love and non-violence, was an individual with internal freedom.

Although, the Beatles barely sang about politics (our country was directly mentioned only once in their repertoire 'Back in the USSR'), one could argue that the Beatles did more for the destruction of totalitarianism in the USSR than the Nobel prizewinners Alexander Solzhenitsyn and Andrei Sakharov. This might seem blasphemous to these victims of the Communist regime, but neither the novelist nor the physicist had an audience in the Soviet Union like that of the Beatles. Solzhenitsyn told the truth about the Gulag, but the population of the USSR in the mass was afraid of his *samizdat* writings. The intellectual trajectory of Sakharov was far from accessible to everyone. Had it not been for his exile to Gorky, which turned him into a martyr, his analytical constructions would barely have escaped the limits of his intellectual circle.

The apolitical Beatles, though, slipped into every Soviet flat, packaged as tapes, just as easily as they assumed their place on the stages of the largest stadia and concert halls in the world. They did something that was not within the power of Solzhenitsyn nor Sakharov: they helped a generation of free people to grow up in the Soviet Union. This was a non-Soviet generation.

In the 1970s and 80s people of the Beatles epoch began to take posts that previously had been occupied by Brezhnevites. Among them were many who had 'furiously applauded' the Komsomol parodies. They had experienced the full influence of the Beatles although they will never admit it. It would be interesting to study the role that the Beatles have played in the lives of those who have influenced the fate of Russia during the last decade.

In 1993 I was invited to the Russian mission to the UN in New York to talk about my research into the death of Rasputin. After my lecture there was a small party with Russian *hors d'oeuvres*. Throughout the evening we listened to the music of George Harrison: clearly all the Brezhnevites had been replaced by people of the Beatles generation. I wondered if Harrison perhaps now meant more to our new managers than he did to Americans, and the following day I went into a large music shop on Broadway and asked where I could find George Harrison's recordings. The assistant replied, 'What kind of music does he write?'

A sceptic will ask if the Beatles generation is also responsible for the disorder currently seen in Russia. Of course they are. Internal freedom cannot be simple. It is a breeding ground for evil, and what we see today around us also developed from internal freedom. This is an unavoidable consequence of emancipation from the slavery of totalitarianism. It is impossible to reconcile this fact, but we can understand the reasons why it is so. What will make the heart calm? As Apollinaire said, 'Happiness always comes after sadness.' And 'damned poets' are always right!

MIKHAIL SAFONOV is senior researcher at the Institute of Russian history at St Petersburg, and is a writer and broadcaster.

This article first appeared in *History Today,* August 2003, pp. 46-51. Copyright © 2003 by History Today, Ltd. Reprinted by permission.

Europe's Mosque Hysteria

Terrorist bombings, riots, and an uproar over satirical cartoons have inspired talk of a Europe under siege by Muslim immigrants. Will minarets rise in place of the continent's steeples, or is this vision of invading Muslim hoards a mirage?

MARTIN WALKER

For the first time since the ottoman turks were hurled back at the siege of Vienna in 1683, Europe has been gripped by dark, even apocalyptic visions of a Muslim invasion. The Italian journalist Oriana Fallaci has sold more than a million copies of her 2004 book *The Force of Reason*, in which she passionately argues that "Europe is no longer Europe, it is 'Eurabia,' a colony of Islam, where the Islamic invasion does not proceed only in a physical sense but also in a mental and cultural sense. Servility to the invaders has poisoned democracy, with obvious consequences for the freedom of thought and for the concept itself of liberty."

Renowned scholars in the United States have sounded similar notes of warning. Princeton professor emeritus Bernard Lewis, a leading authority on Islamic history, suggested in 2004 that the combination of low European birthrates and increasing Muslim immigration means that by this century's end, Europe will be "part of the Arabic west, the Maghreb." If non-Muslims then flee Europe, as Middle East specialist Daniel Pipes predicted in *The New York Sun*, "grand cathedrals will appear as vestiges of a prior civilization—at least until a Saudi-style regime transforms them into mosques or a Taliban-like regime blows them up." And political scientist Francis Fukuyama argued in the inaugural issue of *The American Interest* that liberal democracies face their greatest challenges not from abroad but at home, as they attempt to integrate "culturally diverse populations" into one national community. "In this respect," he wrote, "I am much more optimistic about America's long-term prospects than those of Europe."

These views flourish in the heated context of recent headlines. The crisis earlier this year over Danish cartoons depicting the Prophet Muhammad, with repercussions felt more in the Middle East than Europe, was preceded in October by the eruption of riots in France, in which the children of mainly North African immigrants torched some 10,000 cars and burned schools and community centers in some 300 towns and cities. A terrorist attack by four suicide bombers killed 52 in the London subway in July, and was swiftly followed by a second, abortive

attack. In famously tolerant Holland, the gruesome murder by a young Islamist fanatic of the radical filmmaker Theo van Gogh in November 2004 was followed by the petrol bombings of mosques and Islamic schools. In Madrid, 191 people were killed on the city's trains on March 11, 2004, in a coordinated bombing attack by Al Qaeda sympathizers, an event that was as traumatic for Europe as the September 11 attacks were for the United States.

Less noticed in the United States was the shock that ran through Germany a year ago after the "honor killings" of eight young Turkish women by their own families in the space of four months. The women's crimes were that they refused the husbands their families had chosen for them or had sought sexual partners outside their religion and close-knit communities. This became a national scandal when a school headmaster, outraged when his Turkish pupils insisted of one of the victims that "the whore got what she deserved," wrote to press outlets and to other headmasters across Germany denouncing this "wave of hidden violence" beneath the placid surface of German life. His warning was reinforced by the German government's first detailed survey of the lives of Turkish women, in which 49 percent of them said they had experienced physical or sexual violence in their marriage. One in four of those married to Turkish husbands said they had met their grooms on their wedding day. Their curiosity at last roused, Germans were shocked to find that the homepage of Berlin's Imam Reza Mosque (until quickly revised) praised the attacks of September 11, described women as second-class human beings who must defer to men, and denounced gays and lesbians as "animals."

While these events are disturbing, it is dangerous to merge them into a single, alarmist vision of a Europe doomed to religious division, mass terrorism, white backlash, and civil war. Most immigrants continue to come to Europe to better themselves and to secure a brighter future for their children, not to promote an Osama Bin Laden fantasy of reestablishing the Caliphate and converting the Notre Dame and St. Paul cathedrals into mosques. Most Muslims in France did not riot or burn cars.

Muslim clergy and civic leaders in Britain overwhelmingly denounced the London bombings.

The Islamic immigration of some 15 million to 18 million people is not exactly swamping Europe's population of more than 500 million. Nor is religious violence altogether new for a continent that spawned the Crusades, the 16th- and 17th-century wars between Catholics and Protestants, and the Holocaust. Furthermore, a Europe that within living memory produced Italy's Red Brigades, Germany's Red Army Faktion, France's OAS, Spain's ETA, and the IRA in Northern Ireland is hardly innocent of terrorism.

Despite political scientist Samuel Huntington's warning of "a clash of civilizations," the Arab world is not so very alien to Europe. Judeo-Christian civilization has been shaped by the Mediterranean Sea. Its waters constituted a common communications system from which flowed a shared history. North Africa was a Roman province, and Egypt's Queen Cleopatra was a Greek. Southern Spain was a Muslim province for seven centuries, and the Balkans were dominated by Islam until the 19th century. The Crusades were a kind of civil war between two monotheist belief systems that originated in the deserts of the Middle East. More than just a war, the Crusades were also a prolonged cultural exchange from which Europe's Christians emerged enriched by "Arabic" numerals and medicine, the lateen sail, and the table fork. The Arabs, having already benefited from the wisdom of Greece and Rome mislaid by Europe in its Dark Ages, returned it to Europe while Venice and Genoa grew rich on the Levant trade and spurred the growth that fueled Europe's great surge of oceanic exploration.

Despite warnings of a "clash of civilizations," the Arab world is not so very alien to Europe.

At that point the European and Arabian-Islamic histories began to diverge, only to converge again in the 19th century in the poisoned relationship of colonial rule. The British, in India and the Persian Gulf and along the Nile, and the French and Italians, in North Africa, imposed notions of racial and cultural superiority that deeply complicate the assimilation of today's immigrants into the homelands of the old colonial masters. Those complexities have been sharpened by the urgencies of policing and domestic intelligence-gathering against the evident threat of terrorist attack. In this unhappy context, several alarmist myths are defining the debate about the impact of mass Islamic immigration into Europe. It is important to examine each one with some care.

The first myth is that there is any such phenomenon as European Islam. This misapprehension may be the most pervasive, and the most easily exploded, for, once examined, the various waves and origins of the Islamic immigration reveal themselves as remarkably diverse. In Germany, although the immigrants are usually described as "Turkish,"

they include not only ethnic Turks, but Kurds, who speak a different language and come from a significantly different culture. Neither Kurds nor Turks can communicate with the newest wave of mainly Moroccan immigrants in any language but German. In France, the immigrants are usually described as being "of North African descent," but this is misleading. At least a quarter of the estimated six million such immigrants and their descendants in France are Berber, primarily Kabyle and Rif. They are mainly Sunni in their religion, but few of them speak the Arabic of Algeria or Morocco. Many more, from Mali and Niger, countries separated from the Maghreb by the Sahara, identified themselves to me during the French riots of last autumn as "blacks" rather than "beurs" (the French slang term for young Arabs).

The rich variety of Muslim immigration is most evident in Britain, where the ethnic and linguistic divisions among British Muslims mean that they form several distinct communities whose only common language and culture (outside the mosque and the Qur'an) is English. According to the 2001 census, 69 percent of Britain's 1.6 million Muslims come from the Indian subcontinent, and just more than half of them were born there. The rest were born in Britain. Recent research at the University of Essex by Lucinda Platt suggests that the British melting pot is working rather well, and producing considerable social mobility. She found that some 56 percent of children from Indian working-class families go on to professional or managerial jobs in adulthood, compared with just 43 percent of those from white, nonimmigrant families.

The largest group of Britain's Muslims, more than half a million, are of Pakistani birth or descent, and of them almost half come from the poor district around Mirpur where the building of the Mangla dam in the late 1950s and early 1960s created a vast pool of homeless, landless, and barely literate peasants, who were then recruited to low-wage jobs in the textile industry of northern England. They clubbed together to bring over imams from home to run mosques and teach the Qur'an, imported wives from Mirpur through arranged marriages, and created urban versions of their traditional Mirpuri villages under the gray English skies. When the British textile industry declined, this community of poor and ill-educated people was locked into a grim cycle of unemployment, welfare, female illiteracy, and low expectations. The rust belt that stretches across Lancashire and Yorkshire is the region where the anti-immigration British National Party, a thuggish group with neo-Nazi links, gets up to 20 percent of the vote from an almost equally ill-educated and hopeless white working class. This is also the area that produces most of the dozen or so honor killings carried out each year by angry fathers or brothers, when a Pakistani girl falls in love with a British boy.

The next largest cohort, nearly 400,000, comes from Bangladesh, mostly from the Sylhet region. These people are very different: They speak Bengali rather than Urdu, eat rice rather than roti, apply less rigid dress codes to women, follow a notably more relaxed form of Islam, and are concentrated in East London rather than northern England. They tend also to be more entrepreneurial and open to educational opportunities for their children, who have a far better record of university attendance than the Pakistanis.

The third major group is the Muslims of Indian origin, many of whom came to Britain in the early 1970s as refugees from East Africa after being expelled by Uganda's dictator, Idi Amin. Along with the 16th-century Huguenots from France and the 19th-century Jews from Russia, they have become one of the most desirable and successful immigrant groups that Britain ever welcomed. They have produced more millionaires and college graduates than any other ethnic group—the British included. One in 20 is a doctor.

The 31 percent of British Muslims from outside South Asia are mainly from Somalia and Turkey, each cohort totaling about 60,000. Another 100,000 come from Nigeria, Malaysia, and Iran. The students, refugees, political exiles, and Arab intellectuals who have come from all over the Islamic world and given the city the nickname "Londonistan" make up most of the rest.

So the reality behind the monolithic term "British Muslim" is a potpourri: the wealthy London surgeon, the unemployed and barely literate textile worker in Oldham, the Malaysian accounting student intent on attending business school, the fiery newspaper columnist who dares not return to Saudi Arabia, the government clerk living with her English boyfriend and estranged from her outraged Iraqi family, the prosperous Bengali restaurant owner in East London.

These are the individuals that Prime Minister Tony Blair hopes to rally—after the cultural and political shock of the London bombings—to the common identity of Britishness, by which he means a full-hearted commitment to democracy, and the freedom of speech and religion and lifestyles that it involves. And in these days of Al Qaeda, Blair has sought to convince such individuals that being British may include detention of terrorist suspects without trial for up to 90 days, closed-circuit television cameras in their mosques, and government licenses for their imams. An estimated 1,800 of Britain's 3,000 full-time imams come from overseas, mainly from Pakistan, and many arrive with Saudi funds and sponsorship and after some study in Saudi Arabia, which usually means a commitment to that country's puritanical and dominant Wahhabi creed.

One of the great myths is that Muslim immigrants' higher birthrates threaten to replace traditionally Christian Europe with an Islamic majority.

Many of the moderate elders of Britain's Muslim community go along with Blair's plans, which also have the backing of the Muslim members of Parliament. The mainstream of Muslim opinion is now prepared to admit that the four British-born bombers of the London transport system were influenced by extremists at their mosques in Britain and during visits to Afghanistan and Pakistan, and that this radicalization of some young Muslims is a community problem.

"The Muslim communities are not reaching those people who they need to engage with and win their hearts and minds," says Sadiq Khan, the Muslim Labor MP for the London suburb of Tooting. "What leads someone to do this? The rewards they are told they will get in the hereafter—it is incumbent on Muslims to tell them that nowhere in Islam does it say this, and in fact what you will get is hellfire."

It is ironic that in the wake of the London bombings, the British political establishment and media, and even many Muslim groups in Britain, are now speaking of the Muslim community as a single entity. This may yet emerge, especially if others persist in viewing all Muslims as one mass, although so far various Muslim groupings seem to compete for the title of spokesman, and to criticize one another for being more or less radical or devout or co-opted by the British government (a phenomenon that is also evident in France, as it was in the 1960s civil rights movement in the United States). The fact is that the various Muslim associations in Britain, speaking Urdu or Pashtun or Bengali at home, have little in common except the sense of alarm that somehow they will share in the blame, or suffer the backlash, for the bombings.

But some of the things they do have in common are striking. Around 15 percent of Muslims, both male and female, are registered as unemployed, compared with four percent of the rest of the population. The British government's Labor Force Survey found that Muslims are more likely than any other group to be in long-term unemployment or not even seeking work—in either case, not reflected in unemployment data. In the same survey, 31 percent of employed Muslims had no qualifications and, therefore, little prospect of advancement from menial work. Muslims are five times more likely to marry by age 24 than other Britons. Muslims have the youngest age profile of all religious groups: 34 percent are under the age of 16, compared with 18 percent of Christians. Muslims tend to live together; nearly two-thirds of the 600,000 Muslims who live in London reside in the two East End boroughs of Newham and Tower Hamlets. And Muslims are more likely to reside in rented public housing than any other ethnic or religious group.

Figures such as these have seeded a number of misleading submyths, of which the most common is that the "Pakis" live in ghettos and are beginning to dominate in a significant number of parliamentary constituencies. A by-election in the northwest London suburb of Brent East shortly after Blair's government invaded Iraq alongside U.S. forces became the prime exhibit of this argument. Traditionally a safe Labor constituency, Brent East fell to the Liberal Democrats when many Muslims voted against Labor in protest of the war. In the general election of last year, a former Labor MP, George Galloway, who had been expelled from the party after his outspoken attacks on the war and on "Tony Blair's lie machine," narrowly won reelection in East London as an independent MP, unseating the only MP who was both black and Jewish, the Labor Party's pro-war Oona King. In his first two election victories, Blair carried more than 70 percent of the Muslim vote, but in the 2005 election, exit polls suggest that he got just 32 percent. This seems to have been a direct result of the Iraq war and draws a sharp limit on previous assumptions of common ground between Islam and Blair's Labor Party.

But the fact is that there are only 17 electoral constituencies in Britain, out of 646, where a complete shift of the immigrant vote would be sufficient to unseat the incumbent MP. Although television images depict whole districts where most shop signs are printed in Urdu or where Sikhs and other immigrants predominate, there are few places that fit the classic definition of a ghetto. In some detailed research at the University of Manchester, Ludi Simpson analyzed the 1991 and 2001 census data for 8,850 electoral wards in England and Wales. A ward is a subdistrict of a constituency, containing roughly 10,000 voters. Simpson found that the number of "mixed" wards (defined as wards where at least 10 percent of residents are from an ethnic minority) increased from 964 to 1,070 over the decade. In only 14 wards did one minority account for more than half the population, and there was not one ward where white people made up less than 10 percent of the inhabitants.

The reality is that as immigrant families become established and their children get education and jobs, they tend to move out to more prosperous districts with better schools and housing. In short, just as Britain learned with its West Indian immigrants in the 1960s and 1970s that what was defined as a problem of race was just as much one of social and economic class, so it is finding with its Muslims that race and class and religion all play into a context of social and economic mobility. Britain has been fortunate—this mobility has been possible because the country has enjoyed a booming economy over the past decade, with much lower levels of unemployment than France or Germany.

Despite all this, a small number of educated and apparently well-assimilated young Muslims, mainly but not exclusively of Pakistani origin, have been drawn to the extreme militancy of Al Qaeda. Sources in MI5, Britain's security service, cite a formula devised by their French equivalent, the Renseignements Généraux, to calculate the number of fundamentalists in a given population. Based on an extensive analysis of the French scene, the formula says that in a given Muslim population in Europe, an average of five percent are fundamentalists, and up to three percent of those fundamentalists should be considered dangerous. By that calculation, in France's Muslim population of six million, there are 300,000 fundamentalists, of whom 9,000 are potentially dangerous. Applying the formula to Britain's 1.6 million Muslims produces 80,000 fundamentalists, of whom some 2,400 may be dangerous—a figure very close to the number of MI5 agents.

Assessing the scale of the problem brings into focus the second great myth that confuses the issue of Islam in Europe, which is that native Europeans have been so sapped of their reproductive vigor that Muslim immigrants' higher birthrates threaten to replace traditionally Christian Europe with an Islamic majority within this century. The birthrate of native Europeans has fallen sharply since the baby boom of the 1960s. The usual measure is total fertility rate (TFR), the number of children an average woman will bear in her lifetime. A TFR of 2.1 is required to maintain population stability; the current average level in the 25-nation European Union is just under 1.5, and as low as 1.2 in Italy and Latvia. A study for the

European Parliament suggests that the EU will need an average of 1.6 million immigrants every year until 2050 to keep its population at the current level. To maintain the current ratio of working-age population to pensioners, more than 10 million immigrants a year would be required. Omer Taspinar, director of the Brookings Institution's program on Turkey, suggests that the Muslim birthrate in Europe is three times higher than that of non-Muslim Europeans, and that since about one million new Islamic immigrants arrive in Western Europe each year, by 2050 one in five Europeans likely will be Muslim.

But this is to ignore the clear evidence that immigrant birthrates fall relatively quickly toward the local norm. A recent survey by Justin Vaisse of the French Foreign Ministry, who is also an adjunct professor at the Institut d'Études Politiques in Paris, suggests that, on the basis of French statistics, this change can occur within a single generation. In Britain, Muslims of Indian origin now have a TFR of less than 2.0, and while there are striking regional differences in the birthrates of young women of Pakistani origin who have been born in Britain and educated in British schools, the overall trend is toward fewer children.

Moreover, in Sweden, France, and Britain, the native birthrate has started to rise again, with a marked surge among women who start having children in their early thirties. In Britain, the TFR climbed from a record low of 1.63 in 2001 to 1.77 in 2004, when the number of babies born rose by almost three percent from the previous year. There is no doubt that immigrants tend to have higher birthrates; one in five of those new babies was born to a mother from outside Britain, a significant rise from the one in eight of a decade earlier. But the disparity of birthrates across Europe is so wide—from TFRs of 1.98 in Ireland and 1.89 in France to 1.18 in the Czech Republic—that it is not meaningful to speak of a single European phenomenon.

Furthermore, public policy is not helpless in the face of demographic challenges. Scandinavia has higher birthrates than the rest of Europe, despite relatively low immigration rates, thanks in part to government policies that provide generous maternity leave, family allowances, and good child care for working mothers. Parenting in these days of easy contraception is an essentially voluntary matter. And if a society chooses to have fewer children, it does not have to resort to mass immigration to maintain a high proportion of workers to consumers. Other accommodations can be made, from delaying the age of retirement to accepting lower growth rates and less intensive patterns of consumption.

And thus we arrive at the final myth about Islam in Europe: that a shrinking and aging population of native-born Europeans and a large and growing Islamic population can only be alarming. It certainly looked that way last fall in France during the riots, which seemed to demonstrate, in the ugliest possible way, that something fundamental in the French social system, and thus in its broader European counterpart, is in deep trouble. There are, in fact, two different crises of the European social model, and they collided in the riots. The first is the familiar problem of economic sluggishness that has stuck France, Germany, and Italy with double-digit unemployment for a decade. One cause is the power of the labor unions and the longtime understanding that workers and management are "social partners" in an agreement under which those with jobs are protected, paid well, and given generous pensions and social security. In return, managers get high productivity rates and very few strikes in the private sector. But as a consequence, it is extremely hard to get a secure job, since managers find it almost impossible to lay off surplus employees. The low-wage entry-level jobs that have brought so many of the unskilled British and American dropouts into the workforce barely exist in France, where the minimum wage and employer-paid social insurance costs are very high.

This first crisis has now intersected with the second: that of the largely immigrant underclass, whose young dropouts find it difficult to get any work at all. The problem is most acute in France, where immigrants constitute more than 10 percent of the population, compared with five percent in Britain. They live in what the French now admit are so many ghettos of high-rise public housing blocks with few whites, poor schools, sparse social amenities, harsh policing, and little evidence that they can ever partake of the broad prosperity of mainstream Europe. "They are the lost lands of France," says Jacqueline Costa-Lascoux, a professor at the prestigious school of public administration at the Institut d'Études Politiques. And yet these grim urban nightmares contain, in demographic terms, much of the country's future, even though their precise numbers are not counted under that other French myth—dating back to the revolution of 1789 with its Rights of Man—that there are no ethnic subgroups, only citizens. No affirmative action is necessary, the line goes, because La République has abolished racism.

"France is not a country like others," intoned the prime minister, Dominique de Villepin, in November. "It will never accept that citizens live separately, with different opportunities and with unequal futures. For more than two centuries, the Republic has found a place for everyone by elevating the principles of liberty, equality, and fraternity. We must remain faithful to this promise and to Republican demands."

The best estimates suggest there are now more than five million Muslims and two million blacks in France, and their birthrates are more than twice as high as that of French whites. So while the brown and black inhabitants of France account for one-eighth of the total population, they account for almost a quarter of those under the age of 25. They also account for more than half of the prison population, and close to half of the unemployed. France's future therefore depends on a sullen and ill-educated underclass of future workers and consumers whose taxes are supposed to finance the welfare state and the pensions of French whites, who at age 60 retire after a lifetime of leisurely 35-hour workweeks. After the scenes that disfigured France last fall, this does not seem to be a promising proposition.

And this problem of France is the problem of Europe on a slightly less urgent scale. Alarmists say that without mass immigration, the European social system cannot be funded; but with mass immigration, the European social fabric is visibly and violently tearing apart. And with Jean-Marie Le Pen, the right-wing extremist who leads the Front National, winning almost five million votes in the last presidential election, France has

less room for political maneuvering than most countries. If the myth of de Villepin's Republic is gently retired, and France tries some of the detested Anglo-Saxon remedies of affirmative action to produce a black and Muslim middle class, and puts black and brown faces onto its television screens as announcers, into the higher ranks of the police and civil service and armed forces, and into the National Assembly and the Senate and the prefectures and the corporate boardrooms, then it risks strengthening the white backlash that has already given the demagogue Le Pen some 18 percent of the presidential vote.

It is, nonetheless, a risk that will have to be taken because no other course is practicable. Modern democracies cannot realistically, or legally, impose ethnic cleansing by mass deportations of Muslim minorities or their permanent subjugation by some odious incarnation of a discriminatory police state. The policy alternatives therefore are assimilation or apartheid. The former will be difficult, since it will require fundamental economic reform to tackle the problems of unemployment, education (of both Muslims and those poor whites most likely to resort to backlash), reform of immigration rules and border policing to control illegal immigration, and profound religious reform by the Muslims themselves. European societies should not be expected to tolerate subgroups that seek to impose sharia within their communities, nor imams who preach anti-Semitism or demand the death penalty for Muslims who convert to Christianity or for writers such as Salman Rushdie. But equally, European societies will have to accept the political implications of a significant and growing electoral vote that will agitate strongly for respect of Islam as well as jobs, opportunities, and affirmative action, and that will demand influence over foreign policy.

The challenge is serious but not hopeless. To suggest that European civilization is too feeble and insecure to survive an Islamic population that is currently less than five percent of the total is a counsel of cultural despair. It ignores the example of the United States, which seems to be successfully assimilating its own Muslim minority, just as the vibrant and open American economy assimilated so many previous waves of immigrants. It also ignores the degree to which European Muslims increasingly think and live like the populations they have joined. An opinion poll conducted in Britain for the BBC after the London bombings found that almost nine in 10 of the more than 1,000 Muslims surveyed said they would and should help the police tackle extremists in Britain's Muslim communities. More than half wanted foreign Muslim clerics barred or expelled from Britain. Fifty-six percent said they were optimistic about their children's future in Britain. And only one in five said that Muslim communities had already integrated too much with British society, while 40 percent wanted more integration.

Muslims are being changed by Europe just as much as they are changing their adopted countries. The honor killings of young Turkish women in Germany are appalling, but the actions of the women also demonstrate that many Muslim women are no longer content to abide by their parents' wishes. They want the same freedoms and opportunities enjoyed by the German girls with whom they went to school. The French-born children of immigrants who rioted in the Paris suburbs were demanding to be treated as French by the police, potential employers, and society in general. The riots, as French scholar Olivier Roy has noted, were "more about Marx than Muhammad."

Is European civilization too feeble and insecure to survive an Islamic population that is currently less than five percent of the total?

Across Europe, there are significant numbers of potential terrorist cells, radical Islamist activists and organizations, and mosques and imams that cleave to an extreme and puritanical form of Islam. Many of these reject the idea that Muslim immigrants can or should assimilate into their host societies, and also reject Western democracy or any separation of church and state. One such group is the well-organized Hizb-ut-Tahir, which seeks to reestablish the Caliphate as a pan-Islamic system of government based on the Qur'an. Hizb-ut-Tahir is outlawed in Germany, where it has been described as "a conveyor belt for terrorism," and Blair threatened to ban it in Britain after the London bombings.

But there are other, more promising currents of modern and reformist Islamic thought in Europe that seek assimilation not only with European societies but also with Western values of individual human and political rights. The best known of these currents is associated with Tariq Ramadan, grandson of the founder of the Muslim Brotherhood and author of *To Be a European Muslim* (1999). Ramadan believes that an independent and liberal Islam is emerging in Europe among young, educated Muslims who have been profoundly and positively influenced by modern liberal democracy with its free press and separation of church and state. He moved from Geneva to Oxford, where he currently teaches, after the U.S. Department of Homeland Security barred him in 2004 from taking a teaching post at Notre Dame University. (He was also banned in Saudi Arabia, Tunisia, and Egypt after calling for a moratorium on sharia's corporal punishment, stoning, and beheading.) Ramadan identi-fies himself as a European born and bred, with Muslim roots, whose modernized Islamic faith needs to uproot Islamic principles from their cultures of origin and plant them in the cultural soil of Western Europe. "We've got to get away from the idea that scholars in the Islamic world can do our thinking for us. We need to start thinking for ourselves," Ramadan insists.

Some Muslims see Ramadan as an apostate, while many Christian and Jewish activists regard him as an Islamic Trojan horse. But he seems to represent a significant current in Islam that seeks reform in the Arab world and accommodation with the West. There are traces of this same current in the speeches of Dyab Abou Jahjah, the Belgium-based trade unionist who founded the Arab European League (though he is denounced by the Belgian government). It is also evident in the extraordinary appeal of the Arab world's first Muslim televangelist, Amr Khaled, who was in Britain during the London bombings and repudiated them as un-Islamic.

There is nothing ineluctable about any clash of civilizations between Islam and the West. Current demographic trends are not immutable, and it would be foolish to extrapolate from them a spurious forecast about Muslim majorities in Europe. That the renewed encounter between Europe and its Islamic minorities will result in terrorism or sectarian and ethnic tensions is not foreordained, and a white backlash is by no means inevitable. But the clear prospect that these poisonous predictions could be realized may itself become the antidote. The countries of Europe and their Islamic minorities have had a series of awful warnings, similar to those in the United States in the 1960s. The American response to the civil rights movement is an example to Europe of how open, liberal democracies may address the problems of Islamic immigration and mobilize public opinion and public policy to resolve them. It will not be easy, and the task will endure for generations, at constant risk of being derailed by spasmodic riots and terrorist outrages. But the alternatives are worse.

MARTIN WALKER, the editor of United Press International, covered the London bombings and the French riots last year. He is a senior scholar at the Wilson Center and the author of many books, most recently the novel *The Caves of Périgord* (2002).

Folly & Failure in the Balkans

Tom Gallagher

Bismarck's opinion that the Balkans were not worth the bones of a single Pomeranian grenadier has long been heeded by hard-headed statesmen from Disraeli to Kissinger who warned against active involvement in the region. A sense of fatalism about the ability of local leaders and their populations to aspire to good government and 'civilised' conduct has long coloured Western policy towards south-east Europe.

But the statements and actions of powerful Western leaders in the recent war over Kosovo suggested that a break with past traditions may be occurring. Madeleine Albright, the US Secretary of State, declared to Congress in May that 'the Continent cannot be whole and free as long as its south-east corner is wracked by ethnic tensions and threatened with conflict'. With maps of the region by his side, President Clinton went on television to show the American people where Kosovo was and why the peace of Europe depended on securing justice for deported Kosovo refugees. Britain's prime minister Tony Blair delighted Albanian refugees by promising that they would all be able to return to their homes. Other leaders promised a new Marshall Plan for the region in order to integrate it economically with the rest of Europe.

A look at the role of the great powers in the Balkans over the last two hundred years shows that such clear statements of principles are uncharacteristic. Statesmen have been reluctant to act as peacemakers in the region, at least for extended periods. Altruistic gestures towards oppressed peoples have been overtaken by the need to preserve a balance of power between states whose interests collide in the region.

The Balkan peninsula is a region where civilisations and social systems have collided and merged for thousands of years. For over four hundred years, the Ottoman Empire headed by a Muslim sultan in Constantinople controlled most of the Balkans. The Ottomans taxed their subject peoples heavily and conscripted their young men to fight in frequent wars. But the west European obsession with ensuring that the religion of the people matched that of the ruler was not shared. The Orthodox Christian Church and the Jews enjoyed freedom of worship. They were allowed to maintain their own courts and judges, applying their own laws to their communities in a whole range of civil matters. Forcible conversions to Islam were rare. But among certain peoples, particularly the Slavs of Bosnia and the Albanians, large-scale conversions took place, not least because of the opportunities for upward mobility in the Ottoman bureaucracy or the military provided for Muslims.

The autonomy enjoyed by the Orthodox Church preserved cultural values pre-dating Islam, particularly memories of the Byzantine Empire which had lasted until 1453. This sense of religious and historical separation would provide the seedbed for nationalism when the Ottoman empire decayed. A Byzantine heritage was also preserved by influential Greek families, known as the *phanariots*, who administered parts of the Empire on behalf of the Sultan.

The Orthodox Church was a supranational body that was non-national in its doctrines and outlook. Sometimes the harshness of church courts and the exactions of the *phanariots* made ordinary Greeks view the Turks as less onerous oppressors. During the seventeenth century Greek peasants in the Peloponnese welcomed the return of the Turks after periods of Venetian rule marked by heavy taxation and forcible conversion to Catholicism.

Memories of the sacking of Constantinople in 1204 by Crusaders who looted and massacred, desecrating churches and fatally weakening the Byzantine empire, created long-term enmity between western and eastern Christianity. Today in Greece these images of western treachery and barbarism enable opinion formers to appeal for solidarity with fellow Orthodox Serbs and condemn what is seen as NATO aggression first in Bosnia and later in Kosovo.

Two hundred years ago, as the Ottoman empire became enfeebled and corrupt, it was the West which appeared to offer the path to modernisation and renewed greatness for local Christian leaders and especially restless intellectuals in the Balkans.

In 1807 the Serbs were the first South Slav people to establish their independence. This achievement encouraged the view among Serb rulers that they were entitled to play the leading role in creating a union of South Slav peoples. When Yugoslavia emerged in 1918, the domineering attitude of the Serb leadership provoked resentment among other peoples, particularly the Croats, who, because of their experience of Austrian Habsburg rule from Vienna, had acquired different governmental traditions and expectations.

Before their current demonisation, the Serbs had long enjoyed a vogue in Europe because of their martial sacrifices in the cause of political freedom as well as the beauty of their poetry. Writers from Goethe and Walter Scott to Rebecca West expressed their admiration for the lyric beauty of Serbian popular songs, while Jacob Grimm ranked Serb poetry alongside that of Homer.

The romantic nationalism pioneered by the German philosopher Herder found a ready audience among restless intellectuals in Eastern Europe. With its emphasis on the unique value of every ethnic group and on each group's 'natural right' to carve out a national home of its own, romantic nationalism was able to undermine the multi-cultural traditions of the Eastern world. When Herder hailed the Slavs as 'the coming leaders of Europe', intellectuals were encouraged to explore the past and all-too-often invent glorious historical pedigrees meant to give reborn nations the inalienable right to enjoy contemporary greatness. If this meant dominating territories shared by more than one ethnic group, then many nationalists justified such a course even if it meant that they were imitating the imperialists whose rule they were seeking to throw off.

Intellectuals were encouraged to explore the past and invent glorious historical pedigrees.

The prospects of cultural nationalism were transformed by the French Revolution and Napoleon's humiliation of dynastic empires. The revolution against the traditional political order legitimised a West European concept of nationalism allowing a people to identify with a territory on which they were entitled to establish a state and government of their own.

The appeal of romantic nationalism for European public opinion was first revealed by the Greek War of Independence in the 1820s. Acts of cruelty were committed on both sides but it was the Ottoman atrocities against the Greeks that moved the liberal European conscience. The Ottoman massacre of Greeks on the island of Chios in 1822, immortalised in Delacroix's painting, enabled European public opinion to overrule governments that might have wished to limit Greek ambitions. It was not just Byron, but Shelley, Goethe and Schiller who unleashed a storm of enthusiasm for Philhellenism that cautious governments found hard to stem. In 1824, a series of privately financed loans, which in effect made the City of London the financier of the revolution, proved critical in ensuring Greek success.

One hundred and fifty years later, philhellenism was still a strong enough force to ensure that Greece entered the European Union even though there were nagging doubts about her real commitment to a post-nationalist agenda based upon European integration. In the 1980s and early 1990s Greece would earn the reputation of being arguably the most nationalistic of the Balkan states, under the populist premier Andreas Papandreou. Persistent interference by outside powers in its internal affairs had produced a culture of suspicion and complaint which helped nationalism to flourish.

After Greek independence was achieved in 1832, Great Power interference combined with local factionalism to weaken the prospects of effective government. Russia and Britain in particular had conflicting interests and ambitions in the Balkans. As a multi-national empire in its own right, Russia was hostile to the pretensions of European small state nationalism. But the tsars claimed to be the legitimate successors to the Orthodox Empire at Byzantium and the defenders of east European Christendom.

In 1774 Catherine the Great of Russia extracted from the sultan the right to appoint consuls in the Ottoman empire who could make representations on behalf of its Christian subjects. Between 1787 and 1792, Russia fought a war with Turkey whose aim was to partition the Ottoman empire and establish Russian control of Constantinople and the Bosphorus Straits. For the first time Britain became aware of conflicting British and Russian interests in the Near East. The realisation gave birth to long-standing international tensions as two rival European powers sought to fill the vacuum left by the retreating Ottoman empire on their own terms.

Britain feared that its imperial possessions in India would be threatened if Russia became a Mediterranean power. Thus the Foreign Office became associated with the policy of propping up the Ottoman empire, or at least preventing its slow decline becoming a rapid collapse that might overturn a precarious balance of power.

An anti-Russian coalition headed by Britain waged war in the Crimea in 1853–54 to foil the tsar's bid to partition the Ottoman empire. Thus the only general European conflict in the hundred years between 1815 and 1914 was due to the Eastern Question. An independent Romania emerged afterwards under the sponsorship of France. The victors in the Crimean War chose to sponsor Romania to prevent Russia controlling the mouth of the Danube. The Romanians claimed Latin ancestry and could act as a bulwark preventing a union of South Slav peoples which Britain feared would enable Russia to clinch its ambitions in the eastern Mediterranean.

Thus the precedent was established for map changes in the Balkans in order to satisfy a precarious balance of power rather than to suit the wishes of the local inhabitants. Emerging peoples threw in their fortunes with a Great Power in the hope that they could achieve their territorial goals. Prospects of co-operation between the Balkan peoples diminished as outside powers were prepared to sponsor rival nationalisms for short-term goals. In 1876 the power of events in the Balkans to galvanise international opinion was shown by the reaction in Britain to massacres perpetrated by Turkish forces against Christian Slavs in Bulgaria. William Gladstone, the leader of the Liberal opposition, published his pamphlet *The Bulgarian Horrors and the Question of the East* in September 1876 and by the end of that month it had sold 200,000 copies. He demanded that prime minister Disraeli use Britain's authority to compel the sultan to grant freedom to the Christian Bulgarians.

Gladstone had earlier earned the gratitude of the Greeks when, after serving as governor of the Ionian Islands, he had persuaded the House of Commons to place them under Greek rule. He wished British policy in the Balkans to be guided by moral criteria, challenging the doctrine set down by Palmerston in 1848 when he argued that

> the furtherance of British interests should be the only object of a British Foreign Secretary... [and] that it is in Britain's interest to preserve the balance of power in international affairs.

In 1994, when addressing the House of Commons for the first time as foreign secretary, Malcolm Rifkind repeated the words of Palmerston and said that they would be his motto. Britain was then under fire for pursuing a policy of minimal engagement in the war in Bosnia. Its refusal to support the lifting of the arms embargo which would have enabled the Muslim-led government to defend itself against its Serb adversaries was widely criticised. The government's most vociferous critic was Gladstone's descendant as Liberal leader, Paddy Ashdown, who visited the Bosnian war zone on numerous occasions and argued that Britain was lowering standards of behaviour in the region by refusing to countenance forceful action against Serbs who had subjected the city of Sarajevo to a three-year siege and 'ethnically cleansed' many other areas populated by Muslims.

Gladstone's 'Midlothian campaign' of public speaking on the Bulgarian crisis contained the advocacy of the underdog and the condemnation of aggressors which was to become a hallmark of Balkan crises in the 1990s. Intellectuals, churchmen and ordinary citizens, moved or repelled by Gladstone's rhetoric, entered the fray. The poet Swinburne, who wrote in 1877 that 'the Turks are no worse than other oppressors around the world,' had his counterparts among leading playwrights and television personalities in the late 1990s who argued that there were many Kosovos around the world for whom NATO refused to act.

In 1877 Tennyson's sonnet hailing tiny Montenegro which had repulsed the Ottomans centuries earlier as 'a rough rock-throne of freedom' got much attention. It was accompanied by a long article about Montenegran history written by Gladstone, no other British leader identifying himself as completely with a Balkan cause until Tony Blair's emotional tours of Albanian refugee camps in May 1999. But Gladstone's campaign failed to move his great rival Disraeli. War with Russia appeared imminent in 1877 when, after a Russian victory at the siege of Plevna, Constantinople seemed to lie at its feet. Britain feared an enlarged Bulgaria would become an extension of Russia and an international conference was held in Berlin in 1878 to arbitrate the dispute.

The diplomatic carve-up of the region that ensued under the cynical guidance of Bismarck ruled out the creation of a viable pattern of states as the Ottoman empire was gradually forced out of Europe. Decisions were made about Macedonia, Bulgaria and Bosnia which would return to disturb the peace of Europe in subsequent decades. Rather than sponsoring a Balkan confederation or large ethnically mixed states where minority rights were protected by international guarantees, the European powers left two South Slav states with unsatisfied national programmes who would clash in wars over the next sixty years: Serbia and Bulgaria. Territory was annexed by the powers to which they had but the flimsiest claim: Bessarabia was taken by Russia despite its mainly Romanian population; while Bosnia had been occupied by Austria-Hungary in 1876. The biggest losers were the region's Muslim peoples, several million of whom were driven out of Serbia, Bulgaria and Bosnia, due to the absence of a powerful protector.

The rise of nationalism in the Balkans had arguably left the region as vulnerable to foreign penetration as it had been before. But communities which had been slow to acquire a national identity, such as the Albanians, quickly asserted their own na-

tional claims so as not to be overwhelmed by competitors. In Constantinople, western-style nationalism was adopted by modernising sections of the Turkish elite to stave off the complete dissolution of their state. One early result was the persecution of minorities deemed to be acting on behalf of Russia, the first of a series of horrific massacres being perpetrated against the Christian Armenians in 1896. These culminated under the cover of the First World War in 1915, when as many as a million Armenians were massacred or died in forced evacuations of their territory.

The powers had sponsored small, unstable and weak states, each based on the idea of nationality.

In a bid to protect trading routes, secure military objectives, or establish client states, the powers had sponsored small, unstable and weak states, each based on the idea of nationality. The Balkan states usually had conflicting territorial claims as well as ethnic minorities that had to be assimilated or driven out. They formed unstable local alliances, sought backing from outside powers in order to guarantee security or satisfy national ambitions and, in turn, were used by these powers for their own strategic advantage.

The term 'Balkanisation' has acquired world notoriety to describe the problems arising from such a fragmentation of political power. Two Balkan wars in 1912 and 1913, as Turkey was forced to give up most of its Balkan possessions, degenerated into a bloody scramble for territory among rival states. International arbitration guaranteed an independent Albania in 1913. But the capacity of the Balkans to trigger a wider conflict was shown by the way the great powers went to war following the assassination of the heir to the Austrian throne, Archduke Franz-Ferdinand, in Sarajevo on June 28th, 1914, by local pro-Serb nationalists.

At Versailles in 1919 the victorious Allied states rejected the precedent of the Congress of Berlin and instead sponsored territorially powerful states in the Balkans: Romania, Yugoslavia, and Greece. A new European order based on the national self-determination of peoples and operating under the aegis of the League of Nations was meant to guarantee the peace. But the self-determination principle often only applied where it weakened enemy states such as Austria-Hungary and it was disregarded where its consequences proved unfavourable to the victors. Thus Italy acquired the South Tyrol and parts of the Dalmatian coast where non-Italians predominated. Meanwhile, Yugoslavia excluded the Albanians of Kosovo. The burning of villages in the 1920s followed by the confiscation of land from Albanians in the 1930s, unless they had Yugoslav documents to prove ownership, was a foretaste of future deportations.

The League of Nations lacked the powers to protect minorities in states where insecure majorities which had gained territory as a result of the outcome of a European war often gave subject peoples the grim choice of assimilation or exclusion. Turkey's success in foiling an effort sponsored by the Allies to create a Greater Greece in parts of Asia Minor encouraged other defeated powers to defy Versailles Europe. In 1922 the deportation of 1.3 million Greeks from Asia Minor to Greece and 800,000 Turks in the opposite direction created an ominous precedent.

The mutual hostility which poisoned relations between the East European states encouraged the effective withdrawal of Britain and France from the whole region in the 1930s. The ascendancy of Germany was only challenged in 1939 by Britain and France as the threat to the balance of power became too great to ignore. But the eventual defeat of Nazi Germany only resulted in a swop of tyrannical rulers. In October 1944 Churchill concluded his famous 'Percentages Agreement' with Stalin which assigned the Soviet Union a dominant role in Bulgaria and Romania, and an equal stake for both powers in Yugoslavia, with Britain enjoying a majority stake in Greece. Despite his great services to the cause of freedom, Churchill was prepared to abandon more countries to a tyrannical fate than Chamberlain actually did at Munich in 1938.

During the Cold War, the West identified with bids by countries like Poland and Czechoslovakia to throw off the Soviet yoke. Lech Walesa and Vaclav Havel were seen as the champions of liberty-loving peoples that had been cruelly severed from the West, their natural home. However, the emphasis in the Balkans was in backing a strong leader or strong regional power capable of keeping 'ancient ethnic hatreds' in check and preserving a balance of power that would prevent the superpowers coming to blows there.

Thus Marshal Josip Broz Tito, the architect of Communist Yugoslavia, became a recipient of Western financial and diplomatic support after he broke with Stalin in 1948. Tito was probably the most enlightened Communist ruler the world has ever seen. But he still ran a police state and Western creditors poured money into Yugoslavia without linking aid to gradual democratisation. Milovan Djilas who went from being Tito's loyal lieutenant to his chief critic, was warning in the 1950s that social democracy and the social market were crucial requirements to prevent the internal tensions which festered under one-party rule, but his long imprisonments produced relatively little concern in the West.

During the last decades of the Cold War the West was even prepared to back Romania's Nicolae Ceausescu, an unsavoury Communist despot, in the mistaken belief that he was a weak link in the chain of Soviet power. But it is not just from the Communist Balkans that the evidence showing a Western preference for authoritarian leaders over democratically-elected ones comes.

After the defeat of the Communists in the 1944–49 Greek civil war, the United States was the main power behind right-wing forces determined to prevent the centre-left opposition winning office. Simultaneously, after going back on a First World War offer to Greece to cede Cyprus, with its Greek majority to Athens, Britain pursued a policy of divide-and-rule which left a bitter legacy of ethnic strife even after it conceded independence in 1960. In 1964, when the moderate left finally won office in Athens, the United States proposed to settle the Cyprus question by partition. When the Greek ambassador in Washington told Lyndon Johnson that such a plan could never be accepted, the president retorted:

F___ your parliament and your constitution. America is an elephant, Cyprus is a flea. If these two fellows continue itching the elephant, they may just get whacked by the elephant's trunk, whacked good.... If your prime minster gives me talk about democracy, parliament and constitution, he, his parliament, and his constitution, may not last very long.

The US Central Intelligence Agency was implicated in the 1967 military coup which extinguished Greek democracy for seven years, just as it was in the attempted overthrow in 1974 of Archbishop Makarios, the leader of Cyprus, which led to a Turkish occupation and partition of the island.

The liking for improvised, short-term solutions to complex problems that ignore the wishes of local populations and are enforced by tyrannical leaders characterised the major powers' approach to the Balkans before and after 1945. It produced some of the biggest American and British blunders of the Cold War and has left two well-armed Balkan states, Greece and Turkey, which several times have almost gone to war.

Similarly, the penchant for diplomatic quick-fixes epitomised the West's engagement with Yugoslavia as it dissolved into fratricidal conflict in the 1990s. A new note was apparently struck in the Kosovo conflict in the spring of 1999 as Nato committed itself to undoing the effects of ethnic violence perpetrated on over a million Kosovar Albanians. Nato leaders also promised to abandon the view that the Balkans are a non-European zone of disorder and recurring hatreds by integrating the region with the economic and security structures that brought peace to western Europe after 1945. Time will tell whether these expensive pledges, made in the heat of war, will be redeemed by those who made them or their successors.

The lazy statecraft of external-policy makers has turned the Balkans into a European danger zone. Unless a new approach based on conflict prevention and permitting ill-used Balkan peoples to enjoy the same opportunities as the West emerges from the war in Kosovo, there is every likelihood that Balkan wars and crises will be a feature of the new millennium as they were of the old.

For Further Reading

Barbara Jelavich, *History of the Balkans* (two volumes; Cambridge University Press 1995); *Unfinished Peace: Report of The International Commission on the Balkans* (Aspen Institute/ Carnegie Endowment For International Peace, 1996); Tim Judah, *The Serbs: History, Myth and the Destruction of Yugoslavia* (Yale University Press, 1997); C.M. Woodhouse, *Modern Greece, A Short History* (Faber 1998). Noel Malcolm, *Kosovo: A Short History* (Macmillan 1998).

TOM GALLAGHER is Professor of Ethnic Peace and Conflict at Bradford University. His *Europe's Turbulent South-East* is to be published in 2000 by Harwood.

This article first appeared in *History Today*, September 1999, pp. 45–51. © 1999 by History Today, Ltd. Reprinted by permission.

The End

Astrophysicists say that now they can finally tell us how the universe will expire—and it's not with a bang!

MICHAEL D. LEMONICK

For those who live in a city or near one, the night sky isn't much to look at—just a few scattered stars in a smoggy, washed-out expanse. In rural Maine, though, or North Dakota, or the desert Southwest, the view is quite different. Even without a telescope, you can see thousands of stars twinkling in shades of blue, red and yellow-white, with the broad Milky Way cutting a ghostly swath from one horizon to the other. No wonder our ancient ancestors peered up into the heavens with awe and reverence; it's easy to imagine gods and mythical heroes inhabiting such a luminous realm.

Yet for all the magnificence of the visible stars, astronomers know they are only the first shimmering veil in a cosmos vast beyond imagination. Armed with ever more powerful telescopes, these explorers of time and space have learned that the Milky Way is a huge, whirling pinwheel made of 100 billion or more stars; that tens of billions of other galaxies lie beyond its edges; and, most astonishing of all, that these galaxies are rushing headlong away from one another in the aftermath of an explosive cataclysm known as the Big Bang.

That event—the literal birth of time and space some 15 billion years ago—has been understood, at least in its broadest outlines, since the 1960s. But in more than a third of a century, the best minds in astronomy have failed to solve the mystery of what happens at the other end of time. Will the galaxies continue to fly apart forever, their glow fading until the cosmos is cold and dark? Or will the expansion slow to a halt, reverse direction and send the stars crashing back together in a final, apocalyptic Big Crunch? Despite decades of observations with the most powerful telescopes at their disposal, astronomers simply haven't been able to decide.

But thanks to a series of remarkable discoveries—the most recent just two weeks ago—the question may now have been settled once and for all. Scientists who were betting on a Big Crunch liked to quote Robert Frost: "Some say the world will end in fire,/ some say in ice./ From what I've tasted of desire/ I hold with those who favor fire." Those in the other camp preferred T.S. Eliot: "This is the way the world ends/ Not with a bang but a whimper." The verdict seems to be in: T.S. Eliot wins.

Why do we care? For one thing, this is a question that has haunted humans for as long as we have walked the earth. A definitive answer—if that is indeed what we have—will force philosophers and religious leaders to rethink their assumptions and beliefs about eternity and how the world will end. For scientists, meanwhile, there are certain details in these discoveries that have profound—and bizarre—implications. For example, the new observations bolster the theory of inflation: the notion that the universe when it was still smaller than an atom went through a period of turbo-charged expansion, flying apart (in apparent, but not actual, contradiction of Albert Einstein's theories of relativity) faster than the speed of light.

An equally unsettling implication is that the universe is pervaded with a strange sort of "antigravity," a concept originally proposed by and later abandoned by Einstein as the greatest blunder of his life. This force, which has lately been dubbed "dark energy," isn't just keeping the expansion from slowing down, it's making the universe fly apart faster and faster all the time, like a rocket ship with the throttle wide open.

It gets stranger still. Not only does dark energy swamp ordinary gravity but an invisible substance known to scientists as "dark matter" also seems to outweigh the ordinary stuff of stars, planets and people by a factor of 10 to 1. "Not only are we not at the center of the universe," University of California, Santa Cruz, astrophysical theorist Joel Primack has commented, "we aren't even made of the same stuff the universe is."

These discoveries raise more questions than they answer. For example, just because scientists know dark matter is there doesn't mean they understand what it really is. Same goes for dark energy. "If you thought the universe was hard to comprehend before," says University of Chicago astrophysicist Michael Turner, "then you'd better take some smart pills, because it's only going to get worse."

Echo of the Big Bang

Things seemed a lot simpler back in 1965 when two astronomers at Bell Labs in Holmdel, N.J., provided a resounding confirmation of the Big Bang theory, at the time merely one of several ideas floating around on how the cosmos began. The

How Does the Universe Curve?

According to Einstein, the universe is a space-time continuum that can take one of three forms, determined by the amount of matter and energy it contains. The best way to visualize them is with a two-dimensional analogy

Positive Curvature The cosmos is like a sphere. Travel far enough and you'll come back to the starting point. Draw a triangle, and it will have more than 180°. Without dark energy, this universe will slow, stop and recollapse; with it, the expansion will continue.

Flat You'll never return to your starting point; triangles have precisely 180 degrees, as they do in high school geometry. Even without dark energy, this universe will expand forever, but more and more slowly all the time. With it, the expansion gets ever faster. This is the shape of our universe, according to the latest observations

Negative Curvature Travelers never return; triangles always have less than 180°. And expansion will barely slow, even without dark energy. Until recently, most of the astronomical evidence favored this shape

discovery happened purely by accident: Arno Penzias and Robert Wilson were trying to get an annoying hiss out of a communications antenna, and after ruling out every other explanation—including the residue of bird droppings—they decided the hiss was coming from outer space.

Unbeknownst to the duo, physicists at nearby Princeton University were about to turn their antenna on the heavens to look for that same signal. Astronomers had known since the 1920s that the galaxies were flying apart. But theorists had belatedly realized a key implication: the whole cosmos must at one point have been much smaller and hotter. About 300,000 years after the instant of the Big Bang, the entire visible universe would have been a cloud of hot, incredibly dense gas, not much bigger than the Milky Way is now, glowing white hot like a blast furnace or the surface of a star. Because this cosmic glow had no place to go, it must still be there, albeit so attenuated that it took the form of feeble microwaves. Penzias and Wilson later won the Nobel Prize for the accidental discovery of this radio hiss from the dawn of time.

The discovery of the cosmic-microwave background radiation convinced scientists that the universe really had sprung from an initial Big Bang some 15 billion years ago. They immediately set out to learn more. For one thing, they began trying to probe this cosmic afterglow for subtle variations in intensity. It's clear through ordinary telescopes that matter isn't spread evenly throughout the modern universe. Galaxies tend to huddle relatively close to one another, dozens or even hundreds of them in clumps known as clusters and superclusters. In between, there is essentially nothing at all.

That lumpiness, reasoned theorists, must have evolved from some original lumpiness in the primordial cloud of matter that gave rise to the background radiation. Slightly denser knots of matter within the cloud—forerunners of today's superclusters—should have been slightly hotter than average. So some scientists began looking for subtle hot spots.

Fire or Ice?

Others, meanwhile, attacked a different aspect of the problem. As the universe expands, the combined gravity from all the matter within it tends to slow that expansion, much as the earth's gravity tries to pull a rising rocket back to the ground. If the pull is strong enough, the expansion will stop and reverse itself; if not, the cosmos will go on getting bigger, literally for-

ever. Which is it? One way to find out is to weigh the cosmos—to add up all the stars and all the galaxies, calculate their gravity and compare that with the expansion rate of the universe. If the cosmos is moving at escape velocity, no Big Crunch.

Trouble is, nobody could figure out how much matter there actually was. The stars and galaxies were easy; you could see them. But it was noted as early as the 1930s that something lurked out there besides the glowing stars and gases that astronomers could see. Galaxies in clusters were orbiting one another too fast; they should, by rights, be flying off into space like untethered children flung from a fast-twirling merry-go-round. Individual galaxies were spinning about their centers too quickly too; they should long since have flown apart. The only possibility: some form of invisible dark matter was holding things together, and while you could infer the mass of dark matter in and around galaxies, nobody knew if it also filled the dark voids of space, where its effects would not be detectable.

So astrophysicists tried another approach: determine whether the expansion was slowing down, and by how much. That's what Brian Schmidt, a young astronomer at the Mount Stromlo Observatory in Australia, set out to do in 1995. Along with a team of colleagues, he wanted to measure the cosmic slowdown, known formally as the "deceleration parameter." The idea was straightforward: look at the nearby universe and measure how fast it is expanding. Then do the same for the distant universe, whose light is just now reaching us, having been emitted when the cosmos was young. Then compare the two.

Schmidt's group and a rival team led by Saul Perlmutter, of Lawrence Berkeley Laboratory in California, used very similar techniques to make the measurements. They looked for a kind of explosion called a Type Ia supernova, occurring when an aging star destroys itself in a gigantic thermonuclear blast. Type Ia's are so bright that they can be seen all the way across the universe and are uniform enough to have their distance from Earth accurately calculated.

That's key: since the whole universe is expanding at a given rate at any one time, more distant galaxies are flying away from us faster than nearby ones. So Schmidt's and Perlmutter's teams simply measured the distance to these supernovas (deduced from their brightness) and their speed of recession (deduced by the reddening of their light, a phenomenon affecting all moving bodies, known to physicists as the Doppler shift). Combining these two pieces of information gave them the expansion rate, both now and in the past.

Dark Energy

By 1998 both teams knew something very weird was happening. The cosmic expansion should have been slowing down a lot or a little, depending on whether it contained a lot of matter or a little—an effect that should have shown up as distant supernovas, looking brighter than you would expect compared with closer ones. But, in fact, they were dimmer—as if the expansion was speeding up. "I kept running the numbers through the computer," recalls Adam Riess, a Space Telescope Science Institute astronomer analyzing the data from Schmidt's group, "and the answers made no sense. I was sure there was a bug in the program." Perlmutter's group, meanwhile, spent the better part of the year trying to figure out what could be producing its own crazy results.

In the end, both teams adopted Sherlock Holmes' attitude: once you have eliminated the impossible, whatever is left, no matter how improbable, has got to be true. The universe was indeed speeding up, suggesting that some sort of powerful antigravity force was at work, forcing the galaxies to fly apart even as ordinary gravity was trying to draw them together. "It helped a lot," says Riess, "that Saul's group was getting the same answer we were. When you have a strange result, you like to have company." Both groups announced their findings almost simultaneously, and the accelerating universe was named Discovery of the Year for 1998 by *Science* magazine.

For all its seeming strangeness, antigravity did have a history, one dating back to Einstein's 1916 theory of general relativity. The theory's equations suggest that the universe must be either expanding or contracting; it couldn't simply sit there. Yet the astronomers of the day, armed with relatively feeble telescopes, insisted that it was doing just that. Grumbling about having to mar the elegance of his beloved mathematics, Einstein added an extra term to the equations of relativity. Called the cosmological constant, it amounted to a force that opposed gravity and propped up the universe.

A decade later, though, Edwin Hubble discovered that the universe was expanding after all. Einstein immediately and with great relief discarded the cosmological constant, declaring it to be the biggest blunder of his life. (If he had stuck to his guns, he might have nabbed another Nobel.)

Even so, the idea of a cosmological constant wasn't entirely dead. The equations of quantum physics independently suggested that the seemingly empty vacuum of space should be seething with a form of energy that would act just like Einstein's disowned antigravity. Problem was, this force would have been so powerful that it would have blown the universe apart before atoms could form, let alone galaxies—which it clearly did not. "The value particle physicists predict for the cosmological constant," admits Chicago's Turner, "is the most embarrassing number in physics."

Aside from that detail, the Einstein connection made the idea of dark energy, or antigravity, seem somewhat less nutty when Schmidt and Perlmutter weighed in. Of course, some astrophys-

icists had lingering doubts. Maybe the observers didn't really have the supernovas' brightness right; perhaps the light from faraway stellar explosions was dimmed by some sort of dust. The unique properties of a cosmological constant, moreover, would make the universe slow down early on, then accelerate. That's because dark energy grows as a function of space. There wasn't much space in the young, small universe, so back then the braking force of gravity would have reigned supreme. More recently, the force of gravity fell off as the distance between galaxies grew and that same increase made for more dark energy. Nobody had probed deeply enough to find out what was really going on in the distant past.

Or rather, nobody had got enough data. Back in 1997, astronomers Mark Phillips of the Space Telescope Science Institute and Ron Gilliland of the Carnegie Institute of Washington had used the Hubble Space Telescope to spot a distant supernova designated SN 1997ff and, with the help of Peter Nugent, a Lawrence Berkeley astronomer on Perlmutter's team, had determined its speed of recession from Earth. Nugent couldn't figure out the distance, though: determining the brightness of a Type Ia calls for not just one but several measurements, spread over time.

On the rival team, Riess knew of the discovery, but he learned soon afterward that other Hubble photos had also caught the supernova, completely by chance. So one day last summer, he recalls, "I called Peter and began fishing around for information. I guess I wasn't especially cagey. He said almost right away, 'Are you asking about 1997ff?'"

Rather than try to scoop each other, the friendly rivals decided to cooperate—and soon realized they had stumbled onto something truly astonishing. The new supernova, some 50% closer to the beginning of the universe than any supernova known before, was far brighter than had been predicted. That neatly eliminated the idea of dust, since a more distant star should have been even more dust-dimmed than nearer ones. But the level of brightness also signaled that this supernova was shining when the expansion of the cosmos was still slowing down. "Usually," says Riess, "we see weird things and try to make our models of the universe fit. This time we put up a hoop for the observations to jump through in advance, and they did—which makes it a lot more convincing."

Probing the Cosmic Fireball

What makes it still more convincing is that an entirely different kind of observation—the long-standing search for lumpiness in the cosmic background radiation—now suggests independently that dark energy is real. The lumps themselves were first detected about a decade ago, thanks to the Cosmic Background Explorer satellite. At the time, astrophysicist and COBE spokesman George Smoot declared that "if you're religious, it's like seeing God."

But it was more like seeing God through dirty Coke-bottle glasses: the satellite saw lumps but couldn't determine much about them. In April, though, scientists offered up much sharper images from a balloon-borne experiment called BOOMERANG (Balloon Observations of Millimetric Extragalactic Radiation and Geophysics), which lofted instruments into the Antarctic stratosphere; from another named MAXIMA (Millimeter Anisotropy Experiment Imaging Array, which did the same over the U.S.); and from a microwave telescope on the ground at the South Pole, called DASI (Degree Angular Scale Interferometer).

All these measurements pretty much agreed with one another, confirming that the lumps scientists saw were real, not some malfunction in the telescopes. And two weeks ago, astronomers from the Sloan Digital Sky Survey confirmed that this primordial lumpiness has carried over into modern times. The five-year mission of the survey, to make a 3-D map of the cosmos, is far from complete, but scientists reported at the American Astronomical Society's spring meeting in Pasadena, Calif., that it is clearer than ever that galaxies cluster together into huge clumps that reflect conditions that existed soon after the Big Bang.

To the unaided eye, the images are meaningless. A statistical analysis, however, shows that the early lumps—actually patches of slightly warmer or cooler radiation—don't come at random but rather at certain fixed sizes. "It's as though you're studying dogs," says University of Pennsylvania astrophysicist Max Tegmark, "and you find out that they come in just three types: Labrador, toy poodle and Chihuahua."

That turns out to be enormously important. Knowing the characteristic sizes and also the temperatures, to a millionth of a degree, of these warm and cool regions gives theoretical physicists all sorts of information about the newborn cosmos. They were already pretty sure, from the equations of nuclear physics and from measurements of the relative amounts of hydrogen, helium and lithium in the universe, that protons, neutrons and electrons (the building blocks of every atom in the cosmos) add up to only about 5% of the so-called critical density—what it would take to bring the cosmic expansion essentially to a halt by means of gravity.

But when you add Tegmark's "dogs," plus the more esoteric equations of sub-nuclear physics, it turns out that an additional 30% of the needed matter most likely comes in the form of mysterious particles that have been identified only in theory, never directly observed—particles with quirky names like neutralino and axion. These are the mysterious dark matter, or most of it anyway. The cosmic background radiation itself began to shine when the universe was 300,000 years old, but the temperature fluctuations were set in place when it was just a split-second old. "It's pretty cool," says Tegmark, "to be able to look back that far."

The Flat Universe

The dogs also yield another key bit of information: they tell theorists how the universe is curved, in the Einsteinian sense. There's no way to convey this concept to a nonphysicist except by two-dimensional analogy (see How Does the Universe Curve?). The surface of a sphere has what's called positive curvature; if you go far enough in one direction, you will never get to the edge but you will eventually return to your starting point. An infinitely large sheet of paper is flat and, because it is infinite, also edgeless. And a saddle that extends forever is consid-

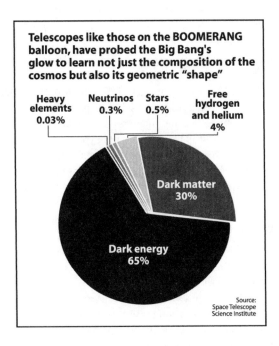

Telescopes like those on the BOOMERANG balloon, have probed the Big Bang's glow to learn not just the composition of the cosmos but also its geometric "shape"

Heavy elements 0.03%
Neutrinos 0.3%
Stars 0.5%
Free hydrogen and helium 4%
Dark matter 30%
Dark energy 65%

Source: Space Telescope Science Institute

ered edgeless and negatively curved. It also turns out that any triangle you draw on the paper has angles that add up to 180[degrees], but the sphere's angles are always greater than 180[degrees], and the saddle's always less.

Same goes for the universe, but with one more dimension. According to Einstein, the whole thing could be positively or negatively curved or flat (but don't try to imagine in what direction it might be curved; it's quite impossible to visualize). "What the new measurements tell us," says Turner, "is that the universe is in fact flat. Draw a triangle that reaches all the way across the cosmos, and the angles will always add up to 180[degrees]."

According to Einstein, the universe's curvature is determined by the amount of matter and energy it contains. The universe we evidently live in could have been flattened purely by matter—but the new discoveries prove that ordinary matter and exotic particles add up to only about 35% of what you would need. Ergo, the extra curvature must come from some unseen energy—just about the amount, it turns out, suggested by the supernova observations. "I was highly dubious about dark energy based only on supernovas," says Princeton astrophysicist Edwin Turner (no relation to Michael, though the two often refer to each other as "my evil twin"). "This makes me take dark energy more seriously."

The flatness of the universe also means the theory of inflation has passed a key test. Originally conceived around 1980 (in the course of elementary-particle, not astronomical, research), the theory says the entire visible universe grew from a speck far smaller than a proton to a nugget the size of a grapefruit, almost instantaneously, when the whole thing was .0000000000000000000000000000000001 sec. old. This turbo-expansion was driven by something like dark energy but a whole lot stronger. What we call the universe, in short, came from almost nowhere in next to no time. Says M.I.T.'s Alan Guth, a pioneer of inflation theory: "I call the universe the ultimate free lunch." One of the consequences of inflation, predicted 20 years ago, was that the universe must be flat—as it now turns out to be.

If these observations continue to hold up, astrophysicists can be pretty sure they have assembled the full parts list for the cosmos at last: 5% ordinary matter, 35% exotic dark matter and about 60% dark energy. They also have a pretty good idea of the universe's future. All the matter put together doesn't have enough gravity to stop the expansion; beyond that, the antigravity effect of dark energy is actually speeding up the expansion. And because the amount of dark energy will grow as space gets bigger, its effect will only increase.

The Fate of the Cosmos

That means that the 100 billion or so galaxies we can now see through our telescopes will zip out of range, one by one. Tens of billions of years from now, the Milky Way will be the only galaxy we're directly aware of (other nearby galaxies, including the Large Magellanic Cloud and the Andromeda galaxy, will have drifted into, and merged with, the Milky Way).

By then the sun will have shrunk to a white dwarf, giving little light and even less heat to whatever is left of Earth, and entered a long, lingering death that could last 100 trillion years—or a thousand times longer than the cosmos has existed to date. The same will happen to most other stars, although a few will end their lives as blazing supernovas. Finally, though, all that will be left in the cosmos will be black holes, the burnt-out cinders of stars and the dead husks of planets. The universe will be cold and black.

But that's not the end, according to University of Michigan astrophysicist Fred Adams. An expert on the fate of the cosmos and co-author with Greg Laughlin of *The Five Ages of the Universe* (Touchstone Books; 2000), Adams predicts that all this dead matter will eventually collapse into black holes. By the time the universe is 1 trillion trillion trillion trillion trillion trillion years old, the black holes themselves will disintegrate into stray particles, which will bind loosely to form individual "at-oms" larger than the size of today's universe. Eventually, even these will decay, leaving a featureless, infinitely large void. And that will be that—unless, of course, whatever inconceivable event that launched the original Big Bang should recur, and the ultimate free lunch is served once more.

Astronomers and physicists are a cautious crew, and they insist that the mind-bending discoveries about dark matter, dark energy and the flatness of space-time must be confirmed before they are accepted without reservation. "We're really living dangerously," says Chicago's Turner. "We've got this absurd, wonderful picture of the universe, and now we've got to test it." There could be surprises to come: an Einstein-style cosmological constant, for example, is the leading candidate for dark energy, but it could in principle be something subtly different—a force that could even change directions someday, to reinforce rather than oppose gravity.

In any case, new tests of these bizarre ideas will not be too long in coming. Next week a satellite will launch from Cape Canaveral to make the most sensitive observations ever of the cosmic background radiation. Supernova watchers, meanwhile, are lobbying NASA for a dedicated telescope so they won't have to queue up for time on the badly oversubscribed Hubble. And lower-tech telescopes and microwave detectors, both on the ground and lofted into the air aboard balloons, will continue to refine their measurements.

If the latest results do hold up, some of the most important questions in cosmology—how old the universe is, what it's made of and how it will end—will have been answered, only about 70 years after they were first posed. By the time the final chapter of cosmic history is written—further in the future than our minds can grasp—humanity, and perhaps even biology, will long since have vanished. Yet it's conceivable that consciousness will survive, perhaps in the form of a disembodied digital intelligence. If so, then someone may still be around to note that the universe, once ablaze with the light of uncountable stars, has become an unimaginably vast, cold, dark and profoundly lonely place.

Why We Study Western Civ

STEVEN OZMENT

A few years ago, I gave a talk to an audience in a small German town based on a book I had written about a prominent but dysfunctional family that had lived there 450 years earlier. When asked how I came upon and researched this story, I described a three-year period in which I spent fully as many waking hours reading and pondering the remains of my sixteenth-century subjects as I did in dealing with my daily life in present-day America. The next morning the headline over my photograph in the local newspaper read: "This is a Man From the Sixteenth Century." Although not such for the local journalist, certainly for a historian there could not have been a greater compliment!

History is every civilization's clinical record of human nature and behavior, for which reason it has always been cautionary and problem-solving for subsequent generations. We study the past not to avoid repeating it but to learn how previous generations survived the same mistakes we make. Historians worthy of the name have an ability to live imaginatively in the past as fully as they do in the present. In doing so they are chameleon-like, but not for the purpose of camouflage and deceit. Only by such abstraction can they become knowing insiders in worlds that no longer exist. In this regard, historians are people with dual or multiple citizenship, only their second and third countries are past civilizations and distant ages.

Who Needs History?

The historian's natural enemy is people who know, and want only to know, their own immediate culture, which they accept as a supreme measure of humankind. It is the civic duty of historians to remind their fellow citizens that they are neither the first nor necessarily the most interesting people to have walked the earth, and that nations that lead their lives as if they were have often suffered terrible consequences.

Today, the distant past is a neglected vital resource. History, fills comparatively fewer shelves in local book stores and libraries, and the history that is most prominent there is about familiar subjects within our contemporary culture. Of the 16 books on the mid June 2004, *New York Times* nonfiction best-seller list, only two were history, both well-worn American (Ron Chernow's *Alexander Hamilton* and Cokie Roberts' *Founding Mothers*), while Dan [Brown's] record-breaking misty fiction, *The Da Vinci Code*, led all categories of adult reading by wide margins. History majors in American colleges and universities overwhelmingly

show a similar sensibility. Over the last three years only 20 percent of history majors at Harvard University enrolled in a field-specific tutorial in premodern history (ancient, medieval, or early modern history). For the other 80 percent, the world began in the more comfortable nineteenth century.

A major reason for such provinciality is the pervasive belief that the past is a benighted world of superstition and prejudice, or, less threatening, a world of fantasy and romance, in either case no proper guide for an emancipated modern age. "Bunk" was Henry Ford's famous word for it. Today, history is another word for dead and gone—"toast," as it is said—and any who think it a Rosetta Stone for their civilization risk irrelevance and scorn.

In casting about recently for the right venues for a book tour, my publicist was repeatedly told that "current events," not history, is what audiences want: talking heads and familiar faces, not the ponderous minds of strangers. "Current events" means today's business (national politics, foreign affairs, and popular culture), issues connected with the recent presidential election, an exit from Iraq, and Hollywood's latest. Having become society's most trusted guides, the present and the future, the one ephemeral, the other imaginary, effectively block a long perspective on our times from the distant past.

This, of course, is not a new problem for Americans. Woodrow Wilson, who was a professor and president at Princeton University before becoming the twenty-eighth president of the United States, blamed the historical illiteracy of his contemporaries on "a certain great degeneracy," born of misplaced trust in science:

> We believe in the present and in the future more than in the past, and deem the newest theory of society the likeliest. This is the disservice scientific study has done us; it has given us agnosticism in the realm of philosophy and scientific anarchism in the field of all politics. It has made the legislator confident that he can create and the philosopher sure that God cannot. Past experience is discredited and the laws of matter are supposed to apply to spirit and the makeup of society.

There have been times, however, when people believed "today" to be the last day to date in the history of human civilization, a profound legacy of baggage and proven ways. Our age is not one of them. "Today" has rather become the first day of the rest of one's life: an untrammeled fresh start, endlessly experimental, and with little need to look back. The longest shelves in local bookstores and libraries are filled with fiction, self-help, and current events (mostly the lives and politics of American leaders)—immediate, self-referential information serving personal amusement and struggle.

The battle between the ancients and the moderns has accordingly become far more difficult for the ancients. In this hermeneutical turn, a waxing present without much of a track record holds greater authority than a well-documented but waning past. Skeptical of history's inescapability and utility, not a few modern historians believe their calling is to sever the dead hand of the past rather than pore over its vital remains. For the reading public, the study of the past often seems a search for forerunners and blockers of modernity, a parade of people, ideas, and crises either lauded for having prepared the way to truths we hold to be self-evident, or excoriated for having opposed them—history as self-confirmation.

In the best historical science, one becomes an expert on a particular age by gaining mastery of preceding ones. That is because human life in individual cultures is interconnected from generation to generation and century to century. Subsequent events and developments root themselves in and incorporate previous ones, not unlike the way the early years in an individual's life continue to inform and shape the later ones. The most crucial and reliable information new generations need to seize their future effectively does not lie before them, but behind them. The past is more powerful and controlling than any future we can contemplate. This side of eternity, we are more the residues of history than the stuff the stars are made of.

Western Civ and Its Discontents

For new generations of high school and college students, rescue from present-day historical escapism and its great informational loss may begin in the mighty European or Western Civilization survey, which leaps over and through 25 centuries, from Mesopotamia onward, in a single academic year. Conceptually born in nineteenth-century European efforts to distinguish the culture and values of a presumedly superior West over those of a presumedly inferior East, Western Civ has been both a beloved and a hated introduction to the study of history in post-World War I America.

Three universities—Harvard, Columbia, and Chicago—played essential roles in creating this American original, appropriately born as an academic course of study in a nation that has believed itself to be a beacon to the world. Of the three universities, Columbia's required general education course ("Contemporary Civilization"), introduced in 1919 and expanded in 1929, and the teaching and writings of Columbia professor James Harvey Robinson, were key. In 1912, Robinson defended a long social, scientific, narrative history focused not on "fortuitous prominence" but on "the normal conduct and serious achievements of mankind in the past," peaking in modern Europe and America. Although he never taught an undergraduate course in Western Civ, the model he developed in his graduate courses and books between 1903 and 1919, which surveyed European history from the Middle Ages to the present, sowed the

seeds. Between 1925 and 1930, a unified history of these centuries became the textbook we know today as Western Civ.

With a view to both world wars, the Western Civ course in America justified Allied sacrifice by presenting the creativity and glory of that civilization at a time when barbarian Germans threatened to destroy it from within. Ironically, it was the ancient and medieval forebears of those same Germans who originally mixed Judeo-Christian, Greco-Roman, and Byzantine cultures into the civilization we call European or Western.

While modern-day European educators take note of the Western Civ course as taught in America, and occasionally entertain versions of their own, the course has always seemed too thin and audacious for the traditional European university, which prefers a history that takes short, measured, finished strides. For critics on both sides of the Atlantic, impeccable period pieces and boutique courses reflective of academic specialization and the modern scholarly monograph are the rule. To its harshest critics abroad and at home, American Western Civ remains a Whiggish, Eurocentric sham of a course.

Yet no other battery of academic courses fulfills so well the historian's civic duty to inform his fellow citizens of the opportunities they inherit from the past and the burdens they must carry from it into the future. For most non-history majors in colleges and universities, Western Civ is their only chronologically deep, college-level acquaintance with European history. Chronicling, mapping, and explaining Europe's development from antiquity to the present, this sweeping survey has helped untold numbers of undergraduates find their place and time in the world.

Favoring a macro-historical approach around a socio-political narrative, the more recent versions of this bird's-eye view of history can be as open-ended conceptually as they are chronologically. Western Civ is an old-fashioned course that continually shops for new clothes, and over the years it has learned to be both down-to-earth and stylish, able to dig postholes in, as well as scan, centuries. The best textbooks treat events and structures, dates and ideas, message and reception, synthesis and analysis, freedom and determination as two peas in a pod. They also fold recent research into new editions and address the growing interest in the West's previously neglected world profile.

Still, it is difficult to imagine a successful Western Civ survey in which a strongly thematic or theoretical approach predominates, and not just for want of pages and time. Making sense of the past as it exists in contemporary records and is retold by modern storytellers living well after the fact opens many doors to subjectivity and *parti pris,* irresolution and ideology. The great danger to the genre is the loss of the story line of the past amid modern doubt and bias, conjecture and special pleading. Much as colorful loosestrife displaces the more useful but less strongly rooted marsh cattail, so do these four horse men of deconstruction and political correctness threaten to trample the vulnerable European narrative.

Reading History Forward

That is not to suggest that fables should hold priority over criticism or bare facts over grand ideas. The unexamined narrative is no more worthy than the antinarrative. However, if Western

Civ is to continue to achieve its goal, which is to spark lasting curiosity about the past, traditional narrative must be the sun and modern theory the moon. With regard to basic information about the formative forces of history, Western Civ presents a highly credible narrative. No knowledgeable person can doubt that Martin Luther laid the foundation stone of religious freedom and pluralism in Wittenberg in 1517, or that the French Revolution changed the relationship between the individual and the state forever. These are watershed events to be handed down to new generations, even though Luther's success came in spite of himself and the French Revolution was quick to undermine its own ideals.

On the other hand, there is no hard and fast consensus on what either the Reformation or the French Revolution meant to contemporaries, who were divided into two sides. Nor is there any sure agreement why those events should be important to an even more opinionated modern age. Over the last two decades, a prominent, theory-driven new historiography, smitten with popular culture and fighting notions of early modernization, has argued that no sharp breaks with the past occurred in the great Protestant lands of Germany and England, and also that where the Reformation was most successful, namely, in iconoclastic fury and embrace of the state, its legacy was harmful to posterity.

The medieval Crusades and family life raise similar issues of meaning and legacy. Contemporary Christians, Jews, and Muslims left different assessments of the Crusaders, and modern scholars of family and gender draw diametrically opposed accounts of spousal and parental love from surviving criminal records and family archives. Between contemporary perceptions and the resifting of evidence by historians, a sense of futility in dealing with the past threatens. But given such sources, one need not manufacture virtual histories to get at the truth. Counterfactual questions are endemic to the smallest historical event; for the wide-eyed and willing, history opens its own alternative paths.

As a rule, Western Civ has treated history's contradictions as more enriching than undermining of narrative. Exploring the reasons why medieval Christians, Muslims, and Jews held differing views of the Crusaders, students receive a lasting lesson in cultural dissonance. In much the same way, conflicting texts and contexts reveal the variables and constants in the family life of the past.

The great strength of the Western Civ survey within the history curriculum is that it reads history chronologically forward, not backwards from a commanding latter day event or popular modern theory, a strength that may excuse its sometimes plodding narrative. Since history is not an equal opportunity employer, what is possible and deemed good in one era is not necessarily such in another, a truism to bear in mind when one evaluates the past, or, more ambitiously, sets out to change the world.

The modern inclination to read German history backwards from the 1930s, or to read premodern history generally in the light of the civil rights movements of the 1960s, is a highly prejudicial perspective on the past that can only find fault. Being German, or being free, has not meant the same thing in every time and place. For most of their long history, Germans success-

fully embraced authority and order without totalitarianism and pursued freedom and equality without liberal democracy. Totalitarianism and democracy have been twentieth-century experiments for Germans, not their mainstream historical polity. Only the historian's carefully cultivated contemporaneity with the past, his ability to "be there" in imagination and the language of an age, makes clear both the great difference and continuity between the past and the present.

In the postmodern world, many can imagine nothing worse than the infringement of individual liberties. Yet throughout most of history, when a choice had to be made, every age and culture has recognized that physical security is more basic to life than the freedom to come and go as one pleases. Before free and vibrant societies can exist, there must first be safety in the streets, productive work, and food on the table. Freedom is not everything; it is only the icing on a very large cake, which is the essential thing. That cake is a mix of stable political institutions, effective educational systems, and fluid social organizations. Freedom is the easy part; the discipline to build and maintain the pillars that support it is what is hard. Liberty and democracy are utterly meaningless concepts if all one is doing is trying to feed oneself and stay alive.

For this reason, we find few homilies in the past extolling egalitarian ideals of freedom. Most societies in the past believed a perverse egalitarianism to be their major problem: too many self-absorbed people and groups doing as they pleased, fragmenting and provoking society, making it impossible for strong cultural bonds to unite rival groups. What has been missing, according to history's contemporary critics, is the citizen's or subject's sense of obligation to a larger world beyond the individual, the family, and the clan. Even the Athenians, who created democracy and arguably loved it most, did not hesitate to suspend their constitution and allow despots to rule over them when aristocratic factions and peasant revolts threatened to destroy civilization. In the rural societies of the Middle Ages, the great problem of life was not to overthrow a tyrant, but to find an effective one. Resort to such rule in time of crisis became an honored political tradition in Europe down through the Renaissance. And therein lies a vital lesson of history for a Western world puzzled by other cultures' rejection of liberal democracy.

Western Civ Meets Global Civ

As an academic dean in the 1980s, I recall the student who protested having to take courses outside of her major. When I asked why, she explained that she had to tutor the alien classes in Michel Foucault's philosophy before there could be any fruitful discussion or proper conclusion! Having grown up with the Internet, the present student generation, to its credit, likes to gather its own information. Unfortunately, it also wants that information delivered in bottom-line fashion without difficult labor and circuitous argument. Yet the same students recognize that their professors' theories and models, while capable of sparking cool, consensual discussions, lack legs and, in the end, indoctrinate.

Given this situation, it is better to give students a variety of contemporary keyholes onto the life of the past than to extend to them a presumed magical key to human nature. There, in the past, they may behold, firsthand, struggles not unlike those of their own age and watch their own lives being played out in different times and places, even romantically, as in the riveting twelfth-century love story of Abelard and Heloise. In present circumstances, merely whetting an undergraduate's appetite for historical perspective and precedent may be challenge and accomplishment enough. How skillfully students ultimately swim is not as important as their initial jump into the great pool of the past. For it is only in their thrashing about there that life-sustaining historical thinking is born.

In introducing undergraduates to the study of history, the Western Civ survey has generally spared them heavy doses of modern theory. It has rather suited them up in basic chronology and geography, immersed them in the most accessible document pools (translations), and let them sink or swim on the buoyancy of their native intelligence and the course narrative, a rewarding exercise at any age. Responding to student interest, publishers today increasingly provide auxiliary readings compatible with the textbook narrative, while remaining independent of it. Such aids now compete with the once sovereign textbook narrative, which increasingly appears in briefer versions. And even the condensed narrative faces stiff competition from enterprising "make-your-own-Western-Civ-course" packages assembled from publisher-supplied sources. All of which is further evidence of the adaptive nature of this old, yet ever young, genre. From the beginning too full of itself, Western Civ today still wants to be more.

The Western Civ textbook has long surrounded its socio-political narrative with hundreds of illustrations, scores of primary-source documents, numerous maps and timelines, and a variety of alternating special effects. These great battleships of the history curriculum are well-equipped to respond to the changing conceptual and virtual history interests of students while sustaining a strong narrative. In the textbook to which I contribute. *The Western Heritage*, one special feature ("Art and the West") discusses the works of artists as commentaries on both themselves and their times, ranging from an ancient Akkadian victory stele to present-day minimalist art. Another ("The West and the World") compares the endeavors of European and world civilizations to develop new weapons of destruction and find new sources of energy. Still another feature ("Encountering the Daily Life of the Past") illustrates the pastimes people have shared across class lines, from divination in ancient Mesopotamia to modern European toys.

Although these add-ons threaten to become gimmicks and clutter the text, they also meet two powerful needs: that of students to venture beyond the mainstream textbook narrative and that of editors and authors to document their ingenuity on the textbook battlefield. In such features we also find the cutting edge of macro-historical scholarship and can sense the influence of history's invisible hand.

Today, World Civ competes with Western Civ, while a new Global Civ challenges them both. Can Western Civ survive such competition? Western and World Civ focus on the genesis and evolution of national cultures, while Global Civ targets the crossroads of civilizations where cultures interact and commodities, capital, techniques, slaves, ideas, and even germs are traded. Here, the key interests are not the essence of individual cultures and civilizations but rather who influences whom, who gets what from where, what one culture or civilization owes another—in a word, how the world's civilizations intersect. Although interesting and certainly *au courant*, a history that preoccupies itself primarily with the boundaries of civilizations runs a risk of becoming marginal history.

If the reach of all three exceeds their grasp, surely Western Civ grabs more, and grabs it more firmly. Students must first know their own history in some depth before they can presume to study those of faraway lands, otherwise, how can they recognize a civilization, much less compare it with their own? If Western Civ is Eurocentric, World Civ and Global Civ seem to have no defining center at all. And if World Civ and Global Civ are more inclusive, they are also far more elusive.

What students need to know first and foremost about European and world civilizations is what inspires and haunts them: what each has made of its opportunities and how it has suffered over time. Students want the big picture, blurry though it may be, but they need surer footholds even more. In the end, all history, like all politics, may be local; surely, it will be such if students have only small, modern segments of their own history to compare with the world around them. Before World Civ and Global Civ began their circumnavigations, the pedagogical goal of the Western Civ survey was to interest students in some part of that long history by showing them as much of it as possible. The hope was that each might somewhere, anywhere, become engaged and make history a lifetime guide to one's place and time in the world. Instead of rushing pell-mell to the fiction, self-help, and current events sections of their local bookstores and libraries, the graduates of Western Civ would make a bee-line to the mighty history shelf.

Reprinted with permission from *The Public Interest*, Winter 2005, pp. 111-122.

Index

A

abolitionism, 71, 72
Africa, slave trade and, 70, 73
agriculture: Cinchona trees and, 112; slavery and, 18, 71; Thirty Years' War and, 10
Albert, Prince (England), 75, 76, 77
Albright, Madeleine, 174
Alembert, Jean d', 47
Alexander II (Russia), 87–88, 89–90, 91
Al Qaeda, 171
Amis, Martin, 141
Anglo-Spanish Treaty, 4
Anthony, Susan B., 64
antigravity. *See* dark energy
anti-Semitism, 163–64
archaeology, 53, 124–27
architecture, 128, 129–30
art deco, 128–30
Art Nouveau, 128
arts, the: art deco, 128–30; the Beatles, 165–67; theatre, 11–12, 13–14, 116–19
Asia, trade with, 15–16
astronomy, 178–82
Auschwitz-Birkenau concentration camp, 131–33
Austria, Otto von Bismarck and, 80

B

Bacon, Francis, 47
Baker, Josephine, 129
Balkans, the, 88–89, 174–77
Beatles, the, 165–67
Belgium, invasion of, 122
Bell, Gertrude, 124–27
Belloc, Hilaire, 14
Bernhardt, Sarah, 116–19
Big Bang theory, 178–79
birth rates, in Europe, 171
Bismarck, Otto von, 79–82
black holes, 182
Blair, Tony, 170, 174, 176
Blenheim, Battle of, 39
Blunt, Anthony, 142
bookmaking, 48–49
Boomerang experiment, 180–81
Brezhnev, Leonid, 166, 167
Bulgaria, 88
Bulwer-Lytton, Edward, 13, 14
Burgess, Guy, 142, 143
Burke, Edmund, 28, 62
Bye Plot, 4

C

capitalism, 153. *See also* commerce
Cartesian philosophy. *See* Descartes, René
Catesby, Robert, 2, 4
Catholic Church: the *Encyclopédie* and, 48, 50; Gunpowder Plot and, 2–6; Pope John Paul II, 152–55; Thirty Years' War and, 7–8

censorship, 41, 48
Central Intelligence Agency (CIA), 143, 177
Champollion, Jacques Joseph, 52–54
Chapman, Mark, 165
chemistry, 56–57
Christianity. in the Balkans, 174; slave culture and, 72–73; social reforms and, 77. *See also* Catholic Church
Chrysler Building, 129
Churchill, Winston, 122, 132, 133, 134–38
Churchill Museum, 134–35, 135–36, 137–38
Cinchona trees, 110, 111, 112
Civil Code (France), 67
civilians, Thirty Years' War and, 9–10
Clairmont, Claire, 63
Classical philosophy, 33, 36–37
Clement VIII (pope), 3, 4
Colbert, Jean-Baptiste, 16–17
Cold War, 123, 138, 177
Comédie Française, 117, 118
commerce: Cinchona trees and, 112; East India Company, 20–24; global trade and, 15–19; Great Britain and, 44–45; slavery and, 70–73; state power and, 42–43; surplus extraction and, 157; Voltaire on, 41
communism, 142–44, 153, 177
Communist Party (Soviet Union), 140
Condorcet, Marquis de, 49
Congress of Berlin, 91
consciousness, Descartes and, 33, 35–36
Considerations on the Causes of the Greatness of the Romans and Their Decline (Montesquieu), 41–42, 43–44
Constantinople, control of, 87–92
Corn Laws, 104
cosmological constant, 180
coups d'etat, Napoleon III and, 84
Cox, Percy, 125, 126, 127
creationism, 93, 95
Crimean War, 76–77, 87, 99, 101, 175
Crusades, the, 169, 185
curvature, of the universe, 179, 181
Cyprus, 177

D

dark energy, 178, 180
dark matter, 178, 179
Darwin, Charles, 77, 93–98
dates, French Revolution and, 55, 56
democracy, 185; John Locke and, 25, 27; Napoleon III and, 83, 84
Descartes, René, 32–38
Descent of Man, The (Darwin), 77
deterrence, naval power and, 121–22
dictatorship: Joseph Stalin and, 139–41; Napoleon Bonaparte and, 65–67
Diderot, Denis, 46, 47, 49
Discourse on the Method (Descartes), 33, 34, 35
Disraeli, Benjamin, 88, 89, 90, 91, 103–6

Dreyfus, Alfred, 119
Druze, the, 124
Dumas, Alexandre, 14

E

East India Company, 20–24
economics, study of, 18–19
economy, the: Benjamin Disraeli and, 104–5, 106; Cinchona trees and, 112; East India Company and, 20–24; European, 171–72; global, 15–19; slave trade and, 70–71, 73; state power and, 42–43; surplus extraction and, 158–59; Thirty Years' War and, 9, 10
Eddington, Arthur, 163
Eden, Anthony, 132, 133
Edict of Restitution (1629), 7–8
education, 62, 184, 185–86
Egyptology, 51, 52–54
Einstein, Albert, 161–64, 178, 179, 180, 181
elites, surplus extraction and, 156–59
Elizabeth I (England), 2, 4
empires, 39–45, 156–60
Empire State Building, 129
Encyclopédie, ou Dictionnaire raisonné des sciences, des arts et des métiers, 46–50
England. *See* Great Britain
entertainers: Beatles, the, 165–67; Sarah Bernhardt, 116–19
Essay concerning Human Understanding (Locke), 25, 26
ethnic tensions, 159
Europe: Islam and, 168–73; study of history and, 184; Thirty Years' War, 7–10
evolution: Charles Darwin and, 93–94, 96–97; H.G. Wells and, 146
Exposition Internationale des Arts Décoratifs et Industriels Modernes, 128

F

Fabian Society, 147
Faisal I (Iraq), 125, 126–27
fascism: Napoleon III and, 85; Nazism, 45, 131–33, 134
fashion: art deco, 129; the Beatles and, 166
Fawkes, Guy, 2, 3
feminism, 26, 124; Mary Wollstonecraft and, 60, 61, 64; Queen Victoria and, 74
Ferdinand II (Holy Roman Emperor), 7, 9
Ferme Générale (Tax Farm), 57, 58
films, 119, 130
Fitzgerald, F. Scott, 129
FitzRoy, Robert, 93, 97
folklore, 107–8, 110
foreign affairs, Benjamin Disraeli and, 106
Fracastoro, Girolamo, 108
France: Cardinal Richelieu, 11–14; empire and, 39–40; the *Encyclopédie* and, 46–50; French Revolution, 55, 56–58, 60, 62–63, 185; global economy and, 16–17; Great Britain and, 120; Islam in, 168, 172–73; Na-

Index

poleon Bonaparte and, 65–67; Napoleon III, 83–86; Thirty Years' War and, 8, 9; World War I and, 122

Franco-Prussian War, 85–86

freedom, 185

French Revolution: Antoine Lavoisier and, 55, 56–58; *Encyclopédie* and, 49–50; Mary Wollstonecraft and, 62–63; Napoleon Bonaparte and, 65; study of, 185; women's rights and, 60

G

Galápagos Islands, 93–98

Garnet, Henry, 2, 3

German Confederation, 80, 81

Germany: Islam in, 168; Nazism, 45, 131–33, 134; Otto von Bismarck and, 79–82; Thirty Years' War and, 9; Winston Churchill and, 134, 135; World War I and, 120–23

Getty, J. Arch, 140, 141

Gladstone, William, 88, 90, 105, 106, 175, 176; Queen Victoria and, 77, 78

global civilization, study of, 186

Godwin, William, 63

Gorchakov, Alexander, 87–88, 91

Gould, John, 97

government, forms of: democracy, 25, 27, 83, 84, 185; dictatorship, 65–67; monarchy, 74–78, 79–80, 81, 84, 85, 158

Great Britain: the Balkans and, 175–76; Benjamin Disraeli and, 103–6; East India Company and, 20–24; empire and, 40–41; global economy and, 17–18; government of, 44; Gunpowder Plot and, 2–6; Islam in, 169–70; Kim Philby and, 142–44; Queen Victoria, 74–78; Russia and, 87–92; slavery and, 70–73; World War I and, 120–23

Great Exhibition (1851), 76

Greece, 175, 177

Grey, Edward, 121, 123

Gunpowder Plot, 2–6

H

Hanssen, Robert P., 144

health, 107–9, 110–13

heat exhaustion, 95–96

history, study of, 183–86

History of Woman Suffrage (Stanton and Anthony), 64

Hizb-ut-Tahir, 173

Holocaust, the, 131–33

Holy Roman Empire, 39

honor killings, 168, 169

Hooker, Joseph, 97

Hubble Space Telescope, 180

Hugo, Victor, 117, 118

humanists, 33, 34

human rights, 60

I

I.G. Farben chemical plant, 131, 133

Imlay, Fanny, 63, 64

Imlay, Gilbert, 62–63

immigration, in Europe, 169, 171

India: East India Company and, 20–21, 22, 23; Florence Nightingale and, 101

Indian Mutiny, 77

intelligence services, Kim Philby and, 142–44

Iraq, 125–27, 137

Ireland, Queen Victoria and, 76

Islam, 168–73, 176

J

James, Henry, 147, 148

James I (England), 2, 4

Jaucourt, Louis de, 47

Jeanneret, Charles-Édouard, 128

Jesuits, 2, 3, 4, 5; Descartes and, 33, 37; Pope John Paul II and, 155; as scientists, 111

jingoism, 90, 91

John Paul II (pope), 152–55

Johnson, Joseph, 61, 63

Johnson, Lyndon, 177

Jones, William "Oriental", 52

Judaism, 103, 154, 163

K

Khrushchev, Nikita, 139

Kircher, Athanasius, 37

Korean War, 143

Kosovo, war in, 174

L

Lacépède, Bernard-Germain-Etienne de, 55–56

Lagrange, Joseph Louis, 55, 58

Lavoisier, Antoine, 55–59

law, rule of, 66–67

Lawrence, T. E., 124–25

League of Nations, 147

Le Breton, André-François, 46–47

Le Corbusier. *See* Jeanneret, Charles-Édouard

Lempicka, Tamara de, 129

Lenard, Philipp, 163–64

Lennon, John, 165

liberalism, 27, 29, 101–2

Liberal Party (Great Britain), 100, 101, 104–5

Ligne, Henri de, 116, 117

linguists, 51, 52

literature: art deco and, 129; Benjamin Disraeli and, 103, 104; H.G. Wells, 145–49; history and, 183–84; Victorian era, 77

Locke, John, 25–29

London, East India Company and, 21

Louis XIII (France), 11, 12

Louis XIV (France), 39, 40, 42

Lycée des Arts, 58

M

Maclean, Donald, 142, 143

Main Plot, 4

malaria, treatment of, 110–13

Malesherbes, Chrétien-Guillaume de Lamoignon de, 48

Marat, Jean-Paul, 57

Maria Alexandrovna, Duchess of Edinburgh, 88, 90–91

Marlborough, Duke of (John Churchill), 39

marriage, Queen Victoria and, 74, 75–76

Marx, Karl, 83, 101

mathematics, 34, 35, 162

Meister, Joseph, 109

Melbourne, Lord, 74

merchantilism, 15–19, 23

Mesopotamia. *See* Iraq

Middle East: Europe and, 169; Gertrude Bell and, 124–27

military classes, surplus extraction and, 157

military intelligence, 131, 132

modern responses: to Descartes, 33, 37–38; to Locke, 25; to Winston Churchill, 134–35

monarchy: Napoleon III and, 84, 85; Prussia and, 79–80, 81; Queen Victoria and, 74–78; Sarah Bernhardt and, 116; surplus extraction and, 158

Montesquieu, Baron de La Brède et de (Charles-Louis de Secondat), 41–45

Mott, Lucretia, 64

N

Napoleon Bonaparte, 45, 65–67, 79

Napoleon III (France), 81, 83–86

national debt, Great Britain and, 22

nationalism: in the Balkans, 174–75; in Germany, 79–82

nation states, origins of, 156–57

naval power, Germany and, 121–22

Nazism, 45, 131–33, 134

Netherlands, the, 17–18

Newton, Isaac, 161, 162

Nicholas I (Russia), 87

Nightingale, Florence, 99–102

North America: global economy and, 17–18; slavery and, 70–71, 71–72

nursing, profession of, 97, 99

O

On the Origin of the Species (Darwin), 77, 94

opium trade, 15–16

Ottoman Empire, 87, 125–26, 174

P

Paris Treaty (1856), 88

Pasteur, Louis, 108–9

Peel, Robert, 74, 104

penal laws, 2–3, 4

Philby, Kim, 142–44

Philip III (Spain), 2

Philosophical Investigations (Descartes), 32

Philosophical Letters (Voltaire), 40–41

philosophy: John Locke and, 25–29; René Descartes and, 32–38

photography, 74

physics, 51, 52, 161–64, 178–82

plantation system, 71

police, Napoleon Bonaparte and, 66

political parties, 100, 101, 103–4, 121, 170–71

political philosophies: Benjamin Disraeli and, 103; empire and, 39–45; John Locke and, 25–29

politics: Islam and, 170; Napoleon Bonaparte and, 66–67; Otto von Bismarck and, 79–82; Pope John Paul II and, 152, 153; Queen Victoria and, 75; warfare and, 39–40

polymaths, 52
press, the, 11, 12
professional classes, surplus extraction and, 157
propaganda: Cardinal Richelieu and, 11–12; Napoleon Bonaparte and, 66; Queen Victoria and, 76; surplus extraction and, 157
Protestantism, Thirty Years' War and, 7–8
Prussia, 79–80, 85–86
public health, 99–102
publishing: the *Encyclopédie*, 46–47, 47–49; Mary Wollstonecraft and, 61

Q

quinine, 110–13

R

rabies, 107–9
racism, 71, 136–37, 172
Ramadan, Tariq, 173
Ratzinger, Joseph, 154–55
Reflections on Universal Monarchy in Europe (Montesquieu), 42, 43, 44
Reformation, the, 185
Reign of Terror, 55–56
relativity, theory of, 161, 162
religion: Albert Einstein and, 163; in the Balkans, 174; the *Encyclopédie* and, 48; Great Britain and, 40; Gunpowder Plot and, 2–6; Islam, 168–73; Pope John Paul II, 152–55; slavery and, 72; surplus extraction and, 157–58; theology and, 35, 36; Thirty Years' War and, 7–10
revisionism, historical, 85, 136–37, 141
Revolution of 1848 (France), 83–84
Revolution of 1848 (Germany), 79
Rhodes, Cecil, 120
Richelieu, Cardinal, 8, 9, 11–14
Robinson, James Harvey, 184
Roman Empire, 40–41, 41–42, 43–44
Romantic movement, 12–13, 14
Rosetta Stone, 51, 53
Rousseau, Jean-Jacques, 60, 62
runaway slaves, 72
Russia, 87–92, 120, 122, 175. *See also* Soviet Union, the
Russo-Turkish War (1877-1878), 90–91, 106

S

Sakharov, Andrei, 167
Schlieffen Plan, 122, 123
science fiction, H.G. Wells and, 145–49
scientific method, 46, 47, 49, 50, 100–101, 108–9
scientists: Albert Einstein, 161–64; Antoine Lavoisier, 55–59; Charles Darwin, 93–98; Jesuits as, 111
Scythian lambs, 46
Secondat, Charles-Louis de (Baron de La Brède et de Montesquieu), 41–45
Second Empire, the (France), 85
Secret Intelligence Services (SIS), 143
September 11 attacks, 137

Serbia, 174
Shelley, Mary (Godwin), 63–64
Shelley, Percy Bysshe, 63–64
silver, global trade and, 15–16
Skepticism, philosophy of, 36
skyscrapers, 129
slave labor, Joseph Stalin and, 140
slavery: global economy and, 17–18; Great Britain and, 70–73
Smith, Adam, 15, 18–19
social classes, 76, 105, 171
socialism: H.G. Wells and, 147; John Locke and, 27–28
social reforms: Benjamin Disraeli and, 105–6; Florence Nightingale and, 99–102; Victorian era, 77
Society of Jesus. *See* Jesuits
Solzhenitsyn, Alexander, 167
Soviet Union, the. *See also* Russia: the Beatles and, 165–67; Joseph Stalin, 139–41; Kim Philby and, 142–44
Spain, 3, 4, 15, 16
Spanish Civil War, 142
spies, Kim Philby and, 142–44
Spirit of Laws, The (Montesquieu), 42, 44
Stalin, Joseph, 139–41
Stanton, Elizabeth Cady, 63
statistics, 100–101
stocks and bonds, 21, 22
Suez Canal, 88, 106
supernovas, 180
surplus extraction, role of, 156–60
Sweden, Thirty Years' War and, 8, 9

T

Tabor, Robert, 111
Tarkovsky, Andrei, 167
taxation: French Revolution and, 57; surplus extraction and, 157; Thirty Years' War and, 9, 10
Tax Farm, 57
terrorism, 137, 168, 169, 170, 171, 173
Tesimond, Oswald, 2
theatre: Cardinal Richelieu and, 11–12, 13–14; Sarah Bernhardt and, 116–19
theology: Descartes and, 35, 36; Pope John Paul II and, 154–55
The Wealth of Nations (Smith), 18–19
Thirty Years' War, 7–10
Thoughts on Education (Locke), 25
Tito, Broz, 177
tortoises, Darwin and, 95, 96
torture, in Elizabethan England, 3
Tory Party (Great Britain), 25–26
trade. *See* commerce
treaties and conferences, 88, 89
Turkey. *See* Ottoman Empire
Two Treatises of Government (Locke), 25

U

U-boats, 122
United States of America: global economy and, 18, 19; John Locke and, 25; Sarah

Bernhardt and, 118; surplus extraction and, 156, 159
universe, end of, 178–82

V

vaccines, 109, 112
vampires, rabies and, 108
Victoria, Queen, 74–78, 90, 106
Vindication of the Rights of Men (Wollstonecraft), 62
Vindication of the Rights of Women (Wollstonecraft), 60, 62
Voltaire, 12, 40–41, 45
voting rights: Benjamin Disraeli and, 105; Napoleon III and, 84, 85; Prussia and, 79, 81; for women, 77, 124

W

Wallenstein, Albrecht von, 9
warfare: changes in, 8, 42; financing of, 8–9, 16; politics and, 39–40; Roman Empire and, 43; spies and, 143; World War II, 132–33
War of the Spanish Succession, 39–40
wealth, surplus extraction and, 158–59
Wells, H. G., 145–49
werewolves, rabies and, 107–8
West, Rebecca, 147
Western civilization, study of, 183–86
Whig Party (Great Britain), 25, 103–4
Wilhelm II (Germany), 121–22, 123
Willard, Emma, 64
William I (Prussia), 80, 81
Williams, William Carlos, 161
Wilson, A.T., 126
Wittgenstein, Ludwig, 32, 34
Wollstonecraft, Mary, 60–64
Women's Anti-Suffrage League, 124
women's rights. *See* feminism
workhouses, 99–100
world government, H.G. Wells and, 147, 148, 149
World's Fair (New York), 128, 130
World War I: the Balkans and, 176; causes of, 120–23; Constantinople and, 91; Middle East and, 125–26; Sarah Bernhardt and, 119; Winston Churchill and, 136
World War II: atomic bomb and, 164; Auschwitz-Birkenau concentration camp, 131–33; the Balkans and, 177; quinine and, 112; Winston Churchill and, 134–37

Y

Young, Thomas, 51–54
Young England movement, 104, 105
Yugoslavia, 176, 177

Z

Zionism, Albert Einstein and, 163–64
Zola, Emile, 119

Test Your Knowledge Form

We encourage you to photocopy and use this page as a tool to assess how the articles in *Annual Editions* expand on the information in your textbook. By reflecting on the articles you will gain enhanced text information. You can also access this useful form on a product's book support Web site at *http://www.mhcls.com/online/*.

NAME: _____ DATE: _____

TITLE AND NUMBER OF ARTICLE: _____

BRIEFLY STATE THE MAIN IDEA OF THIS ARTICLE: _____

_____

LIST THREE IMPORTANT FACTS THAT THE AUTHOR USES TO SUPPORT THE MAIN IDEA: _____

_____

WHAT INFORMATION OR IDEAS DISCUSSED IN THIS ARTICLE ARE ALSO DISCUSSED IN YOUR TEXTBOOK OR OTHER READINGS THAT YOU HAVE DONE? LIST THE TEXTBOOK CHAPTERS AND PAGE NUMBERS:

_____

LIST ANY EXAMPLES OF BIAS OR FAULTY REASONING THAT YOU FOUND IN THE ARTICLE: _____

_____

LIST ANY NEW TERMS/CONCEPTS THAT WERE DISCUSSED IN THE ARTICLE, AND WRITE A SHORT DEFINITION:

We Want Your Advice

ANNUAL EDITIONS revisions depend on two major opinion sources: one is our Advisory Board, listed in the front of this volume, which works with us in scanning the thousands of articles published in the public press each year; the other is you—the person actually using the book. Please help us and the users of the next edition by completing the prepaid article rating form on this page and returning it to us. Thank you for your help!

ANNUAL EDITIONS: Western Civilization, Volume 2

ARTICLE RATING FORM

Here is an opportunity for you to have direct input into the next revision of this volume.
We would like you to rate each of the articles listed below, using the following scale:

1. **Excellent: should definitely be retained**
2. **Above average: should probably be retained**
3. **Below average: should probably be deleted**
4. **Poor: should definitely be deleted**

Your ratings will play a vital part in the next revision.
Please mail this prepaid form to us as soon as possible.
Thanks for your help!

RATING	ARTICLE	RATING	ARTICLE
	1. The Gunpowder Plot: Terror and Toleration in 1605		22. The Incurable Wound
	2. The 30 Years' War		23. Quinine's Feverish Tales and Trails
	3. Cardinal Richelieu: Hero or Villain?		24. The Divine Sarah
	4. From Mercantilism to 'The Wealth of Nations'		25. Germany, Britain, & the Coming of War in 1914
	5. 400 Years of the East India Company		26. Queen of the Sands
	6. John Locke: Icon of Liberty		27. Art Deco: High Style
	7. Descartes the Dreamer		28. Auschwitz: The Forgotten Evidence
	8. Empires Ancient and Modern		29. Contemplating Churchill
	9. Declaring an Open Season on the Wisdom of the Ages		30. The Mystery of Stalin
	10. Thomas Young: the Man Who Knew Everything		31. Kim Philby Had a Remarkable Long Career with British Intelligence—Spying for the Other Side
	11. The Passion of Antoine Lavoisier		32. The World According to Wells
	12. The First Feminist		33. Beloved and Brave
	13. Napoleon: A Classic Dictator?		34. The Rise and Fall of Empires: The Role of Surplus Extraction
	14. Slavery and the British		
	15. Victoria		35. The Maestro of Time
	16. Bismarck, Prussia, & German Nationalism		36. 'You Say You Want a Revolution'
	17. Napoleon III: 'Hero' or 'Grotesque Mediocrity'?		37. Europe's Mosque Hysteria
	18. The Russians Shall Not Have Constantinople		38. Folly & Failure in the Balkans
	19. The Evolution of Charles Darwin		39. The End
	20. Florence Nightingale as a Social Reformer		40. Why We Study Western Civ
	21. Benjamin Disraeli and the Spirit of England		

(Continued on next page)

BUSINESS REPLY MAIL
FIRST CLASS MAIL PERMIT NO. 551 DUBUQUE IA

POSTAGE WILL BE PAID BY ADDRESEE

McGraw-Hill Contemporary Learning Series
2460 KERPER BLVD
DUBUQUE, IA 52001-9902

Ililuuliilliuilluuilllliulilulliuulilulil

ABOUT YOU

Name   Date

_____

Are you a teacher? ☐   A student? ☐
Your school's name

_____

Department

_____

Address   City   State   Zip

_____

School telephone #

_____

YOUR COMMENTS ARE IMPORTANT TO US!

Please fill in the following information:
For which course did you use this book?

_____

Did you use a text with this ANNUAL EDITION? ☐ yes ☐ no
What was the title of the text?

_____

What are your general reactions to the *Annual Editions* concept?

_____

Have you read any pertinent articles recently that you think should be included in the next edition? Explain.

_____

Are there any articles that you feel should be replaced in the next edition? Why?

_____

Are there any World Wide Web sites that you feel should be included in the next edition? Please annotate.

_____

May we contact you for editorial input? ☐ yes ☐ no
May we quote your comments? ☐ yes ☐ no